CHEYENNE HISTORICAL EPISODES
VOL. 1.

PREVIOUS WORKS BY THE SAME AUTHOR.

The Battle of Rainy Butte. "The English Westerner's Society." 2008.

Red Was the Blood of Our Forefathers. "The Caxton Press," Idaho. 2010.

Making Pacts with Old Enemies. "The English Westerner's Society." 2012.

A Double Defeat for the Atsina. "The English Westerner's Society;" 2014.

"Apsarokee" "The Choir Press," Gloucester, England. 2014.

My Good Friend Joe Medicine Crow. "English Westerner's Society;" 2016.

Ma'heo's Children. "The Choir Press," Gloucester, England. 2018.

Raven Men of the Yellowstone. "The Choir Press," Gloucester, U.K. 2020.

Crow Indian Episodes of the Old Frontier, "The Choir Press," England. 2025

Cheyenne Historical Episodes. Vol. 1, 1800-1840. "The Choir Press," England, 2025.

Copyright Brian L. Keefe 2025.

All rights reserved. This book or any portion thereof may not be reproduced or used in any manner whatsoever without the express written permission of the publisher except for the use of brief quotations in a book review or scholarly journal.

First Published byt the Choir Press 2025

ISBN 978-1-78963-582-9

Cover Design. Cathouse Art.

CHEYENNE HISTORICAL EPISODES
OF
INTERTRIBAL WARFARE AND RELATIONS.
VOL 1.
1800 – 1840
By
BRIAN L. KEEFE.

FORWARD

In a previously published volume entitled *"Ma`heo`s Children,"* the present Author analysed both oral and documented traditions from the Cheyenne and linguistically related tribes, pertaining to mythological and religious aspects regarding the latter's origins and migrations and intertribal relations in their ancient and historic periods. The Author's analysis and conclusions chart the likely progress of Cheyennes across the Northern Hemisphere and various places of permanent residence on what is now the North American Continent before terminating their migrations on the Great Western Plains. The current volume entitled *"Cheyenne Historical Episodes,"* continues from where *"Ma`heo`es Children"* leaves off around A.D.1805, and carries the reader in the guise of selected Cheyenne episodes to the period, A.D. 1890. The present volumes contain additional information not seen in previous studies of Cheyenne intertribal warfare, which come from the Author's own Tribal informants repeating oral history, along with fresh documented research.

INTRODUCTION

Forward…………………………………………………………………….iv

Contents…………………………………………………………………….v

Introduction………………………………………………………………..vii

Chapter 1. Four "Sacred Arrows"…………………………………………1

Chapter 2. The "Buffalo Hat"…..………………………………………...19

Chapter 3. Early Horse Days on the Western Plains [1800-'05] ………..29

Chapter 4. Cheyennes in Victory and Defeat [1806-1819]……………...38

Chapter 5. Eight-Hundred Crow Captives Taken [1820]………………..54

          Aftermath……………………………………………………...72

Chapter 6. Government Emissaries Meet Cheyennes [1820]……………79

Chapter 7. Crow Vengeance on Cheyennes [1821]………………………85

Chapter 8. Raiding Pawnees, Crows and Mandans [1822-'24]…………..99

Chapter 9. Friendship Treaty, and Red-Dog-Rope Affair [1825]……....116

Chapter 10. Move to South Platte and Bent's Fort [1828]……………...125

Chapter 11. Cheyennes Defy Crows and Shoshoni [1829]…………….139

Chapter 12. The Sacred Arrows Are Lost [1830]……………………....148

Chapter 13. Big-Head Returns From the Dead [1831]…………………160

Chapter 14. Cheyennes Kill Dangling-Foot and Crow Revenge [1832-'33]166

INTRODUCTION

Chapter 15. Skidi Sacrifice, and Death of High-Backed-Wolf 1st [1833]...181

Chapter 16. Crows Trick Cheyennes; Cheyennes Defeat Kiowas [1835]...187

Chapter 17. Cheyenne Peace with Pawnees [1835]............................ 194

Chapter 18. High-Backed-Wolf 2d Raids Pawnees [1836].....................214

Chapter 19. Raid on Kiowas and Mouse`s-Road Killed [1837]...............218

Chapter 20. Forty-Eight Cheyenne Bowstings Wiped Out [1837]............231

Chapter 21. Cheyenne Medicine-Snake is Killed [1837-`38]..................252

Chapter 22. Preparations against the Kiowa [1838]...........................257

Chapter 23. Big Fight at Wolf Creek [1838]....................................263

Chapter 24. Intertribal Peace on the Southern Plains [1840]..................284

Notes and Sources...295

Index..300

INTRODUCTION

INTRODUCTION.

The Cheyenne Nation is composed of two related tribes, namely the *TsisTsisTsas* [Cheyenne-proper] and *Suhtaio*. Although speaking varied dialects they have, since the mid-eighteen-thirties, been incorporated as one people. Centred in the town of Lame Deer on the Tongue River Reservation, Montana, and at various locations throughout west-central Oklahoma, the majority of the Nation reside. Together they constitute around fourteen thousand persons [as of the year 2013], known as Northern Cheyenne and Southern Cheyenne respectively. Today they strive to retain their tribal identity as descendants of big-game-hunting equestrian nomads; clinging to their old religion and philosophy in an alien environment. Once their young men had raided far afield for horses, scalps and captives, and their vast herds and mixed blood in their veins had been testament to their ability in such pursuits.

Regrettably, yet inevitably, their assimilation into white American society dominated by its material values, has now become the greater part of their present existence, and soon, their age-old traditions will be as far removed from these people, as are now those of the legendary King Arthur to his British descendants.

It is, however, but a comparatively short time ago when Cheyennes were both feared and respected by Indian and White man alike, and their condition typical of the Plains nomad, who hunted the shaggy buffalo for his subsistence and stretched its hide over a conical frame of poles for his shelter. During the Nineteenth century Cheyennes were noted for their cleanliness; the virtue of their women; superb horsemanship and the indomitable will and pride of their warriors. Indeed, Cheyenne manhood bedecked in eagle-feathers and paint, constantly exhibited their prowess in warfare with enemy tribes, and engaged themselves in a prolonged and bloody struggle against unlimited resources of the American military machine. All those acquainted with them spoke highly of their valour and of the integrity of their chiefs.

Underlying these physical attributes was a deep sense of spiritual awareness, in which all tribal members were involved. Among the Cheyennes, as compared to most other nomadic Plains Tribes, religious indulgence and sincerity was of a very high degree, revolving around their concept of a Supreme Being known as *Ma'heo*, and culture-hero prophets, Sweet-Medicine and Erect-Horns.

INTRODUCTION

At their height of power; circa, 1840, Cheyennes were divided into ten proper bands, each of which had stemmed directly or indirectly from a common nucleus, having broken away from a parent band at different periods in favour of a particular hunting territory or preferred alliance with another tribe. Always, they considered themselves Cheyenne and one people, and at least once a year during midsummer, reunited as a tribal body in order to conduct important religious ceremonies together. At other times they joined in communal war ventures against common foes, and at ten year intervals, came together to select the forty-four chiefs of their people, who were to lead them both in war and peace through the ensuing decade.

These separate bands grew larger or smaller depending upon importance or circumstance, so that whilst some became less significant, others rose to prominence. Subsequently, band names were constantly changing, although all Cheyenne informants agreed that during the middle years of the Nineteenth century, the bands in existence could be listed as follows.

Omissis (Eaters). Largest band, aka, Northern Cheyennes.
Heviqsnipahis (Burnt Aorta). Most important band.
Heviatanio (Hair-Rope-Men).Also, collective name for Southern Cheyennes.
Oivimana (Scabby). Offshoot of *Heviatanio.*
Issiometanui (Ridge Men). Mixture of *Heviatanio* and *Suhtaio.*
Oktouna (Jaws). Offshoot of *Masikota.*
Hofnowa (Poor People). Offshoot of *Oktouna* and *Oivimana.*
Masikota (Prairie Men). Part of Dog-Soldier Band.
Suhtaio (Buffalo Men?). Aka as "Dogs." An adopted tribe.
Watapio (Those who eat with the Sioux). Half Sioux or Half-Breed Band.

An eleventh band the *Moiseo* [pronounced *Mo-wee-see-o*], had of old been of paramount significance as one of the original Cheyenne-speaking components. But by the 1850s owing to diminished population and admixture of foreign blood, they survived only as one of several small extended family groups. During the period in question [circa, 1800 -`40], they had lost much of their earlier importance with no precise place in the tribal circle, being attached to one or another band as circumstance dictated.

At times when the entire Nation united, the people pitched their tepees in the shape of a large horseshoe several ranks deep, its opening toward the east

INTRODUCTION

and rising sun. If one faced the horseshoe from the east, the *Heviqsnipahis* or Burnt Aorta band occupied the opening of the circle on its south or left side, the other bands being positioned around the arc in their particular order of significance, now forgotten, but with the *Omissis* band occupying the north or right side of the opening opposite the Aorta.

In the centre of the circle stood two lone tepees, wherein were housed the Nation's most sacred tribal talismans, i.e., four Sacred or Medicine Arrows *[Mahuts]* of the *TsisTsisTsas*, and a Sacred Buffalo Hat *[Issiwun]* of the Suhtaio. Around these talismans both religious and cultural life of the people were inexplicably linked. The power from such objects ensured the continuation of the Tribe both in hunting and in war, and in all other things pertaining to the well-being of the people. Such is still the belief today regarding these sacred icons, both of which have mythological origins, having been given long ago to the Cheyenne and Suhtaio at separate times by their personal culture heroes, Sweet-Medicine and Erect-Horns respectively. They have been, and yet remain, the most important and revered objects among the Nation. Successful war-parties once made offerings to the "Arrows" or " Hat" as tokens of gratitude and at times, both palladiums were carried to war against an enemy tribe to guarantee success. Such occasions were rare and occurred only when the whole fighting force of the Nation was involved.

This fighting force consisted of several military societies or clubs, each of which competed against each other for tribal prestige and renown. They were not age-graded in their makeup and any youth of fighting age was eligible to join. Although admittance was usually by invitation, few were turned away from their society of choice. As a rule, although by no means always, son or nephew followed father or uncle into a particular society and remained a member all his life.

Each society had its own songs, dances and regalia and took turns in policing the camp; organizing tribal hunts; camp movements and combined war ventures. There were four original societies later expanded to eight, and these have remained the only important ones throughout. Some were known by a variety of names and the list below gives the most commonly used terms.

Whkesh`hetaniu. Kit-Fox; aka, *Motsounetaniu*, i.e. Flint Men.
Hi-mo`weyuhks Elks or Elk-Horn Scrapers; aka, Crooked-Lances.
Mahohe`was. Red Shields, aka, Bull or Buffalo Soldiers.

INTRODUCTION

Hota`mita`niu.	Dog or Dog-Rope Soldiers.
Himatanohis.	Bowstrings; aka, "Bows" and Wolf Soldiers.
Whiiu`Nutkiu.	Chief Soldiers or Chief's Band.
Hotami`-Massau.	Crazy-Dogs; aka, Northern Bowstrings.
Hohnuhk`e.	Contraries; aka, Clown Society.

The ten bravest young warriors within the Kit-Fox Society [aka, Swift Hawks or simply, Hawks.], regarded themselves as a subsidiary society. They were once well-known, but no longer extant by the latter years of the Nineteenth century.

Together these tribal bands and warrior societies, [the last named at times being recognized as bands in their own right], were always included as integral participants in the Nation's two important religious ceremonies; that of the Sun Dance [also known as The Medicine Lodge or Willow Dance], adopted originally from the Suhtaio and held once a year in midsummer, and the *`Massaum`* [also called Animal or Crazy Dance], which was of ancient origin among the *TsisTsisTsas* or Cheyenne-proper, not usually held annually, but whenever need arose, such as times of drought, famine, pestilence or migration. Both were Earth Renewal ceremonies, the performance of which guaranteed the continuity of creation, while at the same time, the participants sought the benevolence of the Great *Ma`heo* and subordinate unseen powers of the Above World and Below World, in order to ensure not only the personal well-being of the tribe, but for the whole of Mankind in general, and for every living thing including plants and animals, all of which the Great *Ma`heo* had created.

- 0 - 0 - 0 - 0 - 0 - 0 - 0 - 0 - 0 - 0 -

FOUR "SACRED ARROWS"

CHAPTER 1.

FOUR "SACRED ARROWS"

The beginning period of Cheyenne Nationhood, coincides with that given by Cheyenne informants for the coming of the `Sacred Arrow` talismans among them. When, according to tribal tradition, *"There was famine and pestilence over all the land."* [1]

The coming of the Sacred Arrows and of a Cultural Prophet named Sweet Medicine, are the most important episodes in Cheyenne history. Such events appear to have occurred out of necessity, following a movement of proto-Cheyenne bands south from the southern Ontario region [Canada], and into the Upper and Lower Red Lakes area of what is now the west-central part of the present-day State of Minnesota.

It is not within the scope of the present study to give a detailed analysis of Cheyenne religion, although the coming of the `Sacred Arrows` is particularly relevant. Not only does their appearance corroborate the positioning of Cheyenne peoples in the Upper Mississippi country in the mid-sixteenth century, but they embody all that pertains to Cheyennes as a Nation. They have also been instrumental in subsequent Cheyenne migration and social organization since that time, and warrant a brief synopsis at this point.

It was during the mid-1540s, ostensibly, plus or minus a few years, when the revered prophet Sweet-Medicine brought the Sacred Arrows to the people wrapped in a kit-fox skin. Eventually, there were four such `Arrows`, each with different-coloured feathered flights of red, black, yellow and white, and the shaft of each `Arrow` painted the same colour as its respective flight.

Before this event, so tribal tradition relates, the Cheyennes had no hard and fast laws and no elected chiefs to lead them. Only those who proved the strongest ruled the people according to their own whims, which were often selfish and cruel. These Sacred Arrows [*Mahuts*] being four in number, were and still are, considered the most holy objects the Cheyennes ever possessed. They are held in great reverence and awe, both as a symbol of `Male Power` and of the Nation's unity and continuance as a separate cohesive entity in an alien environment. The shafts of two of these `Arrows` are painted black, and

FOUR "SACRED ARROWS"

are regarded as mediums through which the great *Ma'heo;* the all-powerful Creator along with its associated supernatural powers of the "Above World" and "Below World," bestow their benevolence upon the people. These black painted shafts are commonly called "Buffalo Arrows," for by the enactment of appropriate rituals in the Sacred Arrow ceremony itself, they supposedly have power to bring forth the buffalo and other game in order to provide both material and physical sustenance to the people.

The second pair of `Arrows` have their shafts painted red, and likewise, are regarded as the receptacles of those same unseen powers above mentioned. Whereby, they protect the people from their enemies and if the attendant `Arrow` rituals are observed correctly, ensure the Cheyennes achieve victory in battle. At the same time, it is thought that the powers of omnipotent unseen spirits which are transmitted through the medium of the `Arrows,` can preserve the people from disease and all other natural and man-made calamities, which might cause them to become extinct as an independent body. In short, the periodic enactment of a `Sacred Arrow Ceremony` which lasts four days, guarantees the well-being of the people and their continued unity and strength. Failure to treat the `Arrows` with due reverence, or by neglecting to hold the ceremonies connected with them, would, it is believed, herald the destruction and subsequent demise of the Cheyennes, and thus, these most revered of tribal talismans represent the very essence of the Nation; embracing all that is Cheyenne both in body and in spirit along with the people's very existence. Every so often it is necessary to renew the `Arrows,` especially when an act of homicide occurs within the tribe, but also, in order to replace the feather flights which are of a perishable nature, along with glue and sinews that bind the feathers to the shafts. The shafts themselves cannot be renewed more than the sacred number four times throughout their existence. Today the `Arrows` reside in the care of their present Keeper among the Southern Cheyenne tribe in Oklahoma.

In brief, the coming of the `Arrows` being the most sacred Cheyenne story, tells how the original prophet Sweet-Medicine during an altercation with a fellow tribesman, killed his opponent and fled camp in fear of retribution from

* **Sweet-Medicine is also known as Eagle`s-Peak, Rustling-Corn-Leaf, Standing-Medicine, Standing-Sweet-Grass and Sweet-Root-Standing.**

FOUR "SACRED ARROWS"

his victim's relatives. He remained in exile several years, after which he returned to the tribe a reformed and transformed person, now possessing potent holy powers, and bearing instructions by which to organize the Cheyenne people into a Nation with a singular identity.

It is further mentioned that at the time of his return to the tribe, Sweet-Medicine gave the people corn, and also, brought back the buffalo from their underground refuge to alleviate the people's hunger. He then showed them how to conduct communal buffalo drives with the help of an appropriate ceremony, along with teaching them new skills in both the method of skinning and utilizing hides of the animals killed. In addition, he now had the ability to prophesy forthcoming events, which included the coming of horses; the appearance of cattle and of white-skinned people, each of which the Cheyennes would meet in a future time.

Sweet-Medicine, it is said, had been given the Sacred Arrows personally by the Underworld Spirits that reside within *"Novah-vus,"* or `Bear Butte` as it is designated on modern-day maps. This being the "Holy Mountain" of the Cheyennes and hence, regarded as the center of their Universe. It stands in the western part of South Dakota northeast of the Black Hills near the present-day town of Sturgis. The site is a long way indeed, from the Mississippi headwaters country of northern Minnesota, and before the Cheyennes had horses of any description, it would have taken many months for Sweet-Medicine to reach and return from there on foot.

Other tribes, that include the Mandan, Kiowa-Apache, Kiowa and most important to our present theme, the Hidatsa, also regard Bear Butte as a very sacred place and the Hidatsa, we know, have a Sacred Arrow cult which although not exactly the same as that practiced among Cheyennes, does bear not a few remarkable similarities to it.

Perhaps, then, the Cheyenne innovation to adopt such a cult came originally from the Hidatsa, who being sedentary hunters and agriculturists and likely, once connected with the old Mound-builder culture peoples of earlier times in Michigan and Wisconsin, no doubt had a more solid religious concept and ceremonial life before the less sophisticated nomadic Cheyenne groups arrived in the Upper Mississippi country from the Ontario lakes district of the north.

That Hidatsa were in contact with Cheyennes of the Red Lake's and headwater district of the Upper Mississippi, is substantiated by the fact that in addition to assertions from both the Hidatsa and Cheyennes themselves, the Hidatsa anciently called the Cree *"Shahe"* or *"Scha-hi,"* which is but a variant of an old name for the Cheyennes of *Chaa*. This might serve to show that when Hidatsa and Cheyennes first met, the Hidatsa supposed the latter to have been a Cree faction, which because of the dialect and fashion of dress Cheyennes then employed, would not have been surprising. Certainly, migrant Cheyennes from the southern Ontario region must have been in reasonable proximity to the Cree and probably still associating if only sporadically, with the Monsoni branch of that people [as Cheyenne tradition asserts], and also with the Hidatsa.

This indicates that the territory then inhabited by these early Cheyennes was far north of the Minnesota River, for when at a later date, Cheyennes did reside in the last-named locality, they had very little in either dress or character to immediately identify them with the Cree. Neither were they then likely to have had much contact with the Hidatsa, who during the period of Cheyenne occupation along the Minnesota River of circa, 1640 onward, were themselves far northwest in the Devil's Lake district of the Coteau des Prairies in northeastern North Dakota.

That this was the case, does suggest that the *"lake and prairie"* country then claimed by Cheyenne-proper bands as mentioned in tradition, did embrace both the Upper and Lower Red Lakes and Mississippi headwaters district, ostensibly, in the vicinity of "Bowstring Lake." It is clear that the names Bowstring Lake and Bowstring River are derived from very old Algonquian terms, and during the early period of Cheyenne occupation along Minnesota River further south, the Cree were already referring to the Cheyennes as "Bowstring Men."

We can see also in the Hidatsa equivalent of the Cheyenne Sacred Arrows cult, that among the Hidatsa, their `Sacred Arrow` also has the power to protect one and all from harm and bestow benevolence upon the people as a whole. However, what is more important perhaps, is that the Hidatsa Sacred Arrow`by its 13 component parts, represents the unification of the thirteen clans originally constituting the Hidatsa tribe. Perhaps as the Cheyennes then constituted a number of separate bands rather than specific clans, the said Sweet Medicine received a corresponding number of Sacred Arrows, rather than only one arrow to represent the whole group as was the case with the Hidatsa.

One of the most important attributes of the Cheyenne Sacred Arrows,

FOUR "SACRED ARROWS"

JOHN STANDS IN TIMBER.
Northern Cheyenne informant
And tribal Historian. 1960.
[Margot Liberty Collection].

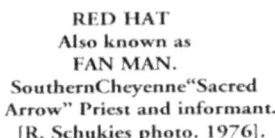

RED HAT
Also known as
FAN MAN.
SouthernCheyenne"Sacred
Arrow" Priest and informant.
[R. Schukies photo. 1976].

FOUR "SACRED ARROWS"

like that among the Hidatsa, is that they symbolize the unity of the Cheyenne people, and in olden days, whenever the `Arrows` were to be ritually renewed or propitiated, the entire population was obliged upon pain of eternal ostracism from the rest of the tribe, to gather together as one body. In such a way, all the Cheyenne people congregated at regular intervals and by so doing, continued to be united both in a physical and spiritual manner.

Conversely, it may have been that the sacred butte known as "Dog Den," was the place where, originally, the Cheyennes obtained their Sacred Arrows, if not from yet another site far to the east of Bear Butte and much closer to the Red Lakes district of northern Minnesota.

It is worth noting that the shafts of the Sacred Arrows are fashioned from wood belonging to an East Woodland variety and two of these shafts, at least, are said to be originals brought to the tribe by Sweet-Medicine himself. It is also indicative that the feathered flights of these Sacred Arrows are always attached to the shafts with sinew and a fish-based glue, rather than the more common animal hoof glue as used when on the Western Plains. This seems to suggest that the talismans first arrived among the Cheyennes when they inhabited the lake country of northern Minnesota, at which time, unlike when in the buffalo country to the west, fish provided a great part of their diet.

It is indicative that the same Dog Den was also sacred to the Mandan, who state that one of their own traditional cultural heroes known as *Okipa*, released the buffalo from an underground refuge at that place. Here, of course, we see a comparison with the Cheyenne cultural hero Sweet-Medicine, who also brought the buffalo to the people after the animals likewise, had been released from their underground confinement.

It seems that only after all Cheyenne-speaking groups had left the Minnesota region and crossed the Missouri to become nomadic equestrian buffalo hunters of the Western Plains, that the mythological account of Sweet-Medicine`s holy journey to *"Novah-vus,"* the Sacred Mountain, was transferred from an original more eastern location to that of a more convenient and perhaps, more relevant site in the west, such as that of present-day Bear Butte, and which same site was already regarded as a very holy place by the then resident tribes of that territory including the Kiowa, Hidatsa, Mandan and Kiowa-Apache among others.

A severe climatic change did effect the aforesaid Ontario area during the time circa, 1535 - 1540, and it is indicative that in 1534 and throughout the succeeding years until 1543, far to the east on the Lower St. Lawrence, the French explorer Jacques Cartier made contact and traded with certain Algonquian and Huron groups in the latter's great towns of *Hochelga* and *Stadacona*, which then stood on the present-day city sites of Quebec and Montreal respectively. There had been much intimacy between the Indians and white men at those times, and it is not unlikely that some type of European disease such as smallpox or even a common strain of influenza, was thus passed on by these Frenchmen to their Native customers who having no natural immunity and lacking even a basic knowledge of contamination, could not prevent its deadly effects from sweeping through their populations, carrying off many thousands in its wake.

This appears to have been the case, for soon after 1543, the Huron apparently, abandoned their towns completely and disappeared from where Cartier had previously found them.

Any such contagion, undoubtedly, would have been transmitted by the infected Huron and their Algonquian allies to neighbouring peoples, causing it to spread far and wide from one tribe to another. Eventually, even Cheyennes in their remote Ontario habitat would likely have suffered the same decimation to their numbers, although they remained far removed from the original source of contagion.

As a result of the proto-Cheyennes [the *Moiseo*] and cognate bands experiencing a similar catastrophic event, it is likely that their people scattered into many, much smaller family camps in an endeavor to escape the same silent enemy of disease.

If there had existed any earlier sacred tribal talismans believed to have power to safeguard the people from harm, then it must have seemed they had lost their potency. Probably the people would not have recalled suffering a comparable devastating calamity within living memory, and there would have been an urgent need to obtain some other form of medium through which, by the enactment of certain *newly* devised rituals, the great *Ma'heo* and its associated benevolent spirits of the "Above World" and "Below," would again bestow their blessings on the people; to preserve them from yet another catastrophe and in some way, unify the *Moiseo* and their cognate groups, to make them again strong and independent and a complete tribal entity in their own right.

FOUR "SACRED ARROWS"

This becomes evident by the fact that long before the Sacred Arrows came among them, the Cheyennes had indulged in an elaborate religious ritual known as the *"Massaum"* [also known as the "Animal" or "Crazy" Dance"]. This was, predominantly, a ceremony of regeneration, the enactment of which persisted into the early years of the Twentieth century. During the performance of the *Massaum* rites, a number of participants disguised themselves as various species of animals in order to propitiate the spirits of all living things. According to some, it was also a ceremony which gave the practitioners both power and guardianship over a certain area of land and over all living things that dwelt thereon. The actual concept surrounding the *Massaum,* appears to be of ancient origin, and had its counterpart among the Siberian nomads of northern Siberia and Kamchatka, in which regions it likely originated during a past millennium.

After the Cheyennes adopted the Sacred Arrows along with the cult associated with them, the *Massaum* lost a good deal of its earlier importance, as the newly inaugurated ceremony of `Sacred Arrows` now achieved a similar end. The *Massaum* continued to be performed, although not on a regular basis, the last occasion being in 1927, and then in association with the *New Life Lodge* ceremony more commonly known as the Sun Dance, which was adopted by Cheyennes from the Suhtaio at a later date after entering the Western Plains. It seems, however, that in olden times; before the introduction of the Sacred Arrows and Sun-Dance, the *Massaum* had been regarded as the most important ceremony practiced by the Cheyenne-proper, and - albeit in varied form - by the latter's closely related Cree kinfolk. The time of *"...famine and pestilence in all the northland"* as mentioned in Cheyenne tradition, which had caused the people to pull up stakes and migrate south into northern Minnesota in the first place, had probably decimated the *Moiseo* and other bands associated with them, as indeed, it did with their Algonquian cousins to the north and east, and threw any age-old social organization and religious observances associated with pre-existing sacred objects into disarray. Perhaps, then, this was the event or events, that diminished the earlier importance of the *Massaum* within the tribe, and when in a later century, Cheyennes as a Nation adopted the Sun-Dance as a regeneration ceremony, the relegation of the *Massaum* to a much lesser position in the Nation's religious life became complete. Although it is true to say that in a later century, the then small remaining remnant of the original

FOUR "SACRED ARROWS"

Moiseo band did alone persist in the importance of the *Massaum,* as an alternative to their adopting the Sun-Dance in its stead.

Certain holy objects of the olden time, evidently, did also survive into the new era of the Sacred Arrows, such as those termed *"Hokhtsin"* or `Wheel Lances` as they are sometimes called, which seem also to have evolved from an ancient northern Siberian concept. Supposedly, these Wheel-Lances had power to protect its owner and followers from harm in much the same way as did the Sacred Arrows, i.e., by causing those behind the lance to become invisible to their enemies. These objects, although not requiring a hereditary chain of custodians as did the Sacred Arrows, became intimately associated with the `Arrows` and had to be renewed at the same time as were the `Arrows` themselves. In one sense, Wheel-Lances also became somewhat superfluous by their having very similar properties to the `Arrows` and thus; as was the case with the *Massaum* rites, the Wheel Lances` themselves eventually lost much of their earlier importance within the tribe as a whole.

According to Cheyenne testimony collected by George A. Dorsey during the early Nineteen-hundreds, the Cheyennes first acquired their Sacred Arrow talismans between eighteen and twenty generations prior to 1905, when the statement was made.

There are several versions in current Cheyenne oral tradition of what might be termed "The Sweet-Medicine cycle," much of the contents of which tends to border on the mythological. Hence, Sweet-Medicine is reputed to have lived for an extensive period - "445 winters" to be precise, and in the ilk of the "Green Man" of ancient Celtic mythology, every winter he would grow old and haggard, but come spring, would rejuvenate into a much younger man. It must be remembered, however, that two of our conventional years correspond with three winters in the Indian idiom, so that the statement "445 winters" in reality, refers to 296 of our conventional years.

Of course, no human being can be said to have lived 296 years by our way of reckoning, and the original Sweet-Medicine of Cheyenne tradition is not regarded as anything other than a mortal human being, albeit, one who showed a remarkable ability to both create and innovate and possessed the power to prophesy important coming events. Indeed, Sweet-Medicine is not only said to have given the Sacred Arrow bundle to the Cheyennes, but in addition, is attributed to having given the tribe its four original warrior societies and also,

FOUR "SACRED ARROWS"

the "Chief's" society, along with many of the tribe's later cultural assets that since the time of Cheyenne residence in the Mississippi headwaters country, have been adopted during various periods by the people throughout their subsequent history.

We should not doubt from this that Sweet-Medicine was not at one time a real historical figure, only that since his demise at an advanced age, a successor had taken the name and embraced the same role as a symbolic personification of the original Sweet-Medicine himself, so that even today, there exists the position in current Cheyenne hierarchy and tribal government of a Sweet-Medicine-Chief. This being one who still personifies in spirit his illustrious namesake of olden times.

SWEET MEDICINE CHIEF, HIGH-BACKED-WOLF.
[After an original line drawing from life by George Catlin in 1832.]

FOUR "SACRED ARROWS"

Obviously, this particular Cheyenne informant was not referring to the original person of that name, but rather, to a personification of him endowed with the title Sweet-Medicine-Chief, and whose demise coincided with the end-phase of what we should call the "Traditional time" in Cheyenne history which terminates around circa, 1820. Hereafter, the Nation's oral history takes on a much more definite format with precise names, dates and events, and which are recounted in their proper chronological sequence. Thus we know, that a man named High-Backed-Wolf 1st was elected to the position of Sweet-Medicine-Chief either in, or just after the year 1820.

If we accept, therefore, that the number *"445 winters"* given as the extent of the original Sweet-Medicine's life span, actually includes those personages who came after him until the end of the traditional era [e.g. 1820], whilst remembering that three winters in the Cheyenne idiom compares with only two conventional years in our modern reckoning, then by subtracting 286 years from 1820, i.e., when the last of the successive Sweet-Medicine Chiefs of the traditional era expired, as Michelson's informant asserted, we have a working date for the period of the original Sweet-Medicine's coming of around AD.1534.

Having said this, we know that Dorsey calculated a period of only twenty years as representing the average length of a generation, and which by counting back 18 generations as mentioned by his Cheyenne informants in 1905, gives us a date of around 1545 as being the time when the `Arrows` were first brought to the people, or perhaps, more precisely, when the first Arrow Keeper was inaugurated into that office by Sweet-Medicine himself.

In corroboration of these dates, the Cheyenne informant Ralph White-Tail, a noted Sacred Arrow and Sun-Dance priest during the early 1960s, listed 12 keepers of the Sacred Arrows prior to and including Chief Little-Man, who, in 1908, was the last of the long-serving Arrow Keepers from the time of the old buffalo days.

In 1838, the then Arrow Keeper named Grey-Thunder, was killed during a big fight between allied Cheyennes and Arapahoe on one side and the Kiowa, Kiowa-Apache and Comanche on the other. Grey-Thunder is noted as number nine on Ralph White-Tail's list of Arrow Keepers. Thus if one calculates thirty years as being a more realistic period corresponding to the average length of a generation and as being the average length of time of any one Keeper's term of office, then deducts the time span of nine Keepers prior to and including the office of Grey-Thunder [which totals a period of 270 years], one arrives at the date of the first Arrow Keeper's inauguration as circa, 1568.

This proposed period also corresponds with the assertion, previously mentioned, that Sweet-Medicine on his return from the Sacred Mountain, foretold the future coming of horses among the people, which, coincidently, match the dates 1540 and 1541, when the Spanish Conquistadors Francisco Coronado and Hernando DeSoto respectively on their separate expeditions, brought the first horses since Prehistoric times onto the Southern Plains. Additionally, the mention by Sweet-Medicine of the future appearance of the white man's cattle, coincides with the first such animals which, having earlier been deposited on Sable Island in the Gulf of St. Lawrence by Baron de Lery in 1518 but long since abandoned by their owners and left to their own devices, by 1545 had multiplied into a significant number. Indeed, parties of French and Basque fishermen both visited and explored the Gulf of St. Lawrence several times during the first half of the sixteenth century, and had made intermittent contact with Natives on the Labrador coast. These events, surely, were known to Algonquians belonging to Montagnais and Naskapi peoples of that region [who were closely related to Cheyennes], and transmitted by word of mouth further inland so that Sweet-Medicine, who, according to the Cheyenne informant John Stands-in-Timber, had been a great traveler south, east, west and north, was made aware of these hitherto unknown newcomers, such as white men, horses and cattle.

In 1910, another of Michelson's Cheyenne informants named American-Horse, stated that during the early days of Cheyenne residence in the north [here referring to the headwaters country of the Upper Mississippi before the people crossed to the west side of the Missouri], there were only two Cheyenne-speaking bands, although Michelson did not designate them by specific names.

One assumes therefore, that one of these two original bands was that known as *Moiseo* or Arrow Men as they were also called, and among whom so we are told in Cheyenne testimony, the Sacred Arrows were first introduced. It does not appear that American-Horse was implying that the Suhtaio should be included as one of the two bands of which he spoke, for he mentioned the Suhtaio as a separate tribe when giving additional information regarding this early period in Cheyenne history. Neither, however, does it appear that he was referring directly to the small remnant of *Moiseo*, but to an old-time breakaway band from them known as *Masikota* and among whom the Arrow Men faction of the original *Moiseo* parent band had since amalgamated. The other Cheyenne-speaking group then resident in the Mississippi headwaters country was the *Omissis* also known as Bowstrings, and both names of *Masikota* and Bowstrings; albeit during different periods in time, were each used as collective terms to include under their respective headings all the later-date Cheyenne-speaking bands.

The traditional account surrounding the culture hero Sweet-Medicine, declares that it was he also, who brought the four original warrior societies to the Cheyennes, and we know that one of these military fraternities was known as Bowstrings. Furthermore, Suhtaio statements given to Michelson in 1910, specifically state that the societies of Elks, Red-Shields and Dogs were originally inaugurated among the Suhtaio, while present-day informants state that only the societies of Kit-Fox and Bowstrings actually originated among the Cheyennes.

Perhaps then, both the band and warrior society of Bowstrings were so named, in memory of a remarkable feat conducted once by the original Sweet-Medicines with a buffalo-sinew bowstring, and it is highly indicative that the Southern Cheyenne Sacred Arrow priest named Red-Hat [also known as Fan-Man], asserted that, traditionally, the Arrow Keepers had always belonged to the Bowstring warrior society.

This particular fraternity of Bowstrings having originally been founded among the Cheyennes, was later adopted by other tribes in contact with them, eventually becoming a pan-tribal society on the Western Great Plains. By this it might be deduced that one of the two early Cheyenne-speaking groups as mentioned by the informant American-Horse, was indeed that of Bowstrings, which offers a clue as to where exactly these particular Cheyennes were then positioned in the northern Minnesota country.

It is no coincidence that slightly southeast of Lower Red Lake - just above the headwaters of the Mississippi, - we find a Bowstring Lake and Bowstring River. These names are derived from translations of very old Algonquian Indian place names and are indicative that long ago, a group of people who evidently were Algonquian speakers and ostensibly Cheyenne, were known by the name Bowstrings who once resided in the aforementioned localities.

FOUR "SACRED ARROWS"

It seems to be also that in 1742, when the LaVerendrye brothers met a band of "Horse Indians" in the Great Plains west of the Missouri and called them *Gens L'Arc,* i.e. "People of the Bow," they were merely employing an old Algonquian name for that tribe, which should more properly have been rendered; "People of the Bowstring." Certainly, an alternative name given for the *Gens L'Arc* of *Atchapeivinioque* in the Bourgainville report of 1757, is a Cree term for the Cheyennes, which translates as *Bowstrings, not Bow.*

The logical conclusion then, deduced from the American-Horse statement, is that those known as *Omissis,* who during these early years were also known as Bowstrings, represented one of the two bands of which he spoke. Thus, the two original Cheyenne component bands of the American Horse statement quoted above, most likely comprised on the one hand the Arrow Men - later incorporated among the *Masikota,* - and on the other, the *Omissis,* later known as Bowstrings.

As regards the Arrow Men component group, they likely represented a breakaway part of the old-time *Moiseo* which some time later, joined the Cheyenne-speaking group known as *Masikota.* These Arrow Men separates thereafter, adopted the Kit-Fox as their personal warrior Society owing to a kit-fox skin being connected to the Sacred Arrows, and became the most important Cheyenne-speaking faction paramount to all other bands. This is apparent by the fact that the proper name of the *Masikota* in the guise of 'Grasshopper' and among whom the aforementioned Arrow Men amalgamated, was also adopted as a collective term for the Cheyenne Nation as a whole, while the specific role of the Kit-Fox society itself, was to protect the Sacred Arrow Keeper and his priestly retinue.

The *Masikota* Kit-Fox Society during this early period, was regarded as the fighting element among the combined Cheyenne-speaking bands, they were thus represented by the *"Man"* arrows in the Sacred Arrow bundle. The Bowstrings Society on the other hand, which included descendants of *Wheskerinni* [Algonkin-proper] tribal extraction comprising the more horticultural element of the tribe in addition to their semi–sedentary habits which, in some ways, caused them to become practitioners of a more regulated and less belligerent lifestyle as opposed to the more erratic and nomadic habits of the *Masikota,* were represented by the *"Buffalo"* arrows. Hence the successive Keepers of the Sacred Arrow bundle itself belonged to the more settled and industrious Bowstrings, while the original Kit-Fox Society represented the Arrow Men of tradition and, after associating with the *Masikota*, became the specific protectors of the Arrow Keeper and his priests. This is why Kit-Fox Warrior Society members of a later date, wore an old-time flint arrowhead along with a kit-fox stole as part of their fraternity regalia, in recognition of being included among the first two bands that received the original Sacred Arrows brought by the revered prophet Sweet-Medicine.

However, as the *Moiseo* or Arrow Men are said to have been the original recipients of the Sacred Arrows, it must be construed that the *Masikota* were then already separated as an independent group from the *Moiseo*, and as the *Moiseo* strengthened their ties with the Monsoni Cree in the north, the *Masikota* moved southeast into the headwaters district of the Upper Mississippi, whereupon the Arrow Keeper and his adherents later known as the Kit-Fox band, left the parent *Moiseo* group and joined the *Masikota* so as to remain independent of the Cree.

At an even later date, this newly formed separatist group of mixed Arrow Men and *Masikota*; by including the Arrow Keeper and his priests, caused the *Masikota* population to increase substantially by further secessions from the parent *Moiseo*, and the main *Masikota* village thus became the focal point whenever the Cheyenne people gathered as a united body. At the same time, the much smaller *Moiseo* remnant although aligning themselves with the Sioux, still represented a separate Cheyenne-speaking band, albeit of greatly diminished importance after the Sacred Arrow people among them had joined the *Masikota*. *

Together with the *Masikota*, they then moved closer to their *Omissis*-Bowstring cousins in the Mississippi headwaters country, and thus, unlike the successive Sweet Medicine Chiefs whose status and commitments debarred them from belonging to any warrior elite, the serving Keepers of the Sacred Arrows have all been members of the Bowstrings fraternity, as the informant

---

* Although the Sweet-Medicine cycle states that the prophet appeared at different times to the people, alternatively dressed in the regalia of each of the four original warrior societies of Kit-Fox, Elks, Bowstrings and Red-Shields before his pilgrimage to the Sacred Mountain to receive the Sacred Arrows, it is nevertheless, clear in the accounts that the military fraternities were not actually inaugurated into the tribe until many years after Sweet Medicine`s return to the people.

FOUR "SACRED ARROWS"

Red-Hat asserted.

At the same time, the protectors of the Arrow Keeper and priests, have always been members of the Kit-Fox Society and separate to the other later-formed Cheyenne societies of Elks, Dogs and Red Shields, each of which were originally adopted from the Suhtaio.

If, of course, both locations of Lower Red Lake and Bowstring Lake were simultaneously occupied by Cheyenne peoples, then there must indeed have been two main groups of Cheyennes at that time, as American-Horse stated. Probably these two main groups of *Masikota* and *Omissis* comprised several villages each, and this much is evidenced by the mention in certain Cheyenne stories which relate to the people's occupation in northern Minnesota when, it is said, they were being attacked by enemies from the north and northeast. Such stories often refer to the existence of several separate Cheyenne villages within reasonable traveling distance of each other. This would also explain how pottery shards of the so-called *"Black Duck"* focus which was predominantly Suhtaio, but includes an abundance of early Cheyenne-proper ware, are found in both the Lower Red Lake and Bowstring Lake areas.

Certainly, for a prolonged period, each of the three Cheyenne groups then in existence [i.e. The *Moiseo, Omissis and Masikota*], remained in contact with one another, merely preferring to camp apart due to economic considerations. But by the early 1700s, the remnant of the *Moiseo* parent band had lost its prominence and prestige and eventually, by the opening of the Nineteenth Century, had become a small hybrid conglomerate, being an admixture of Cheyenne-proper, Suhtaio and even of Teton Sioux extraction.

It seems therefore, that originally, there would have been only two Sacred Arrows brought by Sweet-Medicine; one each for those two early Cheyenne-speaking groups of Arrow Men and *Omissis*, and that a part of the Arrow Men [i.e. the Kit-Fox band] then separated from the *Moiseo* parent group and amalgamated with, by then, the first breakaway group from the *Moiseo*, later known as *Masikota*.

This is corroborated by the Suhtaio statement given to Michelson in 1910, that when the Suhtaio first crossed into the Upper Mississippi country from the east, they met with the Sioux and Cree and three [bands] of Cheyenne. Obviously this Suhtaio statement was referring to those Cheyenne bands in existence during the time in question, and which must have comprised the then three separate bands of *Masikota, Kit-Fox-Moiseo* and *Omissis*-Bowstrings.

By the much later date of circa, 1740, as inferred by Truman Michelson's Suhtaio informant Bull-Thigh, the Cheyenne component groups of *Masikota* [including the Kit-Fox band] and *Omissis* had amalgamated with the related Pipe-Stem-Men [then enjoined with the Ridge Men], and also with the *Watapio* [a mixed band of *Masikota* remnants and Sioux known as *Sheo*], and thus the Nation then comprised four confederated groups from which all the later Cheyenne bands are said to have evolved. Because of this, two additional Sacred Arrows must then have been added to the `Arrow` bundle which, thereafter, contained two *Buffalo Arrows* and two *Man Arrows* making four in total. These in turn represented the unification of the above-mentioned four Cheyenne groups which during the late historic time [circa, 1830s], included the Aorta [originally known as the Kit-Fox band], the *Omissis, Masikota*, and Pipe-Stem Men / Ridge Men band. Together they were then known among themselves by the collective term of *TsisTsisTsas*, and had the totemic names of four separate warrior societies including the Kit-Fox, Bowstrings, Elks and Red-Shields respectively. Suffice to say, these earlier separate groups after amalgamating with the Suhtaio among whom the Dog soldier Society was predominant, formed the basis for the ten bands and five warrior societies of the Cheyenne Nation of more recent time.

The importance of the coming of the Sacred Arrows is that previously, when in central and southern Ontario, the *Moiseo* and their cognates had likely been scattered across the region in numerous separate camps, in order to facilitate in a more practical manner their hunting and gathering potential. They then included among their number a hybrid admixture of *Moiseo, Monsoni, Montagnais* and *Wheskerinni* extraction, whose commonality was that all were refugees, having fled from Chippewa-speaking enemies in the east and that they spoke intelligible dialects one to the other. The predominant dialect of the collective group and its characteristics in general would, though, have been overwhelmingly *Moiseo*, e.g. proto-Cheyenne, albeit altered somewhat from the dialect spoken by the remnant of the original *Moiseo* parent band, whose members continued to use the more archaic and proper form.

The coming of the Sacred Arrows and their associated rites, offered the means by which Cheyennes could alleviate their recent period of suffering and restore a connection with the cosmic and natural order of things, temporarily

FOUR "SACRED ARROWS"

disrupted so as to cause chaos and discord among the people and their environment. In addition, tribal unity symbolized by the "Arrows," thereafter allowed the people in their separate groups, to wander further afield than previously dared, and follow their own whims of fortune without fear of becoming irretrievably separated one from the other. From this time on, the various Cheyenne-speaking bands always regarded themselves as a united people; protected by the benevolence of unseen powers through the medium of the Sacred Arrows, and which obliged each of the bands to keep in contact and assist each other in times of need. Certainly, the unification of the Arrow Keeper's Arrow Men band with the cognate *Omissis* [Bowstrings] and *Masikota*, created the foundation by which that known as `The Cheyenne Nation` came into being. Through the people's collective devotion to the Sacred Arrows, the powers emanating from them even today, allow the Cheyennes to resist all oppressors and - notwithstanding that the current Northern and Southern divisions now have their own respective governments and separate political agendas, - they yet regard themselves as a singular people who through the medium of the `Arrows,` will always be Cheyenne.

- 0 - 0 - 0 - 0 - 0 - 0 - 0 - 0 - 0 - 0

CHEYENNE, LITTLE-BEAR 1875

THE "BUFFALO HAT"

CHAPTER 2.

THE "BUFFALO HAT."

By the Cheyenne's own account, they lived about the large watery expanse of Lower Red Lake in western Minnesota with adjoining prairie for many years. How many, we can only surmise. Certainly, by the date 1640 or thereabout, one Cheyenne-speaking band at least, was in permanent residence much further south, either along or very near the Minnesota River. Tribal tradition recalls that the people's residence about the aforesaid Lake with adjacent prairie preceded any Cheyenne settlement along the Minnesota, and therefore, from the time the *Moiseo* had been pushed from or in any event, obliged to leave the district adjacent to Sault St. Marie in the east around A.D. 1450 to that of the first Cheyenne settlement along the Minnesota of circa, 1640, two-hundred years had elapsed and somewhere between these two dates, the *Moiseo* had roamed the lake country of central and southern Ontario and the northern part of Minnesota. In the interim, they had occupied a position of some permanency within the vicinity of Lower Red Lake. [1]

Assertions made by Cheyenne informants to James Mooney [1907], that the Cheyenne people had actually been created in the cold lake-filled *"Northland"* above the Mississippi Heads, leads one to suppose that by far the longest period of residence in these two areas, [that is, the Province of Ontario and Minnesota], was in effect the Ontario country. Whilst inhabiting this latter region according to tradition, the *Moiseo* were almost constantly on the move in their never-ending quest for food and a more comfortable lifestyle. Accordingly, the people generally moved in a southwest direction, and it may not have taken many years before the *Moiseo* reached the Red Lake's district of west-central Minnesota, although during that period of wandering, they apparently forgot many details regarding their ancestry, along with earlier cultural and historical affiliations with more eastern Algonquian groups.

Evidently then, the time span of Cheyenne residence in the *"Northland"* of tradition, was not a short period in their history. But as the traditional accounts recall clear descriptions regarding the people's residence and lifestyle when in the vicinity of the *"large lake and adjoining prairie"* [e.g. Lower Red Lake], it does suggest a long period of residence in this latter area also. It is more likely that the assertion by Cheyenne informants that their tribe originated somewhere above the Mississippi Heads, in reality, applies merely to the time of their becoming completely separate from the Cree and their having a singular identity, which may be thought of as evolving in the aforesaid region as a separate tribe.

Before this, the component groups which comprised the Cheyenne Nation of late historic time, had originally constituted an admixture of Algonquian-speaking peoples claiming *Moiseo, Montagnais* and adopted *Wheskerinni* ancestry, albeit sharing a common culture and history with only slight variations in dialect. Now, however, these once small autonomous bands had at last come together as a united people, made manifest by their collective adherence to the Sacred Arrows and the new innovative cult connected with them which bound the people together as one. As a result, the coming of the Sacred Arrows became in time, to be thought as being the origin of the Cheyennes as an independent entity, and which, of course, in an indirect way - it was.

Regarding the lifestyle of the early Suhtaio when in northern Minnesota and around the Upper Great Lakes, tribal tradition has preserved some details. Beginning about the year 1895, the eminent ethnologist and historian George Bird Grinnell began obtaining stories from several of his Cheyenne informants, which they in turn had heard from an old Suhtai named Standing-All-Night. This old Suhtai had died in 1867 and was; reputedly, more than one-hundred and forty years of age. He was, however, even during his years of dotage, regarded as a very reliable tribal historian, and often related how the Suhtaio and Cheyennes had once lived before becoming permanent residents in the buffalo country west of the Missouri River. In essence, Standing-All-Night used to say that during those far off days when in the Northeast, the people would often travel to great lakes which were so vast, one could not see across to the other side. The Sioux, he said, were close to the Mississippi to the east and it was from that direction that the Arapahoe also came. The Suhtaio dialect was at that time quite different to that of Cheyenne-proper, but after many years of close association, the Suhtaio came to speak broken Cheyenne. This old Suhtai historian also told how the people in those days made axes of stone and knives of flint. He mentioned the making of earthenware pots and dishes and described their process of manufacture. First, he said, fires were lit in holes in the ground and when the fires burned down, the ashes were partly raked out and the pots placed in the hole then covered with ashes, the heat from which baked them hard. He even told of the old-style lodges the Suhtaio once used. These were not lodges in the proper sense, but merely small shelters covered with bark or grass. At times, he said, when the people went camping, they had short poles dragged by dogs, and these poles were stuck in the ground and bent over to form a framework over which they spread their robes or bundles of grass. Many would then crowd into one shelter for protection from the cold. It was a long time later, after they began hunting buffalo that they made better shelters, although they then took the form of willow frames covered with hides. These lodges did not have smoke flaps and when the occupants wished the smoke to escape from the hearth-fire within, they partly removed the hide coverings from the top of the rounded roof.

Standing-All-Night always said that the first time the Suhtaio and Cheyennes came together, was somewhere far to the northeast of the Missouri River, near the same Great Lakes that are often mentioned in tradition, and that the second time their two peoples united was on the south [west] side of the Missouri, a long time after the Cheyennes had already crossed that river.

At a much later date, according to present-day tribal tradition, a large part of the Suhtaio allied themselves to the Cheyennes when west of the Missouri, whilst the remaining Suhtaio went north and joined the Cree. That group which opted to remain in the Western Plains, continued thereafter in close association with Cheyennes, although still as an independent tribe and were known as "No Colds," as opposed to those of their kinfolk that had retired to the north where winters were much more severe. Although the Suhtaio proved themselves important allies and associates of these early Cheyennes, it was not until around the date 1833, that the Suhtaio became a regular part of the Cheyenne camping circle and fully adopted members of the Cheyenne Nation.

Certainly, the Suhtaio were always a prominent component group when acting as confederates to the Cheyenne-proper and throughout their last years of freedom on the Great Plains, the Suhtaio produced not a few of the most outstanding chiefs and warriors among the so-called, *"Fighting Cheyennes;"* men such as Roman-Nose, High-Backed-Wolf, Sun`s-Road, Black-Shin, Little-

THE "BUFFALO HAT"

Wolf, Black-Kettle, White-Bull [also known as Ice] and Gentle-Horse among others. They were also an important group as regards religion, both respected and honoured by the rest of the Nation. It was the Suhtaio who introduced the Sun-Dance or Medicine Lodge ceremony to the Cheyennes along with that of the "Sacred Buffalo Head" or Hat [*Issiwun*], both of which religious assets were embraced conscientiously by the Nation as a whole.

The Sacred Buffalo Hat as it is more commonly called, or in Cheyenne, *Issiwun*, is unique to the Suhtaio, being connected with the supernatural powers deemed necessary to renew the buffalo herds, in order that the people might continue to procure sufficient meat and material for both their physical and domestic needs. The Native name for this object *"Issiwun"* or *"Essevonuh"* has been translated by Father Peter Powell as something to do with the female buffalo, being compatible in its analogy, he said, with that of "The bearer of new life." However, a more definite connotation of the term *Issiwun*, is derived from the much older ceremonial compound term of *Issi-whun*. The first part *Issi,* meaning "it is dark," and suggests the appearance of a herd of buffalo when covering the prairie. The term *whun* on the other hand, is said to pertain to the rhythmic grunting sound made by buffalo when on the run, and which incidentally, would explain how the name Suhtaio was misconstrued by some other informants as referring to the grunting sound made by buffalo in the rutting season, and thus, rendered in the vernacular as *"speech hard to understand."*

In essence, the Hat - as opposed to the Sacred Arrows of the Cheyenne-proper - represents `Female Power` and embodies all that was deemed essential to the Suhtaio, it being the integral object used during the performance of sacred ceremonies by which the spirits of buffalo and other game animals when in their underground refuge, were enticed into the open in material form to allow themselves to be hunted, and thereby, continued to fulfill the people`s requirements which enabled them to exist.

Even today as a sacred icon, the Buffalo Hat is still regarded as a powerful medium through which; as in the case of the Arrows, the omnipotent supernatural forces of both the Above World and Below World can bestow their benevolence upon the Suhtaio, and when special attention and devotion is paid to the Hat by offering one's personal prayers and suitable gifts, then the powers embodied therein, can bring success against one's enemies and when actually

THE "BUFFALO HAT"

carried to war as a tribal palladium before the people, it insures victory and the total destruction of the foe.

Unlike the Sacred Arrows, the `Hat` is composed of more durable material and so does not require its component parts to be periodically renewed, notwithstanding that the original porcupine-quill decoration on the brow band has, in all probability, been replaced with beadwork, as also deer horns on the original when resident in woodlands, seem later to have been replaced with those of the buffalo when resident on the Plains.

Thus, as the Sacred Arrows are the most important holy talismans among the Cheyenne-proper, so *"Issiwun"* is the most revered ceremonial object among the Suhtaio, and as members of the Kit-Fox warrior society are guardians of the Sacred Arrows, so members of the Elk warrior society are the special guardians of the Hat. It now resides in the care of its present keeper among the Northern Cheyennes at Busby, on the Tongue River Reservation, Montana.

One legend has it that the Suhtaio's own culture hero named *"Tomsivsi"* or "Erect-Horns," [with the alternative names of Standing Horns and Red-Tassels] was given the Hat by the powerful Spirit Beings of the Underworld and at the same sacred mountain of `Navah-hous` [Bear Butte], where the *TsisTsisTsas* or Cheyenne-proper had earlier received their Sacred Arrows. This was also at a time, so Suhtaio tradition asserts, *"When the people were starving and a great famine covered the land."* The Suhtaio, it is said, were unable to move to more provident hunting grounds because they were surrounded by fierce enemies. It was at that period, during the people's dire time of need, that a certain shaman came among them and made *medicine*, which induced the buffalo to come near the camp so the people could hunt and fill their bellies with meat. After this the people again had sufficient food and warm robes to protect them from hunger and cold and, as a consequence, the people survived. This statement refers in reality, not only to the inauguration of the *Issiwun* or Sacred Hat rites among the Suhtaio, but also to that people's migration west of the Mississippi into the buffalo and tall-grass prairie country, wherein Cheyenne-proper groups then already resided.

Indeed, a prolonged period of warm temperatures with more than adequate rainfall, had existed in the Upper Mississippi and inland Canadian regions between circa, A.D. 800 and circa, A.D. 1250, known as the Neo-

THE "BUFFALO HAT"

Atlantic period. The latter phase of this period had encouraged the Proto-Cheyennes and Proto-Suhtaio to practice agriculture on a more intensive scale. However, an era of drier summers between circa, 1250 and 1450; known as the Pacific period, likely instigated the initial Cheyenne and Suhtaio movement from their then less productive environments, and migrate deeper into the Upper part of Minnesota which country supplied wild rice and was more conducive to raising crops. At an even later date during what is termed the Neo-Boreal period [between circa, 1450 and 1880 intensifying around 1550], the growing season in the Upper Mississippi region was shortened. Summers became much cooler and there were fewer frost-free days to allow crops such as beans and squash to mature. This event did not, though, effect the native grasslands, so that grazing animals such as buffalo and antelope etc.; continued to flourish. This in turn induced a greater dependency by the now redundant crop-growing northern Minnesota peoples, to become, at least for the large part of the year, traveling hunters following the herds for their subsistence.

Another version relates that Erect Horns actually received the Hat through his woman or wife, who had sexual relations with a *Mih'n,* i.e., an Underwater Monster, and during which event, the *Mih'n* had passed a small shell from its mouth into hers. The shell in the story represents the supernatural power attributed to the *Mih'n* in question and thus, the peculiar beaded inverted fret design above the brow band on the `Hat` symbolizes the aforesaid Underwater Monster. This same design was typically used as a representation of such a creature among other tribes of the Great Lakes region, among whom were once included the Algonqian-speaking Sauk, Fox and Chippewa. The Hat itself also represents the personification of the Head chief of all the buffalo, which among the Suhtaio is regarded as having a female nature, and can be associated with the concept of *Eyhopsta*, the Yellow-Haired Maiden of the *TsisTsisTsas* [i.e. Cheyenne proper], who is also the `Keeper of the Game.`

Additionally, the Buffalo Hat is connected to the Northeast direction, which does, of course, point to the region of the Upper Great Lakes where the old-time Suhtaio once lived along with their then neighbors, the Fox, Sauk and Chippewa. Certainly, the inclusion of the shell element in the origin story of the `Hat,` suggests something compatible with the "Great Megis Shell," so prominent in Chippewa ceremonialism, so that the Hat of the Suhtaio may well have derived from an earlier Chippewa or other Upper Great Lakes Algonquian tribe's innovation. Indeed, although in the John Stands in Timber account the "Sacred Head" [i.e. the Hat] is said to have been received somewhere in South Dakota, and which in other accounts is designated specifically as the same Bear Butte where the *TsisTsisTsas* received their Sacred Arrows, alternative accounts place the site of origin at either Black Mountain near the Pipestone Quarries in south-western Minnesota, or at a height known to the Suhtaio as Stone Hammer Mountain, close to the western districts of the Upper Great Lakes.

Whatever the case, the Suhtaio Hat is fashioned from the complete crown of a buffalo head with both hair and horns attached, albeit that the horns are shaved thin, tapered and flattened. The whole is designed to be worn on the head, although this has occurred only when taken into battle as a guarantee of success or during attendant ceremonies for war, which was the usual procedure to activate the Hat's specific protective properties.

The aforementioned decoration above the brow-band is composed of large blue and white `Pony` beads, once common trade items obtained from the white man during the 18th and first half of the 19th centuries, and one assumes that, originally, dyed, flattened porcupine quill-work had earlier served the same purpose. Certainly the Hat is regarded as being very old; some tribal informants having stated it was first brought to the Suhtaio at the same time as the Sacred Arrows were introduced among the *TsisTsisTsas* between circa, A.D.1540 and 1560, and before the Suhtaio became confederated with Cheyennes. This, though, is unlikely to have been the case regarding the Hat's original conception by the Suhtaio, although it does suggest that the Hat and its symbolism when inaugurated at Black Mountain in Minnesota, had merely been re-adopted by the Suhtaio as a later variation on an older theme, once founded upon the same fundamental innovation as was the "Medicine Dance" and *Midewiwin* ceremonies along with their associated rituals among other Central Algonquian tribes.

Thus the earlier concept for the Suhtaio Sacred Hat ceremony of later times, may well have been associated with the time of the winter solstice, and only when being reinstated among the Suhtaio, did it become a midsummer ceremony connected specifically with the buffalo when on the Western Plains. The Hat in its original form would likely have been designed with deer horns or antlers, rather than buffalo horns as employed at the later date after the Suhtaio had become a fully-fledged Plains people, and certainly, the names of

THE "BUFFALO HAT"

Erect Horns and Standing Horns would indicate deer antlers, rather than the curved horns of a buffalo.

It may then be that the actual Sacred Hat ritual as later practiced by the Suhtaio, was not inaugurated among them until after the Suhtaio had left the Upper Great Lakes region, at which time they were no longer confederated, or perhaps, even in harmonious contact with other Great Lakes Algonquian tribes. The ceremony was likely to have been merely a revival of an older religious expression, which the Suhtaio had modified to accommodate their new lifestyle and environment after entering the prairie country west of the Mississippi and at which time, buffalo became a more important dimension to Suhtaio existence as a food and utility source. Subsequently, the buffalo replaced the moose, elk and deer of the eastern woodlands and Great Lakes regions as their predominant asset for survival.

In short, the original concept that inaugurated the Suhtaio reverence for the Sacred Hat, had derived - in part at least - from either the Sauk, Fox or Chippewa, which must then place the early Suhtaio in the vicinity of Sault St. Marie at the junction of the Upper Great Lakes, where we know that at one time, each of the aforementioned tribes resided in close proximity to one another.

Likewise, the Sun-Dance as introduced among the *TsisTsisTsas* by the Suhtaio, seems also to have had a northern origin, being a regeneration ceremony indispensable in an area where the seasons occur in the extreme, i.e., in winter ice-bound with deep snow and below freezing temperatures; in summer, as high as ninety degrees Fahrenheit, balmy, humid and wet. We do know from *Blackduck* archaeological remains which likely represent ancestral Suhtaio, that Suhtaio peoples were frequenting the area at the western tip of Lake Superior, if only sporadically, as early as the middle years of the thirteenth century, and by circa.1450, the Suhtaio had moved further east along the northern shore of Lake Superior as far as Sault St. Marie. However, attacks from the Iroquois and perhaps from Ottawa bands [although not as allies] from the east and southeast during the early sixteen-hundreds, forced the Suhtaio west and not until circa, 1680, did the Suhtaio move back east between the western tip of Lake Superior and the Mille Lac region of the Upper Mississippi, as certain contemporary map references assert.

THE "BUFFALO HAT"

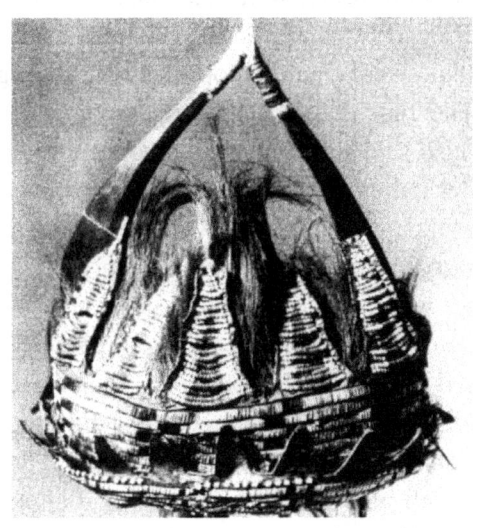

**HORNED HEADDRESS FROM REGION OF THE GREAT LAKES C. 1750.
[MUSEE DE L`HOMME. PARIS.]**

**JAMES LITTLE BIRD WITH THE SACRED HAT.
[PHOTO BY FATHER PETER POWELL. HARPER AND ROW PUBLISHERS. 1981]**

THE "BUFFALO HAT"

Cheyenne tradition further states that the Suhtaio and Cheyenne-proper [i.e. *Moiseo, Masikota* and *Omissis* bands], came together and separated three times before the Suhtaio were finally adopted as fully-fledged members of the Cheyenne Nation. The first time the Suhtaio became confederated with the Cheyennes, so it is also said in tradition, was during the time of the people's wandering in the Great Lakes and rice-marsh country far northeast of their later High Plains habitat, which would fit well with the period during the first half of the seventeenth century, when both peoples were in the northern Minnesota country and in contact with the Sioux.

It must be then, that the Suhtaio during those early colonial days, were very closely associated with both the *Moiseo* and Monsoni Cree and at one time, were probably included under the aforementioned Joliet's *Alimouspigoiak.* By circa, 1660, i.e., around the same period as Pierre Radisson's visit, this particular Suhtaio branch of the *Alimouspigoiak* had already established itself in the marshlands of the Upper Mississippi. They were then allied to the *Moiseo* and Sioux of that region on the one hand, and to the Cree and Chippewa of the Upper Great Lakes on the other. All these peoples at that time, knew the Suhtaio by the colloquial term of "Dogs" or "Dog Village People" [i.e. *Chongaskiton*], albeit there were other designations, one of which was *Neutrals,* and it is also likely that this was the time when the Suhtaio first embraced the original concept of the Sacred Hat and its religious significance. Having said this, it appears that the `Hat` keeper himself was not accorded the same reverence as was the keeper of the `Sacred Arrows,` as the Suhtaio today recall that in a past time, one `Hat Keeper` when old and decrepit had actually been abandoned by his people to die alone on the prairie, having been considered too much of a burden to warrant the people's continued support.

It will be seen, however, throughout the course of the following narrative, how *Issiwun* or the "Sacred Buffalo Hat," was also regarded as an integral part of serious war paraphernalia in conjunction with the "Sacred Arrows" of the Cheyenne-proper.

- 0 - 0 - 0 - 0 - 0 - 0 - 0 - 0 - 0 - 0 - 0 -

EARLY HORSE DAYS ON THE WESTERN PLAINS

CHAPTER 3.

EARLY HORSE DAYS ON THE WESTERN PLAINS [1800-`6]

By the white man`s year of 1740, Cheyenne-speaking Indians after centuries of wandering across south-eastern Canada and the North American Great Lakes regions, were permanently entrenched in the short-grass prairies between the Middle Missouri on the east, and Black Hills on the west. The people then owned a number of horses; lived in conical buffalo-hide dwellings and moved from one hunting ground to another as equestran nomads. They were in close contact with other equestrian nomadic groups and also, sedentary earth-lodge-dwelling riverine tribes such as Mandan, Hidatsa and Arickara, some friendly, others hostile. All, however, practiced a culture based on hunting large game such as buffalo and elk and harboured a similar world view. Cheyennes were then friendly to the Crow, Kiowa and Arapahoe tribes, each of which were enemies of Shoshoni-speaking peoples further west incorporating those later known as Comanche, and hostile to all Pawnee-speaking peoples of the Mid-West Plains. Tribes of the Middle Missouri region also residing in permanent earth-lodge towns and including the Kansa, Omaha and Ponca, were intermittingly at war or peace with Cheyennes and the latter`s allies in the Black Hills region, and Cheyennes were either at peace or war with most Sioux-speaking peoples of the east. [1]

In late 1742, a grand Allied hostile crusade comprised of Cheyennes and Kiowa was launched against the Shoshoni or `Snakes` of the west, but which enemy was not actually met in force. However, during the latter decades of the same century, countless battles between the Black Hill`s tribes which included Cheyennes, took place with various Eastern and Teton or Western Sioux bands until A.D.1800, when the pipe of peace was finally smoked between most Cheyenne groups and Teton Sioux factions. Five years later, all Cheyenne-speaking bands including the Suhtaio which by then had allied with Cheyennes, were themselves also fully at peace with the Sioux and together, they separately and as allies, assaulted Crow and Shoshoni-speaking peoples and drove the Crows west of the Black Hills; the Shoshoni across the Rocky

Mountains, and Shoshoni-speaking Comanche south to and below the Arkansas River.

It was in response to an episode in summer of 1800, at which time Crows wiped out thirty Oglala Teton Sioux, that throughout the coming snow-filled moons, Oglala chiefs decided to eliminate the Crows as a military power on the Northern Plains. Subsequently, they offered a war-pipe to other Sioux bands of Miniconjou, Sans-Arc and Brule and even their recently acquired Cheyenne allies, inviting all to join together and avenge the loss of the thirty Oglala. The chiefs and headmen of each band accepted the pipe and inhaled its symbolic smoke, thereby pledging themselves and warriors to accompany the proposed crusade.

Thus, come mid-summer, 1801, the grasslands around the Oglala camp on Cherry Creek flowing into the Big Cheyenne River between the Middle Missouri on the east and Black Hills on the west, became a moving mass of colour, as the various allied bands congregated in preparation for a grand offensive against the Crow.

From east, south and north the war bands came, all eager to shed the blood of a common foe. Gorgeous feathered bonnets nodded in the breeze, whilst gaudy patterns of dyed porcupine quills and beads decorating hair-fringed war shirts and leggings, splashed bright hues amid hundreds of conical smoke-tanned tepees pitched in their respective band circles, and which covered many acres on a verdant sea of grass. Close to each camp vast herds of ponies milled around, looking from a distance like a huge patchwork of brown, black and white.

The congregating of the various bands was treated as a festive occasion, and at the same time, new arrows were made; lance points and battle-axes re-ground, and among those who had not received protective Spirit Helpers, war *medicines* were earnestly sought to watch over them during the coming conflict, and give them power to bring honour to themselves and their people.

It was to be a large force to invade the very heart of Crow country, and the camps buzzed with anticipation of how many heads [scalps] they would take, along with the vast number of ponies and women and children captives they would drive home before them. So it was after several weeks of singing, dancing and feasting, the grand war-party started out on its *"Red road to war."*

This must have been one of the largest host of warriors seen on horseback west of the Missouri since many a year. Certainly, the largest the

Crows themselves were yet to see sent against them by their now combined Sioux and Cheyenne enemies. Here were gathered over one thousand allied warriors; many armed with bows and arrows, lances and stone-headed war clubs, whilst in addition, some carried short barrelled, smoothbore trade muskets, iron headed axes and even French and English sword blades, and all were of a mind for vengeance; all set against the Crows.

As the huge cavalcade moved forward it followed a course northwest, and when reaching what today is designated Powder River, scouts were sent out to locate the nearest Crow village.

It was not long before the scouts returned, reporting they had discovered a Crow camp of thirty lodges nestling peaceably along a river bank, and that the occupants appeared to be ignorant of impending danger. A council of war was convened, during which the allied chiefs agreed their forces should march out that very night; surround the Crow camp and launch a surprise attack at dawn. In response, the entire conglomerate of allied warriors immediately prepared themselves for battle, and when all were ready, the grand host started forth heading directly towards the foe. Come dawn, the Allies were positioned in a long colourful line, almost encircling the still sleeping Crow village.

As the first rays of sunlight appeared above the eastern hills and lit up the prairie floor, a single high-pitched war-cry rang out, instantly followed by a tumultuous roar arising from a thousand throats. Then was heard the thunder of four thousand hooves pounding the earth, as the entire allied host urged their ponies forward and charged headlong toward the camp. The sound of war-whoops coupled with the clatter of weapons beating on hide-covered shields, along with the shrill of eagle-bone whistles amid the random discharge of guns, brought the villagers from their lodges and panic seized them all. Some of the older Crow warriors called on their comrades to stand and fight, at least in an attempt to save the women and children, who began running in every direction in frantic efforts to escape, and a number of Crow menfolk did indeed, sacrifice their lives by making a stand and facing the overwhelming number of enemies merely that their non-combatants might have a better chance of survival.

Such, however, was the complete surprise attending the attack, the Cheyennes and Sioux carried their charge right in amongst the tepees. Smashing into them and other camp paraphernalia, trampling all and sundry under hoof. The Crow warriors who along with teenage boys and old men constituted little more than one-hundred persons bearing arms, were, of course, grossly outnumbered. Very soon the Crows were falling back under the sheer weight of enemy pressure. In fact, many of the fleeing Crows were obliged to leave their kinfolk where they had fallen, although others continued to fight desperately in bitter hand to hand struggles before one by one they sank to the ground - either dead or dying - until all resistance was subdued. Some Crows escaped, but they were few, and these went running to another Crow village further west along the Yellowstone with word of the attack. But their brother Crows were a long way off from being able to give immediate or practical military assistance.

In the meantime, the Allies dispatched the enemy wounded then cut the bodies into pieces, and after indulging in such gory acts of mutilation, they looted the tepees then set them ablaze along with all domestic belongings they themselves deemed worthless. Following this, they packed their plunder on the backs of little less than one-hundred Crow women and children captives and vacated the scene, driving their prisoners before them like a herd of wild ponies.

Among the aforesaid female captives taken during the event, were two young women having been stolen by Crows from the Shoshoni some short time previously, and who were later traded by the Allies to the Hidatsa. The Crows had known one of these women as Frog-Woman, who was a sister to another Shoshoni captive already among the Hidatsa and known by the name of *Sacagawea*. The same who later accompanied the Lewis and Clark expedition on its epic journey from east to west across the Continent.

After returning to their base camp from whence they came, the victorious Allies dismantled their lodges; packed the covers on pole drags and hastily returned to their own country east of the Black Hills. Before, that is, the whole Crow Nation could organize a formidable war-party and exact revenge.

Cheyenne oral tradition states it were they, Cheyennes alone, who drove the Crows west around this date of 1801, and true it is, as a direct result of the above disaster in which Sioux were also involved, the Crows did temporarily take up residence west of Powder River as far as the Pryor country, in order to escape further raids from both Cheyenne and Sioux enemies.

To the Sioux and Cheyennes on the other hand, it was considered an important victory, and the Oglala American-Horse's "winter-count" for that year records,

> "Winter 1800/1801. Oglala, Sans-Arc, Miniconjou, Brule and Cheyennes destroyed thirty Crow lodges." [2]

EARLY HORSE DAYS ON THE WESTERN PLAINS

Following this, in 1802, Arapahoe allies accompanying Cheyennes, made their own peace with the Sioux and next year [1803], Crows achieved a degree of retribution by killing between twenty-five and thirty Cheyennes in another pitched battle between their opposing forces. Meanwhile, peace having been effected between Cheyennes, Arapahoe and Sioux, allowed all three to visit and trade freely with each other`s allies and friends. And so it was two years later [1805], contingents of the same three tribes just happened to be at an Arickara town on the west bank of the Missouri near the mouth of the Big Cheyenne, and where they planned yet another crusade against the Crow.

It had happened due to some misunderstanding now forgotten, that Crows and Arickara who had once been friends, renewed hostilities against each other, and in Mid-August, 1805, a great body of warriors including Sioux, Cheyennes and Arapahoe visited an Arickara town carrying a war-pipe. The pipe was offered to their Arickara hosts to join them in a grand offensive against their now mutual Crow enemies.

The reason for this visit seems to have been in part, a response to a recent defeat of Teton and Yankton Sioux the previous summer when Crows, by their personal involvement, had assured the Teton and Yanktons suffering a crushing and humiliating defeat. The Cheyennes, of course, had their own reason to want vengeance on the Crows, owing to several recent defeats suffered at that people`s hands which had brought much grief to their lodges, such as the twenty-five or thirty Cheyennes killed two years earlier. In fact, it was Cheyennes who had first proposed the idea of another hostile crusade, as during the previous winter [1804], Cheyenne delegates had carried their own war-pipe to several tribes, among whom were included both the Arickara and Sioux, and even to the Mandan, when first they had contemplated such a venture.

As regards the Arapahoe, during the month of August the previous year when in company with Cheyennes, Padaux [Lipan Apache] and Gattacka [Kiowa-Apache] along with contingents from other tribes, they had visited the Arickara towns for the first time, ostensibly on a trading expedition, and whilst there the Arapahoe at the instigation of Cheyenne allies, made peace not only with the Arickara, but also with a band of Sioux which happened to be visiting the Arickara at that time. Thus, in order to show both the Arickara and Sioux their personal commitment to the recent pact, the Arapahoe included themselves in the proposed crusade against the Crows who only recently had also been the latter's erstwhile friends. The Arickara, likewise, had suffered recent reverses from the same enemy and being at peace with Cheyennes, Arapahoe and Sioux, the Arickara willingly accepted the pipe, and agreed to travel with their newly-found Allies along the *"red road"* against the enemy.

Somehow the Crows themselves had word brought them of such an impending attack by a greatly-superior force. As a consequence, it was agreed among the Crows that each of their scattered bands should be called in and together, move without delay to a canyon-like gap in a range of sandstone bluffs a short distance from what the Crows knew as "Shoots-the-Arrow Rock," overlooking what today is designated Pryor Creek, south-eastern Montana.

This accordingly was done. And so it was the whole Crow Nation congregated as a single body where; it was supposed, they could better defend their families and safeguard their vast herd of ponies.

The site chosen by the chiefs to make their stand had a particular advantage. At the south end of the river valley, the aforesaid 'Gap' forms a low-walled narrow defile or canyon running east to west, and it was here in the deep recess of the canyon itself, that the Crows erected their tepees, while at the canyon mouth at its east end, they placed bushes and small trees to hide the opening from view. Having done this, all able-bodied Crow men folk with the exception of fifty hand-picked warriors, positioned themselves in battle array along each side of the canyon and awaited the arrival of the foe. The remaining fifty warriors were instructed to act as a decoy force, intending to lure the enemy into the narrow defile where they could be fought in smaller groups, and hopefully, slaughtered piecemeal by the main Crow body which would then take the Allies by surprise.

In the meantime, Crows scouts were sent out at all times, so adequate warning could be given as soon as the enemy host appeared.

It was two days later before the enemy did come in sight. The fifty hand-picked Crow warriors mounted their war-ponies and rode ahead from the mouth of the canyon and into a wide grassy valley where a small herd of buffalo was grazing. Just before the allied force drew near, these Crow warriors started to ride in amongst the herd in the pretence they were starting on a hunt. The Allies saw the fifty Crows scattered here and there across the valley, and thinking they could easily run down and kill them all, they at once urged their ponies forward, and yelling war-cries at the tops of their voices charged headlong towards them.

The fifty Crows waited until the Allies were only forty or fifty yards distant, then bunched themselves together and rode pell-mell towards the canyon mouth, as yet still hidden from the foe.

The Crows appeared to be running, *"...like scared rabbits,"* [3] it is said, and the enemy in premature jubilation sent a cloud of arrows after them, while those who carried fire arms of some description shot wildly, and thus expended their first shots before the battle proper began. Suddenly to the Allies' bewilderment, the fifty Crows rode right through the trees and foliage concealing the canyon mouth, but convinced that they themselves would close up with their quarry in another moment, the Allies rode blindly on, still shooting arrows and musket balls into the fleeing bunch ahead.

On they rode following the retreating Crows, straight into the mouth of the canyon and soon were between the canyon walls on either side. The fifty Crows who until this time had appeared frightened with no stomach to fight, suddenly pulled up their mounts; wheeled them smartly around and not only faced the oncoming foe, but charged straight at them.

At this date the Crows owned very few guns, but as their fifty comrades bravely confronted the enemy, a number of gunshots rang out and hundreds of arrows whistled through the air from each side of the canyon. The Crow missiles smashed into allied riders and horses, toppling many a warrior from the saddle and creating general confusion among their ranks. The enemy could only turn and flee in an endeavour to escape the trap and this they managed to do, although leaving many of their comrades dead or dying in the wake of their retreat. The whole fighting force of Crows then joined in the affray; some shooting arrows and guns from the cover of rocks dotting the landscape; others charging on their war-ponies in amongst the throng of enemies in order to count *coup*, or to perform reckless and sometimes, suicidal deeds.

A number of teenage Crow boys between fifteen and sixteen years of age, were not content to remain in the comparative safety of the Crow village protected by the women and old men. Instead, they ran onto the battlefield, capturing loose horses of the enemy whose riders had been killed; seriously wounded or simply unseated from their saddles, and these animals the Crow boys drove deep into the far recess of the canyon as the spoils of war.

Several times during the day-long contest the Allies regrouped and charged anew. But having lost so many of their number both dead and wounded, along with many put on foot and unable to resist Crow cavalry in a significant manner, they could make no serious inroads on the field.

It was late afternoon when the entire Crow force made one last exerted effort led by the latter's indefatigable Chief Long-Hair, and this time they routed the Allies completely. The latter turned their horses around and rode back the way they had come as fast as they were able, many riding double after picking up unhorsed companions as they fled.

Numerous Sioux winter-counts commemorate this fight, referring to it as, *"...a running battle with the Crows"* [4] and in which event, a number of mounted allied warriors were forced to ride double, rendering them at a great disadvantage to those pursuing them. Conversely, a Hunkpapa Sioux winter-count entry for the same year, states that it had been a large Crow war-party consisting of warriors both mounted and on foot which had assaulted a Sioux village, and in the event,

> "The battle was long and well fought, but as the Crows were mounted two on a horse [so they could easily run down the Sioux, many of whom were on foot having had their horses killed from under them], the Crows were the victors and many [Sioux] were killed." [5]

Here it seems, the interpreter of this particular `count` misconstrued the true meaning of the entry, and it should rather be compatible with those other `counts` which state specifically, it was the retreating Cheyenne, Arapahoe, Sioux and Arickara who were forced to ride double in order to escape their pursuers on this occasion.

These same `counts` further mention that a white man trader among the Cheyenne or Arickara force was also killed, while during another stage of the fight, eight warriors made a stand in some kind of enclosure or "dugout," but were surrounded by the enemy and eventually wiped out, although it is also said that *"...The Sioux killed many enemies also."* [6]

However, as is often the case regarding the earlier entries in the winter-counts themselves, there is here as elsewhere, some discrepancy as to whether the mention of eight surrounded and killed, actually refers to Allied warriors or to Crows.

EARLY HORSE DAYS ON THE WESTERN PLAINS

What is remembered by the Crows, is that most of the dead and seriously wounded from among the allied ranks were left where they had fallen, to be abused, humiliated and eventually butchered and mutilated by the victors. To leave one's comrades on the field whether they be alive or dead, was considered a dishonourable act among all Indians, and if having done so, it shows how completely demoralized and in such a state of disarray the retreating Allies must have been at that time.

Nevertheless, the Crows did not let up. They rode after the fleeing foe; raced alongside them and fought hand to hand as they galloped across the prairie, and continued a running fight for several hours until, that is, it became too dark to distinguish friend from foe. Only then did the victorious Crows give up the chase, and return to the original scene of conflict at the canyon's mouth.

It is further said that in the aftermath of the fight, the Crows collected together the bodies of their own slain kinsmen, and even those of their enemies left on the field of battle. These they buried in several pits which they covered over with dirt and stones, creating a number of small cairn-like structures in order to protect the remains from scavenging beasts.

For many years after this time, any Crow - and indeed, members of those Allied tribes involved - when passing through the canyon, were apt to place a small stone on one or more of the cairns in commemoration of the event and to appease the spirits of the dead. Today these piles of stones can still be seen at the place called Pryor Gap.

- 0 - 0 - 0 - 0 - 0 - 0 - 0 - 0 - 0 –

CHEYENNES IN VICTORY AND DEFEAT

CHAPTER 4.

CHEYENNES IN VICTORY AND DEFEAT [1806-`19]

It was soon after the above-recounted fight, that Crows made a pact with the Arapahoe and the latter's Atsina cousins along with a band of Pikuni [Piegan] Blackfoot. Having done this, the Crows endeavoured to extend the hand of friendship to Cheyennes, - who were close allies and associates to both the Atsina and Arapahoe, - along with an invitation to join the Crows in yet another intertribal peace-gathering the following summer. [1]

Accordingly, a delegation of twelve Crow braves was sent into Cheyenne country east of the Black Hills, intending to offer their long-time Cheyenne enemies the calumet of peace, lest the recent escalation of hostility between them should increase even further, and at a time when Crows were already fully engaged defending their hearths against the Assiniboine and more powerful Blood and Siksika [Blackfoot-Proper] tribes from the north.

Unfortunately, at this period, Cheyennes were not inclined to terminate their feud with the Crows, or relax in their endeavour to wrest the eastern portion of Crow country for their own use. Indeed, Cheyennes could afford to be brash now having the powerful Teton Sioux as allies, while at the same time, Cheyennes themselves were conducting a vigorous war against the Shoshoni with whom only a few years earlier, the Crows had also made peace. As a consequence, Cheyennes now regarded Crows as allies to the Shoshoni and thus, by association, were still enemies of the Cheyenne.

What the actual details surrounding the fate of the twelve Crow emissaries were, we are not told in either documented or oral accounts. Crow tradition merely states that somewhere on route to Cheyenne country, the Crow delegation was confronted by a large Cheyenne party and the entire Crow embassy wiped out.

Seemingly oblivious to such a treacherous act as then perpetrated by Cheyennes, in early summer that same year [1806], Hidatsa cousins of the Crows and supposed allies, undertook a friendly trading trip to a Cheyenne tepee village south of the Hidatsa towns, and among which people were then encamped contingents of both Arapahoe and Sioux. The subsequent trip and meeting between the Hidatsa visitors and other tribes present was successful.

Some trading with each other took place, and pacts effected between them which lasted a sort while at least.

Such a move by the Hidatsa initially, was in no small part in response to having previously been persuaded by Captains Meriwether Lewis and William Clark, whose joint expedition just happened to be on its return journey east after traveling across the Continent to and from the Pacific Ocean. Whilst again among the Arickara, Lewis and Clark once more held council with the Arickara along with several Sioux, Arapahoe and Cheyenne chiefs then visiting the Arickara town.

Two years prior to the above-recounted fight at Pryor Gap, the same white explorers when ascending the Missouri and domiciled at an Arickara town on that river's west bank, had met a small number of Cheyennes trading among the Arickara. Captain Clark commented in his journal for October 16th 1804, that Cheyennes were then actively raiding and stealing horses from Spanish Provinces further south, and mentioned that three young Crow captives were then among the Cheyennes.

Now, in August 1806, the same white explorers on their return journey down the Missouri, were again domiciled among the Arickara and again met Cheyennes, albeit a small twelve-lodge group trading corn from their Arickara friends. Included also at the same town was the Head Mandan chief known as Big-White, and together, the various chiefs present sat in council with William Clark and discussed promises earlier given by the Indians in 1804, that while in the explorer's absence, they would make lasting pacts with all their neighbours and foes.

Thus, the explorers urged all chiefs present to keep the peace between themselves, and even extend the hand of friendship to their Mandan and Hidatsa neighbours further upstream. And so it was in accordance with the explorer's wishes, the Hidatsa had set out on a mission to make appropriate pacts with Cheyennes and contingents of Arapahoe and Sioux then encamped alongside the latter.

In another place of Clark's journal of 1806, he recorded some personal observations regarding Cheyennes at that time.

On August 21st, Clark was introduced to a Cheyenne chief who appears from the said journal to have had the name of Grey-Eyes, but which was also the name of the head Arickara chief then present. Whatever the case, Clark wrote that the Cheyenne chief in question was *"...stout and jolly,"* [2] and after council with other Cheyenne, Arickara and Mandan present, a pipe of peace was smoked between them all. Clark was then invited by the Cheyenne chief to join him in the latter's own buffalo-hide tepee which was composed of twenty buffalo skins, being one of the largest tepees among twenty others of the same tribe erected on a hill overlooking the Arickara town. The main group of Cheyennes, Clark was told, was expected to arrive the following day, and Clark offered to give the said chief a small medal to commemorate the meeting, one of many the explorers carried with them. However, the chief refused to take it as he did not like to accept such things from white men who were mysterious to him. Clark also invited the same Cheyenne chief to go the white man's Capitol in Washington D.C. along with the Mandan Chief Big-White and meet the Great White Father President Jefferson. But to this request also, the Cheyenne chief refused. Clark could not persuade him further, but in good spirit, he presented him a coloured ribbon as a token of the white man's continued friendship.

In a later passage of the journal, Clark also noted that Cheyenne menfolk were large and their dress in summer was a light buffalo-skin robe with or without hair, along with breech-clout and moccasins. Their ornaments were few, Clark continued, and consisted of blue beads, shells, brass rings and broaches, although he also noted a number wearing bear-claw necklaces while strips of otter skin were tied around their heads and trailed down their backs. Others, he said, had their hair cut across above the eyes with small plaits above each shoulder, the rest entwined with buffalo or horse hair also in two plaits or flowing down their backs. Of Cheyenne women, they wore loose habits in two pieces with a string over each shoulder and lapels falling half way down the body in front and behind. They also wore blue beads in each ear.

Not aware of the whole Cheyenne Nation, the explorer Clark went further to estimate Cheyenne numbers in their entirety as comprising only between 350 and 400 men with a total of 130 to 150 lodges, and that they were considered rich in both horses and dogs. For the Cheyennes' part, the chief requested Clark to send white traders among them as they [Cheyennes], had lots of beaver in their country.

Lewis and Clark then left their hosts, but throughout the following years as indeed had been done before, several white traders continued to visit Cheyenne camps. Intertribal warfare on the other hand soon after the explorers left, ensued again, albeit somewhat sporadically between Cheyennes, Mandan,

Hidatsa, but moreover, with more-eastern Sioux bands such as Sissiton, Santee and Yankton.

Throughout the period 1812-'13, a clerk named John C. Luttig working at Manuel Lisa`s new *Missouri Fur Company* post not far below an Arickara town at the mouth of Grand River on the Missouri`s west bank, mentions Cheyennes in his journal several times as trading at that post, and includes the names of several Cheyenne chiefs. Notably, those then known to the traders as Lesharroco, Medicine-Man, Papillion [Butterfly] and Poor-Little-Wolf. Some Cheyenne bands were, at that date, still very familiar with the Upper Missouri earth-lodge tribes, although, apparently from Luttig`s journal, they themselves were alternatively at peace or war with the Mandan, and at times, in friction with all Sioux peoples both west and east of the Missouri. Other Cheyennes were residing predominantly near the headwaters of the Big Cheyenne River further west, and were, of course, still in hostility with both Crows and Shoshoni northwest of that point, and continued to be so for many years to come.

Meanwhile, further south, roamed several allied tribes commonly known collectively to white men who had contact with them as "The Trading Indians." These included members from the Arapahoe, Kiowa, Comanche, some friendly Shoshoni from Columbia River, and Cheyennes. Together, they were in the habit of holding grand intertribal trading fairs near the mouth of Horse Creek, being a branch of the North Platte River near what is now the Wyoming – Nebraska State line. Such events since 1803, if not earlier, had become annual ones, whereat the above tribes traded between themselves horses and Spanish goods in return for guns, steel implements and other European artefacts obtained from the resident Missouri tribes. Overall, those Trading Indians in attendance, were under the leadership of an Arapahoe head chief named Bear`s-Tooth and come summer of 1814, a visiting Cheyenne contingent brought with them a number of Brule Sioux, these latter having been persuaded by Cheyennes to make peace with the Kiowa and Comanche with whom, for a long time, the Sioux had been at war.

The Kiowa particularly; ever on precarious terms with Sioux since having been driven from the Black Hills by them twelve years earlier, showed utmost caution and tact in an endeavour to carry off the meeting amicably. The tension, however, was enormous and the scene like a powder keg ready to blow sky high. All was going well until a Kiowa buck began arguing with a Brule.

CHEYENNES IN VICTORY AND DEFEAT

The argument was quickly settled by the Brule, who picking up a war-club, split the Kiowa's head wide open. All hell broke loose as both Sioux and Kiowas grabbed weapons and faced each other in battle array. For a moment, both sides screamed and shouted abuse at each other, whilst others at the gathering, namely Comanche, Kiowa-Apache, Shoshoni, Cheyenne and Arapahoe, sided with one or another as the preference took them.

As it was, the Sioux and Cheyennes together suddenly charged forward and a general melee ensued. The result being that the Kiowa and those supporting them were driven west towards the mountains at the head of the North Platte. The neutrality of the trading camp was thus shattered and as a result, disbanded. Those in sympathy with the Kiowa followed in the wake of the latter, and those agreeing with the Sioux and Cheyennes remained with that people. Of the Cheyennes, some stayed behind on Horse Creek, while others wandered off north in company with the Sioux and so continued a peaceful Sioux-Cheyenne relationship. Having said this, a significant number of Cheyennes thereafter, associated themselves with Bear-Tooth's Arapahoe and a short time later, met in a friendly manner a remnant of Kiowa who remained in the Black Hills region and who were subsequently referred to as 'Cold Men' by their more southern Kiowa kinfolk. With the Cold Men Kiowas, certain Cheyennes again roamed, hunted and socialised with as they had of old, and continued to do so for a number of years following.

In the meantime, those Cheyennes remaining further north in league with bands of Western or Teton Sioux, continued raiding both Crows and Shoshoni, while the Arapahoe, albeit joining Cheyennes against the Shoshoni, were sometimes neutral as regards the Crow and with whom oft-times, they and Arapahoe were socialising with one another.

Come August 1816, a Cheyenne war-party raided a Crow camp and escaped with several ponies, some of which were still covered with Crow blankets. The Crow village occupants had been suffering from the ravages of Smallpox, and the Cheyenne thieves, unknowingly, carried the disease back to their own people. On their entry into camp one of the returning party broke out in spots and only hours later, dropped to the ground a dead man. The Cheyennes were much alarmed. In panic as more and more of their people succumbed, they left their lodges standing and dispersed over the prairies and hills in different directions, endeavouring to out-run an evil which they could not see or defend themselves against. They remained dispersed until whatever unseen evil had betaken them, it finally burned itself out.

How severe Cheyenne population suffered during sickness that year is not known. But no longer were they as populous as they had been, and consequently, those remaining aligned themselves even closer to the Sioux, both as allies and confederates to protect themselves from several more populous foes.

Hereafter, Cheyennes as allies to the Sioux, often became embroiled in altercations with the latter's own foes, such as Mandan, Hidatsa and at times, the Arickara themselves.

With regard to the Shoshoni, Cheyennes had been fighting against them for many years, although now, with the aggressive and powerful Sioux at their side, they took an even more serious approach when attacking them.

Thus it was summer 1817, when according to Cheyenne informants of both George Bird Grinnell and George Bent, that due to some perceived catastrophe perpetrated by the Shoshoni on Cheyennes – details of which we are not told, - Cheyennes launched a grand crusade against the Shoshoni and the latter's Bannock allies, and during which, the Cheyenne Nation's `Sacred Arrows` and `Sacred Buffalo Hat` were carried with them to ensue victory.

The whole Cheyenne-speaking population was then involved, and all their people including warriors, old and young men, women and even children, were included on the march into the very country of the foe. The Sacred Arrow Keeper himself led the way, while his wife walked beside him carrying strapped to her back the kit-fox bundle itself, in which the `Sacred Arrows` were kept.

Each morning scouts were sent out searching for a Shoshoni village to raid. But each time no enemies were found. The Cheyennes, though, travelled on through the heart of Shoshoni Country, notwithstanding it was evident that their quarry was steering well-clear of confronting such an imposing force. The latter seemed to be merely playing will-o-the-wisp with an enemy host which knew little of the country it was in.

Nevertheless, not having sighted any villages of the enemy, three Shoshoni, – one man, a woman and her child - were accidently discovered crossing a stretch of open ground and given chase by two to three-hundred howling Cheyennes all painted and dressed for war, and eager to count the first coup of the expedition for the `Arrows.` The fugitives were soon overtaken and the man promptly killed, while the woman and child were spared death and taken into captivity. Some Cheyenne informants declare that the lone Shoshoni man in question had been carrying a metal shield, like Spanish Conquistadors once carried one-hundred years earlier, and this too, was also taken as booty.

That same night, however, whilst the warriors were dancing and singing victory songs over the single Shoshoi scalp, the two captives slipped quietly out of camp and escaped into the darkness.

Next day, the Cheyennes continued meandering through the unknown terrain still looking for a much larger group of the enemy. But at length, the Cheyenne chiefs and head warriors convened a council to discuss their current situation. It was agreed they had been in Shoshoni country long enough, and so far had obtained only one Shoshoni scalp for their trouble.

It was decided that their search could not go on indefinitely, as not enough game could be found in such mountainous country to suffice their large congregation. They should go home, the chiefs said, as an enemy had been killed and the potency of the `Arrows` not been undermined as enemy blood had been spilt to atone for whatever the Cheyennes` original loss had been. So the crusade came to an end, and all the people returned east to their own domain.

This is, however, the first remembered `move` of the `Arrows` as told by old Cheyenne informants of the Buffalo days, and the only `move` when the enemy in significant number was not met.

It was also at this date, that war between Cheyennes and Mandan re-erupted and in 1818, a battle between parties of both tribes took place and during which, warriors employed the use of Dog-Ropes and stayed their ground alone facing the enemy, until either they were over-whelmed and killed, or forcibly whipped away from their posts by rescuing comrades.

During the same year, although Cheyennes were not officially at war with the Pawnee, Cheyenne horses had been stolen by Pawnee thieves and visa-versa, and if the culprits were caught, they had invariably been killed. Previous to this, Cheyennes on their return from Shoshoni country after the somewhat failed crusade recounted above, were a little disheartened that a greater conflict with the intended foe had not then occurred. Thus, any other foreign party was prone to attack from restless Cheyenne bucks, eager to regain prestige.

Thus when early the following year [1818], one such Cheyenne war-band discovered a small party of Skidi Pawnee, regardless of consequence the Cheyennes attacked the party head on. Only one Pawnee escaped while all his companions were slaughtered, their bodies then mutilated by the victors who cut off the limbs and scattered them across the grassland to camouflage them among bones of buffalo, so not to be immediately discovered by any larger Skidi party looking for their missing kinfolk.

Maybe the dead Skidi were not discovered, for even this event had not immediately inaugurated determined war between Cheyennes and Pawnees at that time. Indeed, it took another two years of depredations against each other before dirt was thrown in the air, and all-out war commenced between them.

So it was early in 1819, with deep snow on the ground, a horse-stealing party of Skidi Pawnee led by a brother of the Skidi head chief and on foot, was traveling south to the camp of the previously mentioned 'Trading Indians' on Arkansas River and who then included Cheyennes among their number. Together, the Trading Indians owned some of the finest horses on the Plains, having been stolen from other tribes and Mexican *rancheros* and *haciendas* further south. Unfortunately for the Skidis, their party was discovered before it reached its objective, but not knowing the danger it was in, had continued along the trail with confidence.

When near the Trading Indians' camp, the Pawnee thieves began preparing horse-hair ropes to lead stolen animals away. But while thus engaged, numerous groups of horsemen came galloping over the hills around them, and in an instant, the Skidis were surrounded.

Hastily, in spite of intense cold, the Skidi stripped to the waist as was their custom, to avert pieces of clothing entering a wound and to allow them to move more freely, and readied themselves to meet the foe which happened to be a host of combined Cheyenne and Arapahoe from the same Trading Indian camp. The Allies circled around their Skidi enemies and poured a hail of arrows and musket balls into the latter's midst, the result of which proved disastrous to the Skidi. The Allies then charged directly at them.

In one great sweep almost half the Skidi were dropped like so many blades of grass under a sickle's edge. The Skidi partisan fell to the ground staining the earth around him red, but for a while, he was still alive, and even from his prone position, continued to direct the defence.

Not only were the horse-thieves grossly outnumbered, they were out-gunned, and it was this fact that made them easy prey for the well-armed Allies. In a fan-like manoeuvre, the horde of mounted warriors closed in for the kill and when nearly upon their prey, the remaining Skidis ran headlong into them in a desperate effort to break through the allied ranks and reach a timbered creek a little way off, and from where they could make a stand.

Such was the latter's determination, they broke clear through the Allies surrounding them and some did manage to reach the shelter. But fifty-three Skidi lay dead on the field, including all the leading men among them.

Of those endeavouring to seek safety in the timber, soon only one Skidi was left standing and he; bloody all over, turned in his tracks and staggered back to where his companions lay to be killed amid their corpses by enemy missiles. Of the few Skidi who did extricate themselves from the carnage, only seven were not seriously wounded. Despite this, they did keep the Allies at bay until nightfall, and at which time at last, they succeeded in escaping under cover of darkness, thus saving themselves from complete annihilation.

Indeed, as twilight was falling, the allied Cheyennes and Arapahoe had themselves retrieved their own dead and wounded, which was no small number, and retired from the scene. The surviving Skidis for their part, when darkness finally fell, constructed a number of crude travois; pilled their dead and wounded on them, and dragging the contraptions by hand and still half-naked despite the cold, followed the course of the North Star which led them home. It was the month of March before the Skidi survivors arrived back at their earth-lodge town on the Loup Fork of the Republican from where they had originally started from.

After this event, all Cheyennes were fully at war with all Pawnee tribes and while such was going on, further north above the Arkansas, predominant among enemies harassing the more northern Cheyennes, were Crows, residing between the Tongue and Powder River north of the Platte. These particular more northern residing Cheyennes, were then encamped on the Belle Fourch branch of the Big Cheyenne north of the Black Hills, and were congregated with their confederates the Suhtaio which at that date, still comprised an independent element variously known to other tribes as either *Staihitans, Skutani* or *Flyers*. More often the Suhtaio when on their own, were apt to come off worse in conflicts with the Crow. But notwithstanding their own inferiority in number and some recent reversals, they were determined still to claim the Lower Powder and Tongue River country for themselves. Thus they continued to engage in persistent warfare with the Crows, and seldom did a week pass that did not witness some bloody confrontation between the two.

CHEYENNES IN VICTORY AND DEFEAT

At times, one side or the other would get together a large party and move deep into their opponent's country, either to exact revenge for some recent defeat, or more simply, to antagonize the other in return for some lesser slight upon their honour.

Each victory nonetheless, generally had its price to pay, and the following episode is yet another case in point.

Due to a typical yet unsuccessful raid by a war-party of Cheyennes and Suhtaio, which had merely intended to steal horses from a Crow village, Mountain Crows under the strategic direction of their paramount chief, Long-Hair, wiped out thirty or more Cheyenne-Suhtaio Crooked-Lance warriors. Only one of the vanquished party survived, and he took news of the slaughter back to his people.

It had seemed as the Crooked-Lance party travelled on at a leisurely dog-trot, that the powers of the Suhtaio holy-men who had previously given prayers and blessings for the party's success, were strong, for they managed to reach the enemy country without miss-hap and everything was going to plan. The entire party was in high spirits and confident of success.

In one account of the affair recorded by the Northern Cheyenne historian John Stands-In-Timber, which he put together from recollections of old Crow and Cheyenne story-tellers early in the 1920s, it is stated that the Cheyenne [i.e. Suhtaio] party was traveling along Tongue River upstream with a scout out on both flanks. These scouts came in and reported that the Crows must also be on a war-trail, for they had seen a lot of sign, although they themselves had no idea where the enemy might be. Stands-In-Timber added that the Crows had in fact already discovered the Cheyennes, and intended to ambush them at the forks of a tributary of the Tongue now known as Prairie Dog Creek. The two scouts went out for a second time, but in a short while one returned saying that again he had seen plenty of sign but not the enemy themselves. The other scout meanwhile, a man named Two-Bulls, remained ahead of the party on the east side of the creek and as it transpired, viewed the ensuing events from a concealed position some distance from where they occurred.

The rest of the party thus continued up Prairie Dog Creek to its fork, then travelled along the crest of a wide but low ridge separating the two streams. It was at this point that the party was suddenly attacked by Crows; quickly surrounded and forced into a desperate fight for their lives.

CHEYENNES IN VICTORY AND DEFEAT

In yet another version obtained by George Grinnell from several Cheyenne and Crow informants, it is asserted that as the Cheyenne party was traveling through the hilly country over by Tongue River with scouts reconnoitring the area, they came upon a lone Indian also on foot, and immediately gave chase. Being hotly pursued by the Cheyennes, the Indian was soon overtaken and killed. Joe Medicine Crow added that upon examining their victim, the Cheyennes knew at once he was Crow by his fashion of jewellery and pompadour hair-style, but whether he had been scouting for a larger force in hiding, they could not determine. However, no sooner had his scalp been lifted, a great body of Crow warriors appeared; some on horseback, many on foot, and the Cheyennes themselves were obliged to flee. All accounts agree, however, it was after the Cheyennes had continued their trek between the forks of the creek and reached an area of flat land 200 yards by 300 that Crows suddenly appeared; whooping and singing, and at first merely sat their ponies in a static position in full view of the Cheyennes before launching their attack.

In the meantime, the Cheyennes had at once taken to their heels. They ran towards a nearby hill and where, on its shale-strewn summit overlooking Prairie Dog Creek, they prepared to make their stand.

Seeing their quarry in flight before them, a large body of Crows charged headlong in pursuit in an effort to cut off their enemy's retreat. Their feathered bonnets streamed out behind them in the wind, as half-naked bodies; daubed with red and yellow ochre, strained forward in the saddle in their eagerness to reach the foe. But the Crow response had come too late. By the time they attempted to actually charge up the hill, the Cheyennes were ready to meet them from behind hastily built, but as to prove effective breastworks, and had dug-in, anticipating a long and determined contest.

The hill itself was a kind of natural fortress easy to defend. Most of the way around its base was very steep, but in one place it slopped gently from the summit down to the valley floor, and here horses could be ridden up to the crest without difficulty. The Cheyenne defenders entrenched along the top paid particular attention to this slope, and the Crows for all their endeavours, could not gain the height and over-run the position with their cavalry. As the Crow horsemen thundered up the slope, a barrage of well-aimed Cheyenne arrows broke the charge and forced the enemy back down into the valley below.

The failure of their first charge brought the Crows to their senses. They foresaw the folly of continuing a direct assault on the hill, for other than the loss of many Crow warriors which such an action would undoubtedly incur, it would almost certainly be in vain. All the while, that is, the Cheyennes remained behind their defences and had a plentiful supply of ammunition. Instead, the Crows surrounded the position and sniped at the defenders from cover with their smooth-bore trade muskets, which the Crows just happened to have in abundance due to a recent trading excursion to their Hidatsa relatives. In this manner they kept the Cheyennes pinned down preventing their escape, and gallopers were dispatched back to the Crow camp with a request that more warriors should come out and assist them.

Other Crow camps since leaving a Medicine Lodge gathering were still in the vicinity, and the Crow head chief, Long-Hair, sent runners to inform them what had happened. The entire Mountain Crow division was thus aroused. War clothes were hastily donned; faces and bodies painted and soon, hundreds of warriors, whooping and yelling, were racing their ponies pell-mell to the scene of conflict. Following behind came the Crow women and children and old ones, all eager to watch the fight and witness the annihilation of their mortal foes.

Long-Hair the Crow chief then spoke,

> "We ourselves have plenty of time. We need not sacrifice our brave men by engaging in rash actions to finish off the enemy too quickly. Let us instead say to our women, return to your camps, take down the lodges and bring them hither, and set them up on the flat land which surrounds this hill where sits the enemy supposing themselves secure. We shall remain in camp at this place until the battle is done, and these Stripped-Arrow People are no more." [3]

The Chief's suggestion was met with unanimous approval, and the tribal crier told the women to do as Long-Hair requested. The women obeyed and within an hour returned, bringing with them pack-horses and travois loaded down with tepee covers, lodge poles and all other domestic paraphernalia. The chief then instructed the lodges be pitched evenly around the base of the hill, thus cutting off all avenues of retreat for the besieged Cheyennes.

The Cheyennes meanwhile, viewed these goings on with apprehension from atop their rocky refuge, mingled, no doubt, with a degree of curiosity, but could only wait and ponder what might happen next.

Once the tepees had been erected the Crows began treating the affair like a festive occasion. Old men beat drums and blew on eagle-bone whistles, while the women sang Brave-Heart songs in praise of their husbands and sons to give them courage in the coming fight. Cooking pots were put to boil, and many non-combatants took up favourable positions to get a better view of the impending conflict in order to satisfy their morbid interest.

Having thus taken time in preparation, it was not until past mid-day before the Crows eventually resumed the fight. It was a Crow war-chief named Sore-Belly who then directed the warriors to let lose a barrage of arrows and musket balls towards the defender's position, and soon, it seemed, every surrounding rock and bush concealed a Crow warrior.

Throughout the afternoon the barrage continued, and the Cheyennes responded in kind. They also shot back arrows fired by the Crows to supplement their own dwindling supply. Every so often a single musket shot would explode from the gun of the Cheyenne partisan One-Eyed-Antelope, but the Cheyenne response appeared to have little or no effect on the Crows. As one Crow musket was silenced, there was another to take its place. Several Cheyennes were wounded, some mortally, and their comrades knew well that their own demise was assured.

At length, the sun began to sink over the western horizon. As the light diminished, so did the firing of guns and arrows until it ceased completely and most of the Crows retired to their lodges. Crow guards kept watch on the hill throughout the night in case the enemy should try to escape, while at the same time, the beating of drums and singing of war and victory songs reverberated over the hills emanating from the valley below. Some Crows including men and women, hurled obscenities at the besieged and the latter in turn, sang loud their own Brave-Heart songs and retorted in defiance that when their fellow tribesmen heard of their deaths, they would send a great force into Crow country and rub out the entire Crow Nation.

So the night passed, and early next morning not long after the sun came up, the battle was resumed.

Periodically, lone Crows would make brazen dashes up the hillside in endeavours to reach the defenders and count coup, but few ran down again, and by mid-day, the Cheyennes were still holding their own and could not be budged.

It was about this time that a Cheyenne in full regalia of scalp-shirt, beaded leggings and eagle-feathered bonnet, jumped over the low breastworks and commenced running back and forth inviting the Crows to kill him. He was making a "caw-caw" sound and flapped his arms in imitation of a bird in order to ridicule the foe. The noise was deafening as every Crow musket, it seemed, was discharged almost simultaneously at him, and a cloud of arrows whistled through the air. By some miracle the lone Cheyenne was not hit, and he went back behind the breastworks to the welcoming cheers of bravado from his comrades. Soon after his return, he again leapt over the breastworks and repeated his actions in an expression of contempt for his enemies. Three times he did this thing, but on the third time he was cut down by another blanket volley of Crow missiles and killed.

It was not long after the death of this brave Cheyenne that the showers of arrows coming from the breastworks became more sporadic. Eventually the last Cheyenne arrow was spent, and only the partisan One-Eyed-Antelope was occasionally still shooting with his gun.

There was a Crow sniper lodged in a crevice between two rocks close to the Cheyenne position. His deadly aim had created some havoc within the breastworks, causing the Cheyennes to lose several of their number to his marksmanship alone.

The position of this Crow was pointed out to One-Eyed-Antelope and the next time the Crow exposed himself to view, the Cheyenne chief fired and blew the sniper's brains out. With cheers of adulation around him, One-Eyed-Antelope reloaded his gun, raised it to the sun and sang a *medicine* song. He then struck the butt on the ground [moreover to seat the ball rather than an assurance of success] and singling out another of the enemy, he fired again and killed a second Crow outright. Twice more One-Eyed-Antelope repeated the procedure, and each time he killed a Crow. But after the fourth shot there was silence from within the breastworks, for this was the last of the ammunition among them.

The Crows soon realized the predicament of the Cheyennes, and were determined to finish them off completely before day-light should fade again. Sore-Belly thus regrouped his forces and prepared at last to make another charge up the hillside, supposing only a few defenders were still alive.

Before such was done, however, a mournful wail suddenly emanated from the hilltop, and the Crows knew well its meaning. Their opponents were getting ready to die, for this was a Crooked-Lance death-song.

Not desiring to tarry longer, Sore-Belly raised the solitary Crow war-cry of *"Koo-Koo-Hey"* and in response, a mass of Crow braves most of whom were on foot and led by Sore-Belly also on foot, assaulted the height from all directions, scrambling over the rocks and over each other in their eagerness to get at the foe.

A popular Crow medicine man [whose name has been forgotten] wearing a buffalo-horned headdress and mounted on a fine steed, rode out in front of his comrades, and galloping up the slope of the hill was first to reach the Cheyenne position. Bravely he leapt his mount over the stone barricade and landed in the midst of the defenders. All at once the Cheyennes ran up to him and began flaying about him with tomahawks and slashing with their knives. One Cheyenne jumped up on the Crow`s horse behind him and tussled for supremacy of the seat, and with the aid of his fellows, managed to topple the rider from the saddle. The Crow medicine man was dead before he touched the ground, and such was the unbridled frenzy of the Cheyennes, they dragged his body over the rocks and literally hacked it into pieces.

The next instant the rest of the Crows were on the crest, tearing down the stone breastwork and screaming vengeance for the death of their medicine man.

In response, the remaining Cheyennes bunched themselves together and with knife or tomahawk in hand, prepared for the end. Suddenly they let out a series of wild ear-piercing war-cries and in unison, threw themselves headlong into the mass of Crows around them, stabbing and slashing blindly as they grappled with their enemies in a number of desperate hand to hand struggles. But one by one the remaining Cheyennes were dropped to the ground, either dead or dying, until all at last lay low.

Two Cheyenne brothers son of a well-known Suhtaio chief named Red-Painted-Robe were in this fight standing side by side, and at the end they lay together in death on the blood-soaked ground, as once they had been together in life.

The last Cheyenne to fall, it is said, fought most valiantly. He slew and disabled several Crows before he himself was over-powered by sheer weight of numbers and killed. His body was later found by Cheyennes nearly at the base of the hill. Apparently he had broken right through the Crow ranks, but finding no further place to run, had made his stand, and there he stayed, fighting unto death.

The jubilant Crows, including a great number of women and children who had been watching the contest from safe vantage points, then flooded onto the hilltop, and began dispatching the Crooked-Lance warriors who were still alive and stabbing those already dead. They stripped the clothing from the corpses, and gleefully hacked off the heads and limbs of their victims. These grisly trophies were then attached to the ends of lances and musket barrels to be paraded around the tepees during the victory celebrations to come.

All this activity on the hillside had been viewed by the surviving Crooked-Lance scout Two-Bulls, who had remained in a concealed position on a height not far north from the forks of Prairie Dog Creek.

Sometime later after darkness had fallen, Two-Bulls crept away unobserved by the Crows, and started his long and hazardous journey home.

When finally the scout did reach his home village and burst out news of his party`s slaughter, the whole population lapsed into a prolonged and excessive period of mourning. Arms and thighs were gashed; hair cut short and covered with ashes or torn out in hanks. Clothing and tepee covers were ripped and shredded and heart-rending lamentations filled the air. At once promises were made among the grieving kinfolk to mount a grand crusade against the Crows to avenge their loss. But in the meantime, there would be much sorrow within many Stripped Arrow lodges throughout the coming snows of winter.

- 0 - 0 - 0 - 0 - 0 - 0 - 0 - 0 - 0 - 0 –

EIGHT-HUNDRED CROW CAPTIVES ARE TAKEN

CHEYENNE, SCABBY-BULL.

CHAPTER 5.

EIGHT-HUNDRED CROW CAPTIVES ARE TAKEN [1820]

With the passing of winter 1819 /´20, and spring sunshine melting snow on the hillsides, to the east of Crow country along timbered streams flowing through the Black Hills, the occupants of scattered Cheyenne and Suhtaio villages began to stir from inertia through the winter season. [1]

Now it had happened in a certain Suhtaio village there lived the man Red-Painted-Robe and his wife White-Buffalo-Woman. Their two sons having been killed in the aforementioned Crooked-Lance slaughter the previous summer, caused their hearts to lay heavy on the ground. Perhaps in Crow country their scalps were still being sung and danced over, yet no vengeance raid on the killers had yet been contemplated by the Cheyennes themselves. It was because of this that Red-Painted-Robe begun ostracising himself from tribal society. He also gave away his horses and most prized possessions thus making himself a poor man. Two-Twists, however, a young Suhtaio of the remaining Crooked-Lances, would allow no one to accept the discarded

EIGHT-HUNDRED CROW CAPTIVES ARE TAKEN

belongings, for he knew the old man was trying to tell the people something by his actions. One day Two-Twists went to the lodge of Red-Painted-Robe and asked him why he had `thrown away` his horses and belongings.

Red-Painted-Robe replied, he had thrown them away in grief for his two sons whose bodies still lay in enemy country and had not been covered. By this he meant no act of retribution had been enacted on the killers. But still no vengeance raid was forthcoming.

Soon after this, Red-Painted-Robe gave away his tepee and the rest of his possessions and started sleeping under the stars at night. Again Two-Twists spoke to the old man. It is not known what words passed between them, but when Two-Twists returned to his lodge his mind was made up. He would get together a formidable war-party and avenge the sons of Red-Painted-Robe, and if the enemy be behind breastworks, he declared, then he alone would drive them out or die in the attempt.

Two-Twists was pledging himself to take the role of a suicide warrior, willing to sacrifice his life to bring defeat upon the foe. From here on, he could take victuals from anybody`s kettle and whip up laggards on the trail without rebuttal, and was offered other men`s wives as reward for his commitment.

Two-Twists was a Suhtaio band member and the hostile expedition now being planned against the Crows was, from the beginning, a Suhtaio initiative. Thus the head chief High-Backed-Wolf 1st, who was half Suhtaio and half Cheyenne, took up the war-pipe and carried it to each of the Cheyenne-speaking bands to elicit their chiefs and warriors in joining the proposed venture.

Throughout the snow-bound moons whilst sat around flickering fires, there had been much Kill-Talk voiced against the Crows. High-Backed-Wolf thus additionally, carried the war-pipe to the Cheyenne`s Sioux allies, and a number of Oglala Sioux puffed on the stem. Some Brule Sioux also took it up, along with a few Miniconjou from lower down Cheyenne River.

The fact that all Cheyenne and Suhtaio chiefs along with some Sioux did accept the pipe, and a very large number of warriors had promised to join the venture, the whole Nation was buzzing with excitement.

Such was the people's enthusiasm, it was decided that the two most sacred talismans among the Cheyennes and Suhtaio, consisting of four Sacred Arrows [*Ma`huts*] and a Sacred Buffalo-Horned Hat [*Issiwun*] respectively, would be carried in front of the grand war-party to ensure its success. So it was

EIGHT-HUNDRED CROW CAPTIVES ARE TAKEN

that War-Path-Bear, keeper of the Sacred Arrows, and Sun-Getting-Out of-Bed, keeper of the Sacred Hat, each also took up the war-pipe and inhaled four symbolic puffs, signifying that the two great tribal palladiums would be carried against the foe. In addition, the whole tribe; women and children included, would actually join the march into the very heart of Crow country, for truly, Cheyennes were determined that on this occasion, the Crows would pay dearly for their exultant scalp-dances over thirty and more Crooked-Lance topknots.

During the forthcoming battle a distinguished warrior would wear the Buffalo Hat and lead the Suhtaio warriors, although he would not be expected to get too close to the enemy, lest the `Hat` fell into the hands of the foe. Two-Twists asked the Hat keeper to let him be that man, but as he had previously vowed to risk his life, his request was refused. Another Suhtai named Whistling-Elk was given the honour of doing so instead.

When came the *"Moon when buffalo are fat,"* the beginning of June 1820, the entire Cheyenne and Suhtaio-speaking Nation led by High-Backed-Wolf 1st, along with a sizable contingent of Sioux Allies under renowned Oglala chiefs named Bull-Bear and Old-Smoke, started on their bellicose venture against the Crows.

After several weeks journey, the allied cavalcade reached a point along the Lower Powder not far from its junction with the Yellowstone. Here the Allies set their base camps; the Cheyennes and Suhtaio on the west side of the river, the Sioux on the east side about one mile distant.

It was whilst encamped at this place early next morning, that Two-Twists appeared riding around the inner-circle of Cheyenne and Suhtaio lodges mounted on a magnificent black and white pony. He himself sported a gorgeous eagle-feathered bonnet on his head, and wearing a beaded and quill-worked war-shirt, deer-hide leggings adorned with numerous black horizontal stripes, and beaded moccasins with wolf-tails trailing from the heels. The horse he was riding was led around the inner circle by a camp crier who proclaimed aloud to the people that here was their champion Two-Twists who had pledged to offer his life in the coming confrontation to bring victory over the Crows. Two-Twists himself was at the same time, professing aloud,

EIGHT-HUNDRED CROW CAPTIVES ARE TAKEN

"I will give our people a chance to destroy the foe. I alone will clear the way for our brave men to charge and make the ground muddy with Crow blood." [2]

And the onlookers responded with shouts of *"Ha'ho, Ha'ho."*

Meanwhile, even before the Allies had erected their hundreds of tepees, the Crows in camp on Tongue River not far west must have known of their coming. They could not, though, have known then if their enemies were coming merely to hunt or with hostile intent. The presence of women and children among the Allies would usually signal peaceful motives, as very seldom did Indians put their families at risk by including non-combatants as part of an invading force. Nevertheless, as the Crows were resolved to stay their ground, they, too, began preparing for a fight.

This was the Crow village of the *Ashalaho* [i.e. Many Lodges], the band of the Mountain Crow Head Chief, Long-Hair, and which only recently had played host to the entire Crow population, comprising at this date somewhere in the region of one-thousand lodges. The respective Crow bands had been together holding annual religious ceremonies, but had since split again into at least three separate bodies, each of which had gone off in a different direction to conduct its mid-summer hunt. As a consequence, this same Many Lodge village on the Tongue, being that nearest the Allies, was now reduced to around two-hundred and fifty lodges, which included members from each of the thirteen Crow clans, and contained about fifteen-hundred persons, including between four to five-hundred males of fighting age.

Being aware of the presence of a large enemy force within striking distance of his village, Long-Hair called together his subordinate chiefs and held a council of war.

Long-Hair told those assembled to send out scouts in a specific direction, and at a certain place which he then described, they would find the enemy camps. His personal *medicine* helpers `Bear Spirit` and `Morning Star,` he said, had told him this, and would also prevent the invaders moving away until the scouts had gathered whatever intelligence they wished to obtain.

The scouts duly set off to reconnoitre the allied camps. The result being they were discovered by the enemy and forced to make a precipitous retreat, leaving one of their number dead in the process. The Cheyenne High-Backed-

EIGHT-HUNDRED CROW CAPTIVES ARE TAKEN

Wolf, now fearing the Allies would lose the initiative once the surviving Crow scouts reported their position, immediately called together the headmen of the Cheyennes and Suhtaio along with their Sioux confederates, in order to re-appraise the situation.

During the course of deliberations, it was unanimously agreed they should attack the Crow village as soon as possible, before that is, the Crows had time to react to their scouts' report of the size and location of the allied camps, and take appropriate evasive action.

So it was only a few hours before midnight that the great allied war-party, numbering at least one thousand warriors, all be-feathered and painted and mounted on wiry ponies decorated in a similar manner, started from their two camps along the Powder in search of the Crow village. In addition, a host of women and other non-combatants followed some distance behind in order to watch the contest from safe vantage points, and in the expectation of carrying off much plunder from the camp they hoped to see destroyed

That same night in the Crow village, the surviving scouts came loping in on their exhausted mounts. A small pile of dried buffalo chips was hastily erected in the centre of the camp, and the leader of scouts had first to kick over the pile before reporting to the chiefs. Such an act was tantamount to making a vow that what he was about to relate would be the truth, and after complying with custom, the scout leader burst out news of his and his comrades' ill-fated brush with the Cheyennes. He also mentioned the great size of the allied camps, along with added intelligence that the number of ponies belonging to the enemy scattered along both banks of the Powder could be counted in their thousands. Long-Hair was alarmed. Again he called his chiefs together and held a second council of war. The Crows could still not have known for sure if the Cheyennes and Sioux had come into the country specifically to fight or to hunt. Nevertheless, so the Crow chiefs reasoned, the Sioux and Cheyennes had now drawn first blood, and the chance of raiders sallying forth to harass their camp, was a more certain threat to contend with.

Expediently, Long-Hair dispatched runners to take word of the great allied presence to the other Crow camps, with an urgent request to organize large war-parties and join the warriors of his own village, whereupon, they could go forth and attack the foe together. However, as an afterthought and thinking the Allies might, even then, be preparing to march against them, the subordinate chiefs decided not to await the arrival of their kinsmen. Instead, this time they countermanded Long-Hair's directive and ignoring his advice, sent word to the various Crow camps that their respective war-bands should set out directly against the foe on their own initiatives. The chiefs further decided to move their village to Otter Creek [known to the Crows as Badger Creek] an eastern tributary of the Tongue, and at the same time, would send out their own warrior force to attack the allied camps before the enemy could start.

To this last proposal the other Crow camps did as suggested, and each of the warrior societies in eight large war-bands led by their respective pipe-holders, started out in separate bodies against the foe. They set off independently of each other, although all travelling in the same general direction. Among these several war-bands the largest belonged to the Half–Shaved-Heads Society led by Sore-Belly, and he, perhaps more than any other, was confident of achieving a great victory over his people's mortal foes. Long-Hair on the other hand, had previously advised caution. After hearing that nearly the entire fighting force of the Nation had been instructed to go out at the same time, he berated the council for not leaving behind an adequate force to protect the camp, lest it be attacked while the warriors were away. But his warnings fell on deaf ears, and the war-bands were soon far distant in the blackness of the night.

It was intended that a number of formidable Crow war-parties would assault the allied camps from different directions if, that is, their forces did not unite before reaching their objective. Either way, by so doing the Crows might gain the advantage of surprise. Their plan was to kill as many allied warriors as possible; capture a large number of women and children along with the horses, and drive the rest of the invaders back across the Powder, expelling them from Crow country once and for all.

Now, however, in the opposing camps of Crow, Sioux and Cheyenne, there were only women, children and old men and their civil chiefs [whose duty it was to stay with the non-combatants] left behind to defend the tepees if they themselves should be attacked. But, ironically, neither side's rank and file imagined for one moment that their own villages were under immediate threat. All were certain their respective war-parties could successfully deal with any eventuality.

It was not long after the several Crow parties had started from their separate villages that a young Crow warrior named Red-Owl, having been away

EIGHT-HUNDRED CROW CAPTIVES ARE TAKEN

at the time, came into the relocated camp on Otter Creek. Learning of the departure of the war-parties, he at once took up bow and quiver; mounted his war-pony and rode off into the night in an endeavour to catch up with the warriors. He was obliged to ride slowly as he tried to figure out the trail made by his kinsmen with only a pale moon to give light.

At this time the young Suhtai named Whistling-Elk [later known as Spotted-Wolf] out scouting far ahead of the allied force, saw the lone Crow riding slowly along looking hard at the ground. For some reason Red-Owl dismounted from his horse, probably to inspect the trail more closely, and it was then that Whistling-Elk charged upon him. Before the Crow could reach for his bow and arrows carried in the quiver slung across his back, the Suhtai had knocked him twice on the head with his war club. Red-Owl fell to the ground and was lying quite still, apparently dead. Whistling-Elk then took the Crow's weapons and horse and rode back to the allied war-party to report what he had done.

When the Allies heard of Whistling-Elk's deed they were in high spirits, thinking that yet another of the enemy had been killed, and supposing the man was likely a scout from the Crow village, they thought their own passage towards it would now go undetected and they themselves would take the enemy by surprise. As it transpired, the lone Crow who Whistling-Elk attacked was only stunned. After his assailant had ridden off, Red-Owl soon regained consciousness, whereupon, he headed straight back to the village he had recently left. Even as Red-Owl was returning to the village he could hear the sound of many horses - like the rumbling noise of buffalo on the move - and knew there must be a very large enemy war-party nearby heading in the same direction as himself.

It was shortly past midnight when Red-Owl came running, almost breathless into the Mountain Crow village in which were now only old men, and women and children, all the warriors having gone in search of the allied camps. Red-Owl was still bleeding profusely from the head wound where he had been hit by the Suhtai Whistling-Elk, although he told the camp occupants he had been set upon by a number of enemy warriors who had counted coup upon him and stolen his weapons and horse. He also told of the many horses he had heard coming towards the village, and advised the people to flee at once because of the imminent danger they were in.

EIGHT-HUNDRED CROW CAPTIVES ARE TAKEN

Now it happened that Red-Owl had only recently stolen another man's wife and had eloped with her in order to escape the husband's wrath. This was the reason he had been absent from the village when the several Crow war-parties first started out. Because of this, Long-Hair and most of the people were not convinced by his story. Knowing of Red-Owl`s adultery, they agreed among themselves that the man whose wife he had stolen had come across him in the dark and beat him about the head with a pony quirt, as indeed, would not have been uncommon in such instances among the Crows, when a man's wife had been stolen or compromised and the injured party sought satisfaction.

Surely, the people said, if the enemy had in truth attacked him, they would have killed him and taken his scalp, and besides, if there were any Cheyennes or Sioux nearby, then their own Crow war-parties would have found them. The people made the decision therefore, to remain where they were, although just in case there was an element of truth in Red-Owl`s words, Long-Hair commanded that a barricade of logs and brush be placed around the camp. This was duly done, `though in a haphazard manner and of somewhat flimsy nature as a half-hearted precaution against attack. Red-Owl did not bother to argue. Instead, he went immediately to the lodges of his friends and clan relatives and told them to quickly get their most prized possessions together and move away as soon as possible, for the whole village was doomed to disaster.

Altogether, around fifty families were persuaded to leave the camp. They left their lodges standing, abandoning everything that was too heavy to carry or deemed of little value. They mounted their ponies and leading pack horses behind them, went out into the night with Red-Owl to seek a place of safety in the hills.

In the meantime, the allied war-party was making good progress and drawing ever closer to its objective, even though their actual route of travel was slightly off-course from the exact location of the Crow village. On the other hand, the Crow forces lost their bearings completely, and seemed to be heading away from the allied camps rather than toward them.

It was now but a few hours before dawn. Each of the two great war-bands, one composed of eight parties of Crows; the other of allied Cheyennes and Sioux, were travelling in opposite directions and actually passed one another without the least inclination of doing so. Only many years later, when Crows discussed the affair with the Cheyennes and Sioux and compared the different routes of their respective war-bands during the night in question, did

EIGHT-HUNDRED CROW CAPTIVES ARE TAKEN

they realize how close they had come to actually bumping into each other in the dark.

By a stroke of providence on the part of the Sioux and Cheyennes, the Crow forces failed to find the allied camps, although the latter by then may have moved to a different location from where the first body of Crow scouts had initially found them. The allied warriors for their part, found their objective, but had difficulty doing so, and the sun was already up before the Crow tepees along Otter Creek were sighted.

This, of course, was the same village of Long-Hair, the occupants of which due to the episode with Red-Owl the previous night, were still curled up on their pallets deep in slumber.

The Allied warriors reined in their ponies among a surrounding stand of trees about one hundred yards distant from the outer perimeter of lodges, and thus positioned in many tight mounted groups, they faced the camp on three sides. Suddenly, there appeared on the far side of the village a procession of Crow women and children, along with a few old and middle-aged men coming leisurely towards the tepees. Some were horseback and others on foot leading pack animals, but all oblivious to the presence of their enemies. These were, in fact, a body of those who had gone out with Red-Owl during the night and now thought it safe to return.

Apparently, Red-Owl and his followers had gone just so far into the hills when they started quarrelling among themselves. Several of their number had been moaning it was too cold to stay out and when the sun came up and they could hear no sound of battle, they said that perhaps Red-Owl had been lying after all and nothing was going to happen to the village. As a result, about half these people; some twenty-five families in total, had left their more cautious companions and started back towards the camp.

The Cheyennes and Sioux saw them coming, and remaining hidden from view among the trees, allowed them to enter the village before making their presence known.

A young Crow girl then between ten and twelve years of age who was taken captive that day by Cheyennes, and later known by the name of White-Haired-Killer, was a member of this Crow party returning from the hills. She always said, they had no sooner got back to the village and were unloading their horses when the Cheyennes suddenly charged, taking them completely by surprise.

EIGHT-HUNDRED CROW CAPTIVES ARE TAKEN

Having said this, according to the Cheyenne version, the Allies themselves had only just arrived on the scene, at virtually the same time as the returning non-combatants were approaching from the far side of open ground surrounding the camp. The sun had been up some short while, but there seemed to be no activity within the camp itself. The Cheyennes also say they had been surprised that no Crow warriors had come out to meet them.

On this occasion, there appeared to be no determined opposition to the allied force and the latter were confident of an easy victory now they had the Crows at their mercy. Consequently, the allied host watched and waited in silence until the last of the returning Crows entered the sleeping village and began unloading packs from their horses.

One important man among the allied host on this occasion, was a Suhtaio warrior named Ice. He belonged to the Contrary Warrior Society, whose members were apt to speak and do things backward and had pledged themselves never to retreat in battle, even if it meant certain death. This man was positioned on his war-pony a little in advance of the Cheyennes, looking conspicuous by the stuffed skin of a prairie-dog owl tied to his forehead, and red paint of his society order covering his entire body which was naked, but for breech-clout and moccasins made from remnants of old lodge skins. In his left hand he held striped of its wolf-fur covering, a holy `Thunder-Bow` lance, thought to embody the power of `Thunder` itself, and it was this man who, by passing the lance behind his neck from left hand to right, actually gave the signal for the allied host to charge.

In response, the Allies in a long colourful line all at once charged from the timber and into the open, almost completely surrounding the camp. The Allies, however, stopped some fifty yards from the camp perimeter, whereupon at first whilst sat upon painted ponies, they began singing and whooping, but which soon gave way to the fricative cry of *"Shi, Shi, Shi,"* the sound a cat makes when angry and in this case, to indicate that their hearts were very bad towards the Crows. At the same time, others beat quirts on hide-covered shields to arouse the sleeping occupants of the camp.

This sudden commotion did arouse the camp. It brought the Crows running from the lodges and the sight which met their eyes threw many into a panic. Some stood for an instant gazing with a fixed stare as if dumbstruck at the sight of the enemy host around them, and clapped a hand over their mouth in the customary expression of horror. Their chief Long-Hair assisted by some of the old men, tried desperately to calm the people and restore some sense of order within the camp and they did, at length, manage to get the people in a defensive frame of mind. The flimsy barricade of logs and brush erected during the night was hastily re-enforced, and gaps between the tepees filled with camp baggage and anything else the occupants could lay their hands on. All those who could use or hold a weapon took up positions facing the enemy, ready to defend themselves as best they could against the expected onslaught, whilst mothers with small children in their arms prepared to make their escape; if chance allowed, into the surrounding countryside.

The Allies waited, meanwhile, for certain rites pertaining to their `Sacred Arrows` and `Sacred Hat` to be duly performed.

Holding the Sacred Arrows wrapped in a kit-fox skin in one hand with arm outstretched towards the Crow camp, War-Path-Bear sang a holy song and every now and then spat juice from a plant he was chewing. He then took one of the `man` or `war` arrows from the bundle and holding it horizontally before him, its flint-headed point directed at the foe, he repeatedly raised his left foot and hopped about on one leg. As he continued to hop and sing, he several times stamped his raised foot on the ground and all the on-looking warriors uttered their war-cries in unison as he did so, while with their own weapons of clubs, lances and bows, they made stabbing motions at the enemy camp in front.

While this was going on, the Cheyenne and Suhtaio women among the fighting men and all those who had come merely to observe the impending conflict, turned their backs to the Arrow Priest, for if any female looked upon these, the most holy of tribal talismans, then the power transmitted through them, it was believed, would be nullified and lost.

Twice the `Arrow` priest performed the ritual, one time each for the two `man` arrows in his care, and then returned them to the bundle. Next he tied the bundle itself to the lance of a young Cheyenne *medicine* man, and whose duty it would be to carry the lance with Sacred Arrows attached against the enemy at the head of the allied charge. Now the enemy having supposedly been blinded by the power of the `Arrows` would not be able to shoot their missiles straight, while the Cheyennes by the same power would be invisible to the foe and, as a consequence, could not be harmed by the enemy or their weapons.

The young man who carried the bundle tied to his lance then rode out in front of the Cheyenne line, whilst he with the Sacred Hat upon his head rode to the front of the Suhtaio. After chanting a few holy incantations, each of these two suddenly raised their war-cries, and urging their ponies into a gallop, began riding towards each other at oblique angles from their respective ranks. As they raced across the open ground their paths crossed diagonally and after this, they each circled the enemy camp and passed each other a second time as they whirled their ponies around and returned to their own lines. Thus having made the pattern of a double loop.

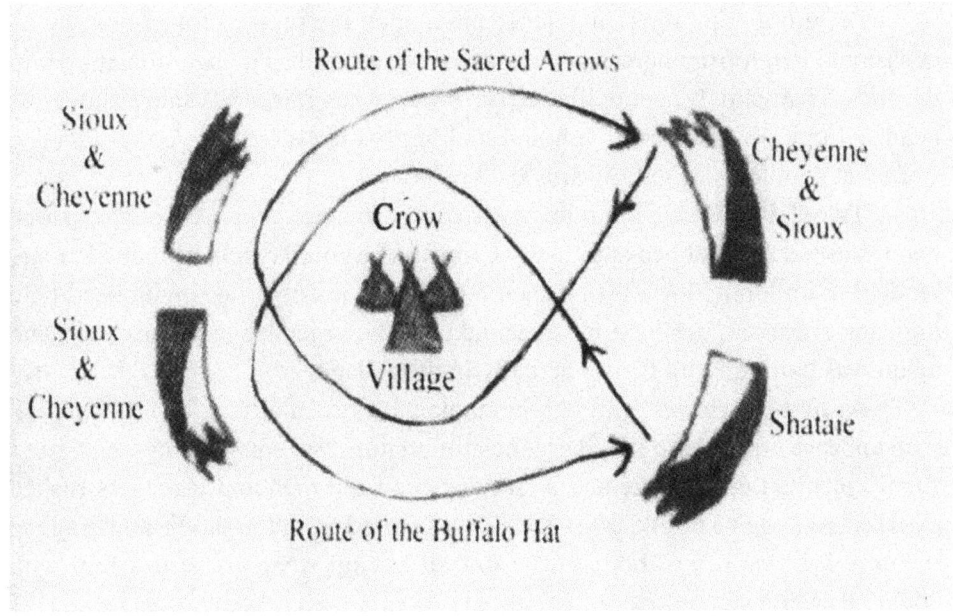

ROUTE OF SACRED ARROWS BEARER AND OF SACRED HAT.

As soon as the carriers of the tribal palladiums returned to their respective lines, Two-Twists nosed his mount out a few yards in front of the Cheyenne and Suhtaio warriors. He reigned up erect in the saddle in full view of the Allied warriors and the Crows. His body was stripped to the waist, his arms, chest and face daubed in bright ochres of red, green and yellow. Two or three eagle feathers with red horse hair flying from their tips were entwined in his raven hair, which signifying his intention to fight to the death, was left un-braided, to flow thick over his shoulders and down to his middle. Hanging on one arm was his *medicine* shield emblazoned with his personal protective totem, along with pendent eagle feathers attached to its rim gently fluttering in the breeze. He held his reigns in his left hand while with his right, he gripped the hilt of a Spanish sabre, its blade pointing to the ground. A red strip of strouding-cloth sufficed for a breech-clout and his horse was covered with sacred paint while eagle feathers were braided into its mane and tail, the latter cut short and tied in a bob fashion as was customary when being ridden into battle.

At length, Two-Twists raised his head to the blue Montana sky and sang a song to his dead companions of the Crooked-Lance Society. He called to their spirits saying, *"Look over your shoulders, this one is coming behind you."* [3]

For a lingering moment silence enveloped the scene, broken only by an occasional neigh from horses which pawed the ground as if eager to gallop into the fray. Then slowly, yet deliberately, Two-Twists raised his sabre above his head; let out a high-pitched yell and kicking his heels into his pony's flanks, started at a gallop straight towards the breastworks.

Two-Twists leapt his pony over the barricades and with sabre in one hand, slashed and stabbed at as many Crows as he could reach, be they old men, women or children. Two-Twists then returned to his own lines with head held high and chest out, but soon for a second time, he urged his mount forward and again was battling with Crows actually in the village.

At first the Crows – all non-combatants – stared at this lone thunderball who appeared to want to kill everyone around him. But some among the Crows finally plucked up courage and a large body of old men and teenagers rushed over to assist their kinfolk. Two-Twists was pulled from the saddle and dragged under a writhing sea of bodies who not all having weapons, struck him with sticks, fists and stones.

When the Cheyennes and Suhtaio saw their champion go down, the countryside reverberated to their screams of anger. Their eyes fell upon the Contrary warrior Ice waiting for him to give the signal to attack, and in response, Ice quickly passed his Thunder Bow behind him from left hand to the right. A great cry arose and immediately, the whole allied host in one great engulfing wave surged their ponies forward, and followed in the path of Two-Twists.

As the Allies drew near they were amazed to see their champion Two-Twists reappear from among the struggling mass of bodies, his torso, face and limbs covered with blood, but continuing to wield his sabre with as much ferocity as before. The Allies charged the camp on three sides and moments later, a host of them were also jumping ponies over and through all obstacles before them; smashing into hide lodges and riding down everyone in their path,

EIGHT-HUNDRED CROW CAPTIVES ARE TAKEN

trampling them under hoof. Breaches appeared in every part of the breastworks, and as more and more allied warriors and horses crowded through them, the gaps grew even wider until nothing blocked their way.

Careering their ponies around within the inner circle of tepees, the Allies bludgeoned their way through huddled groups of Crows; war-clubs and arrows flying; their lances dealing death to any who resisted their wrath. The scene within the camp was one of utmost confusion, as the occupants first ran this way then that in desperate endeavours to extricate themselves from the trap.

Some of the defenders did manage to mount horses and succeed in breaking through the enemy line, only minutes before the bulk of the latter came pouring through the breastworks and completely infested the camp. Others were not so lucky. White-Haired-Killer, the Crow girl taken captive that day, told her daughter Standing-In-The-Lodge many years later, that just before the Cheyennes and Sioux broke through into the camp, her mother had put her and her sister on a horse ready to flee into the hills. As mentioned earlier, White-Haired-Killer was then between ten and twelve years old, but her sister was a lot younger, perhaps only three or four and White-Haired-Killer was accustomed to looking after her especially when travelling from one place to another. At such times the younger sister was always tied onto the horse to prevent her falling off. Unfortunately at this particular time, she did fall off and White-Haired-Killer was obliged to dismount in order to pick her up. Whilst in the act of doing so the Allies came charging through the camp making a great hullabaloo. The Crow horses took fright which was probably the Allies` purpose in the first place, and that belonging to White-Haired-Killer became unmanageable. It reared up on its hind legs then took off to join the rest of the animals which together, were then stampeding around the camp interior searching for an exit. White-Haired-Killer was suddenly left on her own and on foot, and was taken captive by a Cheyenne warrior even before she had a chance to run.

Of those who did manage to get out of the camp before all avenues of escape were cut off, most were women and children, although a few Crow men including the latter`s head chief Long-Hair, were among them.

These men were not cowards, but after defending their ground for a while, they had realized they alone could not resist the overwhelming onslaught from such a vastly superior force. As an act of expediency, they joined the stream of fugitives as the latter raced both on foot and on horseback for the safety of distant hills.

In reality these men with Long-Hair at their head, had at first fought a desperate rear-guard action in order to give the fleeing fugitives a better chance to escape. A number of Cheyennes and Sioux saw these Crows now racing for the hills, and pulling themselves away from what was going on in the camp, took off in hot pursuit.

Long-Hair was lagging behind. Seeing that a few of the allies were drawing close he suddenly reined in his horse; jumped unhesitant from its back and stood alone facing his oncoming attackers who he threatened to shoot with his short-barrelled trade gun. Almost at once his pursuers also reined up, not daring to venture near and instead, though still mounted, they hovered tentatively around whilst shouting abuse at the lone Crow and challenging him to come forward and fight. Long-Hair stayed his ground and returned the verbal challenges, but after a short while he vaulted onto his waiting horse and galloped off again, following the path of the fugitives.

The Cheyennes and Sioux immediately resumed the chase and being mounted on war-ponies, whereas the Crow chief rode nothing more than a pack horse, the Allies were soon again at his heels and pressing him hard. It was a desperate race that followed, but it was not long before two Sioux warriors caught up, and riding alongside the Crow chief on either side, tried to pull him from the saddle. In the ensuing tussle Long-Hair was eventually thrown to the ground, but in an instant he was back on his feet and braced again to defend himself with gun at the ready. Long-Hair`s aggressive stance and look of determined resolution on his grim visage, caused his two nearest antagonists to draw back and await their comrades to come up and join them. Meanwhile, several Crows following in the rear of the fugitives but ahead of Long-Hair, happened to glance behind them, and seeing the imminent danger their chief was in, they turned their horses around and yelling the Crow war-cry, raced back to give their assistance.

This small group of Crows composed of old and middle-aged men, and armed with only the basic of weapons such as stone headed war-clubs and lances, reached their chief just as the rest of the pursuing Allies came into view.

Fortunately for Long-Hair his enemies had no chance to finish him off. The returning Crows quickly surrounded him and by their belligerent behaviour, indicated to the Cheyennes and Sioux they were resolved to protect the person of their chief, no matter what the cost. The number of Allies in this opposing group was not large, although they evidently had the advantage in age and weaponry. Even so, they decided that on this occasion discretion was the better part of valour and merely hurled a barrage of insults at the Crows, telling them they were going to take their women captive and describing in minute and lurid detail what sexual treats they had in store for them. They then rode back the way they had come and allowed the chief and his loyal followers to escape.

Another bunch of Crows, however, had also managed to escape the camp and were fleeing toward the hills, but in a different direction to Long-Hair's group. These people were passing around the foot of a nearby butte [now known as Taylor's Butte], when a mixed band of Cheyennes and Sioux got after them. In the running fight which ensued, the allies killed them all including the old men, women and even some children. The Sioux later recalled the fight as *"When they [Crows] fled around it,"* [4] referring to the slaughter of fugitives around the butte in question. Only one small Crow boy survived this particular episode of slaughter and being on the back of a fast pony, he raced off in search of the Crow warriors whose several war-parties were still looking for the allied camps on both sides of the Powder.

Meantime, in the Crow village the fight was in full swing, although all was now mayhem and confusion. The mass of horses and bodies seemed never ending, as the Allies continued to career around the interior of the camp, striking down without mercy all the old and middle-aged men and scalping them. Dead Crows lay on top of one another and very soon their corpses littered the ground. The victors rounded up the surviving women and children in great bunches, whilst clouds of choking dust churned up by the galloping horse's hooves further impeded the Crows from offering any practical resistance. It is said that not a few of the Crow non-combatants simply resigned themselves to their fate and offered no resistance whatsoever. The Allies ushered them this way and that and the Crows obeyed without complaint [which to do so would likely have meant instant death], going along with whomsoever claimed them as their captive.

Winona Plenty-Hoops, the present Author's Crow informant, remembered that when a small girl, some very old Crow persons whose mothers or fathers had been children at the time of the fight, would repeat what they had been told. They would emphasize the great number of horses charging around the interior of the camp,

EIGHT-HUNDRED CROW CAPTIVES ARE TAKEN

"... `Iichilaa, Iichilaa, Iichilaa;` [horses, horses, horses], bumping into one another, knocking down people and lodges and raising great clouds of dust that the defenders found it hard to see before them. At the same time, they were constantly being showered with stones and clods of earth thrown up by the thousands of flying hooves." [5]

The Cheyenne account states that one among their warriors that day named Bob-Tailed-Bull, then a noted war-chief, rode his pony right through the beleaguered village, striking both left and right with his lance killing and wounding many Crows, and it was he, it is said, who counted the most coups on Crow menfolk during the fight. Another Cheyenne named Island [Killed at Camp Supply by Government soldiers in 1868] was almost just as prolific with his coup stick, and charging among the huddled groups of Crows, counted nearly as many strikes as did Bob-Tailed-Bull. But of all the allied warriors battling within the camp, none was more conspicuous than Ice the Contrary. Making a cry like the hoot of a Prairie Dog Owl which stuffed skin he wore on his forehead, he careered his mount around the tepees touching every Crow he could reach with his Thunder Bow. It is recalled that on this day he counted more than one-hundred coups. At the same time High-Back-Bear a Suhtai, counted so many coups upon the Crow women and children, none knew for sure the proper number.

As for the old man Red-Painted-Robe, he was always where the fighting was thickest. His hatchet seemed to be everywhere at once. Crying over the death of his two sons, he hacked off a Crow arm in the traditional Suhtaio manner, and so obtained a grisly trophy with which to dance over in the victory celebrations to come. His wife White-Buffalo-Woman skulked around the ruined camp wielding her gigantic wooden club, bringing it down on Crow heads, both dead and on those merely wounded, smashing them to pulp.

A number of Suhtaio and Cheyenne women accompanying the allied party were actively engaged in the carnage, and it were they who first began plundering the lodges and destroying them. They ripped the tepee coverings to shreds with knives and broke the lodge poles into pieces so they could not be reused. They even smashed clay cooking pots such was their hatred of the Crows. And when the majority of fighting was over, the rest of the Cheyenne and Suhtaio women who had been watching the unequal contest from a safe distance, ran into the camp on foot, wielding knives, clubs and axes. They screamed with savage glee as they pounded and stabbed those of the foe lying wounded and even those already dead. They stripped the bodies naked then hacked them to pieces limb by limb, some parts of which they paraded on high attached to the end of their husband's lance-points as grisly trophies of their victory.

While all this was going on, there was one particularly prominent figure among the Cheyennes. This man paraded around the ruined lodges wearing a strange shirt covered with small metal discs and wore an iron helmet to match. Years later, Crow survivors recalled they had been much afraid of this man, and wondered if he was Human or a Spirit Person sent to aid their enemies. They further recalled, he was mounted on a big Spanish pacing mule and created an imposing spectacle, a sight to behold. He sat so upright in the saddle, they said, they thought he must have had some kind of wooden frame or brace strapped to his back in order to keep him so ridged.

In one part of the invested village a group of Crows, predominantly old women and children but with a few old men among them, stood huddled in a bunch cowering in the midst of the carnage going on around them. For some unknown reason the allied warriors left them alone and seemed to take no notice of them. Perhaps, though, they had already been claimed as captives by others among the Allies, or were considered too old and decrepit to even be bothered with. The Cheyennes themselves did say later that they had not wanted the old Crow women for they were thought to be of little use. They thus set them free, telling them to go find the rest of their people and inform them what the Allies had done.

One very old Crow woman almost totally blind, made her way over to the grandmother of White-Bull [who was the son of the Contrary Ice], and communicating with signs, asked the grandmother to give her back her granddaughter so to guide her, for, she said, her own eyes were dead and she would not be able to find the rest of her people on her own. The wife of Ice took pity on her and when a younger woman came out of the crowd of Crow captives, the wife of Ice allowed her to go free and assist the old woman.

The battle over, the Cheyennes and Sioux asked the Crow women why there were hardly any Crow warriors in the village, and were told that several big war-parties had gone out the night before to attack the allied camps along the Powder. Apparently the Allies still did not think their own camps were in immediate danger, probably because their villages had since been moved from their earlier location. Nevertheless, they quickly packed their plunder on spare horses captured from the Crows and prepared to leave the scene, lest the Crow war-parties should return in force. It was thus around midday when the triumphant Allies finally set off heading back to their base camps, driving a great herd of captured ponies before them along with all their Crow prisoners. Most of these latter were on foot, and were hurried along, even though forced to carry heavy loads of plunder on their backs.

The Allies left behind a scene of utter ruin. Not a few lodges had been set ablaze and amid the scattered debris of the camp, lay countless mutilated and mangled corpses some pin-cushioned with arrows, while a trail of dead bodies lay scattered along the several routes which groups of Crow fugitives had taken in their efforts to escape.

A sizable number of camp occupants notwithstanding, had managed to escape into the hills, but the victorious Allies still took a very large number of prisoners. George Bent the half-White half-Cheyenne informant, asserted that Cheyennes alone had captured well over two-hundred and fifty of the enemy - all young women and children - and that the Sioux had taken many more captives themselves. My own Crow informants agree that the number of Crow captives and deaths together amounted to around one-thousand persons in total, eight hundred of that number having been taken captive, and hence, why the event has ever since been remembered among the Crows as, *"When eight-hundred were stolen.* [6]

This last number is verified in a Hudson's Bay Company journal which pertains to the post at Lake Traverse for the date November 9th 1820, and wherein it is recorded,

"…the Tetons went last fall to war, and returned a few days ago with 1100 horses and 800 prisoners of the Crow Indians." [7]

AFTERMATH

According to the Cheyennes, it was not long past mid-day whilst the Allies were on their way back to their base camps, that Cheyenne scouts riding ahead of the column looking for sign of Crow war-parties, suddenly came

EIGHT-HUNDRED CROW CAPTIVES ARE TAKEN

galloping back at great speed. They reported a small band of Crows was heading towards them from the hills.

These people appear to have been the rest of those Crows who the night before, had gone out with the aforementioned Red-Owl, for the party comprised only women and children and a few old men. They were on horseback and like their predecessors earlier in the day, were leading pack ponies loaded down with personal belongings. Evidently, they, too, now thought it safe to return, having no idea that their village had already been taken and destroyed.

A large body of Cheyennes quickly hid among the trees and bushes lining both sides of the path the Crows were traveling, and when the unsuspecting party came abreast of the hidden warriors the trap was sprung. Yelling their fearsome war-cries a horde of mounted Cheyennes converged on the Crows from both sides, taking their quarry by surprise. The Crow men-folk were killed outright and the women and children along with the pack-ponies taken captive. Some Crow children taken at that time and who remained thereafter with their captors, marrying into a Cheyenne or Sioux band and raising families of their own, later said,

> "The Cheyennes and Siouxs [sic] swept down upon us and drove all our returning ones before them. We had not time to dismount, but were driven along like a herd of wild horses to their camps." [8]

The victorious Allies had then continued their journey home, now with their extra captives in tow.

Whilst on route, a single Crow brave appeared atop the crest of a hill overlooking the allied column below. He had shouted down to the Allies and using signs, asked if they had harmed the Crow village on Otter Creek. Now among the Cheyennes was a young man who had been captured during an earlier attack, ostensibly, during the allied Cheyenne and Sioux assault of a small Crow village in 1801. This particular Crow who the Cheyennes had named Big-Prisoner, had since been fully adopted into the Cheyenne tribe and spoke both his captor's and his mother's tongue fluently. So it was that when the lone Crow called down from the hill-top, it was Big-Prisoner who turned off from the column and conversed with his fellow tribesman. The lone Crow hollered down saying his name was Long-Jaw, then asked if the Allies had killed the women and children in the village recently assaulted. Big-Prisoner replied that most of the women and children had been spared, although now captives of the Cheyennes and Sioux. Upon hearing this, the lone Crow then turned his horse around and disappeared from the crest, and the Cheyennes later said, they could hear him crying and bewailing the fate of his people as he rode away.

During all this time, the Crow boy mentioned earlier, who had escaped the beleaguered village and survived the massacre of the fugitives, had been following up the trail of one of the Crow war-parties which had gone out the night before in search of the allied camps. We have noted that for some reason the Crow warriors had failed to locate their target and when the boy finally caught up with one of the parties and burst out news that their own village had been attacked, the warriors became distraught. Riders were dispatched to locate and inform the other Crow parties the terrible news, and they in turn were distraught. They thought at once of their wives and families left to the dubious mercy of their mortal foes. They cried aloud to *Akbaa-tadia* the Great Spirit, and to their personal totems - begging them to preserve their kinfolk.

The Crow pipe-holders could not keep the war-parties together. Groups of warriors and even lone individuals, all at once raced off at high speed back towards Long-Hair's village in an effort to save their people. Thus, the Crow force which only moments before had been a match for any foe, broke up into two dozen or more separate bands, each warrior heeding only his personal fears and commitment to his loved ones. They completely disregarded the strength of their unity, the one real hope of achieving anything against their enemies. Their war-chief Sore-Belly, it is true, did exert all his powers of persuasion in order to keep the warriors in a cohesive body. But even his own great standing could not deter them from pursuing their individual designs.

Unfortunately, the horses the Crows were riding were already tired, having been ridden all night in search of the allied camps. Now, racing at breakneck speed back towards the village, their animals quickly became exhausted, and it was long after the allied host had left before Crow warriors in one group after another began arriving at the scene, a smouldering, corpse-littered ruin. As each of the exhausted groups of warriors came in and beheld the carnage before them, they screamed aloud their grief and swore oaths of vengeance over the bodies of their dead and mutilated kinfolk. The whole atmosphere was a mixture of abject despair and anger.

EIGHT-HUNDRED CROW CAPTIVES ARE TAKEN

When at last all Crow warriors had returned and it was clear the Allies had definitely left the vicinity, the surviving Crow fugitives who had been lucky enough escaping to the hills, came treading gingerly back to the dilapidated camp. For many there was only heart-rending sorrow as the men-folk searched among the ruins, discovering the dismembered corpses of close relatives, or alternatively, the realization dawned that a missing child, mother or wife had been led into captivity to suffer a fate they knew not what. Death Songs and hideous screams of anguish filled the air as blood flowed freely from gashed arms, legs and breasts. Others stabbed foreheads with knives or sharp stones and pulled hair from their heads in great hanks, all in expressions of grief.

In the meantime, the cavalcade of Cheyennes and Sioux driving their Human captives and great herd of captured ponies before them, continued wending its way across country back from whence they came. When arriving at their camps, the women took down the lodges and the whole ensemble moved further upriver to a small tributary of the Powder, and it was here, the second night after the battle, that the Allies held a grand victory dance which, Cheyenne veterans of the intertribal wars used to say, was the biggest dance of its kind ever held by their tribe. Such was the excitement of the occasion that the Cheyenne women, it is said, appeared to go crazy, offering sexual favours to any of their choosing. Hence, the tributary along which the allied camps were then pitched, has ever since been known among both Cheyennes and Sioux as "Crazy Woman Creek."

Throughout all, the captive Crow women huddled in darkened lodges, wailed their mourning dirges and cried aloud over their slaughtered loved ones, whose grizzled remains were being abused before their eyes. The captured children of which there were many, sat together in bunches bewildered by all that was going on around them. The Cheyennes and Sioux traded off their booty with one another, haggling over every transaction, as they exchanged a captive for a horse or some other item of plunder obtained from the vanquished village.

At the same time, a Sioux warrior who had suffered serious wounds during the actual attack, finally succumbed to his injuries. As an act of vengeance his relatives set upon one of the female Crow prisoners with their knives; threw her still breathing body onto a camp fire, and whooped with fiendish delight as she slowly roasted to death.

At first the Cheyennes and Sioux had been united in their victory celebrations. But as often when Indian groups came into close proximity with one another for a prolonged period, congenial relations soon became strained. Arguments increased over the distribution of captives, as the informant George Bent averred, and the situation became decidedly heated. To the extent that warriors on both sides grabbed weapons and opposed each other in battle array, ready to clash in deadly combat as if facing mortal foes. Fortunately, the chiefs and headmen of the two camps intervened and after much difficult persuasion, managed to calm the situation and prevent a full scale conflict erupting among the lodges. As it was, one or two Cheyenne and Sioux warriors had already been either killed or seriously injured during the brief, but heated melee, ironically by their own tribesmen, and certainly, several Crow captives had also lost their lives, having been murdered out of hand through spite by one side or the other.

It was because of this dissension that the very next morning, the women of both camps again took down their lodges; packed the covers along with their domestic belongings on pony-drags, and in separate bodies began moving off in different directions.

So it was that the grand allied expedition to punish the Crows came to an end. An end of the matter, that is, as far as the Allies were concerned.

For the time being, the Crows remained fragmented and irreparably divided. Truly, it would take the persuasion of a great chief to instil again into that people the pride and confidence which had marked them high above their neighbours, both friend and foe alike. Yet none at present could foresee the rise of such a man, who alone could heal the great wound now tearing the Nation apart? Surely, thought the Crows, their totems had forsaken them. The star of their ancestors which once shone bright, was dimmed.

The aforesaid attack by Cheyennes and Sioux, proved itself the worst calamity ever to attend the Crows regarding inter-tribal conflicts, and the largest number of Crow captives ever taken by the enemy.

As late as 1876, the Cheyennes still had forty-four lodges belonging to their Nation, composed predominantly of Crow captives and their descendants [between 200 and 250 persons]. According to Bradley, these people by then, had intermarried within the Cheyenne tribe and at the time of his writing formed a separate camp or clan. Generally, they were to be found upon the headwaters of Powder River and usually kept aloof from most other Cheyenne bands, and even from the Crows. At that time [1876], there was a good deal of mixed blood among them, but the older members still spoke fluent Crow, even though their everyday language was Cheyenne. Bradley further stated that the Crows still thought of them as members of their own people, and declined to pursue hostilities against them, save their sometimes stealing their horses. The Cheyennes also desisted from harassing this band, but did not readily include them in the tribal politics which governed the rest of the Cheyenne Nation. The band apparently disintegrated shortly after 1879 or thereabouts, when the reservation system `kicked in` so to speak. Some band members joined the Mountain and Kicked-in-the-Belly Crows in southern Montana; others joined the Northern Cheyennes, whilst a few families went south to be absorbed among the Southern Cheyennes in Oklahoma, and there now remains little trace of their once separate identity.

However, it appears likely that the small group of people once residing at Lame Deer on the Northern Cheyenne reservation and known as "Black Lodges," represented the remnant of the band in Montana, being so named owing to their close friendship and association with the "Black Lodge band of River Crows, whose own descendants yet reside around Crow Agency on the present-day Crow reservation.

It is interesting to note that in 1850, when Thaddeus Culbertson acting for the American Government undertook a survey of the "Western Tribes," he reported the existence of a Crow clan or band then known by the name *"Those whose camp is charged upon."* There seems to be no other reference to a Crow band or clan by that name either before Culbertson's comment or after. Assuming that the name is correct, and the band itself was extant at that date [1850], then perhaps the members were, in fact, survivors from the same band of Mountain Crows under Chief Long-Hair, whose village had been assaulted and destroyed some thirty years earlier and its population drastically reduced by the allied Cheyenne and Sioux. More specifically, the name may have referred to that group of Crows which had gone out with the adulterer Red-Owl the night before the village was attacked, and returning to the Crow camp next day, had been "charged upon" by the Allies and taken captive.

Whatever the case, as Culbertson obtained the name from the Crows themselves, the band or clan referred to was probably the same mentioned at a later date by James H. Bradley, whose members, he said, were then of mixed Cheyenne and Crow parentage residing in a separate village somewhere near the headwaters of Powder River.

– O – O – O – O – O – O – O – O – O –

SUHTAIO–CHEYENNE HEAD CHIEF, HIGH-BACKED-WOLF 1st

[Painted from life by George Catlin, 1832]

CHAPTER 6.
GOVERNMENT EMISARIES MEET CHEYENNES [1820-21]

Soon after the above recounted Cheyenne-Sioux victory over the Crows, in mid-July somewhere on the Loup Fork of Republican River, Nebraska, a Skidi Pawnee earth-lodge town was offering hospitality to a group of white men under Major Stephen H. Long. The Major was undertaking an expedition from St. Louis on the Missouri to the Rocky Mountains of Colorado, and he and his party of white men had paused at the Skidi Pawnee town at the invitation of the head Skidi chief at that time, known as *Petalasharo*. The Pawnee had recently suffered a concerted attack from the earlier-mentioned Trading Indians among which were a number of Cheyenne, the same who had been with the mixed conglomerate of tribes on Grand Camp Creek in 1816, but now also included certain outlaws from the main body of Cheyennes, having been exiled from their tribe due to internal killing of tribal members during celebrations following the aforesaid victory over the Crows. [1]

Before this date [1820], Cheyennes, for the most part, had been at peace with the `People of Wolves` as they called the Pawnee, probably because they had little cause for contact owing to distance between them. But as has been noted, sometime during the previous winter both peoples had been plunged into bitter war with each other, which notwithstanding intermittent short periods of truces, continued for another fifty years. Perhaps previous victory celebrations by Cheyenne allies the Arapahoe and Kiowa over Pawnee scalps, and many horses the latter stole from Pawnee herds, had at last been too much a temptation for Cheyennes not to follow suit, and thus, had joined in such attacks or raided Pawnee stock on their own initiative. There again, Cheyennes may have been killed or seriously injured while visiting the Kiowa or Arapahoe when those peoples had been attacked by Pawnees, and in such a way, Cheyennes had been forced into war. Either way, by 1820 Cheyennes were certainly out to get their share of Pawnee hair.

In the war's initial phase, Cheyennes appear to have treated it somewhat as a game. It was not until a decade later when Cheyennes along with Sioux and Arapahoe allies, went all-out to wipe the Pawnee Nation from the face of the Earth, and by the late 1850s, the aforesaid allies together, had almost succeeded.

GOVERNMENT EMISARIES MEET CHEYENNES

On the other hand the Suhtaio, who in the early Eighteen-hundreds were merely Cheyenne confederates and an independent tribe, themselves became embroiled in war with Pawnees around this same time, and the Pawnee themselves retaliated by attacking all Cheyenne-speaking peoples when and wherever found regardless of one's innocence or not. The Pawnees as a Nation then numbered between some ten to twelve-thousand persons, although it seems, only the Skidi Pawnee tribe was at first actively engaged in constant fighting with Cheyennes. It is likely, however, Pawnees from other bands were also losing hair to Cheyenne scalping knives, and the latter numbering only around three-thousand five-hundred souls in total, according to an estimate by Captain Morse in 1822, suggests that Cheyennes by being at war with the Pawnee, were biting off more than they could chew. In fact, one might go as far to say that few raids were then actually conducted on Pawnee towns by Cheyennes themselves, that is, not without Cheyenne numbers being augmented with Sioux or Arapahoe allies, and at a later date after 1840, Cheyenne numbers were again expanded by the inclusion of Kiowa and Comanche confederates who then also, were at war with all the Pawnee-speaking tribes.

Pawnees therefore, had enough on their plate already without adding Cheyennes to their list of enemies, and professed their desire to make peace with the so-called Trading Indians, and especially with their now new-found foes the Cheyenne. Thus, the Skidi Pawnee chief *Petelasharo* requested the aforementioned Major Long to act as intermediary by carrying a message of peace from the Pawnee chiefs to those among the Trading Indians, and to which the Major agreed. Yet before he even met the Indians in question, a war-party of the latter among which was a large number of Cheyennes, had already started out against the same Pawnee town from where the said General had just left.

It had been early July when the white men started southwest from the Skidi town. Whilst on route, they stumbled across the remains of a very large Trading Indian camp and shortly afterwards, came upon a formidable band of the same Indians on the Arkansas south of the Platte, comprised of Arapahoe, Kiowa, Kiowa-Apache, Lipan-Apaches [probably Jicarilla], Snakes [Shoshoni] and Cheyennes. No Sioux were present, they having worn out their welcome back in 1814 at Horse Creek. A French half-breed named Bijeau who had been with Manuel Lisa's brigade of trappers in Crow Country as early as 1807, was with the Major's expedition, and now acted as Major Long's interpreter by

GOVERNMENT EMISARIES MEET CHEYENNES

talking both signs and in the Crow language to a Crow woman captive then among those Cheyennes present.

These Cheyennes with the Trading Indians informed Bijeau of their origins and that they were then at war with the Spanish Provence of San Antonio [present day Texas] and the Mexicans, and that recently, they had commenced hostilities with the Pawnee. If the Pawnee peace wishes were then relayed by the Major or not, it was to no avail, for it was then Bijeau was told of the severe conflict with Skidi Pawnees the previous winter [already recounted], and that the very band of Cheyennes involved, had actually been on its way home after the fight when they decided to visit the Trading Indian's camp instead.

Bijeau further learned from his hosts that fifteen days before the white men's arrival, the Trading Indians themselves including Cheyennes, had been in conflict with Spaniards on Red River below the Arkansas, and in which event, some Mexicans had been killed and all their horses run off, the animals having since been sold by the Indians to white men traders at French and Anglo settlements further down that river. One of Bijeau's Indian informants had lost a brother in the aforesaid battle and was still in mourning for him.

In good spirits, the expedition finally left the Trading Indian's camp and again set off on its travels, this time with a Kiowa-Apache and his woman as guides. On July 24th the expedition split, one group led by Major Long exploring the course of Red River, the other led by a Captain Bell, traveling further down the Arkansas as far as a place now known as Belle Point.

Nearing Purgatoire Creek, a tributary of the Arkansas, the Bell party came upon another large encampment containing Kiowa, Kiowa-Apache, Comanche, Arapahoe and Cheyennes, their lodges stretching more than a mile along the river bank. A group of Kiowa rode out to meet the white men and in sign language, told the party they were awaiting the arrival of their leading chief Bear's-Tooth, an Arapahoe, but who's influence extended over all the Allied Indians in camp. Captain Bell declined an offer to stay among the lodges and instead, set up his party's own bivouac-tent camp in a semi-circle around his horse herd about four-hundred yards from that of the Indians.

Hardly had the white men's tents been pitched, when a number of important Indians visited them, including three chiefs from among the Cheyennes, Kiowa and Kiowa-Apache. Captain Bell sat down with them and smoked a pipe as was the custom, while Samuel Seymour the expedition's

GOVERNMENT EMISARIES MEET CHEYENNES

artist, sketched the likeness of the Indians around him. Thus were the first ever portraits of Cheyennes executed by white men long before photography even existed. The Indian guests left just prior to nightfall, but left several Indian guards to protect the white men's horses from thieves. Bijeau, we are told, sat up most of the night conversing in sign language and a smattering of Crow among those Cheyennes present, learning the details of their recent fight with the Skidi and of that with the Mexicans. He was also told that at that very moment, there was yet another Cheyenne war-party out against the Pawnee.

The following day, Bell held council with five chiefs of the gathered Indians, which comprised two Kiowa, one Arapahoe, one Kiowa-Apache and one Cheyenne. A host of warriors, along with women and children also milled around and had to be constantly pushed back from the circle of those in council by stick-wielding Society police. Meanwhile, a second pipe was smoked for around fifteen minutes and after which, the Captain explained that he had not been authorised by the Great White Father to hold councils with the Indians and therefore, lacked worthy gifts to present them. But, he continued, he would report that his Indian brothers had treated him and his comrades well. In response, the chiefs told the Captain they were the first American official white men they had seen, and requested that American traders should be sent among them.

After this, the Kiowa chief gave Bell a magnificent mare and each chief received tobacco, knives, looking-glasses, fire-steel and hair combs in return, and which were promptly distributed by the respective chiefs to certain persons among them as was customary for chiefs to do so. The white men then asked for and were given a large quantity of fresh meat and pemmican to sustain them on their continued journey.

That same night, other Cheyennes raided the Arapahoe part of the Trading Indian village and ran off seven ponies.

Next day, the white men took down their tents and started moving upriver in search of the Bear-Tooth's camp. On route they were met by another group of Cheyennes who also greeted them as friends. The Cheyenne leader told Bell that one of his fellow warriors had been away hunting buffalo, when he was captured by four Mexicans and imprisoned in a Spanish fort at the forks of the Arkansas. The Mexicans, however, had released him in order to take a message to the Trading Indians, requesting their chiefs meet with Mexican officials further down the Arkansas, and where the latter would endeavour to implement peaceful relationships with all the tribes. The Cheyennes informed the Captain that the main Cheyenne village was then along the river of that name to the north, and they themselves had left their kinfolk on that river to live with the Arapahoe. Bell additionally reported in his journal,

> "...This band [Cheyennes] had left their Nation and attached themselves to the Arapahoe...The Cheyennes appear to be of bad disposition, faithless and fond of plunder...They wear their hair tied behind." [2]

These particular Cheyennes were most likely outlaws from the north after the great victory over the Crows. Bell went on to say that the combined strength of Bear-Tooth's Allies consisted of five-hundred fighting men; remained at one place no more than a few days, and that they had recently declared war on the more northern Cheyennes after an Arapahoe comrade had lately been killed by the latter. He further commented that Cheyennes were at war with the Pawnee, Kawas [Kaw or Kansa], Otoe and Osage, but at peace with the Pawnee Picts, i. e. the Witchita another Caddoan-speaking faction.

Later that same day, a strong party of Cheyennes rode up to the white men at full speed. In the party were forty warriors, four or five women and another Crow prisoner who, fortunately, was also able to converse with Bijeau, and Bell reported,

> "...Some of them [Cheyennes] were painted black and had a most horrid and frightful appearance...The whole well equipped with their war implements and decorated with plums and ornaments." [3]

These Cheyennes, apparently, had four days before been against the Pawnees and taken a scalp. They were on their way to join the Arapahoe and were in a hurry, lest Pawnees were pursuing them. Nonetheless, they had time enough to rest their horses which they turned out to graze and then smoked a pipe with Bell. The Captain, though, was wary of the validity of the Cheyenne's declared friendship and stationed armed guards around his party's horses. The Cheyennes likewise, appeared to be suspicious of the white men, and retained their bows with

GOVERNMENT EMISARIES MEET CHEYENNES

an arrow notched at the string in case the whites themselves should prove aggressive.

One of the visiting warriors then claimed the Captain's horse as the same lost to thieves two years prior. But the Captain - having heard the same story from a dozen different Indians in the last few days, - refused to listen. These Indians likewise, asked Bell to send white traders among them such as lived with the Mandan and Hidatsa, and when the Indians were about to leave and go on their way, Bell gave the Indian partisan tobacco and knives which the chief, like his earlier counter-part, gave to other members of his party. He also asked the Captain to give him his handkerchief as a gift and received it, whereupon, the chief embraced the Captain before riding away with the rest of his party. Bell was pleased that the meeting had concluded peaceably and was moved to write,

"A Cheyenne war-party is the most dreaded and feared of all other Indians." [4]

The white men continued on their way, meeting a band of Comanche who Bell referred to as *"Iatans or Comanch,"* and also, a village of Osage and among which, he also had friendly contact.

On September 9th the white men finally reached Fort Smith at Belle Point, where they joined again with the rest of the expedition already there under Major Long. The Major and his group had actually missed Red River and travelled down the Canadian instead without making contact with any Indians.

Having said this, thus was concluded the second official meeting of Cheyennes with American Government officials since the Lewis and Clark expedition in 1803.

- 0 - 0 - 0 - 0 - 0 - 0 - 0 - 0 - 0 -

CHAPTER 7.

CROW VENGEANCE ON CHEYENNES
[1821]

The following summer [1821], combined Mountain and River Crow bands were encamped along the Yellowstone across from present-day town of Billings, Montana. It was then that the latter's head war-chief Sore-Belly declared, he personally was ready to lead a revenge raid against the killers of Long-Hair's people the previous year if, that is, any warriors were brave enough to join him. [1]

In response, many flocked to his call and preparations were made before starting south to *"clean up"* on the Cheyenne.

This must refer to the same episode of which Lieutenant James H. Bradley was told in 1876, and what the present Author's Crow informant Joe Medicine Crow later heard from old-time Indian historians in his youth [1930s], that about one year after the attack on the Otter Creek Crow village, Sore-Belly and a large Crow war-party went into Cheyenne country and killed many of the enemy. It was Chief Sore-Belly who organized the expedition on that occasion and he alone, who planned the strategy employed.

It is said also that the day before the grand party's departure, Sore-Belly requested all those wishing to join the expedition to parade in their best regalia before him, and those wishing to take vows of vengeance, would then be allowed to do so in a ceremonial manner.

It was to be a crusade which Sore-Belly had previously planned and meditated upon for many moons. To the extent that he had become somewhat obsessed as regards its successful conclusion. Often he had proclaimed to those around him of his profound hatred for Cheyennes, and especially his disdain for the particular Cheyenne Chief High-Backed-Wolf who was known to the Crows as Striped-Elk, and of whom Sore-Belly said,

"...Now the man with stench in his hair is forcing our people to be miserable and makes them grieve and cry. Over there, the Cheyennes think they alone are brave. He makes my poor people sit in the lodges in places where the water drips on them. He beats them and kills them at will. Now it will come to an end. We shall meet with the enemy and have a decision be it that the enemy is killed or we Crows are killed. Now is the time we shall have a decision, one way or the other." [2]

This then, was to be a venture dear to Sore-Belly's heart, and would be governed by his personal plan of attack. His strategy was to send a decoy force to the enemy camp, which would entice the Cheyennes into a trap to be executed by the main Crow body positioned in hiding further along the trail. The success of the expedition would at last, Sore-Belly thought, exact retribution upon those who earlier, had wrought so much woe and grief upon his people.

Thus, that same day around mid-afternoon, the occupants of the combined Mountain and River Crow villages, including all the warriors, old men and women, assembled in the large open space within the camp circle. They readied themselves to honour the leading men and chiefs among them and pay homage to the great Sore-Belly himself when he condescended to appear before them. At length, Sore-Belly did appear, bedecked in a long double-tailed eagle feathered bonnet; beaded and scalp-fringed war-shirt and leggings, and beaded moccasins with wolf tails attached at the heels. He was mounted on a magnificent black pony with a prominent white blaze on its forehead, and positioning himself at the south entrance of the tepee circle, he presented a formidable and imposing sight.

Then followed the steady throb of war drums beating, as into the centre of the circle the tribal herald who was on foot, led the war-pony of a popular and distinguished fighter and council chief named Little-White-Bull [aka; White-Buffalo-Calf and Looks-at-the-Albino-Buffalo], sitting proud and erect astride the animal's back. The herald proclaimed aloud to the spectators how brave this warrior would be in the coming fight, while Little-White-Bull himself responded by vowing vengeance on the enemy and thereby, would allow those who had lost kinfolk the year before, to cease their mourning. The warriors whooped war-cries in unison, while the women raised the tremolo and sang praise songs in recognition of their champion parading before them. After this, another mounted warrior named Small-Back was also led into the circle by the camp herald, and the same or similar speeches were made by both. Following Small-Back came several more great Crow fighters, among whom were included Passes-Women, Wants-To-Die, High-Backbone, Two-Face and High-Lance. Each of these was well known as being formidable in battle, and after they virtually reiterated words that had been said before, they, too, were honoured by the people.

Also prominent among the eminent warriors at this time, was a middle-aged Crow man named Plays-With-His-Face. He had lost most of his immediate relatives during the attack on Long-Hair's village apart from his mother and a brother [who was the same Two-Face noted above], and now had little regard for his own safety. He no longer cared to live. Plays-With-His-Face was a Crow Sore-Lip clan member of the Lump-Wood society, and recognized as a brave fighter who knew not the meaning of fear. Often he wore a long-tailed buffalo horned war-bonnet and was regarded as one reckless in battle, likely to be killed at any time. Some declared it was the intervention of divine providence why he had escaped earlier situations which had seemed like certain death, and were not surprised when he asked Sore-Belly to let him be among the proposed decoy party. This would be a dangerous undertaking especially for a person already past his prime. But knowing the dare-devil potential of Plays-With-His-Face, Sore-Belly agreed to the request.

When this part of the ceremony was over, Sore-Belly invoked his personal *medicine* which was the 'Thunder' and this time he actually did so in full view of the people. He thereafter commanded that while on the march, no birds, even of small size and seemingly insignificant, which, it was believed, were connected to 'Thunder' itself, should be killed. For such, he said, would break the potency of his *medicine* and lead to the death of some among the Crows.

Soon after this the warriors prepared themselves for war, and that same night, a grand Crow host of some two-hundred warriors along with a number of women tending to the needs of their men-folk, started out in search of the Cheyennes, all believing the omens were auspicious for the party's success.

The following morning after travelling only a short distance, a young female named Likes-the-Old-Women made a swipe at a meadowlark flying too close to her face. The bird was accidently killed and she told Sore-Belly what she had done. The chief rebuked her for her carelessness saying he could do nothing about it now, but surely, one of their number if not more would subsequently be killed in the coming fight. Still, however, Sore-Belly was resolved to continue on the war-trail and meet the foe in combat. So the grand party travelled on, notwithstanding that the great chief's *medicine* had already been undermined.

After a few more days of hard traveling, Crow scouts discovered a large Cheyenne village on Horse Creek, a tributary running into the south side of the North Platte. Some distance from here, Sore-Belly told his warriors to site their base camp, for this was as far as they should go, and when darkness covered the land, six Crow warriors who had been selected as the aforesaid decoys including Plays-With-His-Face and Hanging-Raven [at a later date known as Four-Dancers], and with the council chief Little-White-Bull as their leader, started out on horseback towards the Cheyenne village. The main body of Crows, meanwhile, positioned themselves some miles distant in two gullies running parallel to each other either side of a narrow stretch of open ground semi-obscured by stands of cottonwood trees. Here they would wait for the Cheyenne force which was expected to give chase to the decoys, who would then lead the Cheyennes into the trap waiting to be sprung by hidden Crows.

It was just before dawn when the Crow decoys came close to their objective, whereupon they dismounted and walked their ponies at a slow pace. This was to allow the animals to get their second wind before charging the enemy camp, and as they continued on, they entered a sunken defile along which they travelled to obscure themselves from view. It was then that Plays-With-His-Face became angry and impatient. He berated his companions for what he thought was their over caution and timidity saying,

> "We are not dogs skulking around, afraid to get to grips with the enemy. Let us go to them in the open and kill them face to face. That will cause them to make a charge upon us. We were not told to creep along hidden from view." [3]

By his words Plays-With-His-Face meant they should bring the Cheyennes as quickly as possible to the place where Sore-Belly and the rest of the Crows were waiting. His blood was hot, he said, and he could no longer wait to carry destruction to the enemy. Little-White-Bull, even though having himself the reputation of a somewhat impetuous and reckless character, this time showed a degree of caution. He refused to do as Plays-With-His-Face suggested, which caused the latter to ride off towards the Cheyenne village intending to confront the enemy alone. In his wake, one of Little-White-Bull's companions, a slightly younger man named Hanging-Raven, the same who had been a mentor to Sore-Belly in the chief's childhood days, raced his pony after Plays-With-His-Face ready to join him in his reckless endeavour, and when coming to the crest of a ridge over-looking the enemy village, both Plays-With-His-Face and Hanging-Raven halted their mounts and surveyed the scene below. *

It being mid-summer, the whole Cheyenne Nation had earlier come together adjacent to Horse Creek, and had just finished conducting their Medicine Lodge ceremonies. Their tepees had been positioned in the shape of a large horse shoe several ranks deep. In this camp there were many Crow persons taken during the attack on Long-Hair's village and some lodges, it is said, contained four or five captives each.

When the two Crow decoys arrived on the scene, the morning sun was just coming up. Some Cheyennes were already taking down their tepees and preparing to move. Others had previously moved off, and were meandering slowly over the prairie with pole-drags and loose ponies in tow.

According to the Cheyenne version, a woman in camp out early collecting firewood, heard the faint sound of a human voice, and casting her gaze towards a ridge-top, she spied a lone horseman positioned on its crest. The horseman then began ridding back and forth along the ridge at a slow gait, evidently hoping to be seen more clearly by the camp occupants, whereupon the woman ran back into camp and called her people to come and look at this strange sight. Many Cheyennes responded and went over to where the old woman had been standing in order to determine what or who it might be.

The lone rider then began making a wailing noise, but the Cheyennes could not decide if he was one of their own people or an enemy, and also, if he was singing a song or crying. Some said one thing, some another, while those of an impetuous nature urged others ride out and get a closer look.

*In another Crow account, the companion of Plays-With-His-Face is named Creeps-Through-the-Lodges, although such was merely an earlier name for the same man later known as Hanging-Raven and Four-Dances. [Plain-Feather to Barney Old-Coyote, LBHC Archives, 1959].

CROW VENGEANCE ON CHEYENNES

The Crow version continues by saying that from their position overlooking the Cheyenne camp, Plays-With-His-Face and Hanging-Raven spied a man in the act of easing himself in the brush some way from the lodges, and at once, the two Crows galloped their ponies down the ridge slope attempting to strike the lone Cheyenne and claim the highest honour by counting the first `coup` of the impending conflict. As they careered towards this man, some village occupants saw what was happening and called to their comrade to run. Hanging-Raven was racing ahead of Plays-With-His-Face, and by following close on the heels of the Cheyenne, allowed himself to be carried into the enemy camp before striking his fleeing foe. Hanging-Raven did manage to return safely and unharmed to the side of his companion, who by then, had already returned to the ridge top. Plays-With-His-Face before this, had himself struck a second Cheyenne discovered outside the camp, but not seen by Hanging-Raven, and so it was Plays-With-His-Face who earned the right to claim the first *dakshey* of the expedition.

After this, Plays-With-His-Face continued to sit his pony on the ridge top in clear view of the Cheyennes, while his companion Hanging-Raven being satisfied with his deed, rode back to where Little-White-Bull and the other decoys were still positioned some distance away. The Cheyennes by then had discerned by the hairstyle and costume of Plays-With-His-Face that he was Crow, and this intelligence was quickly passed from mouth to mouth among the villagers. An excited howl issued from the throats of the young warriors as they psyched themselves up for battle, believing there would be more Crows nearby.

Now among the Cheyennes at this time was a visiting Hidatsa. This man who was fluent in the Crow language, was asked by the Cheyennes to find out from the lone Crow who he was and why he had come to their camp in such a manner. The Hidatsa thus rode out to the base of the ridge and when within hearing distance, repeated aloud what the Cheyennes wished to know, and to which Plays-With-His-Face replied,

> "...Ho, Striped-Feather-People, when I was away hunting you came to my village with a cloud of warriors and killed my kin-folk and took away my wife making me alone and saddened. I came to your camp to get back my wife, or be killed. But I became afraid

and fled, so now I ask you ride after me and kill me, I do not want to live." [4]

When the Hidatsa interpreter relayed these words back to the Cheyennes, a number of warriors were ready to go after Plays-With-His-Face and satisfy his request. But the Hidatsa advised caution, saying the Crow may not be alone, and it was likely there were many Crow enemies waiting out of sight and ready to strike. Such a warning did deter most Cheyennes from going after the lone Crow who; by then, however, had vacated the ridge-top and was no longer in view.

In the meantime, while the Cheyennes dithered among themselves whether to go out or not, the rest of the Crow decoy group led by Little-White-Bull, having moved closer to the Cheyenne village, met up with Plays-With-His-Face whilst in the process of returning to his comrades where he had left them. Having come together again, three of their number continued towards the enemy camp, while the rest including Plays-With-His-Face, Hanging-Raven and Little-White-Bull remained where they were, and instead, waited for their three comrades to bring the Cheyennes in a body towards them.

Also in the Cheyenne camp at this time was the keeper of that tribe's Sacred Medicine Arrows. His name was War-Path-Bear [also known as Feathered-Bear], a wise and respected patriarch among his people. A group of young men, all Cheyenne Bowstring Society warriors who were guardians of the Sacred Arrow lodge and its keeper, after spying the arrival of the three Crows on the crest of another knoll over-looking the camp, mounted their war-ponies and took up arms, and were about to charge out to see if they could capture the three by themselves. Like the Hidatsa before him, War-Path-Bear, too, advised caution. He urged these young men not to go on their own, but to wait until a large party was assembled and all go out together. Perhaps the three Crows were also decoys, he said, as their Hidatsa friend likewise suspected, and that a formidable Crow force might be in hiding waiting to ambush them in the hills.

Some took heed of the "Arrow" Keeper's words, but twelve young men of the Bowstring Society refused to listen. They whipped up their ponies and rode off to confront the Crows, eager to count their coups upon them.

CROW VENGEANCE ON CHEYENNES

Seeing these Cheyennes riding towards them, the three Crows vacated the ridge top and were soon racing back to their comrades with the twelve Cheyennes in hot pursuit. When joining again with the rest of their party, all six Crows galloped off together in the direction of the distant gullies, where Sore-Belly and his warriors were waiting.

While the decoys were racing ahead, Plays-With-His-Face who was bringing up the rear, suddenly reined in his pony and turned to face the foe alone. Again Plays-With-His-Face began singing and wailing and at first did not move from his static position. Calmly he sat his horse until the twelve Cheyenne Bowstrings were no more than twenty-five yards distant. Then he suddenly turned his mount around and drumming his heels smartly into its flanks, sped away across the Plain following in the wake of his comrades. The Cheyennes did not stop. Immediately they spurred their own ponies on faster as they continued their pursuit.

Before Plays-With-His-Face had gone much further, it seemed that his horse was tiring and soon the Cheyennes were rapidly gaining ground. When, however the twelve Cheyennes were almost upon him, the Crow's horse found a new spurt of energy and pulled away, leaving them far behind. Thus the chase continued and soon the distance between pursued and pursuers began to shrink yet again. But once more, just as the Cheyennes thought themselves near enough to strike, the Crow's horse again spurted forward and drew ahead, its rider now appearing to lash the animal ferociously across both flanks with his quirt. By this time it was obvious to the pursuers that the lone Crow indeed, was acting as a decoy, endeavouring to lure them into a trap. But thinking they would overtake him in another moment, they refused to relax their speed or give up the chase. The Cheyennes urged their mounts on even faster and were concentrating so much upon their quarry, they paid little attention to where he was leading them, or what might lay ahead.

As Plays-With-His-Face continued to race across the grasslands, he suddenly jumped from his pony's back and began running alongside the animal with one arm resting on its neck. This caused the Cheyennes to believe that the horse Plays-With-His-Face was riding was now very tired and might soon give out through exhaustion.

By now the open prairie was far behind, as the lone Crow still on foot and only just ahead, led his pursuers through a narrow passage between the two gullies obscured by stands of cottonwood trees on either side.

The Cheyennes were gaining fast. They were almost alongside Plays-With-His-Face when suddenly, up and out of both gullies there simultaneously appeared hundreds of mounted Crows. They shouted "Koo-Koo-Hay" at the tops of their voices, and in an instant, a cloud of Crow missiles had dropped several among the twelve Cheyennes from their saddles. The remaining Cheyennes, still on horseback, bunched themselves together and began battling furiously with those Crows brave enough to charge in amongst them, and for a while, they held the Crows at bay.

In the meantime, a great number of Cheyennes had by then left their camp and were following up their twelve kinsmen for fear of what had already happened. Unfortunately, they were still some distance in the rear, but as they rode they could see rising in the distance to their front a great cloud of dust, and as the Cheyennes later described it,

"A dark shadow lay over the prairie, indicating that a fierce battle was taking place." [5]

During the furious melee then going on, several more Cheyennes were killed before the few survivors made a sudden bold dash through the Crow lines, and began racing back the way they had come. The Crows, after scalping and cutting up the dead Cheyennes, took up the pursuit as they could see that the horses of the Cheyenne survivors were quickly tiring. The Crows would have overtaken and killed them all, had it not been that just when the fleeing fugitives were on the verge of annihilation, the main body of Cheyennes from the village finally came up. They immediately went smashing into the charging Crow ranks and a fierce hand to hand tussle ensued. Lance points and iron-bladed tomahawks flashed in the sunlight; bows twanged and the very ground soon became soggy with the blood of those wounded and dying; both of horses and of men.

Sore-Belly was in the forefront of the Crows. He was wearing this day a double-tailed feathered bonnet and as usual, carried a lance which he wielded with deadly effect, toppling several Cheyennes from their saddles. However, being bunched up in the narrow strip of land between the gullies, neither body could manoeuvre effectively. They were severely hampered by a lack of space and in the close fighting, a number of warriors on each side were killed and others severely wounded, and as more Cheyennes came up allowing an additional number of reinforcements to enter the affray, the Crows were halted in their tracks. They were obliged to fall back in order to put some little distance between themselves and the enemy.

It was then that the Crow champion Two-Face reined in his steed. He dismounted and confronted the oncoming Cheyennes alone and on foot, crying aloud that he for one would not flee in face of the foe. This was a suicidal action on Two-Face`s part, and the rest of the Crows seeing him thus, all at once turned their ponies around and in a body, charged back into the fight in order to protect their comrade. But the Cheyenne force was too strong to overcome, and although Two-Face survived, the momentum of the Crow onslaught was checked. A great melee again ensued with both horses and riders mixed up together and during which, the warrior Wants-to-Die, who also had paraded around the lodges before starting from the Crow village, now attempted to fulfil his vow so the widows of Long-Hair`s people might cease their grieving. This man lashed his pony with his quirt and galloped unhesitant right in amongst a thick bunch of the enemy. Such was his fury that he alone succeeded in forcing the Cheyennes back, after which he returned to his own ranks, escaping from what had seemed like certain death.

Following this, the Crow Passes-Women then charged into the midst of the enemy, and after him the indomitable Plays-With-His-Face followed suit. Whereupon, they were immediately followed by Little-White-Bear, Bear`s-Head, Twines-His-Horses-Tail and Sore-Belly who together, led the rest of the Crows in yet another determined charge. This time the Crows did not falter. They turned the Cheyennes and forced them to flee in such a disorganized manner, that the latter`s retreat quickly became a rout. The Crows harried them relentlessly, killing and wounding an additional number of Cheyennes in the process. The Crows later said,

> "…The battle was like a whirlwind. There was dust everywhere and the sound of gunfire was heard even after the fight was over and the great dust settled, as our victorious Crows continued to swarm over the battlefield, shooting those of the enemy who were wounded and even those already dead." [6]

CROW VENGEANCE ON CHEYENNES

One among the fleeing enemy was the same Hidatsa who, earlier that day, had conversed with Plays-With-His-Face when on the ridge top overlooking the Cheyenne camp. This man was mounted on a near-exhausted pony, and was overtaken by a number of Crows who surrounded him and had him at their mercy. In his desperate situation the Hidatsa began pleading with the Crows, calling them friends and cousins in the hope they would spare his life. The Crows asked him why he had been riding with their mortal foes, to which the Hidatsa replied that he was a poor man and not even worthy of killing. For some reason the Crows did not kill him, but showed their utmost contempt by urinating over him and then copulating with him anally to his great humiliation, and when they had finished, they beat him about the buttocks with the flats of their bows before sending him away disgraced, saying that next time there was a fight, he should remain among the women where he belonged. At length, however, the Crows grew tired and gave up the chase and made a strategic, but organized departure from the scene. In total the Crows had sustained the loss of six warriors dead along with several wounded, and these they carried with them on their journey home. A small number among the discomfited Cheyennes followed at a distance for a few miles before they themselves grew tired; gave up their trek, and returned to their village.

It had not been an over-whelming victory for the Crows, even though they had inflicted more casualties upon the foe than they themselves sustained. Many blamed the earlier killing of the meadow lark by the Crow woman as the reason their great chief's *medicine* had not been fully potent. Nevertheless, after the warriors arrived back at their home camp on the Yellowstone, the event was celebrated with gusto. It was considered their people's first great feat of arms since the disaster attending Long-Hair`s village the previous summer.

As for the Cheyennes, after returning to their own camp from whence they came, the women relatives of those who had not returned, went out to the site of the battle with pony-drags and collected together the remains of their dead. Eight of the original party of Bowstring Cheyennes were among those killed and had been cut up in a most horrible manner. Some were missing their head, whilst others were without arms, legs, hands and feet. The body parts were scattered over a wide area and the women spent many hours searching for all the pieces in order to carry them home.

CROW VENGEANCE ON CHEYENNES

All eight had been servants of the Cheyenne's Sacred Arrow lodge, and it was to that place that their body parts were first taken. There the limbs were put together as best could be, after which each corpse was wrapped in a robe and placed on a raised pallet within a specially enlarged tepee erected specifically for the repose of the dead.

The Cheyennes today admit they then did a terrible thing in the eyes of Cheyenne law. But the relatives of those killed, they say, were wrought with anger and grief which knew no bounds. Some relatives of the eight dead Cheyennes had Crow captives taken during the attack on Long-Hair's village. These captives had since been living in their lodges as adopted members of the tribe. But notwithstanding this, a number of Cheyennes dragged eight of the captives over to the burial tepee, and slew them without mercy by clubbing them to death. They then lay the Crow corpses around the base of the lodge, stacking them one upon the other as if they were logs, commonly used to keep tepee covers down in the advent of strong winds. Not long after this the Cheyennes moved away from the region, as was their custom when blood had been spilt roundabout. They thus left the Crow bodies to the mercy of the elements and to tooth and claw of the prairie creatures.

It must be said that many among the Cheyennes even then, condemned the slaughter of the captives, as it was the custom after a prisoner had been taken into a lodge and nourished, that he or she was then accepted into Cheyenne society as a family member. To kill such a person thereafter, was considered an act of homicide within the tribe, and it is further said that the next time the Sacred Arrow bundle was opened in order to renew its contents, specks of blood were found on the Sacred Arrow flights themselves. The blood, it was believed, of the murdered Crow captives.

Many years later during the so-called Fitzpatrick Treaty gathering of 1851, when Crows and Cheyennes among other tribes, came together at the behest of the American Government and made formal pacts with each other, which in some cases, lasted at least five years, the Crows and Cheyennes discussed past battles between them. It was then that the Crow chief Big-Shadow pointed out to the Cheyennes the Crow warrior Four-Dances [aka Hanging-Raven], the same who had been the companion of Plays-With-His-Face, and one of those who led the twelve young Cheyennes into the trap at the time of the fight in question. The Cheyennes were surprised to see a very old man, his body painted red all over and wearing a necklace of raven feathers with their tips cut off, signifying he had cut the throats of his enemies. The Cheyennes welcomed him among them, saying they had waited many years to speak with him. They asked whether the lone Crow on the ridge top had been singing or crying, as it had caused much debate among the Cheyennes, some declaring he sang and others that he cried, and since then, they had craved a true answer to the question.

The old Crow warrior replied freely, saying the man they were referring to was Plays-With-His-Face and he had been doing both things. He had been crying, Four-Dances said, for those of his people killed by Cheyennes and Sioux during the attack on Long-Hair's village, but had also been singing a war song for revenge. Plays-With-His-Face himself by that date had long since died, having committed suicide after contracting smallpox in 1833, and of which we will speak where appropriate. All being said, this 1821 Sore-Belly inspired attack on the Cheyennes had, primarily, been conducted for revenge, and certainly, it showed the Crows had not been cowed by their tribe's earlier defeat on Otter Creek. Indeed, Sore-Belly had made it known that Crows were still a force to be reckoned with, whose warriors could and would take the offensive against any and all their foes, even deep into the enemy's domain.

In the latter months of 1821, Captain Hugh Glenn and Jacob Fowler led an expedition from Fort Smith on the Arkansas River to what is now Pueblo County, Colorado, high up Huefeno Creek and back again. The expedition's route followed much the same pattern as had that of the Major Long expedition of 1820, and from which reports it had been inspired. Part of the Glenn-Fowler party met with the same group of so-called 'Trading Indians' and in late November, camped with a large encampment of seven-hundred tepees later joined by two-hundred lodges of Cheyennes. Jacob Fowler kept a diary of their eighteen months travel.

The Cheyennes in this instance had split up after their recent confrontation with the Crows, half of the nation remaining north along Cheyenne River not far west of the Missouri, and the rest later known as Southern Cheyennes roaming south of the Platte on the north side of the Arkansas as their current association with the Trading Indians suggest.

CROW VENGEANCE ON CHEYENNES

According to Fowler's diary, these more southern Cheyennes were then trading guns, powder and ball along with other European commodities obtained from their northern tribes-folk near the Missouri, who obtained such items from that river's American trading posts and from the Mandan and Arickara, and in turn, were now bartering such goods to the aforesaid Trading Indians in exchange for horses stolen from the Mexican Provinces. This is what Edwin James of the Long Expedition had reported, and even earlier, Lewis and Clark had mentioned the same in their travels of 1803-'06.

Meanwhile, on the Republican Loup in the Central Plains, a grand congregation was taking place including Skidi Pawnee and Osage. The Osage had recently been a Missouri-dwelling tribe, but having been harried west by more powerful eastern enemies, had been disputing their new domain in Nebraska with the resident Pawnee. However, although having been at war with each other for a generation and more, each was now so harassed by other foes and barely holding their own, the Pawnees for one had expressed a desire to make peace with all their neighbours and especially with the Cheyennes. The Osage had agreed to the Pawnee offer and responded at once, although how long the peace would last was anybody's guess. Either way, the pact was effected and by so doing, Cheyennes became enemies of the Osage also.

- 0 - 0 - 0 - 0 - 0 - 0 - 0 - 0 - 0 - 0 -

CHEYENNE, RED-SLEEVE

RAIDING PAWNEES, CROWS AND MANDANS

CHAPTER 8.

RAIDING PAWNEES, CROWS AND MANDANS [1822–1824]

As previously mentioned, peace wishes conveyed by Pawnees to Cheyennes through Major Long having failed, early in 1822 a strange thing happened contradictory to usual Indian character, but alas, fruitless in its outcome. [1]

A war-party of Cheyennes set out from their village west of the Missouri above the Platte to raid the Skidi town on the Republican Loup. As usual, the Cheyennes were after Pawnee horses and went on foot.

The Skidi Pawnee at this date, were renown for the fine horses they possessed and consequently, were prone to raids from most other Plains Tribes. For this reason the Pawnee kept their favourite horses and mules [the latter of which they owned in large number stolen from Mexicans and southern tribes] within the interiors of their earth-lodges at night and in strong log corrals adjoining the lodges both within and without the perimeter of the town. Thus it was always a dangerous task for potential thieves to wrest Pawnee stock successfully, and many are the tales of enemy raiding parties being discovered in their endeavours and in a few cases, annihilated within the very town.

In the current case, the Cheyenne raiders reached their objective and waited until nightfall when all would be pitch black. Whereupon, they then entered the sleeping town in groups of twos, threes and fours and were groping around the lodges looking for prime animals to steal. Finding what they were after, each slipped a hair-rope noose over an animal's neck and began leading the more gentle of horses and mules out of the circle of lodges and back to a prearranged rendezvous a short distance from the town, being more than careful not to arouse the slumbering owners.

Bear-Feathers, a young Cheyenne warrior, came upon a large corral accommodating the finest horses in the town. As Bear-feathers was in the act of untying the corral gate, a huge Pawnee came up behind him and pinned both his arms behind his back. The Cheyenne could do nothing to free himself, but to cry out to his comrades would call the whole town to arms, and Bear-Feathers was obliged to place his fate in the hands of his captor and his own protective totems. Just then, the Pawnee's wife appeared and came over to assist her husband. The husband, however, told his wife to be quiet and go back inside her lodge. In sign-language the Pawnee, who was a famous Skidi war-chief named Big-Eagle, but known to the Cheyennes as Big-Spotted-Horse, then told his captive to enter his lodge and assured him that he should not be harmed.

Inside his captor's lodge, Bear-Feathers was made comfortable and given food to eat. Although obviously frightened, the Cheyenne did not show fear and did exactly as the Skidi chief requested while pretending not to notice his captor constantly staring at him.

After Bear-Feathers finished his meal, Big-Spotted-Horse who's lodge the Cheyenne was in, filled a pipe and smoked and after which, he gave it to Bear-Feathers who also smoked. The Pawnee man then told his guest in signs of his people's desire for peace with all Cheyennes, and bade his wife throw a saddle-blanket on one of his best mules; place an ornately silver-studded Spanish saddle on it, and after giving the animal as a gift to Bear-Feathers, told him go back unharmed to his own people and tell them the peace wishes of the Pawnees. Bear-Feathers was bewildered by his captor's actions, but needing no more prompting, he mounted up and rode away a free man, and disappeared into the murky night.

When Bear-Feathers finally reached his own village in the north, his people came out to meet him, having believed him dead, and noticing the fine mule and silver-embossed Spanish saddle he was mounted on, they praised his courage for what, they supposed, he had stolen and for the powerful *medicine* they thought he must possess for his preservation. Bear-Feathers was probably embarrassed that both mule and saddle had been a gift instead of having stolen it from the town which would have been regarded by his people as an honourable deed. Perhaps, though, he did not really have a chance to explain the true details before his people jumped to their own conclusions. Therefore, he did not actually then tell his people of his encounter with the Pawnee chief or of the latter's personal offer of peace. Instead, Bear-Feathers agreed that he had entered the enemy town and personally stolen the mount and saddle.

Bear-Feathers had earlier been connected in some way with the Cheyenne Sacred Arrow talismans against the Crows, and was at a later-date known as a Southern Cheyenne chief of the *Watapio* band known as Feathered-Bear, he was generally friendly to all white men, and who knew him variously also by the name of Old-Bark and Ugly.

RAIDING PAWNEES, CROWS AND MANDANS

PAWNEE GOVERNMENT SCOUTS.
[WILLIAM JACKSON PHOTOGRAPH, 1860s].

It was this same year of '22, when hostilities commenced yet again between Cheyennes and Arapahoe on one side and the Mandan and Arickara on the other. The Arickara had been enemies of the Cheyenne on and off since 1800, their bull-boats `bobbing` up and down the Missouri River between the mouth of the Cheyenne and Little Missouri, while their domed-shaped earth-lodge villages dotted the Missouri's steep western banks. The Sioux – especially the western or Teton Sioux bands - had mostly been waring with the Arickara for many years and had often suffered during such contests. Now, however, that Cheyennes were more closely allied to the Arapahoe and Sioux, the Arickara being old foes of the latter, both Mandans and Arickara began raiding Cheyenne camps together. The result being that this same year, a twenty-two strong Arickara war-party was surprised on foot on the open prairie and wiped out by Cheyennes. Only one of the Arickara party survived and in accordance with Indian custom, was set free to take word of the slaughter to his people. This the man did, and hostilities between Cheyennes and Arickara again reached a crescendo. As has been noted, Cheyenne hostility towards the

RAIDING PAWNEES, CROWS AND MANDANS

Pawnees was still constant, and the fact that the Arickara were very closely related by blood and as allies to the Skidi Pawnee, only exasperated the hostile situation.

As it was, at the date in question Cheyennes were actually spending most of their time combating the Crows and Pawnee, and so only now and again did they actually fight the Arickara in pitched battle. Indeed, Cheyennes had often previously been at peace with the Arickara and the blood of both peoples was more than a little inter-mixed due to inter-marriage between them. Before the 1840s and their closer allience with the Sioux, there are no accounts of Cheyennes attacking the Arickara towns themselves, although as the latter's towns were protected with strong palisades and their population numerous with some five-thousand souls, Cheyennes would then likely to have been at a disadvantage.

Likewise, Cheyenne enmity with the earth-lodge Mandans was again inaugurated about this time. The Cheyennes and Mandan for several generations had been at war and peace with each other as circumstance demanded and also, there was a fair degree of mixed blood through inter-marriage between their two tribes. During the 1830s, the artist George Catlin recorded stories of fights between Cheyennes and Mandan, while the observer Prince Maximillian Zu Weid mentioned in more than one passage from an account of his own sojourn among the Mandan in the early 1830s, of Cheyenne–Mandan hostilities then still going on, and commented, "...*Cheyennes are their* [Mandan's] *most virulent foes."* [2]

Several particular Cheyenne–Mandan fights were recorded by the afore-mentioned Catlin from the actual mouth of a Mandan chief named *Mahto-Topa* or Four-Bears. The stories were confirmed by a white trader named Joseph Kipp then residing in the same chief's particular town, and who stated that the Four-Bear accounts referred to the first years when Kipp himself had gone among that tribe which was in 1823 and '24.

The following accounts must then, have occurred within the aforesaid dates, and recount that at that time a band of Cheyennes numbering around one-hundred and fifty warriors, made a dawn attack on a Mandan earth-lodge village of which the fighter *Mato-Topa* or Four-Bears was a leading war-chief. The Cheyennes were endeavouring to steal Mandan horses which, for the most part, were held in pen-like corals just outside the village, while more valuable animals were taken into the earth-lodges at night as a safeguard against thieves. Some among the Cheyennes at that time were audacious enough to enter a number of lodges, and groping around in the dark within, being careful not to trip over and awake sleeping occupants, they untied certain animals from under the very owner's noses. Something happened and the alarm was raised, and immediately the whole village was aroused. By the time the drowsy occupants came fully to their senses, the Cheyennes were already some distance away in their flight back home with a sizable number of ponies being driven at speed before them, along with one bloody Mandan top-knot for good measure.

The Mandans left in the camp gathered together a large party and mounting horses set out to pursue the thieves. They did not know how many enemy Cheyennes they might have to deal with, although fifty braves were considered ample for the chase. Soon these fifty were galloping fast, following the trail of the thieves. The Cheyennes, however, continued driving the captured herd at a rapid gait, and it was noon on the Mandan's second day out before they came in sight of their quarry.

The number of Cheyenne in the party the Mandans had grossly underestimated, which caused the latter to pull up their mounts and talk of giving up the chase and going home empty handed without offering to fight. It appeared that the whole pursuing party was resolved to turn back when their chief Four-Bears kicked his heels into his pony's flanks, and galloped out on the open prairie in front of his warriors and in full view of the enemy. The latter, having seen the hesitation of those following, halted their flight and faced the Mandans across the field.

Four-Bears, meanwhile, still mounted and within hearing distance of his warriors, stuck his lance upright in the ground beside him so its point was buried up to its shaft. Circling his mount around it, he tore from his waist a long red sash [which was probably a type of dog-rope]; reached over his horse's neck and fixed it to the shaft so it fluttered in the breeze like a long scarlet guidon. He then cried aloud to his tribesmen with words of contempt saying,

> "What have we come to this? We have dogged our enemies for two days and now we have found them, are we to turn back like cowards? *Mato-Topa's* lance which many times has been reddened with the blood of his enemies has led you within sight of the foe. You have followed it eagerly, and now it stands firm in the ground

> where it will drink the blood of *Mato-Topa,* for you all may go back and I, *Mato-Topa*, will fight the enemy alone." [3]

The Cheyennes remained static, not being sure if to fight or flee. But at length, a lone Cheyenne resplendent in majestic eagle-feathered bonnet and a war-shirt trimmed with scalps of his several conquests, and cradling a primed musket in his left arm, suddenly nosed the snow-white steed he was riding forward. He then cried aloud to the Mandan chief to know the name of he who had thrust his lance in the ground as a challenge to all among the foe, thus conveying he would not retreat until one was laid low, be it himself or an enemy Cheyenne. In response *Mato-Topa* answered with justifiable pride,

> "I am called *Mato-Topa* of the brave and valiant Mandans." [4]

And the lone Cheyenne replied,

> "I have heard of *Mato-Topa* and his bravery. Yet will he dare face me while our warriors look on?" [5]

Four-Bears, thinking he himself might well be killed in a one to one conflict, would rather it be at the hands of a man with some standing on a par with himself, rather than being slain by an unknown buck intent on counting coup and making a favourable impression on his elders and peers, therefore continued by saying,

> "Is it a chief who speaks to *Mato-Topa*?" [6]

His adversary across the field then retorted,

> " Look now upon the scalps of my enemies that hang from my horse's bit, waiting for that of a Mandan…See here my lance decorated with ermine tails and this, a war-eagle's tail." [7]

So saying, he raised both lance and eagle tail fan so the Mandan chief could see, and *Mato-Topa* accepted the challenge and waited for his contestant to come near.

The Cheyenne chief spanked the rump of his mount with the cold barrel of a musket he was carrying; screamed his war-cry and charged full gallop at the Mandan. Then, when nearly upon him, the Cheyenne wheeled away, made two full circles and then returned near to where the Mandan chief still sat motionless on his steed. The Cheyenne then thrust his own lance also emblazoning a red-coloured cloth into the ground next to that of Four-Bears, before riding off to create a little distance between them.

For a few lingering moments, both contestants eyed each other with the waving prairie between them, and both began singing death-songs and soliciting their protective totems to preserve them. Also, each cried to their people to smile upon them and see the great deeds they intended to do.

The Cheyenne raised his musket to his shoulder; let out a blood-curdling war-whoop and spurred his pony headlong at the other, who at once did the same. They charged their mounts at at break-neck speed and pulled the triggers of their guns simultaneously, although they actually passed each other without serious damage done to either. The Mandan's aim was wild, whereas that of the Cheyenne only succeeded in shattering Four-Bear's powder horn. After this, the Mandan chief reigned up and held up the fragments of the smashed powder horn so onlookers on both sides could see that his protective *medicine* was more powerful than that of his contestant. The Mandan then threw down his gun and instead, drew forth his bow and fitted an arrow to the string, while holding two spare arrows between his teeth in reserve.

The Cheyenne, not having time to reload his piece, discarded it also and likewise, drew forth a bow and arrows.

Again both charged their steeds at one another, letting fly several arrows as they passed each other several times, each time wheeling their mounts around and while so doing, wounded each other in the arms and legs until, at length, a Cheyenne arrow struck Four-Bear's horse square in the chest bringing down both man and beast. Four-Bears was trapped for a moment under his horse's weight and was frantically trying to free himself. Lucky for him, the Cheyenne chief had exhausted his own supply of arrows and now threw away his bow and quiver in disgust. Then, drawing a large flint knife from its scabbard and raising a bull-hide shield to protect his chest, he faced the Mandan who having freed himself and again was on his feet, yelled for him to come forward and fight in hand to hand combat. Four-Bear's, however, still retained his bow although his supply of arrows was spent, and as the Cheyenne came lumbering towards him, he dealt his attacker a hefty blow on the head with the knob end of his bow. As the Cheyenne was reeling from the strike, Four-Bears searched his person for his own knife, but it was not about him. At the same time, the Cheyenne like a wounded cougar, lunged at his opponent with knife raised above his head so to deal a blow with great force, but the Mandan chief caught hold of the naked blade with one hand and holding it tight, began grappling with his opponent for his life.

Blood was streaming down the Mandan's hand and arm, yet undaunted, he managed to get possession of the weapon and eventually, thrust it deep into the Cheyenne's torso several times. The wounded Cheyenne sank to the ground, his life's blood oozing over the grass about him. Truly, thought the on-looking Cheyenne warriors, the *medicine* of Four-Bears was strong. The Cheyennes for their part, picked up the body of their dead chief; placed it over the back of a pony and rode slowly off into the distance towards the valley of Heart River far from the Mandan town. Hereafter, Four-Bears the victorious Mandan chief, always wore in his hair a red-painted stick, in commemoration of his knife fight with the lone Cheyenne.

Not long after this event, probably that same year, a young Cheyenne in a bid to avenge a lost relative killed at the hands of the same Four-Bears, sent a message via the Hidatsa who were then friends with both Mandans and Cheyenne that he wished to meet the famous Four-Bears in a one to one duel to the death. Four-Bears accepted the challenge and along with many of his people including women, children and old men, met a large group of Cheyennes on the open Plain. Both sides were drawn up in battle array not far from the Mandan town on the west side of the Missouri.

The two contestants faced each other on horseback, each with a lance poised above their head ready to strike. The two horses then galloped towards each other and actually collided in mid-field.

The Mandan rider avoided the Cheyenne's thrust, but buried his own lance-point deep into his opponent's bowels, actually lifting his victim out of the saddle in the process. Then, after dismounting from his steed while the animal was still in motion, Four-Bears fell on the prostrate Cheyenne who was yet breathing and writhing in agony, and with a flint-bladed knife, ripped off the Cheyenne's scalp, then held it aloft so all those among the enemy could see.

Now the whole Cheyenne party charged their ponies at the Mandan ranks, trying desperately to retrieve their champion's body, and a bloody hand to hand skirmish ensued. The result was that the Mandans having superior numbers, were victorious, and the Cheyennes were finally obliged to flee the field.

RAIDING PAWNEES, CROWS AND MANDANS

Such was the gore the Indian then thrived upon. Men, it was thought, were born to kill or be killed and enemy blood smeared over their greasy torsos, or to savage the enemy to such extent as to be unrecognisable to even a brother. Such, however, brought the perpetrator a certain thrill which might cause one`s heart to jump, the pulse quicken and bring a gleam to the eye when an enemy`s head was dragged behind a running horse, or a severed arm, leg or other body-part, waved high in the air attached to the end of a willow-stick, lance-point or musket barrel. And withal, a fresh hank of blood-stained hair whirled above one`s head, splattering onlookers with fleshy pellets.

MANDAN CHIEF MATO-TOPA OR FOUR-BEARS
[Painted from life by Karl Bodmer, 1833]

It was indeed, a merciless era, when heroes alive were exalted, but when dead, were not remembered long, after being talked about around lodge fires for one or two winters duration.

RAIDING PAWNEES, CROWS AND MANDANS

There was another time, so Cheyenne tradition states, between 1823 and '24, that another note-worthy fight took place between Cheyennes and Mandan on a Plain in the Upper Missouri country. In this action, both opposing parties again used Dog-Ropes and there was much slaughter on either side, many falling where they stood. The result, however, was stale-mate, and both parties retired from the scene come sundown.

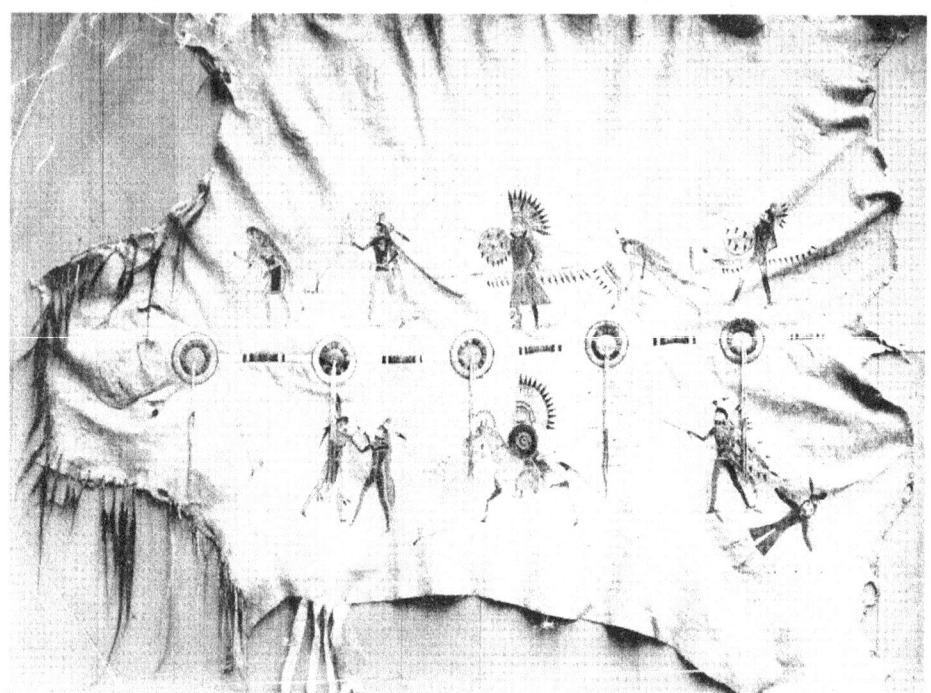

Four-Bear's Mandan Robe. Depicting fights with Cheyennes and others.

It may have been due to the above recounted fight that soon after, it led to one side or the other sending forth a retribution force against the enemy, and which indeed, would have been the usual procedure among warring tribes. In this case it was the same Mandan Chief Four-Bears who set out again against Cheyennes to seek revenge.

Before the Mandan party reached its objective which was a large Cheyenne tepee village, a formidable group of Cheyenne warriors rode out and confronted the Mandans in an effort to check their advance. A fierce battle commenced and during which, the Mandans were obliged to retreat leaving their dead and wounded on the field. One among the wounded was the great Four-Bears himself. This man was so cut-up and bleeding that his fellow warriors supposed he was dying or already dead. They could not at that time get near enough to him to carry the corpse away, and were about to leave him to suffer the contempt and humiliation the victorious Cheyennes were likely to heap upon him.

Four-Bears was not dead. When thirty or forty Cheyennes rushed forwards to count coup on his body and collect his scalp, Four-Bears promptly grabbed his nearby musket which was already charged, and shot dead his first attacker. Whereupon, the rest of the Cheyennes dropped to the ground seeking cover, and themselves began shooting their own pieces and arrows at him.

Still the Cheyennes were kept at bay by the lone Mandan shooting at them, and the withdrawing Mandan warriors knowing that musket balls and powder would not be wasted merely on a *coup-de-grass*, returned to the scene to see what was going on. Seeing their chief still alive and defending himself against the Cheyennes, the returning Mandans made a heroic charge and managed to drag their wounded chief to safety. Truly, even the Cheyennes held Four-Bears in high esteem and even today, declare he was the bravest of all Mandans they met in battle.

In the spring of 1824, a certain Cheyenne band still residing close to the Missouri on the lower part of Cheyenne River, was roaming the grasslands east of the Black Hills in what is now South Dakota State. The party was hunting buffalo and looking for enemies to attack. Somewhere on route, they came face to face with a large Mandan war-party out to raid Cheyennes for horses and led yet again, by the indomitable Four-Bears. At once, upon sighting the enemy, the Cheyennes herded their horses and non-combatants into a bunch, while the warriors formed themselves in a long line in front and made ready to fight.

Both sides sat impressively astride their war-ponies painted and bedecked in coloured cloths and feathers, while green prairie grass shimmered and feathered bonnets fluttered in the breeze. Both sides sang *medicine* songs and some even death-chants while the women-folk raised the tremolo to give their men-folk courage. Then, a powerfully-built Mandan chief garbed in all the savage regalia his rank entitled, rode his mount slowly beyond the van of his tribesmen and cried a challenge to the Cheyennes,

"Are the Mandans drawn up against women and children or against men worthy of our spear-points and are they worthy enough to mingle their blood with that of a Mandan?" [8]

There was silence from the Cheyenne ranks, for all the Cheyenne warriors then present recognised the man before them, and knew well the name and fame of *Mato-Topa* or Four-Bears. They were wary of his warrior prowess and *medicine,* and again the Mandan chief called to the Cheyennes, but this time with contempt.

"Ho Cheyennes, who among you are brave enough to face *Mato-Topa* in combat and darken the ground with his blood?" [9]

Such words struck deep into the hearts and minds of the Cheyennes, and all of a sudden, many returned the insult ferociously. At length, a Cheyenne chief nosed his mount forward into the no-man's land between the two sides, and after plunging his lance upright in the ground, accepted the challenge of Four-Bears. In response, from both ranks war-songs were sung by onlookers for their respective champions and rang out across the Plain.

The Cheyenne contestant was first to charge at his adversary. He wore an eagle-feathered bonnet and carried a feather-trimmed shield and rode right up to the still stationary Four-Bears, and a desperate tussle ensued from horseback as both lunged at each other with laces and swung at each other with iron-bladed hatchets.

As the contest progressed, both became dismounted from their steeds, and soon after, only one warrior was left stranding and that was the Mandan Four-Bears, again with a bloody Cheyenne top-knot in one hand. At this, the dead Cheyenne's wife who had witnessed the event, herself rushed upon the Mandan victor brandishing a tomahawk, but before she could make contact, Four-Bears laid her low with a shot from his musket, and to the humiliation of her people, scalped her also.

In yet an additional hostile confrontation between the same enemy groups during the same time period as recorded in Mandan recollections, and in response to six members of a Hidatsa war-party having previously been killed by Cheyennes, the surviving Hidatsa partisan of the discomfited party named Guts, carried a pipe to a neighbouring Mandan village on Knife River, and offered its stem to the great Mandan Chief Four-Bears then residing at that place. Four-Bears took up the pipe and smoked, and declared he would accompany the party to war, but only as leader of scouts and that the Hidastsa Guts should himself be the party's leader. Thus a large number of both Hidatsa and Mandan started forth to avenge themselves on the Cheyenne killers.

At length, the party met a war-band of Cheyennes in battle somewhere north of Yellowstone River, and during which confrontation, a Cheyenne chief wearing a bright red shirt was killed by Four-Bears himself. The great Mandan chief took the gun, shirt, feathered bonnet and scalp of his adversary as tokens of his deed, and thereafter, both Cheyennes and the Mandan and Hidatsa party gave up the fight and retired from the field.

Indeed, thought the Cheyennes, the *medicine* power of the Mandan chief *Mato-Topa* or Four-Bears was invulnerable, and Cheyennes were forever wary when pitted against him and his warriors in deathly struggles with each other's tribe.

- 0 - 0 - 0 - 0 - 0 - 0 - 0 - 0 - 0 - 0 –

CHEYENNES, IRON-SHIRT and WIFE

CHEYENNE CHIEF, TWO-MOONS. **CHEYENNE WOMAN, POISON, WITNESS TO 1820 EVENTS.**
[Smithsonian Institution Washington D.C.]

AMERICAN-HORSE'S SIOUX WINTER-COUNT FOR 1820 /21.
"WHEN THEY DESTROYED THE CROW LODGES."
[From Garrick Malory's "Pictographs of the American Indian." Smithsonian Institution.]

CHEYENNE CHIEFS, LEFT TO RIGHT, SPOTTED-WOLF AND CRAZY-HEAD. DECENDENTS OF CROW WOMEN CAPTURED BY CHEYENNES AT OTTER CREEK IN 1820.
[WASHINGTON D.C. PHOTOGRAPH, 1873]

MANDAN FOUR-BEARS FIGHTS CHEYENNE. [Depicted by Four-Bears after Karl Bodmer].

SKIDI PAWNEE EARTH-LODGE VILLAGE.

DRAGGING-OTTER, BUFFALO HAT KEEPER

CROW INDIAN, CRAZY POND-ORIELLE

CHEYENNE KIT-FOX WARRIOR.

ARROW KEEPER, MEDICINE-MAN.

"FRIENDSHIP TREATY" and RED-DOG-ROPE AFFAIR

CHAPTER 9.

"FRIENDSHIP TREATY" and RED-DOG-ROPE AFFAIR [1825]

The year 1825 was important regarding Cheyennes, in that they signed their Nation`s first treaty with United States Government officials. [1]

Having perused reports from white entrepreneurs in the Upper Missouri country, the American Government dispatched General Atkinson and Benjamin O`Fallon along with a detachment of army dragoons, to ascend the Missouri River in wheel-boats and make as many treaties with the Western Tribes as they could contact. Such an undertaking was intended to establish a more regulated order of trading in the Indian country, and to secure peaceful relations between the latter`s Native inhabitants and the United States. Thus, such documents became known as "Friendship Treaties."

According to the later-date Cheyenne informant John-Stands-in-Timber, Sioux Indians who knew the head Cheyenne chief, High-Backed-Wolf 1st, took word to him in camp not far west of the Missouri, that army officers were about to hold council with several Sioux bands at Fort Tecumseh on the west bank of that river at the mouth of the Teton, and had requested Cheyennes to attend. Most Cheyennes had little, if indeed, any contact with white men before this time, certainly not face to face. And so it was when High-Backed-Wolf agreed to meet the white officials, none among other Cheyenne chiefs at first agreed to accompany him to the fort. High-Backed-Wolf, however, was a proud man and already had given his word to the Sioux that he would go with them and meet the white men. He was also a wise man and, no doubt, realised the advantage of making certain agreements with the Americans and so was determined to keep his word.

Perhaps he was aware of the disastrous struggles East Woodland Tribes had suffered owing to white encroachment on their lands, and the latter`s subsequent defeat and humiliation. No doubt he had also pondered the military might and resources of these new interlopers, who grew long hair on their faces and kept their bodies covered from the light of day causing their skins to bleach. They could, though, as indeed they had, smash powerful Indian Nations such as the Iroquois and others, and against whom even the powerful Sioux had earlier met their match. For these reasons and ever-thinking of his own people's wellfare, High-Backed-Wolf - Sweet-Medicine Chief of all the Cheyennes - felt he was obliged to go with his Sioux allies to the council, and see what was on offer which might benefit his people.

High-Backed-Wolf had not long left his village when two other Cheyenne chiefs named Leaving-Bear and Buffalo-Head, finally decided that as headmen it was their duty, too, to be present at the meeting. Hastily, they followed up the path of High-Backed-Wolf and soon after this, two other Cheyenne chiefs named Little-Moon and White-Antelope also left the village and joined the emissaries bringing their number to five, and constituted the first ever Cheyenne delegation to officially meet with American Government representatives in order to make treaty agreements with them.

With the arrival of the five Cheyennes at Fort Tecumseh on the west side of the Missouri, the white officials crossed from the east bank in bull-boats and on July 4th 1825, met the said Indian delegates along with Fort Tecumseh's Fur Company personnel.

A council was held and the white officials informed High-Backed-Wolf that they wished permission to go through country west of the Missouri where Cheyennes roamed. The Cheyenne chief replied that such a decision was not for him alone to grant, but must be put to the full Cheyenne council of forty-four chiefs, and their answer would be final. Following this, the five Cheyennes returned to their village and discussed the white men's request whilst holding their own council within the tribe.

As it transpired, the rest of the Cheyenne chiefs approved the matter, and on July 4th a host of Cheyennes, now comprising twelve important delegates returned to the fort. These chiefs included High-Backed-Wolf, Buffalo-Head, Little-Moon and One-Who-Walks-Against-the-Others acting as the tribes' most paramount headmen, while lesser chiefs and warriors among them were White-Antelope, Raises-the-Club, Pile-of-Buffalo-Bones, Little-White-Bear, Running-Wolf, Soldier, Lousy-Man [aka Scabby] and Big-Hand.

That morning, the chiefs and braves of the Cheyennes were seated at the council place. The white Major and an accompanying General explained to the new arrivals their mission of treating with them and, thereafter, the Commissionaires were invited to the Sioux Chief Standing-Buffalo's lodge in the Oglala camp to partake of a noon-day feast. After a meal of boiled puppy-dogs, the Sioux chief requested the white men and Cheyennes in assembly with them, to smoke the `pipe of peace` and this having been done, another feast was offered and accepted by all.

In reality, the actual council with Atkinson and O`Fallon was brief. The officials merely asking for mutual friendship; the cessation of Indian theft from white men traders, and the regulating of those traders already amongst the tribes by application of licensing controls. There were, though, additional Articles written on the treaty paper itself, but which seemed to the Indians to be somewhat incomprehensible and so were actually hardly given a thought.

ATKINSON – O`FALLON `FRIENDSHIP TREATY WITH CHEYENNES.

These additional clauses proclaimed the tribes as each being subject to the Great White Father President Quincy Adams and of the United States. But to the Cheyennes, of course, such conditions put forward meant very little to their natural way of thinking. More important, the Indians thought, was that the council was their first meeting with American Government officials and of the

"FRIENDSHIP TREATY" and RED-DOG-ROPE AFFAIR

Indians themselves receiving gifts for, as they also supposed, merely being present.

Contrary to the above, however, and to the Government's way of thinking, the Indians, having agreed to and signed the treaty articles by each making his mark on the paper itself, Indian lands and behaviour came under American Government control and within its legal jurisdiction. If indeed, Cheyennes had understood what the council had really been all about, then surely, so they later said, there must have been a degree of misinterpretation or certainly errors in what had been declared and outlined. The Great *Ma'he'o* had given the land to the Indian in which to hunt and live, and no Human Being could regard any land as one's personal belonging to the exclusion of all others. Furthermore, the Indian was his own boss, so to speak, and would roam the land 'As long as the grass shall grow.' Certainly, no words on a piece of the white man's paper could change it being so.

Having said this, it was either through expressions of goodwill or merely in order to humour the white officials, that Cheyenne chiefs; as had others belonging to various tribes which the latter had already met, put their marks on the treaty paper in good faith, and for so doing, each chief was presented a medal bearing the inscription "Friendship Treaty 1825" on one side, and the engraved likeness of President Jefferson on the obverse. The Cheyenne chiefs did cherish the medals presented them, although regarded more as illustrious body ornaments, rather than representing what the white men supposed, had been an important occasion when life-long agreements had been solidified. Some medals indeed, were worn as war-charms and as a result, many were lost in battle or taken by enemies as booty after its owner had been killed. Any such medals in existence today are in museums or private collections, although according to the Cheyenne informant John Stands-in-Timber, the actual medal once belonging to High-Backed-Wolf 1st was handed down after his death in 1833 to his nephew High-Backed-Wolf 2d, and who himself, was killed in battle in 1865. The medal next was owned by the latter's sister later known as Old Lady Rondo, and after her, by Medicine-Elk, nephew of High-Backed-Wolf 2d. At length, it was sold to a white man trader named A. C. Stohr who kept it until his death, although today the medal's present owner is not known, and most likely it is lost.

"FRIENDSHIP TREATY" and RED-DOG-ROPE AFFAIR

Before the above meeting with Government Army officials, only small bands of white men either trappers or traders had been in Cheyenne country, and these gave away few secrets of their race. Now, at last, Cheyennes became aware that in some far off place of habitat there must be many such men with more sophisticated arts and materials of war; their number more numerous than the very blades of grass. The Indian should be wary of attacking white men head-on, they thought, but should wait in ambush and attack only in superior force. Later, when white emigrants and settlers came in, Indian attitudes changed somewhat owing to the white man`s ignorance and lack of knowledge when in Indian country. The Indian, however, was ever an apt pupil, and saw the advantage of learning certain things from the white man, some of which the Indian improved upon and successfully, converted to his own environment.

Having said this, the aforesaid treaty of `25 was the dawning of a new era for the Plains Indian. At last, it seemed, the American Government was taking a genuine interest in its savage subjects. Ever since the Lewis and Clark expedition of 1803-`06 had mapped a route west from the Atlantic Seaboard to the Pacific Ocean across the wilds and wastes of the Continent, Congress had been determined to act. To expand its culture and power, that is, and settle every acre of habitable land if it so wished without interference from the rightful Indian inhabitants. Indeed, as it had done already with most Eastern Woodland Tribes. A show of arms, thought the Government, even though small, would be enough to subdue any aspirations of resistance from a people running half-naked over the prairies. They did not ruminate on the progressiveness and resourcefulness of their `savage` subjects, a mistake to cost the white man dear; cause many more treaties to be made and broken, and a much greater show of force before a prolonged compromise would be reached.

Thus it was evident within only a few weeks after Cheyenne chiefs had put their marks on the so-called *Friendship Treaty* paper, the idea of bringing the prairie tribes together in peace proved of little avail. Probably the council did ultimately help put an end to the Cheyenne–Mandan war a few years later, although the prime factor was surely the migration west and southwest of most Cheyennes and, consequently, their stepping up of hostilities with more western and southern foes in whose territories Cheyennes were then encroaching into. In such a way, the Cheyenne–Mandan war simply faded out, as it were, and a

"FRIENDSHIP TREATY" and RED-DOG-ROPE AFFAIR

few years later, Cheyennes abandoned forever their earth-lodge towns and fields adjacent to the Missouri.

Certainly, it was soon after the above-mentioned Atkinson–O'Fallon treaty-signing at the mouth of the Teton, that there occurred yet another Cheyenne brush with the Mandan, albeit the latter then aided by the Arickara and led by an Arickara chief whom the Cheyennes aptly named due to the event, Red-Dog-Rope.

In late summer 1825 due to their own recent agreement with the Atkinson-O'Fallon expedition, a large party of mixed Arickara and Mandan sent word to the main Cheyenne village then on Cheyenne River, that they were coming to meet them in order to smoke the pipe of peace between their peoples. This, so the Arickara told Cheyennes at a later-date peace conference in 1835, was actually a rouse orchestrated by the Arickara and Mandan, in order to get up close to the Cheyennes and attack the occupants within the latter's own camp. Those Cheyennes involved may well have been residing in one of their seasonally occupied earth-lodge camps either adjacent to the Missouri or on Grand River or Cherry Creek not too far west. The Arickara and Mandan would not have had much difficulty investing a tepee village without protective palisade or breastworks, and we know that some Cheyennes were, until 1833 and later, still visiting one or more of their old, then since abandoned but once permanent earth-lodge villages, to harvest still-growing crops. The Cheyennes, coincidently at the same meeting of '35, professed to the Arickara and Mandan that they themselves had, in fact, harboured the same intention of treachery against the latter, by at first agreeing to a peaceful meeting, but only to wait until the visitors were off their guard and then the Cheyennes would slaughter them all. It seems, of course, that these explanations given by one side and the other that they had not been taken in so not to expect a treacherous act, was used merely by both to excuse the real situation as it had been at the time.

Either way, when word reached the Cheyennes of the so-called Arickara-Mandan peace commission's approach towards their village, there was much excitement among the people. The Arickara, say the Cheyennes, were then already known for their treacherous acts and therefore, had caused the Cheyennes to be wary and exercise a high degree of caution. Subsequently, the Cheyenne chiefs agreed among themselves to meet the visitors in friendship, and then, when all were within the camp, to suddenly turn upon them and slaughter them all.

Accordingly, as the Arickara and Mandans approached, Cheyenne bucks as was customary, rode out on spirited ponies to meet the new-comers. When they did meet, several Cheyennes took hold of certain persons among the visitors by the shoulders and even began hugging them as an indication of welcome. The visitors, all of whom were on foot, were then invited to jump up on the mounts the Cheyennes were riding, so to be carried in style to the Cheyenne camp.

There was one Arickara, a chief of some sort, who called to his warriors not to do as the Cheyennes requested as it might be a trap to allay their suspicions of treachery. They should continue on foot, he said, for they could not be sure of the Cheyenne attitude when actually in the camp, and if indeed the Cheyennes wanted to fight, then he and his warriors could kill many Cheyennes including women and children before they themselves were killed. Many Arickara and Mandan fighting men took heed of the chief's proposal, but five men among them did mount up behind Cheyenne riders and were carried into the village.

As the Arickara chief himself walked towards the village, he produced a long scarlet cloth decorated with porcupine quills and eagle feathers from a medicine bundle he was carrying, and the cloth having a loop at one end, he placed over his head so it rested on his body like a long bandoleer. This was a form of Dog-Rope, which only the bravest of men possessed, and was a sign to all that if any fighting occurred, then he for one would stake the cloth's trailing end to the ground with a wooden pin and fight where he stood until killed. Meantime, he continued walking towards the village whilst also fletching an arrow to his bow.

Seeing this, a mounted Cheyenne rode in front of him and attempted to stop the chief from going any further. Whereupon, the chief shot an arrow at the horse the Cheyenne was riding, causing the animal to fall and which broke the rider's leg as it fell. Before the fallen Cheyenne could react, the lone Arickara was upon him and dashed out his brains with the club end of his bow.

By this time other Cheyennes were racing forward, but before contact could be made, the Arickara chief loosed off a second arrow which also found its mark, and so toppled another Cheyenne from his horse. The dismounted

"FRIENDSHIP TREATY" and RED-DOG-ROPE AFFAIR

rider, however, managed to make his escape before being slain and the Arickara chief, rather than mounting the horse, shot it dead instead and continued walking towards the village. The whole body of both Arickara and Mandan now moved in a compact body towards the Cheyennes and were calling to the latter to come on and fight.

The Cheyennes were amazed at the enemy's audacity and raced back to their camp and on-looking people, yelling to them to prepare for a big fight and to barricade the village.

Luckily for the Cheyennes at this time, the village actually appeared too large for the Arickara and Mandan force to attack, and they halted their advance when they came to a nearby timbered creek. The Cheyenne warriors did not charge out, but having fortified their village, stood ready to repel an assault and so left the enemy where they were. Needless to say, the five Arickara and Mandans taken on horseback into the Cheyenne camp were promptly killed.

The Cheyenne so-named the Arickara chief who had been most prominent during the affair, Red-Dog-Rope for obvious reasons, and the event is still remembered among them as *"When Red-Dog-Rope came to fight."* [2]

So runs the Cheyenne recollection of the event, although it is likely that at first the Cheyennes had good intentions towards the Arickara and Mandan, but when seeing the Arickara chief stringing his bow and donning his Dog-Rope, their fears of Arickara treachery made them try to stop him reaching the village. In the excitement, the Arickara chief had released his arrow and the skirmish began. As above mentioned, it was ten years later when Cheyennes, Arickara and Mandans conversed with each other concerning the affair, and the Cheyennes probably wished to cover up their embarrassment of having been taken in by the latter.

Even so, such an audacious raid probably offered more than a little incentive for Cheyennes to attempt to avenge themselves on the Arickara and Mandans, although if so, quite likely it was the last major brush Cheyennes as an entity had with them. Certainly, at about this same date of 1825, Cheyennes as a Nation ceased abruptly their hostility towards the Missouri River tribes of Mandan and Arickara, while at the same time, the Mandan and Arickara broke their own alliance and began warring against each other.

- 0 - 0 - 0 - 0 - 0 - 0 - 0 - 0 - 0 - 0 -

NORTHERN CHEYENNE, WOODEN-LEG.

CHAPTER 10.

CHEYENNES MOVE TO SOUTH PLATTE and BENT`S FORT
[1826-1828]

For many years Cheyennes had heard stories of a populous warrior Nation of the North, their tribal domain stretching from the Upper Missouri in the South to the Bow and Saskatchewan Rivers in the North. They were engaged in bloody wars with Crows, Flatheads, Shoshoni, Nez-Perce, Assiniboine and Cree, yet treated their neighbours the Sarsi and Atsina [Gros Ventres of the Prairies] as friends and allies. At their height of power, they were raiding all points of the compass and became the undisputed masters of the Northern Plains. As a consequence, they were daubed by contemporary white men as `Tigers of the Plains. ` The Cheyennes knew them as *"Po-o-mas"* signifying `Blankets whitened with earth,` and held them in high regard. However, they called themselves collectively Siksika, but more commonly were known as Blackfeet. [1]

Living under Blackfeet protection at that time were the Atsina, also called Big-Bellies, and who themselves, were very close kinfolk to the Arapahoe with whom they also roamed at will. Subsequently, due to the close confederation of Cheyennes and Arapahoe, some Atsina became frequent visitors to Cheyenne camps. In a similar manner, Blackfeet bands when in company with Atsina allies, also came in contact with Cheyennes and likewise, were made welcome in the latter`s camps.

Around the date 1826, thirty or forty Atsina along with twenty Blackfeet warriors came down from the Northern Plains, the Atsina to visit the Arapahoe; the Blackfeet on their way further south to steal horses from one or another southern tribe. Cheyennes were then again encamped somewhere along Cheyenne River east of the Black Hills, and welcomed the northern visitors heartedly as was customary when strangers came in peace.

Some few years earlier, Blackfeet bands had commenced hostilities with the southern tribes of Kiowa, Comanche and Ute owing to an excessive

CHEYENNES MOVE TO SOUTH PLATTE and BENT'S FORT

Blackfeet desire for horses, and which caused their war-parties to fan out in all directions even as far south as Mexico.

While guests of the Cheyennes at the time in question, Blackfeet warriors paraded around within the Cheyenne camp in a long line, proclaiming aloud their ability at stealing horses and their prowess as warriors. They were at that very moment on their way south across the South Platte, they said, to steal from Comanche stock. Cheyenne onlookers urged them to fulfil their boasts, and the following day, all the Blackfeet set out in quest of Kiowa and Comanche herds.

It was not long after this that the same Blackfeet returned, now whooping and singing and shooting their Hudson's Bay trade guns in the air whilst driving a formidable herd of ponies before them groomed in the Comanche fashion. They rode around the Cheyenne camp circle in self-adoration of their deed and proclaimed aloud the countless number of wild horses and buffalo teeming in huge black masses south of the South Platte River. They rebuked the Cheyennes as being non-adventurous and urged the warriors to join them in their next venture south.

The Cheyennes listened, half despising, half with envy. They realised, of course, that if the words of their guests were true, then they were indeed missing out on something advantageous to their people. Here they were scrimping and scraping an existence, relying on chance that buffalo in large enough number would pass through their territory and of which, many times, disappeared as quickly as they had come. Often their hunters had to travel far afield in search of game and frequent were times they had returned to their families empty-handed. Additionally, the natural elements of the northern region above the Platte were fierce and hazardous, and the seemingly easy way of procuring horses in the south, caused the jibes of the Blackfeet visitors to sink deep.

For some it was too much of a temptation, and eventually, the *Hevitanio* or Hair-Rope band of Cheyennes decided to move south and see for themselves what was on offer.

Three *Heviatanio* chiefs led their whole band south, and these were Yellow-Wolf, Afraid-of-Beavers and Medicine-Snake [aka Walking-Whirlwind]. Thus, Cheyennes crossed the South Platte River and took up permanent residence in what is now the southern part of Colorado State. Indeed, Cheyennes acted only as a compact entity when either the Nation's Sacred Arrows were `moved` against an enemy, and annual religious ceremonies were to take place, or every ten years, when the reselection of the Nation's forty-four chiefs was to be held. Tribal law did not otherwise control the wanderings of any band or family clan, and one could go where and when one pleased. This being so, it was no surprise when Yellow-Wolf led his particular band across the South Platte and took up permanent residence on that river's south bank albeit that before this move, no Cheyenne had lived permanently that far south. In a short time, other Cheyenne bands followed suit and became - after the erection of Bent's Fort on the Arkansas River - what the white man designated as Southern Cheyennes. The latter themselves did not at that time distinguish themselves from other Cheyenne bands that remained in the north, not that is until 1851, when due to another treaty gathering with white Government officials, did Cheyennes of the South Platte and Arkansas country become officially recognised as the `Southern Cheyenne.`

    Soon six Cheyenne-speaking bands were scattered in separate camps in the South Platte country, namely the *Heviatanio, Oivimana, Aorta, Issiometanio, Watapio* and a band of Suhtaio. The remaining bands of *Omisis, Mashikota, Oktouna, Hofnowa* and rest of the Suhtaio thereafter, constituted what became known as the Northern division or, `Northern Cheyenne.`

    It is true that regardless of a distant separation between Northern and Southern divisions, Cheyenne language and customs remained the same and always, they considered themselves one people. Their respective environments, however, were completely different. In the north they fought the Crows, Shoshoni, Pawnees and Blackfeet [the last-named after 1856] and allied themselves very closely to the Western or Teton Sioux and Northern Arapahoe, coupling their history with theirs and intermingling their dress and culture. In the south, Southern Cheyennes fought the Utes, Kiowa, Comanche and Kiowa-Apache, Pawnees and most other Caddoan tribes along with those later known as Emigrant Tribes from the east, and followed the dress and culture of the Southern tribes to immediately distinguish them from their Northern kinfolk.

    If all Cheyennes had remained in the north, undoubtedly they would have ran afoul of Teton Sioux encroachment west from the Missouri and again

CHEYENNES MOVE TO SOUTH PLATTE and BENT'S FORT

been in hostility with them. With regards to the number of Tetons as opposed to Cheyennes, the result must have been the diminishing of Cheyennes as a fighting force, and, of course, Cheyennes could not have held out against the white man as long as they did without having the populous Sioux as their allies. Breaking up into two divisions of north and south, enabled Cheyennes to tag along with other tribes also at war with the whites, and thus, enabled them to present a united Indian front when needed.

Here also in the South Platte and Arkansas country were vast expanses of lush green grasslands shaded here and there with milling herds of wild horses and grazing buffalo, along with cool streams boarded by long stretches of timber. It was indeed true what their Blackfeet guests told them of the Southern Plains and which in all things, was certainly conducive as Indian Country.

As previously noted, the intertribal horse trading fair in 1814 had been broken up abruptly due to the killing of a Kiowa by a Sioux. The respective bands had then sided with those they were best on terms with, and Cheyennes and Arapahoe had sided with the Sioux. Conversely, Comanche, Kiowa-Apache and Shoshoni saw reason with the Kiowa and in such a manner, withdrew in their respective groups. Tribal bonds thereafter, were for a time sealed, and not again for several years did the bulk of Cheyenne warriors travel freely with the Kiowa, Comanche and Kiowa-Apache, although all-out warfare had not as yet broken out between them.

During all this time, Cheyennes for the most part were involved in bitter warfare against the Crows and, since the affair of `17, with the Shoshoni also. Kiowas on the other hand, were traditional friends of the Crows and Comanche and with such a fact, it is little wonder that Kiowas and Comanche grew more than a little temperamental against Cheyennes, when the latter crossed the south Platte and began hunting and camping regularly between that river and the Arkansas. Soon, the once harmonious Cheyenne – Kiowa companionship passed into folk-lore. A resolvable matter at first, perhaps, but in reality, one which started a prolonged and gory conflict which took little inducement to ignite.

It must be said that hunting wild horses themselves, was not often the Cheyenne's prime concern, for when a Comanche tepee village with many horses was discovered by a war-party led by a wiley *Heviatanio* horse-thief

CHEYENNES MOVE TO SOUTH PLATTE and BENT'S FORT

Yellow-Wolf, the same who had led his people south, his eyes were turned covertly towards those animals and a short time later, he and his comrades were driving stolen stock back to their home camp. Perhaps the Cheyenne thieves had done such as a daring-do exercise, rather than a deliberate act for commencing war. But the Comanche chief was a famous fighter known as Buffalo-Hump, and was angry enough to retaliate in a vengeful manner.

According to later-day Cheyennes, it was the Comanche who inaugurated hostilities by first attacking Cheyennnes and so igniting a war, although more likely, Yellow-Wolf's party had first stolen Comanche horses and in retaliation, Buffalo-Hump had attacked Cheyennes in their camp. Either way, prolonged war was the result and which endured for another fourteen years, soaking the pages of Cheyenne and allied Arapahoe along with Kiowa and Comanche history in blood.

In spring 1827, Yellow-Wolf left his village on the South Platte and with several young men went on foot on yet another raid after Comanche horses. After a few days travel, the party came upon a Comanche village on the North Fork of Red River, Texas, a favourite haunt of Buffalo-Hump's people. The Cheyennes entered the sleeping village at nightfall, and rode off with a large number of horses without trouble.

On returning to their own village, Yellow-Wolf was widely acclaimed and many young men were anxious to match his deed. Among these last was one named White-Antelope and another, named Rock-Forehead. They went to Yellow-Wolf's tepee and asked him where exactly the Comanche village was sited, and Yellow-Wolf was happy to tell them where it was and also the best way to reach it. The next day both White-Antelope and Rock-Forehead who carried the pipes [led them] started forth on foot with twenty other young braves and headed towards the same North Fork of Red River.

It was only a matter of a few weeks before the Cheyenne party reached its objective, although the Comanche village had since moved further downriver. Meanwhile Cheyenne scouts went out to locate the enemy's exact position and before nightfall, the same scouts came running back now crouching as they ran and waving their heads from side to side while howling like wolves. Then the leader burst out the news of the enemys' whereabouts

CHEYENNES MOVE TO SOUTH PLATTE and BENT'S FORT

and said that the latter's horse herds stretched for miles each side of the Fork. Such news could not have come at a more opportune moment as some among the party were already talking of returning home empty-handed. Instead, they now all hastily prepared themselves for the raid.

That same night twenty-two Cheyennes watched as dying embers in Comanche lodges died down and it became pitch dark as there was no moon. The camp was a large one and White-Antelope told his comrades to concentrate on stealing horses grazing or tethered along the river bank, lest one or more of their number be discovered in the village itself. This the party did, and before dawn broke, they were riding north back to the South Platte driving before them what is said to have been the largest number of Comanche ponies stolen by Cheyennes at one time.

Within a year of this particular raid, Cheyennes going against the Kiowa and Comanche and visa-versa were constantly taking place, most parties returning to their own camps in the same routine, driving scores of stolen ponies before them and, perhaps, waving one or two blood-congealed enemy top-knots above their heads. From this date on, Cheyennes north of the Platte allied themselves with Teton Sioux bands and went to war against the Crows, Shoshoni and Pawnee, whilst Cheyennes on and below the South Platte, allied themselves with Southern Arapahoe and made war upon the Kiowa, Ute and Comanche.

Come spring, 1828, Buffalo-Hump - the aforesaid Comanche chief - made a moonlight raid on The *Heveatanio* Cheyenne village and escaped with a formidable herd of horses. Cheyennes led by Yellow-Wolf pursued the thieves as far south as Cimarron River, Texas, in the very heart of Comanche territory. When Buffalo-Hump thought his party was safe from pursuers, Yellow-Wolf and comrades ambushed the thieves; killed several Comanche and retrieved all the stolen stock. All that summer Cheyennes seemed to be forever raiding both the Comanche and the Kiowa for horses and at one time, it is said, the *Heveatanio* herd consisted entirely of Comanche stock. The famous *Watapio* Cheyenne chief Black-Kettle [killed at the Washita fight in 1868] received his warrior status by such raids, as did other Cheyennes such as Yellow-Wolf, Little-Wolf and Mad-Wolf among many others.

CHEYENNES MOVE TO SOUTH PLATTE and BENT'S FORT

Later that same year, a war-party of Southern Cheyennes led by an up and coming warrior named Big-Foot, started south after Ute horses. Whilst on route, they came across a crude party of white men on the Arkansas with several loaded wagons surrounded by a brush stockade. At first the Cheyennes thought of stealing the white men's horses, but the Indians being inferior in number and with little knowledge of the white race, paraded into the open with heads held high and right hands held up with the palm open in the universal Indian sign of peace.

The white men in camp included none other than William Bent on his way to the town of Santa Fe with merchandise. The white men were actually setting up winter quarters on the river, although their ultimate purpose was to establish some kind of trading house or fort in the heart of Indian country on the Plains and, consequently, William Bent was pleased to meet these Cheyennes which he might use as emissaries to the chiefs of that tribe. Certainly, he realised that the impression he gave these Indians and his actions would determine him as friend or foe, and therefore, he was prepared to make the most of the meeting.

Using a few words of Sioux and Indian sign language, Bent and Big-Foot conversed, smoked, joked and ate together, the Cheyennes all the time pondering over the trade trinkets and coloured beads in the wagons. Soon, however, the party decided to continue on its way, and in good faith towards each other, all but two Cheyennes left the stockade.

The two Cheyenne stragglers were intrigued by such articles they were seeing and with the first white men they had actually come close to, let alone face to face with. William was happy to entertain them. However, it was not long after Big-Foot and the others had left, that over the hills to the south came yet another band of Indians, although all these were horseback, heavily armed and painted for war.

On distinguishing their dress, the two Cheyennes' hearts thumped with fear, as these were Comanche warriors and two Cheyenne scalps would not be passed by. The pair would have been buzzard meat for sure had it not been for William Bent who realizing their plight, quickly hid the two Cheyennes under the pelts on his wagons. Maybe the trader was thinking of future trade with the Cheyennes, and saving their two tribal members would welcome him among

CHEYENNES MOVE TO SOUTH PLATTE and BENT'S FORT

that tribe. Yet it is just as likely that William had a genuine sympathy for them, and, perhaps, he suspected that if the Comanche discovered he was attempting to hoodwink them, he might lose his own scalp also.

Buffalo-Hump the Comanche leader was curious as to the white men's camp, but had undoubtedly met white men before, and would even have stolen the latter's horses were the camp not one of traders. William on the other hand did not want any trouble. If he played his cards right he might succeed in gaining Comanche trade also and with them, that of their southern allies the Kiowa and Kiowa-Apaches. Buffalo-Hump nevertheless, was no fool. It did not take him long to spot moccasin prints in the sand peculiar to the Cheyenne pattern. He demanded to know from whence they came, and William confessed that Cheyennes had earlier visited the white men but had since left for their own village which was, William told them, on the South Platte further north. Buffalo-Hump was satisfied with the answer, and with his warriors started at once towards the village on South Platte.

The white men and especially William Bent, sighed relief as did the two concealed Cheyennes, who hastily thanked William profusely, then set off on foot as fast as they could run towards their own village.

A tie of friendship was thus forged between William Bent and Cheyennes, which would prove itself one of the strongest White–Red relationships in the history of the West. Meanwhile, the two Cheyennes when reaching their village gave their people warning of Buffalo-Hump's intention to raid it. But it was too late. Already the Comanche were re-crossing the Arkansas, driving a large number of captured Cheyenne horses before them.

By a strange coincidence, The Cheyennes Yellow-Wolf, Little-Wolf [later known as Old-Little-Wolf], Big-Old-Man, Walking-Coyote and twenty others had been out chasing wild ponies, and having captured a sizable herd, were on their return home near Sand Creek where it enters the Arkansas. Yellow-Wolf was in the lead and was first to catch the smell of burning Buffalo ribs. All those with Yellow-Wolf agreed that enemy peoples must be nearby and were cooking meat. Yellow-Wolf thus dispatched his adopted son Walking-Coyote and a few others to scout ahead, and determine if the suspected camp contained friends or foe.

CHEYENNES MOVE TO SOUTH PLATTE and BENT'S FORT

The only water around was at a place the Indians called Black Lake, and Yellow-Wolf had told his scouts that if anybody was encamped in the vicinity, then Black Lake was sure to be the place. It was mid-night when Walking-Coyote and comrades came to the lake in question, whereupon, he crawled to the crest of a small hill, while the rest of his fellows waited in silence at the base of the hill, and below which on its far side, sat many Comanche warriors with a number of horses milling around them.

When the scouts returned to the other Cheyennes, Yellow-Wolf decided to attack the unsuspecting Comanche and stampede the latter's horses to add to those the Cheyennes had already captured. To do this, Yellow-Wolf said, they must first get on the other side of their quarry, so if they gave chase, he and his comrades would be racing north towards their own village rather than from it. Then he told some of his braves to start at once north with the wild horses to the South Platte, and told them not to stop even if they heard shooting behind them. To Walking-Coyote and some others, Yellow-Wolf directed them to hold back the Comanche if they should attempt to follow, while himself and remainder of the party, would drive the Comanche herd away.

Come morning, the Cheyennes were on the other side of the hill and those with their own herd were galloping northwards as directed by Yellow-Wolf. The Comanche previously had herders out watching their animals, but as dawn broke, had returned to their camp, supposing the animals to be safe in the light of day.

Suddenly, Yellow-Wolf and his warriors came hurtling down the hillside in full view of the enemy and rode straight into the camp where thirty or forty horses were tethered next to their owners. In the wild melee which followed, the Cheyennes screaming war-cries and waving blankets above their heads to arouse the animals, the Comanche were taken by surprise and were shooting their guns and bows and shouting. Many horses were terrified at the noise. They pulled up their picket pins and joined in one stampeding herd. The Cheyenne said later that they themselves were constantly dodging flying picket pins as they herded the animals north.

Walking-Coyote rode right in amongst the Comanches and dismounted; cut the rope securing a fine horse, remounted and rode away unscathed. Giving his prize to Yellow-Wolf for safe-keeping, he then returned to the scene in an

CHEYENNES MOVE TO SOUTH PLATTE and BENT`S FORT

effort to hold back the enemy, who having caught and mounted some passing steeds, began to pursue the thieves. Soon around twenty Comanches were gaining fast, but without warning, Yellow-Wolf, Big-Old-Man and Little-Wolf and others who carried guns of some description, stopped their horses in their tracks, turned their mounts around and actually charged blindly into the Comanche pursuers. Yellow-Wolf rode up alongside a Comanche, poked the barrel of his musket into his pursuer`s face and pulled the trigger. His victim went crashing from his steed and soaked the prairie red with blood. Walking-Coyote then counted second coup upon him and Old-Little-Wolf the third and also removed the scalp. Another Cheyenne named Stone, dropped another with a musket ball and upon which, the enemy turned their own mounts around and fled the field completely.

The Cheyennes, although amazed that the enemy should have given up the fight so soon, rounded up the stolen animals including the two once belonging to the dead Comanches, and continued to their own village and while on route, caught up with their companions who had gone on before with the wild horses previously captured.

When the victorious party reached home, they each painted their faces black as was the custom when returning in victory, while Yellow-Wolf and Walking-Coyote each tied a Comanche scalp to the end of their gun barrels.

The whole party then galloped their ponies down the hillside and raced around the interior of their camp, singing victory songs and shooting guns in the air amid countless ponies both wild and tame, all mixed up and stampeding around them.

The camp occupants, however, on close inspection of the herd, recognised many among the animals as having first been stolen from the Comanche by Cheyennes, then from Cheyennes by Chief Buffalo-Hump and his Comanche, and now from Buffalo-Hump`s camp by Yellow-Wolf's party.

When some years later at a peace council between Cheyennes and Comanche in 1840, Comanches were asked why they had given up the fight so easily. Buffalo-Hump replied that when his warriors saw the herd of wild horses other Cheyennes were driving in the distance, they thought they were nearing a much larger force of Cheyennes by the size of the dust cloud created, and for that reason, they had given up the pursuit.

CHEYENNES MOVE TO SOUTH PLATTE and BENT'S FORT

Come early spring, 1829, Yellow-Wolf again met William Bent and was introduced to members of the Bent clan and their companions. Even at this date white men were few on the Plains, and Cheyennes appeared to enjoy their company without inclination of the coming storm and bitter tears the encroachment of white men would inevitably bring. Thus when William, traveling with a caravan loaded with goods on route to his newly established trading post on Fountain Creek of the Arkansas, stopped temporarily at Purgatory Creek on the south bank of the Arkansas, he harboured no fears of meeting Cheyennes or other Indians. When a guard shouted that a band of Indians was driving a formidable herd of horses before them and coming over the hills from the south, William at once with eyes that might have been trained by a hawk, recognised them as Cheyenne along with the previously mentioned Yellow-Wolf and Old-Little-Wolf who led them. These Cheyennes were returning home with yet another bunch of ponies stolen from the Comanche or Kiowa.

When the Indians came near and reigned in their horses, Yellow-Wolf went up to William and greeted him heartedly and made good his relations with all other white men then present. Soon coffee was on the boil and Indians and whites sat down and smoked the fraternal pipe together. They talked, ate and smoked, and Yellow-Wolf gave some among the white men each an Indian name. To Charles Bent; the head of that family, he gave the name of White-Hat, being a poetic Cheyenne idiom for a leader of white men. To William, being shorter in height to Charles, he named Little-White-Man, while the latter's brother George, became Little-Beaver, and Robert, regarded by the Indians as handsome, was daubed Green-Bird.

Like their predecessors under the Cheyenne Big-Foot, Yellow-Wolf's party nosed around the Bent caravan in curiosity, taking in everything they saw, for these, too, were probably the first white men many among the Indians in this party had met at such close quarters.

To show their appreciation, the white men gave the Indians presents with promises of continued goodwill between them, and hereafter, discussions became more serious between them, eventually leading up to the building of the Bents' proposed fort. Speaking in pidgin Cheyenne, Indian sign language and a smattering of Sioux, Charles explained that they intended erecting the

CHEYENNES MOVE TO SOUTH PLATTE and BENT'S FORT

said fort on Fountain Creek. Yellow-Wolf expressed his anticipation of having a trading post in accessible country, but was debatable as to its supposed location. Surely, remarked the chief, a place known as `Big Timbers` - a thirty mile stretch of cottonwoods running along the Arkansas River itself about thirty miles south of the Purgatory, - would prove much more beneficial. This being a well-stocked wooded area offering both fuel and shelter for horses, fresh water and a favourite refuge for buffalo. Also, it would be central not only for Cheyennes, but for other tribes such as Arapahoe, Kiowa, Comanche, Kiowa-Apache, Ute, Crows and the occasional Shoshoni from the mountains. Both Charles and William sensed the logic of Yellow-Wolf's words and pondered over them. Soon, however, it was time for the Cheyennes to leave for home, and after conveying their respects to each other, the white men and Indians departed to go their separate ways again with happy hearts towards each other. It is evident that when the Indians left it was in an atmosphere of friendship, and now especially so, after William had saved the two Cheyennes from instant death the previous summer.

What of this man Yellow-Wolf who could win the friendship and respect of all with whom he came in contact? His proper name was *Oh-Kohm-Kho-Wais*, meaning Yellow-Coyote, and was destined to become one of the greatest warriors of his age and always a staunch friend of the white man. Of those who excelled in conflict with the Kiowa and Comanche, none achieved more acclaim than he. Born into the *Heviatanio* Cheyenne also known as the Hair-Rope band in 1779 or thereabout, his warrior schooling was mostly against Crows and Shoshoni and sometimes the Mandan, and it was not long before he became a leading man among the Bowstring Warrior Society and recognised for his fighting prowess and as a leader of men. His horse-stealing raids were constant and successful and his rewards great. In time he gained a large following and when still in his thirties, became head chief of his band. Although he did not obtain the role of a big chief in the Nation as a whole, he carried much weight in tribal councils and his words were often decisive. He was smaller in build then most of his fellow tribesmen, and rarely wore anything other than breech-clout, moccasins and deer-hide leggings, embroidered with beads and quillwork as only Indian women know how. His strategy often

CHEYENNES MOVE TO SOUTH PLATTE and BENT'S FORT

surpassed both Indian and white men with whom he came in contact and who in turn, spoke of him only in terms of the highest respect. Like his contemporary Elk-River, he often disregarded the customs of the war-path. On the war-trip against Buffalo-Hump's Comanche in '28, he had refused to carry the war-pipe [symbolising leadership] and refused to be waited upon by others in the party as was the custom, saying that such customs involved too many taboos which, if broken, would cause the party to turn back or incite so much superstitious fear, it might mar any good luck the party should incur.

An American army officer Lieutenant J. Abert, met Yellow-Wolf and his band at Bent's Fort in 1846. Abert was much impressed by Yellow-Wolf's bearing and character and wrote,

> "He is a man of considerable influence, of enlarged views and gifted with more foresight than any other man in his tribe… He frequently talks of the diminishing number of his people and decrease of the once abundant buffalo…and says that in a few years they will become extinct, and unless the Indians wish to pass away also, they will have to adopt the habits of white people, using such measures to produce subsistence as will render them independent of the precarious reliance afforded by the game." [2]

Yellow-Wolf was born into what later proved one of the most notable families among the Southern Cheyennes, from which came Old-Little-Wolf, a great fighter and tactician and a leading chief; Walking-Coyote a Ponca captive adopted by Yellow-Wolf as a son, and Red-Moon, a wise and respected *medicine* man and one-time keeper of the Nation's Sacred Arrows, being a nephew of Red-Sun also a great warrior among the tribe.

Yellow-Wolf was killed in 1864 at Sand Creek, Colorado, at the age of eighty-five, along with his brother Big-Man during the height of Cheyenne power. If he had survived the aforesaid massacre, he would perhaps have died of a broken heart to see the decadence his people fell into thereafter.

As it was, Charles and William Bent took heed of Yellow-Wolf's words, and did, in fact, move the location of the proposed fort further downstream, but not as far as Big Timbers as originally suggested. A mistake William was later

CHEYENNES MOVE TO SOUTH PLATTE and BENT'S FORT

to regret. Little did William and Yellow-Wolf realise then, that their new-found friendship would bring bitter heartbreak to the Bents and the fall of the *TsisTsisTsas* Nation. However, 1829 was not the time to contemplate the future. There were still buffalo to run, horses to steal, and enemies to fight and kill.

Soon after this, William Bent married the Sacred Arrow keeper's daughter Owl-Woman and sired three half-breed sons, Charley, George and Robert Bent, each of whom became well-known historic personages in their own right.

- 0 - 0 - 0 - 0 - 0 - 0 - 0 - 0 - 0 - 0 –

A WHITE MAN'S SMALL TRADING ESTABLISHMENT ON THE WESTERN PLAINS.

CHAPTER 11.

CHEYENNES DEFY CROWS AND SHOSHONI [1829]

That very summer [1829], the Mountain Man William Sublette's brigade of trappers met a large war-party of combined Cheyenne, Sioux and Arapahoe on Powder River. The Indians, Sublette later recorded, were on a hostile expedition against the Crows and Shoshoni. It is not recorded or remembered what the outcome was regarding the event, although around the same time after meeting Sublette, a memorable fight did take place ostensibly later that summer, when a formidable Northern Cheyenne and Suhtaio war-party was out searching for Crow and Shoshoni scalps and women and children captives. [1]

Earlier that year, a Northern Cheyenne chief [whose name has been forgotten], had been killed by Crows. Perhaps this occurred prior to the same Sioux, Cheyenne and Arapahoe expedition met by Sublette. But whatever the case, in response the *Omissis* and Suhtaio Cheyenne bands then generally roaming the Black Hills of South Dakota, decided to punish the perpetrators, and a large war-party comprising a little over one-hundred braves was organized to do so. The warriors travelled on horseback as it was intended to take scalps rather than horses alone. Among their number was a well-known Suhtaio shaman named Old-Horn [in later years known as Blind-Bull], along with his son Box-Elder [later known as Brave-Wolf]. The shaman Old-Horn was the owner of a powerful *medicine* that had been given him by the wolves, and this, it was believed, would protect both he and any with him from harm.

Now it happened that a mixed war-band consisting of a few Mountain Crows and a large number of Sore-Belly's River Crows along with a contingent of Shoshoni allies, was at that same time traveling from the Wind River region towards the buffalo country east of the Big Horn Mountains. In total, not including non-combatants, this combined group numbered little short of one-hundred and fifty warriors, and having scouts out reconnoitring the route ahead, they discovered the aforesaid Cheyenne war-party and surrounded it, even before the enemy knew what was happening.

CHEYENNES DEFY CROWS AND SHOSHONI

When the Cheyennes did realize their vulnerable situation, they all at once dismounted and hastily erected a kind of barricade with brush and dead timber, and behind which, they prepared to defend themselves against imminent attack.

The first action on the part of the Crows and Shoshoni, however, whose complement of fighting men was not much greater than the enemy, was to stampede the latter's horses, after which they began sniping from cover at the enemy already entrenched behind their breastwork. The defenders returned fire with arrows and musket balls, and throughout the daylight hours the conflict continued, incurring one or two casualties on both sides.

Come nightfall hostilities ceased. But the Cheyennes could not escape due to the vigilance of the Crows and Shoshoni, who kept a close watch on the position, and shot missiles at anyone and anything that moved.

As the sun came up the following morning, reciprocal shooting began again and for another three days and nights, the conflict continued. The Crows and Shoshoni would not give up; and the enemy could not be budged.

During all this time several Crows and Shoshoni had been wounded, whilst the latter had no way of knowing for sure how many – if any – casualties their besieged enemies may have suffered. The Crows and their allies knew too well what great loss to their own numbers would be incurred if they were to storm the position head on. Thus they merely carried on sniping at the foe, while shouting the customary epithets of abuse and insults in an attempt to lure the Cheyennes into the open.

By the fourth day the besieged Cheyennes were suffering greatly from thirst and fatigue, and had fully resigned themselves to being annihilated by the foe. It was at this stage in the siege that a pack of wolves in the vicinity – smelling blood and sensing the human carnage about to transpire - all at once set up a continuous howling, which was interpreted in different ways by the respective combatants at the scene. The Crows and Shoshoni were sure that the sudden gathering of wolves was a sign the enemy would all be killed, while among the Cheyennes, the shaman Old-Horn actually welcomed what he heard.

The wolves, he said, were his sacred protectors and were talking to him in a way only he could understand. He told his companions that the wolves were telling him to send his son Box-Elder outside the breastworks to make *medicine,* and by so doing, their whole party would be saved.

CHEYENNES DEFY CROWS AND SHOSHONI

Whatever his personal misgivings, Box-Elder did as Old-Horn instructed and stepped outside the breastworks in full view of the enemy. He then began blowing on a high-pitched eagle-bone whistle and performed a kind of rhythmic dance in front of the Cheyenne position. The Crows and Shoshoni were at first curious regarding the actions of this lone Cheyenne, and suspecting that some powerful *medicine* was being directed against them, they became apprehensive as to what would happen next. Then all at once the wolves ceased their howling and the lone Cheyenne still blowing his whistle, suddenly charged directly towards the enemy. At the same instant, the remaining Cheyennes leapt over the breastworks and followed in the wake of Box-Elder. The whole force of Crows and Shoshoni seemed to take fright and retreated back, giving room to the charging Cheyennes rather than getting to grips in hand to hand conflicts which would incur many more casualties than the Crows themselves deemed necessary. Thus the Crows and Shoshoni continued to hold back and subsequently, allowed the Cheyennes to make their escape, and albeit on foot, they returned safely to their own country.

The Crows and Shoshoni when retiring from the scene, were satisfied with the number of horses they had taken from the enemy.

SKIDI PAWNEE CHIEF, BIG-EAGLE

WILLIAM BENT. **GEORGE BENT AND WIFE, MAGPIE.**

BENT'S OLD FORT ON THE ARKANSAS RIVER, 1845.

CHEYENNE, CHIEF YELLOW-WOLF.

[DRAWN FROM LIFE BY LIEUTENENT JAMES ABERT IN 1845].

CHEYENNE CHIEF OLD-BARK`S SON AND WIFE. *[DRAWN FROM LIFE BY LIEUTENANT JAMES ABERT, 1845].*

OWL-WOMAN, W. BENT`S WIFE.

[PAINTED BY JAMES ABERT, 1845]

CHEYENNE CHIEF, LITTLE-ROBE.

SOUTHERN CHEYENNE, WAR-BONNET.

CHEYENNE CHIEF, TWO-MOONS

CHEYENNE TEPEE CAMP AT BIG TIMBERS ON THE ARKANSAS RIVER, 1863.

MAD-BULL, SOUTHERN CHEYENNE.

CHEYENNE RED-SHIELD WARRIOR.

CHEYENNE CHIEF BLACK-WOLF.

LEFT TO RIGHT, CHEYENNE CHIEFS LITTLE-WOLF AND DULL-KNIFE.
SMITHSONIAN INSTITUTION, WASHINGTON D.C. 1863.

THE SACRED ARROWS ARE LOST

CHAPTER 12.

THE SACRED ARROWS ARE LOST [1830]

In summer of 1830, Pawnees were still suffering multiple enemy attacks. The enemy this time were predominantly Osage, one-time hereditary foes of all Caddoan-speaking peoples to which stock the Pawnee belonged, and broken only by a temporary truce in 1822 broached by the previously-mentioned Major Long`s exploratory expedition of that year. The truce had been short lived. The previous year of `29, a war-party of three-hundred Osage broiled down from neighbouring hills onto a small village of buffalo-hunting Skidi Pawnee, who on foot for the most part and being chased into a small lake, were butchered with knives and tomahawks. Of the few Skidi survivors, five women were taken into captivity. The victorious Osage then raised the village to the ground and rode off driving eighty-four captured horses before them. [1]

War gripped yet another part of the mid-west Plains and as usual, it was Pawnees who suffered. Again there would be much sorrow and grief among the latter`s earth-lodge towns throughout the coming months. Luck was not with the Pawnee – or was it? As if to compensate for the aforesaid defeat, a number of Cheyenne top-knots soon played into their hands and were tied to Skidi waist-belts.

It had happened when the annual big-freeze covered the land and all once green was blanketed with snow, that there came a tragedy, the second of many to harass the Cheyennes. The event, as believed at that time, marked the genesis of the Cheyenne Nation`s downfall and had followed in a similar fashion to the Crooked-Lance slaughter by Crows in 1819, only this time, the Cheyennes experienced a blow not to heal for many a year.

A party of Cheyennes from both Northern and Southern bands had started on foot on a horse-stealing raid against the Pawnee. When at last the party came upon their quarry in a buffalo-hunting tepee camp somewhere on the Lower Platte, they waited until nightfall then entered a Skidi village and began untying horses from under the very noses of their owners. Something went wrong and the whole village was aroused. The horse-thieves ran amok in both fear and dumbfoundment at being trapped in the village and during the melee which followed, all Cheyenne horse-thieves were killed. It had been an easy-gained victory for the Pawnees, who proceeded to cut up the bodies and throw the severed limbs into an adjacent creek causing it to run crimson red. The victors howled savagely at their gory work and, as usual, made the most of it.

It would be hard news when it eventually reached the Cheyenne camps. Surely as a collective, they would not take such an insult to their prowess lightly. Certainly, so the Cheyenne chiefs professed, the Pawnees would pay dearly for their deed.

The inevitable consequence for the massacre the Skidi knew well, but decided it was too late in the year for a formidable revenge force to start against them for revenge. In the meantime, the Skidi hoped the snows would be a long time melting, yet nonetheless, prepared themselves for just such an attack when time and weather would be more conducive to the enemy.

Throughout the long winter months, the grand earth-lodge villages on the South Loup of the Republican comprising the whole Skidi tribe, was reinforced with breastworks and surrounded with a stake palisade. Women never wandered any great distance from the towns, while war-ponies and favourite mounts were tethered inside the earthen lodges at night as a safe-guard from enemy thieves. Scouts were constantly on lookout to give immediate warning of an enemy's approach, as the Pawnees expected a large Cheyenne party to come against them. But even so, they gravely underestimated the fury and determination of the foe.

It was sometime after the slaying of the horse thieves before the Cheyennes learned of their warriors' fate, and even then, solely by chance. Another Cheyenne party out against Pawnees, accidently stumbled across the bones and skulls of their missing kinfolk and whereupon, they abandoned their original objective and took news of the disaster back to their people. Thus, throughout the snow-filled moons, a war-pipe was carried by a member of the *Omissis* Cheyenne clan to each other Cheyenne-speaking band in turn, and the respective chiefs accepted the pipe and inhaled its symbolic smoke. Doing such was tantamount to the chiefs committing themselves and their warriors to join a grand crusade against the killers of the thieves and bring vengeance upon them. Thereafter, a war-council was arranged and during which, each chief recounted past grievances against the Pawnees, while the women-folk beseeched their warriors to go to war. Emotions became intense and so much

THE SACRED ARROWS ARE LOST

so, the pipe was presented to Grey-Thunder, then Keeper of the tribes' *Mahuts*, the four Sacred Medicine Arrows, and to Sun-Getting-out-of-Bed, Keeper of the Suhtaio's Sacred Buffalo Hat, *Issiwun*. Both these most holy of men smoked as requested, and preparations for a big war-party to start against the Pawnee were made.

The Sacred Arrows had brought good *medicine* to Cheyennes when carried against Crows a decade earlier, and from then on, it seemed, the star of the Cheyennes had shone bright. When the `Arrows` and `Hat` were moved, so was the entire Cheyenne-speaking Nation, including all the men, women and children, horses and dogs, and thus, runners sped across the still snow-covered land and ice-covered streams informing the scattered bands of the time and gathering place for the proposed crusade to congregate. The pipe was also carried north to certain Sioux bands and west to the Arapahoe, and among the Sioux both Oglala and Brule chiefs smoked as also, did some among the Southern bands of Arapahoe, although the latter's Northern Arapahoe cousins declined the offer.

To the Cheyennes, summer did not come a moment too soon. Murmurings of war had by then already begun to die down, as the lust for vengeance and anger became somewhat subdued due to the passage of time since the initial event. Indeed, if summer had come late, then the whole affair may well have been forgotten. But it did come at last, and once again when the bands finally congregated somewhere on North Platte River, the women again implored the respective Warrior Societies for vengeance. Once more they slashed themselves with knives and sharp stones and smeared blood over the bodies of their men-folk, and again, cut their hair short and covered their heads with ashes to show grief while crying hideously at the fighting men so the latter's own emotions were stirred so they too, cried once more for Pawnee blood. Sacred chants and the singing of Brave-Heart songs amid monotonous rhythms from beating drums, were accompanied by stomping feet and bending and straightening of backs along with other weird contortions peculiar to the war-dance. Old men rode around the different groups of lodges recounting aloud their many coups, and giving guidance to young bucks soon to be in their first battle. At the same time, up and coming warriors strutted around on foot bedecked in all their savage splendour, proclaiming themselves the bravest and

THE SACRED ARROWS ARE LOST

most fearsome of all men. It was a time of excitement among all the people, and all were eager to go to war.

Come August 1830, the *"Moon when cherries are ripe,"* a grand body constituting the entire Cheyenne-speaking Nation of nearly four-thousand persons, along with contingents of Sioux and Arapahoe, snaked its way across the prairies heading east from the north bank of the North Platte. It was a long colourful line more than one mile in length heading south to a point on the lower part of the Republican River where several Pawnee earth-lodge towns could be found. Leading the cavalcade was Grey-Thunder, along with his wife carrying the sacred `Arrow` bundle on her back and walking in front of her mounted husband. Next to Grey-Thunder was the Suhtaio holy man Sun-Getting-out-of-Bed also mounted and his wife likewise, walking in front of her husband while bearing the Sacred Buffalo Hat bundle on her back. Additionally, with these two most revered of men, was the Cheyenne pipe-barer High-Backed-Wolf 1st being the leading war-chief of the expedition, and behind him, the Sioux and Arapahoe chiefs and warriors in the customary place for honoured guests at the front of the column. At the same time, the rank and file conglomerate of Cheyenne, Sioux and Arapahoe non-combatants, with the Cheyenne Warrior Society fighters themselves, brought up the rear of the column and on its flanks.

The grand cavalcade eventually crossed the North Platte to its south bank and moving southeast, continued up Birchwood Creek until it came into the country of the foe in what is now the northern part of Nebraska. At this point, four Cheyenne scouts were sent out to locate the Pawnee towns, but somewhere on route in the Nebraska Plains, they were surprised by a large force of Pawnee and running to a nearby stream, the scouts dropped behind its bank which they then used as a kind of breastwork and for a while, repelled the enemy onslaughts against them. The attackers, however, were in large number and finally drove the scouts from their cover and onto the open prairie. It was there that the scouts bravely stood their ground until, that is, being in the open and having spent the last of their ammunition, they were annihilated one and all.

It was not long after this that the cavalcade itself came across the dead and mutilated bodies of the scouts, decomposing and gnawed by wolves and carrion of the sky. But the sight only added to their anger and determination to get even with the killers. Only two names pertaining to the said scouts are now

THE SACRED ARROWS ARE LOST

remembered, that of a man named Light and another named Roasting, the latter being a brother of the Cheyenne High-Backed-Wolf himself, the overall leader of the expedition.

The Pawnees, meanwhile, after slaying the scouts, were put fully on their guard, and all those out hunting or residing in skin tepees on the prairie came into their earth-lodge towns for protection. Having said this, the next day and not having been attacked, the Pawnees supposed the four Cheyennes had merely been a small horse-stealing party and so continued again in their usual activities. The Cheyennes, though, dispatched more scouts to locate the enemy, who this time were more fortunate than their predecessors. They returned with intelligence of the Pawnee position which, they said, was on the headwaters of the South Loup of the Republican. On hearing this, the Cheyennes and their Allies pitched their tepees and rolled up the sides so not to be gnawed by rodents and wolves, and placed domestic valuables on scaffolds out of reach of the same. They then started forth towards the enemy towns, all the warriors leading the way with the host of women, old men and children following behind. Throughout the rest of that day and night the cavalcade travelled, and the following dawn, finally came close to the enemy.

Apparently in the Skidi Pawnee town, the occupants were about to make a sacrifice to one of their deities, e.g. the Morning Star, and since the previous day, a big ceremony had been going on. Probably they already had some inclination of the cavalcade coming against them, but it was not that which alerted them to its advance. Ironically, a group of Skidi buffalo-hunters had left the Skidi town at first light and accidently, came face to face with the drawn-up battle lines of Cheyennes, Sioux and Arapahoe. A brief skirmish ensued and the hunters were completely routed. To the Pawnees first blood was to the enemy, but to the Cheyennes it was a bad omen. The element of surprise which more often was coupled to a victory being gained, was lost. Even more disastrous, thought the Cheyennes, the power of their sacred tribal talismans the `Arrows` and `Hat` had been broken. For at the time the hunters had been attacked, the blinding ceremonies connected to the talismans thought necessary to immobilise the enemy, had not yet been performed.

When returning to the cavalcade, the victorious Cheyenne party which had routed the hunters was severely reprimanded by their chiefs and elders. The whole theme of ``moving` the Arrows and Hat was now entirely invalid. Even

THE SACRED ARROWS ARE LOST

so, it was deemed, it would be a safer bet to either go on or stay put, as a retreating body hampered with women and children and a vast herd of ponies in tow, would likely be prone to guerrilla attacks from the Pawnees and in which event, would result in some kind of catastrophe for the Allies. Added to this, to abandon the attack would be too much embarrassment for the Cheyennes to face from their companion tribes, and thus, it was decided that as they had come this far, they would take the risk of defeat rather than turn back.

The Pawnees for their part were alarmed, and prepared themselves for a big fight.

As it was with most tribes when confronted by an enemy force, the Pawnee fighting men from the latter's Skidi and Picturahat bands moved a short distance from their towns, so to put themselves at the fore to protect their women and children and keep the enemy away from the lodges. The best manoeuvre with such priorities in mind, was to make sure the enemy was not allowed to get within striking distance of the town itself, and instead, oblige them to come to battle on the open Plain. This the Pawnees did, and so it was that two great bodies of warriors; the flower of the Central Plains Tribes at that time, came face to face in conflict on the rolling grasslands of Nebraska.

The Cheyennes and their Allies were arrayed in two divisions north to south in a long line several ranks deep with a gap between the two divisions. The Sacred Buffalo Hat was worn on the head of a chosen warrior at the front of one group, the Sacred Arrows in a bundle attached to a white-painted lance of another, positioned at the front of the second group.

The Pawnees on horseback and on foot, faced the Allies also in a long line several ranks deep, and in all, it was a scene of gorgeous colour. Snow-white feathered bonnets tipped with red and yellow horse-hair nodded gently in the breeze, while brightly-hued beads flashed in a multi-colour like painted stars, and the sun glinted on metallics of lance-points battle hatchets and muskets.

Those among the Cheyennes who had not yet smelt the stench of death or been drenched by the blood of an enemy felled by their hands, waited nervously, but impatiently, to dig their heels into their pony's flanks and hurl themselves at the enemy. To the veteran brave it was a chance to kill Pawnees or if their totems demanded, then to die in the attempt, as for these men it was not just a venture to extract retribution for young men lost on a raid for horses the previous summer, but for more determined reasons than one's pride and loved ones lost. To the veteran Cheyenne, the people they now faced were hereditary enemies against whom there could be no relent. They were fighting for their Nation, for their brothers, sisters, sons and daughters, for their religion and way of life. Only too well the Cheyennes and their allies knew the religion and customs of the Pawnees including one of Human sacrifice. Such ways were not good ways, thought the allied veteran. Such a road was not a good road to follow.

Meanwhile, the arrayed Pawnees looked resplendent with their vermilion-dyed scalp-locks on shaven heads and with buffalo-horned feathered bonnets, while their scarlet robes and breech-clouts contrasted against their deer-hide leggings adorned with black and white vertically-stripped beads and which, was cause for the opposing Cheyennes and allies to look with awe upon the foe. Indeed, each warrior then hoped to look his best, lest he should meet his ancestors that day along the long dark road of no return.

Whilst the opposing groups viewed each other from their respective lines, Cheyenne horse-doctors who concentrated their knowledge and skills on such animals, applied their special *medicines* to protect the mounts from falling and to give them speed by being long-winded in the contest to come. Usually the partisan of a large war-band would always offer a pipe to a respected shaman and to a revered horse-doctor, who while dancing and singing over the tracks of the animals, would implore the deities to protect the horses from falling or getting hurt. Thus Grey-Thunder, although the most important *medicine* man among the allied host at that time, also allowed the horse-doctors to carry out their incantations and blessings before which, the Cheyennes got themselves ready to charge.

If it was Cheyennes or Pawnees who were first to charge, is not determined, although as the Pawnees were fighting a defensive action, it was probably the Cheyennes. Quickly, Grey-Thunder tied the `Arrow` bundle to the lance which a Cheyenne named Bull was carrying, but attached it near the point of the lance, whereas each Sacred Arrow should have been tied to the lance shaft singularly and at intervals one from the other. At this point, however, it was thought there was not enough time for proper procedure to be conducted before the Cheyennes would clash in combat, and so Bull rode off waving the

THE SACRED ARROWS ARE LOST

lance with the bundle attached just below its head, and all Cheyennes could see that the Sacred talismans were with them.

Now among the Plains Tribes, there was a custom where those discontented with life either through illness or bereavement, would take a suicide vow pledging themselves to die. This was performed in many ways and during the fight in question, just such a Skidi Pawnee pledger had positioned himself in the van of his tribesmen. This man had been carried on a robe by his brothers and deposited some fifteen feet in front of the Pawnee line. His only weapon was a bow with an arrow fixed at the string with additional such missiles scattered around him on the ground so to be within easy reach. Sitting on the ground with legs out-stretched, he was intending to be killed during the first onslaught of his charging enemies. And there he stayed alone on the prairie between the opposing forces, prepared to die in battle as a brave man should. When the Cheyennes and their allies did charge towards the enemy line, the lone Pawnee's death-song rang out high above the war-whoops of his antagonists, and seeing him thus, the charging warriors realised his plight and each mounted warrior was eager to count coup on such a prominent, but in his own way, dangerous target.

The leading Cheyenne Bull rode straight towards the lone Pawnee, endeavouring to gain the first coup of the battle for the Sacred Arrow bundle itself. Drawing clear of his companions, the Cheyenne levelled his lance with the `Arrows` attached, and bore down on his quarry, who at first, still sat motionless on the ground in the very path of Bull. The lone Pawnee then began singing a *medicine* song and Bull rode around the man and off to one side before thrusting at him with his lance. The Pawnee, however, suddenly jumped to his feet; avoided the stroke and instead, actually caught the lance Bull was holding, and wrenched it from his grip.

The warrior Bull was now unarmed. He rode away crying over his misfortune while imploring his tribesmen to retrieve the captured `Arrows` from the hands of the enemy. The rest of the Cheyennes and allies reigned up their horses, not knowing if to continue the charge or flee. Such were the lamentations then voiced openly by Bull, that the lone Pawnee suspected there was more than some usual significance attached to the bundle tied to the lance. He called his people to come and see what he had captured.

THE SACRED ARROWS ARE LOST

The Cheyennes were in disarray, and Grey-Thunder himself took charge of the situation. The `Arrows` he said, must be retrieved no matter what, and so he personally would lead the Allies as they charged again towards the enemy in a wild assault. This time the Allies attacked with much more ferocity, but the combined Pawnee force in as great a number if not actually exceeding that of the foe, held their ground, and after a hard fought melee, forced their allied assailants to withdraw.

In the forefront of the Pawnee line then charging forward, was the Skidi head war-chief Big-Eagle, who the Cheyennes referred to as Big-Spotted-Horse due to such an animal the chief often rode. That day he was garbed in his finest regalia as befitted his chiefly rank. He wore his hair roached in a strip along the middle of his other-wise shaved head; a bear-claw necklace about his neck along with striped beaded leggings and black moccasins. He also wore a red calico shirt and two white man`s silver peace medals on his chest. Alone he rode up and down the no-man`s land between the opposing sides, and other than slaying several among the Allies, he chased several Cheyennes back to their own lines after singularly, they had come forward to confront him. At length, the Allies turned to retreat and the Pawnees again pursued them and charged in amongst them, striking additional fear by one of their number carrying before him the very same lance captured from the Cheyennes with the `Sacred Arrow` bundle still tied to it.

At one stage, another Cheyenne raced his pony towards Big-Eagle in an attempt to slay the chief, as such a deed might turn the tide of battle in favour of the Allies and it had already been agreed among the Cheyennes, that he who did so, would be elevated to the status of a chief among their tribe. Big-Eagle realised the intention of his adversary and turning his pony, rode back to his own lines with the lone Cheyenne in pursuit. Just as the Cheyenne was baring down upon him, Big-Eagle again turned his pony smartly around and faced his pursuer, who, without delay, followed suit and attempted to race back among his own people. Only this time it was the Skidi chief in hot pursuit. Big-Eagle was being drawn in very close to the host of Cheyennes, but before he drew nearer, he leaned over his pony`s neck and struck the Cheyenne he was following with his pony quirt in the act of counting coup. After this humiliating event, Big-Eagle rather than kill the man, merely rode back to his own Pawnee lines to wild acclamations from his peers.

THE SACRED ARROWS ARE LOST

The Cheyennes did, however, manage to regroup, then turned and checked the Pawnee pursuit. Yet try as they did, they could not break their enemy's line of defence. After several bloody clashes much of which was hand to hand from the backs of horses, and costing many lives in dead and injured with a number of Allies left on the field of conflict, both sides finally gave up the fight and withdrew in opposite directions across the grasslands. Together they left the intervening ground strewn with human copses and dead and wounded horses, and, of course, the Cheyennes were obliged to leave the prized 'Sacred Arrow' talismans still in the hands of the Pawnees.

The Allies then conducted a slow and despondent march back to where their lodges had been left standing. Hurriedly, they dismantled their tepees; collected their belongings and in all haste, started back to the South Platte and home. If the enemy had followed up the Cheyenne's flight and attacked them again, the latter with their women and children in tow, then the Cheyenne and allies would have been at the mercy of the Pawnees, and another more determined battle would surely have proved disastrous to them all. Without protection from the 'Arrows,' the Cheyennes thought, they themselves had no further hope of victory that day, and indeed, with their talismans in the hands of the enemy, all Cheyenne self-confidence and morale was at a low ebb. They had no further will to carry on the fight.

Back in Big-Eagle's own Skidi earth-lodge, the chef placed two of the captured Cheyenne 'Arrows,' one with its shaft painted black with a black feather flight and another painted red with its red feather flight attached, in the Sacred Morning Star bundle belonging to the Skidi tribe, while of the other two 'Arrows,' he gave one each to the other two Pawnee tribes known as the *Chaui* and *Kitkahaki* for their own safe-keeping.

Meanwhile, the spirit of the Cheyennes as a fighting force for the immediate time was broken. The one thing which had held the Nation together and gave their warriors enthusiasm was torn asunder, while the 'Arrows' themselves were among the enemy and, perhaps, being humiliated by them. How great the 'Arrows' now, challenged the young bucks of the tribe? Having often regarded the talisman's rigid taboos and devotion paid to them dull and laborious. If before they had once helped the Cheyennes so well, now would they help their present Pawnee owners against them? As it was, such a mishap was all that was needed to shatter long-held beliefs among many Cheyennes.

THE SACRED ARROWS ARE LOST

Old doubts as to the sincerity of the tribal religion and its authentication having lay dormant in one's mind, suddenly burst into reality, and logical explanations began to over-run those of theology and fantasy.

This is not to say that the whole Cheyenne Nation felt as such. On the contrary, they were in the minority and among the younger element at that. Old and middle-aged men, having had the religion drummed into them since an early age and who now were drumming it into their off-spring, had been involved too deeply to simply disregard the sanctity of their religion at the first opportunity to do so. As a consequence in their minds, the tribe had committed a grave sin and therefore the `Arrows,` or rather the sacred power transmitted through them, had forsaken the people, leastways, until the wrong, - whatever that might be, - had been righted or, conveniently, they paid for the misdemeanour by some form of communal discomfort along with excessive expressions of self-grief and sorrow.

Such thoughts being the majority, these latter were able to supress sacrilegious murmurings from young hot-heads, and enabled the people as a whole to transfer their devotion temporarily to the remaining `Sacred Buffalo Hat` while four *new* Sacred Arrows were made as a replacement. These, of course, had to be religiously and meticulously prepared with prayers, ceremonies, blessings and purification rites. But even so, the seemingly mock authentication incurred by simply inaugurating of a *new* set of `Arrows,` was not by all tribal members brushed aside. Surely, so the dissidents thought, there could be no substitute for the original talismans which the ancient Cheyenne prophet Sweet-Medicine himself, had first brought among the people.

Meanwhile, winter came again and covered the land with snow. Some bands of Northern Cheyenne moved northwest to the Laramie Fork of the Platte, and the Suhtaio to the headwaters of Cheyenne River. In both locations they pitched their camps amid leas and timbered groves ready to sit out the hoary moons, and throughout that season's duration, sporadic horse-stealing forays were conducted by small Cheyenne and Suhtaio parties foraying west against the Crow and Shoshoni. Southern Cheyenne bands for their part, moved south to the Big Timbers district in what is now eastern Colorado, and splitting into half a dozen separate camps, set their tepees along the north and south bank of the Arkansas. They themselves sent out the occasional horse-stealing parties

THE SACRED ARROWS ARE LOST

further south against Kiowa, Comanche and Kiowa-Apache horse herds, while, moreover, other warriors during the long winter nights, merely sat around blazing fires relating stories of myth and of valour and of their own proposed new hostile ventures they would make come spring. One among them, however, was the revered Grey-Thunder himself, who with a few adherents, thought that after losing their Sacred Arrows to an enemy it should not be the time for kill-talk. But rather, for contemplating thoughts of peace. Having said this, intertribal warfare nevertheless, continued on the Cheyenne front, although not especially so against the Pawnee. Indeed, for those Cheyennes wishing to go to war, for a while they steered somewhat clear of Pawnees and instead, concentrated on the Shoshoni, Crows and other foes throughout the rest of that year and following.

-0-0-0-0-0-0-0-0-0-0-

SOUTHERN CHEYENNE WARRIOR.
[Edward Curtis photograph, 1907.]

BIG-HEAD RETURNS FROM THE DEAD

CHAPTER 13.

BIG-HEAD RETURNS FROM THE DEAD [1831]

Somewhere along the Platte in summer of 1831, near the recently erected Fort John at the mouth of Laramie Fork, * the great Cheyenne-Suhtaio Sweet-Medicine Chief, High-Backed-Wolf 1st, returned from a highly successful raid against the Crows, and young warriors were full of praises for his deed. The chief of the Cheyenne Fox Warrior Society was then a man named Big-Head. He was envious of High-Backed-Wolf's acclaim and at once, got together his own party to go west against the Shoshoni. [1]

Since the tribal move against the Shoshoni in 1817, some Cheyenne bands since that date had no great conflicts with them, owing to the Shoshonie's more northwestern location beyond the Rocky Mountains and the drifting south of certain Cheyenne-speaking bands, which, after the erection of William Bent's first stockade trading post in `28, became regarded as the Southern Cheyenne division. Instead, raids by the latter against both Shoshoni and Crows became few and far between due to distance between them. This is not to say that all Southern Cheyenne raids towards the northwest were nil. There were particular Southern Cheyenne warriors who still continued to concentrate upon their more northern and northwestern foes spawned either from personal grievance or merely, a preference for Shoshoni or Crow horses which included the much desired Appaloosa breed, stolen or traded from other Northwestern tribes such as Flatheads, Nez-Perce and Cayuse.

Big-Head was a famous Southern Cheyenne born around 1812, and in later years was known as Curly-Bear. He had joined the Cheyenne Fox Society at an early age and by the time he reached manhood, had become head chief of that fraternity. A Cheyenne chief named Big-Hand signed the so-called `Friendship Treaty` with American Government officials in 1825, but was probably a miss-translation of the name Big-Head, and was probably the latter's

*Built in 1833 and later, after being sold to the American Government and expanded, was known as Fort Laramie.

BIG-HEAD RETURNS FROM THE DEAD

Father or Uncle. At the date in question [1831], Big-Head of the current theme was a veteran of many battles, although he was noted, moreover, for his powerful *medicine* which, it was believed, made him invulnerable to musket balls and bullets as the following escapade suggests. At a later date, he was several times shot by soldiers in 1856-`57, but always recovered, and when a young man, was himself the owner of a Kit-Fox Warrior Society Bow-Lance, carried only by the bravest members among that Cheyenne fraternity. Such a `lance` forbade its owner to retreat during a conflict, even when remaining on the field meant certain death. Because Big-Head`s *medicine* appeared so strong, he never lacked volunteers to make up a war-party against his enemies.

Of those accompanying Big-Head on this occasion, were the warriors Man-Above, Many-Magpies [also known as Heap-of-Birds], Stone-Calf, Sitting-Bear, Lone-Bear, Walks-Out, and a young son of the *Heviatanio* chief, Yellow-Wolf, a lad of thirteen years old and named Little-Wolf, then acting as servant to his elder brother Man-Above. Altogether, there were some thirty persons in the party, each of whom carried a flintlock musket with plenty of powder and ball and all were on foot, so to ride captured ponies back home.

At first they traveled west along Upper Platte River, then turned north at the first out-crop of the Rocky Mountains and continued west towards the Wind River and Shoshoni country. Big-Head and Man-Above carried the pipes.

They journeyed on for most of the week and at last, reached the hunting grounds of their intended foe. At that stage, three scouts lead by Stone-Calf then a young man, were sent out to locate the enemy`s position, while the rest of the party made camp and awaited the scout`s return. One night whilst partaking an evening meal, the party heard the long eerie whine of a wolf which broke the still night air. This was a signal that the three scouts were returning to camp and the rest of the party knowing this, got ready to receive them.

Soon, Stone-Calf - the scout leader - came into view, twisting his head from side to side as he ran and howling like a wolf. When all three scouts come close to the partisan Big-Head, the latter held out his hand and grasping the hand of Stone-Calf, led him over to where the rest of the Cheyennes were gathered and bade him make his report. Before Stone-Calf uttered a word, however, he and his two companions lit and smoked a pipe, this being a sign that what they were about to relate would be the truth.

BIG-HEAD RETURNS FROM THE DEAD

Stone-Calf then told Big-Head that they, the scouts, had not travelled far when they had come upon the fresh tracks of a pony and began following its trail. A little further on, the horse they were following had apparently stopped and its rider dismounted, as moccasin prints indicated, and which they knew by the pattern of the print, the rider was either Ute or Shoshoni. In excitement, the scouts said, they had followed the tracks at a canter and which led them up a high mountain where they had gained a panoramic view of the surrounding country. In places the mountain path had been precarious and their going slow, and it was noon before they reached the summit. When finally they had looked down, and on the far side of the height, they saw that a buffalo hunt had recently taken place in a green valley below, as carcasses missing their hides lay strewn about, while women were packing meat on pack-ponies and pony-drags and were about to leave the field.

Upon hearing the report, the two pipe-holders called together their whole party and held a council. It was then agreed it was too late in the day to assault the enemy, and therefore, Big-Head said, they would move closer to the foe and dispatch another set of scouts to locate exactly where the Shoshoni camp was located.

Stone-Calf at once volunteered to go out again and four among the onlooking party asked to go with him. Big-Head warned these four not to attempt to raid the enemy camp by themselves, for such an action whether successful or not, would spoil the venture for the others and even though the Cheyennes were about thirty warriors in number, if the enemy was aroused before a concerted attack was made, then likely they - Cheyennes - would be at a disadvantage by being in unknown territory and outnumbered by the foe.

Consequently Stone-Calf and four companions started out to scout the surrounding country, and early next morning, the scouts returned to Big-Head's camp. Apparently, they had discovered a small Shoshoni village while twilight had been ascending and so had waited 'till nightfall before starting back, lest they be discovered in the light of day by the foe, as they had discerned a lone Shoshoni on a pure white horse roaming the area looking for game. When Big-Head heard this new report, he bade his warriors to dress for battle and fix up their war *medicines* for, he said, it was time to make their play. Hurriedly the warriors re-braided their hair; daubed their faces and torsos with paint; uncovered buffalo-hide shields emblazoned with sacred designs, and slinging them over their shoulders to protect their backs from missiles while crawling around the Shoshoni lodges, they started in a body towards their objective.

It was dusk when they reached the same mountain top from where the scouts had spied the village, and whereupon, they waited until it was pitch dark and the occupants asleep on lodge pallets before making their raid. Meanwhile, Big-Head advised the younger warriors not to go after animals picketed close to the tepees themselves, but to concentrate on those grazing outside the camp, as then the stolen animals would not be missed until sometime after the morning's sun had risen.

At length the Cheyennes crawled from the hill-top and crept down into the valley where the Shoshoni tepees were pitched. The occupants were by then fully asleep, and the Cheyenne thieves set about un-hobbling horses outside the camp and leading them quietly away to a pre-arranged rendezvous a short distance ahead. All was going well and soon, those with stolen animals were waiting for the last man of the party to come in to the rendezvous before they set out for home. This last man was named Walks-Out, and when finally he did come in, he was leading four horses each still dragging their picket ropes, showing they had been taken from the inner circle of lodges. According to Walks-Out, he could not find any likeable mounts outside the camp, and not wanting to go back to his comrades empty-handed, had taken these others tied close to the lodges instead.

The rest of the Cheyennes realized the four horses in question would be missed as soon as the owners came out from their lodges, and that the enemy would be after them at once, as it was well-known that the Shoshoni of all tribes, were resolved always to go in pursuit of thieves. Consequently, it was decided by Big-Head that they should race away immediately as fast as they could travel, and trust in their respective *medicines* to protect them.

All next day the Cheyennes rode at a gallop, but actually covered little ground owing to the rough terrain of the country and high spirits of the stolen animals they were driving. Consequently, the loose horses were hard to control as they were apt to take off on their own, some even turning back towards the Shoshoni village from whence they had come. Added to this, the thieves' rocky route offered little if any chance of covering their tracks, and left a broad trail for potential pursuers to follow. Big-Head knew this and was forever looking over his shoulder expecting any moment to see dust clouds behind them indicating their enemies' in pursuit. Soon, the Cheyennes indeed could see a rising dust cloud in their rear, and in even greater haste, they urged their captured stock forward towards some high hills which, they hoped, would afford some kind of cover if attacked.

For a time, the Shoshoni were obscured from sight due to the hilly terrain and the Cheyennes did reach the base of the mountains without being overtaken. But suddenly, whilst they were still racing ahead, a shrill Shoshoni war-cry echoed to the Cheyennes' front, and before they could change mounts and escape in another direction, a band of enemies charged out from behind some rocks and headlong at them. In the van of these Shoshoni was a chief of the latter astride a magnificent all white war-pony and carrying a large brass shield on one arm, whilst waving a feathered lance with the other above his head. This rider spurred his horse towards the Cheyenne ranks, and ridding right through their lines to cheers of bravado from his comrades, came out on the far side without a scratch. Big-Head realized that a running fight would likely prove disastrous to his party. He thus told them to dismount and make for some higher rocks and large boulders from where they could make a stand, and having done so, the party endeavored to save itself from annihilation.

As the Cheyennes ran for the rocks, they acted in pairs and in such a way, fought off their mounted Shoshoni attackers. One Cheyenne would fire his musket at the foe and the other, merely aim his piece as if about to shoot while his companion was reloading, and who then, when reloaded would threaten to shoot whilst his comrade in turn reloaded. Both would then fall back a little and repeat the procedure until they reached the safety of the boulders and where they took up obscured positions sufficient to preserve them.

The Shoshoni force all on horseback then charged forward, and he with the brass shield on the white horse singled out Lone-Bear and Sitting-Bear where they had made their stand. But now Sitting-Bear took more careful aim with his flintlock gun, and shot the oncoming Shoshoni clean out of the saddle. Seeing this, three Cheyennes ran from cover and over to the prostrate enemy to count coup upon the corpse. Lone-Bear was first to reach the body, a man named Plenty-of-Birds [aka Many-Magpies] came after, and Iron-Crow counted the third.

Meanwhile, having seen their man with the brass shield felled from his horse and killed, the rest of the Shoshoni again charged headlong at the thirty

BIG-HEAD RETURNS FROM THE DEAD

Cheyennes, and a fierce determined melee ensued with the firing of guns and arrows at each other from their respective sides.

During this phase of fighting, Big-Head himself received a wound which caused a profusion of blood to issue from his person, but with the help of Stone-Calf who also carried the chief's Kit-Fox Lance, Big-Head managed to gain extra cover behind a big boulder and sit himself against it. However, to all intents and purpose, it appeared that Big-Head was about to die from his wound, and thus, his Lance was placed beside him as was customary at such a time to accompany him to the Spirit Land, and thereafter, he slipped into an unconscious state.

In the meantime, the Cheyennes had brought down at least three Shoshoni horses and wounded two or more enemy riders, and this was enough for the Shoshoni attackers to cease their fighting; pick up their dead comrade with the brass shield, and retrieving all the stolen ponies which the Cheyennes had been obliged to abandon in their flight, they turned their mounts around and vacated the scene, leaving the Cheyennes to themselves without further molestation.

When the Cheyennes reached their home camp, on foot and despondent because their partisan Big-Head was no longer with them, the women folk cried loud their laments and showed excessive grief for the loss of such a man who had been much respected and loved by all his clan-folk.

But Big-Head had survived to fight again. Indeed, it was the following day after his brothers-in-arms had departed for their home camp on the North Platte, that the wounded Big-Head regained his senses, and using his Kit-Fox Bow Lance as a kind of crutch, had regained his feet, and after partaking some water and edible tubers he dug up from the ground with the iron point of his lance, he slowly regained his strength. Thus at length, he started on his long, slow and hazardous journey towards home in the wake of his party.

Indeed, Big-Head lived to later fight Government soldiers during the latter's altercations with Cheyennes in 1857, but was killed at Fort Kearny on Platte River, Nebraska, that same year.

-0-0-0-0-0-0-0-0-0-

CHEYENNES KILL DANGLING-FOOT and CROW REVENGE

CHAPTER 14.

CHEYENNES KILL DANGLING-FOOT and CROW REVENGE [1833]

Now it happened during the early part of the following spring, 1832, the whole Cheyenne Nation came together in a grand encampment adjacent to the Tongue tributary of the Yellowstone. There, the people's head chiefs and holy men sat in council to decide if to abandon their old hunting grounds in the Powder and Cheyenne River country of the north and move south, between the South Fork of the Platte and Arkansas Rivers, which latter region, it was thought, would prove more conducive to their needs. This proposed Cheyenne movement had been encouraged on one hand by the continued encroachment of Sioux into lands which previously, had been regarded as belonging exclusively to the Cheyenne, and on the other, through the persuasions of the white trader William Bent, who suggested to the Cheyennes and Suhtaio they take up residence close to his new trading post on the Arkansas, and from where, he promised, he would supply their whole tribe with all the white man's goods it required. [1]

The result of the council did induce the more northern Cheyenne bands, including the *Watapio, Oivimana, Hevietanio* and one or more Suhtaio group to move south, and by mid-summer that same year, they had vacated their erstwhile more northern districts entirely in favour of the South Platte and Upper Arkansas Rivers of the Southern Plains. In confirmation of this date of movement, William Bent later told his son George that his first meeting with the Suhtaio [as yet a separate tribe albeit closely confederated with the Cheyennes], was while building his new adobe fort on the Arkansas. This was the first time to his knowledge that the Suhtaio had come so far south to camp on a permanent basis.

Word of the Cheyenne migration had at once been carried to the Crows who believed it a permanent move, and it was this intelligence which induced a prominent Crow chief named Dangling-Foot, to lead his small band of followers into the Black Hills along the Belle Fourch branch of Cheyenne River. He believed that his people's mortal enemies the Cheyenne, were then too far south to pose a significant threat.

CHEYENNES KILL DANGLING-FOOT and CROW REVENGE

However, by the end of summer, 1832, the trader Bent had still been in the process of building his new adobe-bricked post, which stood on the American north side of the Arkansas between where the towns of Las Animas and La Junta now stand, twenty-five miles or so west of a thirty mile stretch of cottonwoods known to several tribes as "Big Timbers."

Before the construction of the fort was completed, smallpox broke out among Bent's Mexican labourers, and he was obliged to temporarily abandon his task until the disease burned itself out. He sent runners to the Cheyenne and Suhtaio telling them not to come near the Arkansas at that time to prevent their contracting the contagion. As a consequence, those Cheyenne bands which only recently had forsaken their lands in the north, and who knew from past experience that the best way to avoid infection was to put distance between themselves and its source, took heed of Bent`s advice and fled precipitously back to their old haunts. It was for this reason, moreover, rather than being chased out of the Arkansas country by the Comanche as Edwin Denig supposed, that these particular Cheyenne and Suhtaio bands had expediently returned to their old home to escape the epidemic then raging across the entire Central and Southern Plains. Thus - unbeknown to the Crows at that time, - by early Autumn, 1832, several Cheyenne bands were again roaming and camping in the North Platte country, whilst the Suhtaio were back in the Black Hills, far north of the Arkansas River.

The Crows used to say that Cheyennes were always looking for someone to fight, and especially so the latter`s Suhtaio confederates, if they happened to stumble upon those they regarded as "easy prey." Any people appearing as such would most likely run afoul of that tribe's scalping knives. Such a fate was to befall this small band of Crows led by Dangling-Foot, who, like innocent children, came stumbling on. They were meandering through the Black Hills, completely unaware of the real danger of being assaulted by Cheyennes or Suhtaio.

It was not long before Suhtaio scouts discovered the presence of Dangling-Foot`s small band. At once they took news of the discovery to their main body, whereupon the Suhtaio war-chiefs began preparing for a fight.

The Suhtaio had the element of surprise on their side and were resolved that none of their Crow enemies should escape their wrath. For several days Suhtaio scouts `dogged` Dangling-Foot`s column as it moved disconcertedly

CHEYENNES KILL DANGLING-FOOT and CROW REVENGE

across the region. The Suhtaio were waiting patiently for the Crows to reach what they considered would be a convenient spot to launch an attack, and so, still undetected, Suhtaio scouts continued to watch as the unsuspecting Crows set up their lodges at the end of each days march.

At length, after several more days of close observation, the Suhtaio scouts were satisfied with the location the Crows had chosen to pitch their camp.

The lack of diligence among Dangling-Foot's people, had caused them to site their village where it would be at the mercy of any enemy force which might stumble upon it either by accident or design. Indeed, at a later date, both Crows and Cheyennes agreed that the camp at that time had been situated in a very vulnerable position. This being an open stretch of grassland where a small camp could easily be surrounded, and was some distance from any protective feature where the occupants could have taken cover in the advent of assault. This was close to where the present-day town of Rawlins, Wyoming is now situated near the headwaters of Cheyenne River.

The Suhtaio scouts, meanwhile, raced back to their base camp and reported this intelligence to their chiefs. It was then decided to move out that very night and the following morning, attack the Crow camp and destroy it. Hopefully, they thought, they would then drive off the entire pony herd in the process; along with killing as many Crow warriors as possible and taking the women and children captive.

So it was that the whole Cheyenne force comprising some two-hundred and more fighting men, set out from their war-camp that very night and next day, just as dawn was breaking, the warriors got ready to charge on their objective.

Before they did so, a party of Crow hunters on horseback was observed leaving the camp and the Suhtaio decided to wait until the hunters had ridden a long way off. Then when they assaulted the camp, there would be fewer Crow warriors to contend with.

Such was the Indian philosophy, which always considered it to their credit if they had an overwhelming advantage over the enemy and lost as few of their own fighting men as possible. It was not the intention of the Suhtaio, of course, to offer what might be regarded as "fair play," by allowing the enemy the chance of a more equal contest.

CHEYENNES KILL DANGLING-FOOT and CROW REVENGE

After an appropriate hiatus in order to allow the Crow hunters to put some distance between themselves and the camp, a sudden shrill-pitched Suhtaio war-cry rang out over the shimmering grasslands. This was followed by a horde of painted and be-feathered warriors mounted on fleet war-ponies, all at once converging on the small cluster of tepees.

The Suhtaio rode toward the camp from two directions and moments later, had it completely surrounded. They then began bulldozing their way in and out among the lodges and into the camp interior itself with musket balls and arrows flying. At first the Crows were stunned by the lightening effect. But then a few Crow men-folk who had not gone out with the hunters and had their fastest horses picketed close to their lodges, quickly mounted up and fled the scene along with a sizeable number of women and children only moments before all escape routes were cut off. Their unfortunate kinfolk left in camp, could do naught but suffer the deadly fate now looming over them.

Of the Crow fighting men who did remain in camp, there was no time to don war clothes or *medicine* charms. Almost as quickly as they strung their bows or loaded their fusses, they were laid low. Some few Crows on horseback were toppled from their saddles and whilst the children screamed, several Crow women in fits of desperation, picked up their fallen husband's weapons and bravely carried on the fight for survival. All these women were also either shot or clubbed to death and left lying on the blood soaked ground, their bodies then scalped and pin-cushioned with arrows, as had been done to their slaughtered men-folk.

Miraculously, Chief Dangling-Foot was one who did break out of the beleaguered camp. Single-handed with his trade fusse and an ample supply of powder and ball, he had battled his way through the tightening ring of encircling enemies and managed to entrench himself in a small hollow not far from where most of the fighting was raging. From his position he succeeded in keeping the Suhtaio at bay for a long time. The Cheyennes later admitted to the Crows that this man had been very brave, and had killed and wounded several of their warriors before he himself was finally slain. It is additionally stated by the Crows that after the fighting ceased, the Suhtaio chief had looked down upon the lifeless, bloodstained corpse of Dangling-Foot and said to those around him,

CHEYENNES KILL DANGLING-FOOT and CROW REVENGE

"See this enemy lying stiff and lifeless who has given his body to the wolves. He was a brave fighter. Do not take his scalp. Treat him with respect as befits a fearless warrior." [2]

This, say the Crows, the Suhtaio did, and it is also said that the victors then washed the blood from the body of Dangling-Foot; dressed the corpse in their own fine clothes, and laid it to rest with the same ceremony as would be customary for one of their own.

As for the remaining Crow warriors who had no means of escape, they also had fought as bravely and as desperately as any when outnumbered at least three to one. But it was not long before all resistance had been subdued and Suhtaio moccasin feet stood among the slain. Every adult Crow male trapped within the camp had been killed, along with a number of females, while of those women and children who did survive, they were carried into captivity by the victors. In the aftermath, the Suhtaio ransacked the tepees and camp baggage, taking as booty everything of value and of novelty, and the rest, including the tepees, was put to the torch. The Suhtaio then rode away triumphant, driving scores of Crow ponies and women and children captives before them.

Almost as suddenly as the battle started - it was ended, and only Suhtaio victory songs fading into the distance broke the once again still and peaceful prairie air.

The Crow fighting men in Dangling-Foot's village had originally numbered between seventy and eighty warriors, although at least half that number had been away hunting at the time the battle took place. When finally the absentees returned to their then smouldering, corpse-littered camp, they were filled with grief. Immediately they started south in search of Raven-Face and his Dried-Out-Furs band, whilst two of the survivors returned north to the main camp of Sore-Belly's River Crows then located along the Yellowstone to inform him what had happened. Sore-Belly himself was not in camp at that time, having gone to visit the Flatheads west of the Rocky Mountains, while at the same time, word of the disaster was also carried to Long-Hair's people, then in transit to the Buffalo Pasture and intended wintering grounds about the forks of the Stinking River further west

In reality, according to Joe Medicine-Crow's information concerning the affair, the total number of Crow men-folk actually killed during the fight,

CHEYENNES KILL DANGLING-FOOT and CROW REVENGE

was no more than thirty or perhaps forty persons at most. On the other hand, of between one-hundred and one-hundred and fifty women and children constituting the non-combatants of Dangling Foot's thirty-eight lodges, the Suhtaio took a little over one-hundred prisoners. Of these, several later escaped back to their own people in the north, or were traded to or captured by other tribes with whom the Suhtaio were in contact. A sizable number of captives, however, were taken south by the Cheyennes when the latter returned to Bent's post on the Arkansas later that year. Many of these likewise managed to escape from their captors, and after wandering around for some time in the southern country, eventually joined the Kiowa - then enemies of the Cheyenne – where at last they found succour and safety.

A small number of Crow captives from Dangling-Foot's band did remain among the Suhtaio, and two of these at a later date became important personages among that tribe. One, a boy was later known as Stands-All-Night [not the noted Cheyenne tribal historian of the same name who was Arickara by birth], whilst the other, a young woman called Pretty-Lance by the Crows, but known as Blackbird-Woman among the Cheyennes, also married into her adopted tribe and became the mother of the famous Southern Cheyenne war-chief Lame-White-Man. This man was later killed whilst doing brave things during the infamous "Custer Fight" on the Little Big Horn in 1876.

Over all, the destruction of Dangling-Foot's village was a severe blow to the whole Crow Nation. There was much grieving and oaths of vengeance were taken against those culpable. The most important issue as far as Crow warriors were now concerned, was to wreak vengeance again on the Cheyennes and Suhtaio, and all the people's energies seemed to be directed towards that purpose.

It was early January, 1833. In compliance to the wishes of the Crow head chief Long-Hair, some nine-hundred and more clay-whitened, buffalo-hide tepees were erected in one great camp in several concentric circles, with others scattered among the cottonwoods growing along the south bank of the Yellowstone. Thousands of ponies milled around on the adjacent prairie looking like dark mottled patches, and every hour, it seemed, hunting parties were going out or coming in. For such a large village required a great quantity of fresh meat to sustain its population.

CHEYENNES KILL DANGLING-FOOT and CROW REVENGE

Although several weeks had passed since receiving news of Dangling-Foot's demise, no retaliatory action had been forthcoming. Indeed, the Crows had been so engrossed in lamenting their loss, they had not time even to contemplate what to do next. Now, though, with the full might of the Nation encamped together in one place, the people again felt strong and able to avenge themselves upon any foe in some spectacular manner, and not least, upon the "Stripped-Arrow-People," who since the dissolution of their pact with the Crows, were again considered among the latter's foremost antagonists.

The coming together of all the Nation's fighting men was cause also, for clan relatives and close friends of Dangling-Foot's slaughtered and otherwise missing people to launch themselves into yet another overt frenzy of grief. Bereaved womenfolk with blood streaming from self-inflicted wounds and screeching hideous laments, ran up to the important warriors, beseeching them to avenge their loss that the widows might cease their mourning. They wiped their blood on the warrior's heads and bodies and held up mutilated hands, now missing a recently lopped off finger joint so as to incite more pity.

The warriors could not help but be moved by such gory spectacles, which seemed to follow them everywhere around the camp.

This being so, it was not long before a number of warriors dressed themselves in their finest regalia and with a pack-pony loaded with gifts, carried a war-pipe around the camp before finally stopping at the door flap of the large red and black-painted lodge belonging to the head chief, Long-Hair. The warriors sang a wolf song outside his tepee to indicate they wished to conduct a raid deep into the enemy's own country and avenge the slaughter of Dangling-Foot's people. The Crows alone among other Plains Tribes, actually chose to mount grand hostile expeditions during the depths of winter, at which time enemy camps were often immobile and more likely to be taken by surprise.

Long-Hair summoned the leading men among the party to enter his tepee, wherein, after seating themselves in a half circle upon the buffalo robe covered ground, the war-pipe was charged and lit, then passed left to right from one mouth to the next. The last to be offered the stem was Long-Hair himself. But he refused to smoke. Instead he declared he would not accompany such a raid, as it would only bring more grief upon his Crow people if, it too, should end in disaster. The emissaries were taken aback at the chief's response. They rose to their feet in dejected silence and left the lodge and thereafter, walked around the village bewailing aloud that there was no great man among their people who would lead them to war.

It must be noted with regard to Long-Hair's decision, that an important part of his personal *medicine* power, was that he could not personally advocate the slaying of his own tribal people, and this applied to the Cheyennes as they had so many Crow captives since their victory in 1820 on Otter Creek, that Crow persons were sure to be killed if any Cheyenne village was actually attacked in force by the Crows. This then was the logic behind Long-Hair's refusal to join the raid himself, although it did not prevent him sanctioning such an action by others.

Thus the warriors packed even more gifts on the pack-pony. They then carried the pipe to Sore-Belly's lodge and stood outside the door flap while together, they again sang their wolf songs. The great chief bade them enter and they did so, their leader holding the war pipe in both hands with arms outstretched. After seating themselves around the central fire, they smoked the pipe in turn as it passed from mouth to mouth, and finally, the pipe was offered to Sore-Belly who sat silent and impassive at the rear of the lodge. Unlike Long-Hair, Sore-Belly grasped the pipe with both hands, placed his lips to the mouthpiece and inhaled and exhaled the four required puffs, thus signifying his acceptance of being the elected leader of the war-trip his visitors were proposing to take.

All the warriors shouted in unison, *"Ah-ho, Ah-ho"* as an expression of approval, and left the lodge in a body, joyous in both heart and mind.

So it was the very next day, as a winter sun sank slowly in the west, a formidable Crow force at last started from the great village sited on the south bank of the Yellowstone in the shadow of `Pompey's Pillar;` looming large and evocable on the open Plain.

The grand host travelled through that night and rested the following day. Scouts were then sent out to reconnoitre the surrounding countryside to the front and on the flanks, and in such a way utmost vigilance was employed. Sore-Belly who always rode at the head of the van, considered it imperative for the success of the venture that the Cheyennes did not have warning of their coming. If so, they would be sure to disperse and hide from such a large enemy force which could do them much damage. Truly, the Crows were determined that this time, the Striped-Arrow-People would pay dearly for their exultant scalp dances a few moons earlier.

Before sunset on its second day out, the column was off again. Now it headed specifically towards the Black Hills region, intending to visit the site where Dangling-Foot's village had been destroyed.

After a cautious, slow, meandering march, the party at last came upon the battleground; still littered with the remains of their slaughtered kinfolk. The flesh had been picked and gnawed from the bones by beast and fowl, and withal, previously mutilated and abused by human hands so as to be unrecognizable even to a relative. Each skeleton lay pin-cushioned with arrows, the flights of which were of wild turkey and sage hen feathers which was a peculiarity of Cheyenne manufacture. Every skull had been smashed in; the limbs amputated, and all, of course, missing their scalps.

It was agreed among the Crows that the bones lying asunder, were all that was left of Dangling-Foot's people [the Crows not knowing at this stage that survivors of the battle had taken refuge among the Kiowa]. They further discovered by lingering tell-tale signs that the Cheyenne band responsible belonged to the Suhtaio, and had not long fled the country, perhaps in fear of retribution.

However, upon the sight of the mutilated remains, the onlookers were again overcome with grief and great anguish. Outlandish oaths were retaken as old wounds, self-inflicted during the previous period of mourning, were savagely reopened, and it seemed that the guardian spirits of the Crows now cried with them over what they beheld. It is said that *Akbaa-tadia* then put the spirit of demons into their hearts, causing the Crows to again swear vengeance upon the perpetrators of the deed - or themselves to die in the attempt.

They gathered up the scattered bones and deposited them in large pits in the ground, which they then covered with earth and rocks as a safeguard against further despoilment from passing foes and animals, and when this was done the avenging host started forth again, this time in broad daylight with more vigour and resolve than before.

Having picked up an old trail leading south from the battlefield, the party continued in a southerly direction and followed the trail diligently. They hoped it would lead them to the specific Suhtaio band involved, and woe be to those people, as yet ignorant of their impending peril.

CHEYENNES KILL DANGLING-FOOT and CROW REVENGE

It was mid-January 1833, the tenth sleep after leaving the village on the Plain before Pompey`s Pillar, that the Crow cavalcade set their base camp close to where the town of Cheyenne, Wyoming now stands, and from here, the warriors, having left the non-combatants who had accompanied the cavalcade this far, started forth and headed further south until they came into a snow-covered valley watered by the Arkansas. This was a long way indeed from their own Crow country in the north. Again scouts were sent out, and these soon brought word that a Suhtaio village was near the place known as "Big Timbers." In those days, this was a notable landmark on the Southern Plains. It consisted of a stretch of cottonwoods both sides of the Arkansas for a distance of nearly thirty miles, and about the same distance east from where Bent's new trading post stood on the same river some twelve miles from the mouth of Purgatory Creek.

Upon this intelligence, Sore-Belly sent out more scouts in order to ascertain the exact topography surrounding the village, and also, in order to observe any activity in the camp which might indicate whether or not the latter were aware of a Crow presence in the region. In due course the scouts returned with information that the Suhtaio appeared oblivious to the close presence of enemies. In response, Sore-Belly held a war-council with his leading chiefs and warriors to discuss their next move. And thus it was as the moon rose high in a star-sprinkled heaven, the great war-chief devised his plan of attack.

The Suhtaio at this time, were encamped between two heavily timbered creeks known as Horse Creek and Big Sandy Creek, both of which flowed north to south parallel to each other and into the north bank of the Arkansas. The village itself stood on a stretch of open grazing land between the two streams, and milling around at the southern end of the lodges was the Suhtaio pony herd. It was Sore-Belly`s plan to send two separate parties of Crows along each creek from the south end of the village. These two parties would then drive the herd through the village to its north end and beyond, which action Sore-Belly anticipated, would bring forth the owners from their lodges and in pursuit of the thieves. The main body of Crows, meanwhile, would be positioned further north between the creeks, a large party led by Sore-Belly behind a ridge on one side of the open ground; a second party opposite behind a corresponding ridge and led by the great warrior Little-White-Bear, along with another then simply

CHEYENNES KILL DANGLING-FOOT and CROW REVENGE

known as Blackfoot, but in later years, by the name of Sits-in-the-Middle-of-the-Land. Their forces would be obscured by timber bordering both creeks, and when the Crow decoys who first had stolen the enemy's herd raced along the open land between the creeks and flanking ridges, the Suhtaio in pursuit would be drawn into a trap executed by the two lines of hidden Crows.

Thus, early next morning, as the sun rose above the eastern horizon and lit up the strip of land where stood the Suhtaio village, nearly four-hundred Crow braves were already hidden some distance away, waiting with grim anticipation of their comrades bringing the Suhtaio to them. As they waited, some warriors calmly removed the fringed and beaded covers from their lance-points. Others strung bows and fitted an arrow to the string, while those with guns primed the powder pans of their fusses and waited patiently for the battle to commence.

And then it happened.

The two small parties of decoy Crows, comprising seven warriors in each group and having previously positioned themselves at the south end of the Suhtaio village, suddenly let out ear-splitting war-whoops and charged headlong into the Suhtaio pony herd. They shouted and sang at the tops of their voices and at the same time, waved and whirled blankets above their heads whilst others beat quirts on hide-covered shields, in all creating a terrifying din. All at once - neighing and kicking - the whole herd was aroused and began stampeding through the village towards its north end in a panic-stricken mass, churning up the snow and kicking up large clods of earth as they bolted.

Amid the confusion and commotion, the drowsy Suhtaio quickly summed up the situation as they believed it to be. Merely that the attack was nothing more than a daring dawn raid for horses by a small number of enemy opportunists.

Accordingly, eighty or more Suhtaio braves grabbed weapons and mounted ponies, which having been tied securely to picket pins at the door-flaps of the lodges, had been prevented from joining the stampede. These Suhtaio immediately rode off in pursuit of the thieves followed by others on foot, all exultant in the thought of easily obtaining fourteen enemy scalps. Such was the Suhtaio naivety of the real seriousness of the raid that many of the men-folk remained within their tepees, content to let the younger warriors count the coups on this occasion while outside the village, the chase was on.

CHEYENNES KILL DANGLING-FOOT and CROW REVENGE

The Crows so not to be hampered, were soon obliged to abandon the stolen herd in order to elicit more speed, but still the Suhtaio continued in hot pursuit. However, as the chase went on, it seemed the Crow mounts were slackening speed due to the gruelling pace the pursuers set. But just when it looked as if the Suhtaio were gaining, sudden spurts of energy left the pursuers far behind. Once more the Suhtaio were gaining, and yet again the Crows pulled away from almost arm's reach, and try as they might, the enraged Suhtaio could not overtake their quarry. In such a manner the game was played and replayed, the Crows all the time drawing their enemies further from the village and in the direction of their painted and be-feathered Crow comrades.

As the chase progressed, the Suhtaio were led into a wide area of open ground flanked on either side by the tree-covered ridges, and all at once, those same ridges sprouted feathers as a host of Crows suddenly appeared atop each crest.

The fourteen Crow decoys then veered off in as many different directions, and the next instant, had vanished from sight of the pursuing Suhtaio. Too late the latter realized their blunder. They were caught in one of the oldest; but as to prove most effective traps of Indian strategy, and for a moment the two sides stared at each other - one with a look of triumph - the other in despair. A single Crow cry of *"Koo-Koo-Hey"* resounded from the throat of Little-White-Bear who sat his horse atop one of the ridges, and with it, the whole Crow force suddenly charged down the slopes on both sides of the Suhtaio.

The very ridge flanks seemed to move and the ground tremble and the Suhtaio for the present, could do no more but watch the cavalcade of colour, as four-hundred Crow ponies and riders thundered down the two flanking slopes like raging human torrents. The Crows did not stop. They came on at breakneck speed careering into the midst of the Suhtaio who milled about on their ponies, looking desperately for a way out of the trap. Within minutes they found themselves completely surrounded.

The Suhtaio knew they were doomed, and could only prepare to sell their lives dearly in the advent of their complete annihilation. And so it was after only a short while, agonizing moans of dying braves resounded from among the Suhtaio ranks, as warrior after warrior was dropped from the saddle and lay twitching in death throes on the blood-soaked ground.

CHEYENNES KILL DANGLING-FOOT and CROW REVENGE

The Crows say today that their own warriors concentrated their movements in the manner of a circle, and continually rode around the Suhtaio, hurling arrows, lances and musket balls into the huddled bunch within. In such a way they wreaked a dreadful toll in both dead and wounded upon the enemy, and on their fifth or sixth circumference, the Crows finally reined in their mounts and turned to face those of the enemy still standing. They then threw themselves at them and in one swoop knocked the remaining Suhtaio to the ground and rode them under hoof. It was said by Crow veterans of the fight that when the Crows looked back over their shoulders, not one Suhtaio had been left alive. All had felt the under-estimated might of Crow ferocity, and were well on their way to the Spirit Land of their ancestors. The bordering creeks ran red with blood; many *dakshey* * had been counted, and at least eighty bloody Suhtaio topknots dangled from Crow waist-belts.

By this time, those Suhtaio who had preferred to remain in the village had heard the din of battle, and now came racing to the scene; some on horseback and many on foot. Their additional numbers, however, were still no match for the Crows and many met the same fate as their already prostrate comrades. The Suhtaio expediently soon gave up the fight, their depleted force turning around and racing back to the village in order to protect their women and children. But the exultant blood-crazed Crows harried them all the way, cutting down the stragglers as they went, and soon the Crows reached the village itself. Without hesitation they rode right in amongst the lodges, striking and killing every Suhtaio warrior they could lay hands on, and every woman and child who offered the slightest resistance to their wrath. Today, Crow oral tradition accredits the then aspiring Kicked-in-the-Belly Crow warrior, later known as Spotted-Horse, as having been particularly conspicuous during this part of the fight, counting many *dakshey* and taking at least seven female Suhtaio captives in the event. Indeed, it is also said by the Crows that for the most part, the Suhtaio women and children could only watch helpless as their men-folk were slaughtered and their bodies mutilated before their eyes. Much of the Suhtaio incentive to continue the fight had been quickly lost and their defence turned into a rout.

A number of the village non-combatants managed to flee including a small group of men-folk, although a significant number of Suhtaio warriors did

* **Crow word for war-honours or `coups.`**

stay by the women and children, valiantly; but vainly, resisting the Crow's mad onslaught. At length, they were either shot down or in some other way killed where they stood. Some few others actually left the line of retreat and bravely returned to throw themselves into the thick of the blood-bath still raging, merely in the hope of preventing a direct pursuit of those fleeing the scene, knowing of course, they would never again look upon the faces they were endeavouring to save, least ways, not in this world. No quarter was asked or given. The Suhtaio had done the same when rubbing out the village of Dangling-Foot.

It was not long before noon when the fighting finally ceased. Perhaps the fleeing Suhtaio did not stop to look behind them. If they did, they would have seen the glowing flames of their lodges which the Crows put to the torch, and heard the piercing screams and wailing of their now captive womenfolk and children among the victors as they lamented their fate. The Suhtaio had taken a whipping not to heal for many a year, as long as intertribal warfare blighted the Plains. Too well the Suhtaio had paid the price for their earlier victory, and the philosophy of the Indian – death for death and blood for blood - had been exacted in full.

The victorious Crows claimed as booty hundreds of Suhtaio ponies along with warrior equipment in weapons and shields, and had looted the domestic paraphernalia of the camp before setting the tepees ablaze. According to the trader, Edwin Denig, the Crows killed over one-hundred of the enemy in total, and took around two-hundred and fifty women and children into captivity. The Crows themselves, he added, lost only five warriors killed and between ten and fifteen wounded.

Whatever the real number of enemy killed and of captives taken, the Crows then returned to their temporary base camp in a jubilant manner. They were filled with confidence regarding their own warrior prowess, due alone; they thought, to their indomitable Chief Sore-Belly and his omnipotent all-protective *medicine*.

Of the Suhtaio including men, women and children who survived the attack by escaping from the village, they waited until late in the afternoon when they were sure the enemy had left the region. Only then did they come out from hiding and return to the site where once stood their camp. An old man among them walked around the ruined scene calling to the remnants of the people, and

CHEYENNES KILL DANGLING-FOOT and CROW REVENGE

continued calling until, it was thought, all the survivors were assembled together. The Cheyennes at a later date [1930s], told Stanley Vestal that the people then had no horses to ride and that all their food, bedding and tents had been destroyed. Some of the survivors were almost naked, not having had time to dress before fleeing the camp. The weather was very cold, it being in the depth of winter. But notwithstanding, they started out on foot, and enduring much hardship, they travelled in a northwest direction towards the South Platte, hoping to find others of their Nation who would take them in.

-0-0-0-0-0-0-0-0-0-0-

CROW INDIAN HAVING KILLED AND BEHEADED A CHEYENNE
[Painting by Author]

PAWNEES SACRIFICE CHEYENNE WOMAN
And DEATH OF HIGH-BACKED-WOLF 1st

CHAPTER 15.
PAWNEES SACRIFICE CHEYENNE WOMAN
And DEATH OF HIGH-BACKED-WOLF 1st [1833]

According to the Northern Cheyenne informant White-Bull to George Bird Ginnell, the Cheyenne chiefs High-Backed-Wolf, Limber-Lance and Bull-Head visited the white man's Capitol of Washington D.C. sometime in 1832. However, regarding such an occasion the present Author has been unable to verify. Perhaps, though, White-Bull was referring to a visit at the time specified, to Belle Vue on the Lower Missouri, and where the Government appointed Superintendent for tribes west of the Mississippi then resided. This man would not have been the American President himself, but rather, one named William Clark of the famous `Lewis and Clark Expedition` of some years earlier. He was indeed, often referred to by his Indian wards as `Great White Father,` and was known to have several times during his tenure of office, himself visited and been visited by numerous important tribal chiefs within his jurisdiction. Whatever the case, Indian warfare continued as fervently as ever, and not least, were hostilities still raging between all Cheyenne bands and all Pawnee-speaking tribes. [1]

With the coming of spring [1833], a Cheyenne woman having been captured by Skidi Pawnees the preceding winter, was made ready by the latter's priests to be sacrificed to their Morning Star deity. At this time, the four Pawnee tribes were under the jurisdiction of a Government Agent named John Doughty, although as yet, they were not restrained by reservation limits and laws.

The first thing their Agent did when taking up his appointment, was to outlaw the Morning Star ceremony in an effort to assimilate the Skidi into the white man's culture and values. Thus, a Pawnee half-breed employee residing among the Skidi rode his pony hard to the hamlet of Belle Vue on the Missouri where the said Agent was then living, taking word to him of what the Skidi proposed to do. On receiving the news, Doughty immediately saddled up and with five companions set out for the Skidi town hoping he would not be too late

PAWNEES SACRIFICE CHEYENNE WOMAN
And DEATH OF HIGH-BACKED-WOLF 1ˢᵗ

to halt the procedure. Not that the Agent had any love for Cheyennes, or for that matter, his wards, but because he personally abhorred the idea of Human sacrifice and it was his job to stamp it out.

As it was, he reached the town on the Loup Fork of the Republican before the woman in question had been harmed. In fact, she had previously been made comfortable by her captors and had been given no inclination as to her intended fate. The Agent's arrival, however, was greeted with scornful looks and an ominous silence from most of the town's Pawnee inhabitants. A milling horde of Skidi had already worked themselves up in a frenzy in preparation of the ceremony about to take place, and were not likely to have the ritual stopped without a fight. The Skidi head-Chief named Big-Eagle [or Big-Axe as he was sometimes called], saw at once the Agent and his companion's peril and welcomed them into the town. He further agreed to assist the Government employees in ransoming the intended victim, and for a while, the authority of Big-Eagle prevailed. That night the woman was brought into the earthen-lodge where Doughty and his retinue and some Skidi chiefs were gathered.

Big-Eagle then told the chiefs to let the Agent have the said woman and take her safely away, but was answered with a flat refusal by another group of warriors present. Big-Eagle now took complete charge of the potentially hostile situation and defied anyone to molest the woman, and placing two trustworthy guards on each side of her, assured the Agent that she would not be harmed. The chiefs and indignant warriors then left the lodge, albeit in an ugly mood.

That night was quiet, but with an eerie atmosphere and trouble was in the air. This being so, Big-Eagle advised the Agent and his companions to take the Cheyenne woman and flee the town before day-break, lest certain Skidi priests incited the warriors to rebellion and who might then slay them all. The Agent agreed, and placing the woman on horseback between two stout companions while he and the rest of his retinue and now including a number of sympathetic Pawnees led by Black-Chief, surrounded the three and started as silently as possible on their precarious journey out of the town and across the Plains to freedom.

PAWNEES SACRIFICE CHEYENNE WOMAN
And DEATH OF HIGH-BACKED-WOLF 1st

By now, though, in the early morning light, the tops of every Skidi earth-lodge was covered with howling Pawnees, armed and ready to respond to any signal from the priests to massacre the whole absconding party. Indeed, the priests were mingling among the crowd planting seeds of hate and propaganda against the white men, and exhorting the supposed need to sacrifice the captive woman to ensure the future of their crops and well-being of the people.

Slowly nonetheless, the small party wended its way through the maze of domed earth-lodges, expecting any moment to hear the order given for their deaths. Then, as they were passing the largest lodge, a well-known warrior named Spotted-Horse who was standing in its vestibule, let fly an arrow which struck the Cheyenne female in the chest, causing her to slump forward over her horse's neck. The next instant, other Skidi who had been waiting for just such a moment, grabbed the woman's bridal while the dense crowd of onlookers suddenly opened up, and they slipped through them into obscurity. When Agent Doughty tried to follow, the crowd automatically came together again and presented a wall of resistance. Black-Chief saw the assailant standing in the shadow of the vestibule and without hesitation, sprang upon him and proceeded to strangle the man with his bare hands.

Now the whole tribe began taking sides and a wild blood-letting melee seemed imminent. The Agent knew that if the assailant was killed, it would mean certain death for his party. Miraculously he with the help of his accompanying Pawnees fought his way over to the struggling man named Black-Chief, and managed to stop the fight, thus sparing the assailant Spotted-Horse's life. By this time, however, the other complicit priests had slipped away with the dying woman, and somewhere out on the prairie, they cut her up into little pieces. Very soon, all the Skidi were rushing over the grassland outside the town, while some warriors rode their horses around in circles and waving bloody bits of Cheyenne flesh and body parts above their heads. Agent Doughty knew then there was nothing more he could do, and that his own life along with that of his companions was very much in danger. As it was, while the majority of Skidi were preoccupied in their gory revelry, Doughty and his comrades made good their escape.

PAWNEES SACRIFICE CHEYENNE WOMAN
And DEATH OF HIGH-BACKED-WOLF 1st

It was not long, of course, before the Cheyennes themselves heard of the affair and so infuriated were they, a considerable revenge force started out against the same Skidi town without delay. At the same time, Arickara cousins to the Skidi Pawnee, had vacated their own towns on the Missouri and moved west to camp alongside the Skidi owing to pressure from the Sioux, and had by so doing, swelled Skidi numbers to that of a multitude.

In due course, atop a distant hill of the Loup Fork of the Platte and the circle of Skidi Pawnee earth-lodges below them, a long line of Cheyenne warriors suddenly appeared from the west, resplendent in all their savage attire. The warriors sat their horses like a row of toy soldiers and waited to be discovered. It seemed that the entire Southern Cheyenne fighting force in one continuous line, rising and falling as the escarpment demanded, had come to chastise the `People of the wolves.` However, Upon such a sight being discerned by some towns folk, it was not long before the alarm was given and the whole Pawnee town became a hub of excitement and activity.

Suffice to say, the Cheyennes were then formidable enough to have given the Skidi alone a hard fight if not a crushing defeat, but the advent of the recently-arrived Arickara now acting as allies to their cousins, counteracted any such outcome. Indeed, when the Cheyennes charged, the Pawnees and Arickara did not take merely a defensive stance, but being arrayed in a predetermined battle order, they acted on the offensive and were more than eager for conflict. The Cheyenne attackers came thundering forward on their ponies down from the hills and over the Plain, howling and whooping, and singing Brave-Heart songs while beating quirts and tomahawks on their shields. The Skidi and their allies surged forward to meet them, and both sides clashed in bloody mortal combat.

For several hours the opposing hosts pushed backwards and forwards without advantage to either side, and many men and horses were laid low. Try as they might, the Cheyennes could not break through the Skidi and Arickara line, and likewise, the combined Skidi and Arickara could not force the Cheyennes to give way. Indeed, it had become evident that the conflict would prove indecisive and stale-mate if allowed to continue in such a manner.

PAWNEES SACRIFICE CHEYENNE WOMAN
And DEATH OF HIGH-BACKED-WOLF 1ˢᵗ

Thus after nearly a whole day of fruitless and sometimes costly charges and counter-charges at each other's ranks with all the fury they could muster, not to mention single combats, which themselves had taken its toll of once highly regarded persons among each side, the Cheyennes as did their enemies, finally retired from the field and slowly drifted back to their respective homes. Had not the Skidi been aided by the Arickara, the affray may well have turned into a rout for the Skidi, but this time it was not to be.

So in general, it was a bloody year on the Plains in 1833. Kiowas while most of their menfolk had been out hunting, suffered a disastrous attack on one of their villages by the Osage, who slaughtered everyone in camp; cut off the heads and left them in the Kiowas' own cooking pots, and added to this, a smallpox epidemic swept the Southern Plains that summer and was only just dying out, although it had carried off many Indians of all ages during its course. Further south, an army of Navaho exacted long-overdue retribution on the Utes killing a large number of the latter, while as noted above, a large number of Suhtaio-speaking Cheyennes had been discomfited by the Crows. Such wanton spilling of Indian blood stirred even white men as yet uninvolved in such conflicts, and Government officials were urged to try and stem this constant flow of crimson.

Then during the night of November 12ᵗʰ that same year of `33, Cheyennes thought the world was coming to its end, and all Indian peoples would vanish from the earth. A *Leonid* Meteoric star shower, which lit up the whole night sky across the open Plains was seen all over the United States, and which phenomena paralysed the Indians with awe. The Southern bands of Cheyennes then camped outside Bent's Fort on the Arkansas, translated it as a sign from the Great Spirit that their people must have done a great wrong, and as a consequence, many were stupefied with fear all the time the `shower' lasted. Some warriors donned feathered-bonnets and war regalia; painted their faces, and mounting war-ponies, rode single file around their village ready to die like warriors should if they could not adequately defend themselves and families against such an occurrence. The women wailed and sang death-songs,

PAWNEES SACRIFICE CHEYENNE WOMAN
And DEATH OF HIGH-BACKED-WOLF 1st

while children cried throughout the night. Surely, thought the Cheyennes, the end of the world was nigh.

Come morning, the sun rose in the east as usual, and the sky again was calm and bright. All at once, the people's fears were forgotten and very soon, `The Night the Stars Fell` passed into Indian myth and folk-lore. Although the Cheyennes themselves declared, the stars falling from the sky must have been a portent for some future catastrophe, or even a warning that one or another great man among them was soon about to die.

Indeed, it was after this event in late '33, that the great Cheyenne Sweet-Medicine-Chief, High-Backed-Wolf himself, met his own demise. It was probably when his whole Cheyenne camp was intoxicated, that the aforesaid chief, while running to assist a relative named Flint fighting outside his tepee over a stolen wife, was promptly stabbed to death in the ensuing tussle.

The great chief who had led the great attack on the Crows in 1820, and signed the first treaty between his people and American Government in 1825 was dead. And with him died an era. Even though he had brought his fate upon himself, as being a chief he had no right to interfere in tribal quarrels, nevertheless his passing was deeply mourned by the whole tribe and which thereafter, broke up into many disoriented bands and family camps, and for a while, wandered the Plains in separate bands and in confusion.

It was believed by many Cheyennes that stars had fallen the sky that November night was to be taken as a portent, and thus, had heralded the death of such a great man as High-Backed-Wolf 1st.

- 0 - 0 - 0 - 0 - 0 - 0 - 0 - 0 - 0 - 0 –

CROWS TRICK CHEYENNES and KIOWAS DEFEATED

CHAPTER 16.

CROWS TRICK CHEYENNES and KIOWAS DEFEATED [1835]

During the winter of 1834 -'35, those Cheyenne and Suhtaio bands remaining north of the Platte had, as usual, moved to the Laramie branch of that stream and western headwaters of Cheyenne River. They pitched their camps amid timbered groves ready to sit out the hoary months and conduct hostile sorties against Crows and Shoshoni simply to relieve tribal boredom through the season's duration. Further south, other Cheyenne bands moved to the Big Timbers area on Arkansas River and splitting into several camps, set their tepees at various points along that river's north bank. Here through the long wintery nights sitting leisurely around central fires, warriors retold stories of valour, and proposed new forays into enemy country when again would come spring, and grass once more be lush with buffalo in abundance. [1]

For one, however, it was not the time for Kill-Talk, but for contemplating peace. This, of course, was Grey-Thunder, the renowned holy man and keeper of the Nation's `Sacred Arrow` talismans, and indeed, since the loss of the talismans to Pawnees four years earlier, and even though four *new* `Arrows` had been instigated in their place, only the original set, believed Grey-Thunder, contained the omnipotent mystic powers connected to them. Still he yearned their safe return, and long was he prepared to wait and see such happen. Although how that would occur, he was undetermined. *

At this same time, word was carried by the proverbial moccasin grapevine, declaring that some Central Plains Tribes were about to make peace

---

*   **Owing to High-Backed-Wolf's death, the Sacred Arrows were bound by Cheyenne custom to be renewed, as their shafts were thought to have been soiled with blood. There were, of course, at that time, no Sacred Arrows among the Cheyennes, having earlier been captured by the Pawnees. Thus, four *new* `Arrows` were made to replace those lost. Two revered Cheyenne holy men named Crazy-Mule and Box-Elder were chosen to make the new Arrows, and which; after great ceremony and prayers, were interned within a new Sacred Bundle itself.**

with one other, and among these last were Pawnees. Could this be the opportunity Grey-Thunder had been waiting for? Maybe not, but now he was resolved to act in a more positive way. He would go into the very country of the Pawnees, he declared, and personally solicit the return of the `Arrows` to his tribe.

A large party might arouse suspicion among the Pawnees as to the proper Cheyenne motive for such a visit, and Grey-Thunder decided to take only a small retinue with him, these being his wife, another woman and two other holy men named Old-Bark and Doll-Man.

So it was one fresh morning before snow had cleared away, the five emissaries started from the *Aorta* Cheyenne village outside Bent`s Fort. They left without customary praises or well-wishing from the people and rode horseback northeast on their perilous mission. All five knew the journey might be their last in the world they then knew, but for the welfare of the Nation they felt it must be done. Once in the Pawnee village they could claim sanctuary as guests, as no Indian would dare violate such a custom lest they tempt the wrath of their ancestors. The real danger was getting to the Pawnee village safely across the open Plains, and of getting back to Cheyenne country alive. As there were more enemies than Pawnees to contend with.

Winter thus passed, but there came no word of Grey-Thunder or his companions. Perhaps, thought his people, Grey-Thunder`s little group was dead. Nevertheless, Cheyennes as a whole refrained from raiding Pawnees ere they were still alive and such actions might impair the group`s safety. Instead, those Cheyennes wishing to go to war, concentrated on raiding Crows and Shoshoni northwest of the Upper Platte, and Kiowa and Comanche pony herds south of the Arkansas.

Early in the new year of `35, a large war-party of Crows was roaming south of the South Platte River as far as the Arkansas. Generally, they were creating mayhem among the resident tribes, looking for horses to steal and any foreign tribesmen to kill. Now it happened around this time that a Crow war-party led by a chief named Yellow-Belly and including the frontiersman James P. Beckwourth [a Mulato in the employ of the American Fur Company but living with the Crows], came upon a *Yamparika* Comanche village under a renowned chief named Buffalo-Hump. One night, Yellow-Belly`s Crows raided the camp and escaped in a northwest direction with a considerable herd of stolen Comanche horses which they drove before them at a rapid gait.

The dispossessed when discovering their loss, called together an equally large party and before mid-day, were in full pursuit of the thieves, although ignorant of the latter's tribal identity.

For three days the Crows kept up a gruelling pace, but still Buffalo-Hump and his Comanche braves continued following the trail, and soon were only a few miles behind the thieves. The Crows knew they would have to shake off their pursuers or turn and fight to save their lives, let alone to retain the herd. When all hope was almost gone of eluding their foes and a fierce battle appeared imminent, as they topped the summit of a ridge which rolled down to the south bank of the Arkansas, they suddenly observed a cluster of Cheyenne tepees in a valley below.

Caught between two large enemy groups, the Crows had but one chance to save themselves, which was to veer off from the course they were traveling, and execute a long detour around their Cheyenne foes, who themselves, were encamped in numbers far exceeding that of both Crows and pursuing Comanche in total.

The Crows thus continued through a kind of hollow with all the captured ponies, and by the time the Comanches topped the same summit where a short time before they had spied the thieves, not a Crow or stolen horse was in sight. The Comanches, of course, could plainly see horse tracks leading up the ridge and also see the tepee village on the far side of the hill, and this, thought the pursuers, was the thieves' village. Without further ado, the pursuing Comanches made preparations to attack it.

Meanwhile, in the valley below, the Cheyennes had not let these actions go unobserved. They had spotted the Crows when first the latter had exposed themselves for an instant against the sky-line, although the distance between the Crows and village occupants had been too great for Cheyennes to distinguish the tribal stock of the thieves. They knew they were not Cheyennes and since then, their own warriors had been donning feathers; stringing bows and loading muskets ready to defend themselves. When soon after this, the Comanche pursuers appeared as had the Crows on the same ridge-top against the sky-line, the Cheyennes naturally supposed them to be the same group as previously seen.

CROWS TRICK CHEYENNES and KIOWAS DEFEATED

So it was that the Comanches careered their mounts down the ridge slope and over the Plain towards the village, but were met with a solid wall of resistance by hundreds of Cheyenne fighting men, already prepared for just such an attack upon them. The Cheyennes then galloped at break-neck speed towards the Comanches and went crashing into their ranks, toppling warriors from the saddle and lancing them through. The Comanches, having a moment earlier been full of confidence of taking the village by surprise, were instead torn apart and scattered, and as the wily Crows later said, they could hear the report of muskets and screams of both contending parties as they themselves continued racing on, not slackening speed, but taking full advantage of the ongoing melee to escape with the stolen herd.

The Comanches were at a disadvantage. At length, they turned their ponies around and raced back over the ridge-top and back the way they had come in a somewhat disorganised rabble. As the Comanches hued towards their own country they were hotly chased by a horde of Cheyennes, who continued after their quarry as if chasing a herd of buffalo.

Come nightfall, the Cheyennes gave up the chase, having killed a few more Comanche stragglers and were jubilant when returning to their own village on the south bank of the Arkansas. The Crows – instigators of the whole affair – also made it safely home to their camp far north on the Yellowstone, and where the Crow chief Yellow-Belly was highly acclaimed for his party's deed, and for taking so many horses at one time from the Comanche.

It seemed with regard to tribes of the Southern Plains, there was only one friend the Crows could turn to. These latter were Kiowa, and had been Crow allies for several generations past. Now, however, being at war with Cheyennes, the Kiowa found it precarious to continue regular visits to their old-time Crow allies in the north, and for Crows to travel south in order to reciprocate those visits unless in formidable number. When at such times Kiowas did go north or when returning south, they usually kept to the eastern foothills of the Rocky Mountains to escape being noticed by enemies. Of such excursions, however, Cheyennes were fully aware and as a consequence, were forever on the lookout in the hope of surprising just such a Kiowa or Crow column on the move, for at such times, the said column would be unprotected and encumbered with women and children, travois and a vast herd of loose ponies. Cheyennes recall in their

CROWS TRICK CHEYENNES and KIOWAS DEFEATED

traditions only one attack by their people on such a traveling Kiowa band, although the Kiowa calendars actually record at least three similar hostile events, when either going north or returning south after visiting the Crows.

In early summer of `35, just such a village of Kiowa was traveling north towards the Tongue and Big Horn River to trade with the Crows. The Crows would trade black-tipped white ermine tails, beads and dressed animal-skin clothing and guns, these last-named having been obtained from trading posts along the Missouri, in exchange for Kiowa horses captured from Mexicans and Anglo-Americans south of the Arkansas. The Kiowa village in question at this time, contained some one-hundred lodges and was moving north close to the tree line east of the Rocky Mountains to protect its village occupants from the elements and marauding bands of enemies. Occasionally, the occupants would be obliged to traverse open expanses of treeless prairie and at which times, the cavalcade would be open to attack.

By coincidence, the Cheyenne chief Yellow-Wolf and his *Hevitanio* band along with Black-Shin`s Suhtaio, were following a buffalo herd with their entire villages in tow, and were actually moving along a parallel route as were the Kiowa. Having no idea that enemies were near, the Cheyennes were traveling in a carefree manner. Nevertheless, a Cheyenne scout out ahead of the column scanning the horizon for buffalo, discerned the moving Kiowa village and quickly made his horse gallop backwards and forwards as a signal to his tribesmen behind him that enemies were near. His tribesmen knew what he was signalling and in response, Yellow-Wolf and Black-Shin at once called to arms their warriors, and bade them change their mounts for war-ponies and ready themselves for battle.

Within minutes, two-hundred and more Cheyennes and Suhtaio fighting men were riding pell-mell to the brow of the hill where still sat their scout. They could see that the Kiowa column was half way across an open stretch of grassland flanked on one side by a stream now known as Scout Creek shrouded on both banks with timber. When the Cheyennes topped the crest, they were spotted by the Kiowa menfolk and immediately Kiowa women, old-folk and children automatically broke off from their line of travel, and herding together their extra horses, raced the animals they were riding towards the protection of the timber. Meanwhile, the Kiowa fighting men turned their mounts to face the enemy and prepared themselves for a fight.

CROWS TRICK CHEYENNES and KIOWAS DEFEATED

One Kiowa woman racing towards the trees had strapped to her back a cradle board in which was a very young child. Unfortunately, she fell off her horse and lay on the prairie at the mercy of oncoming Cheyennes. The Suhtaio chief Black-Shin was first to ride up to her and counted coup with his lance, albeit inflicting only a flesh wound. Two more among the charging warriors also counted coup on her person, but these likewise did not kill her. Whereupon Black-Shin pulled her up behind him on his horse and claimed her as his captive. The rest of the attacking force then threw themselves at the bunch of Kiowa warriors who were bravely attempting a stand between the attackers and their fleeing kin-folk. After a short time, however, pressure upon them became so great that the Kiowa warriors were forced to cede their ground and draw back in order to adopt another position. This procedure was repeated several times until finally, the Kiowa warriors themselves reached the timber and where they took cover among the trees and continued shooting to protect their people.

During all this time, a brave Kiowa mounted on a splendid snow-white stallion and wearing a Dog-Rope over one shoulder and across his chest decorated with dyed porcupine quills and armed with only a lance, held his mount outside of the protection of the timber in front of other Kiowa warriors also outside the timber, and made many charges at the Cheyennes. Several times he rode right in amongst the latter and succeeded knocking several Cheyenne braves from their ponies, one of whom was the *Hevitanio* Old-Little-Wolf's brother named Man-Above, a noted Cheyenne fighter. This same lone Kiowa was very brave, the Cheyennes later said, and seemed to bear a charmed life. He was in fact, a kind of suicide warrior of the Kiowa *Kotisenko* warrior society, which included only the ten most formidable fighting men among that tribe, and thus, he attacked the Cheyennes time and again. The final charge he made caused him once more to go smashing into the enemy ranks, and although being carried by his steed clear through the Cheyenne line to its far side, he collected three arrows in his back. Still he managed to ride his war-pony back through the Cheyennes, but before he reached his own people, he finally slid from his horse a dead man. Witnessing the fall of their champion, the rest of the Kiowa fighting men lost spirit to carry on the contest. In one body, they themselves took extra cover in the timber where their non-combatants had been digging rifle-pits and erecting a kind of barricade with brush and camp baggage against a potential frontal assault.

CROWS TRICK CHEYENNES and KIOWAS DEFEATED

Here the best horses of the Kiowa were tied securely among the trees, lest they be stampeded by Cheyennes, and who themselves lost no time regrouping their forces and charged directly at the barricade itself.

The beleaguered Kiowas nevertheless held fast, and after many valiant yet costly assaults, the Cheyennes realised the folly of trying to drive the entrenched enemy from its position. The attackers instead, concentrated on stampeding the Kiowa horses including most of the animals intended for trade with the Crows, and these were eventually driven off, while the Kiowa war-ponies and prized mounts remained secured to their tethers among the trees. The horses captured, however, sufficed the Cheyennes for the present, and being somewhat contented they retired from the field, leaving the discomfited Kiowas to pick up their belongings along with their dead and wounded and at length, continue on their journey.

A young Cheyenne girl at the time named Snake-Woman, said that after the fight, the Kiowa woman who had fallen from her horse during her people's dash for the timber, was seen sitting despondently outside Black-Shin's lodge with a young girl-child in her arms. The said child, Snake-Woman further declared, was white, having brown hair and blue eyes and at a later date in 1840 when Kiowas, Comanches and Kiowa-Apaches made peace with the Cheyennes and Arapahoe, the captive woman was reclaimed by the Kiowa, but they did not want the child. Thus the girl subsequently remained among the Cheyennes until her death of old age. She was known simply to her captors as Kiowa-Woman, although more correctly in Cheyenne, as *Enu-tah*, meaning, "Woman member of a foreign tribe." At a later date she was known more popularly as White-Cow-Woman, and was still alive among the Cheyennes as late as 1912.

The Kiowa brave on the white stallion is, for his part, still talked about by present-day Cheyennes, as having been a most daring and great warrior among their enemies.

- 0 - 0 - 0 - 0 - 0 - 0 - 0 - 0 - 0 - 0 –

CHEYENNE PEACE WITH PAWNEES
CHAPTER 17.

CHEYENNE PEACE WITH PAWNEES [1835]

Regarding Grey-Thunder and his emissaries, earlier rumours the latter heard regarding peaceful overtures broached between several Plains Tribes, had not been unfounded, as the presence of American troops on Arkansas River was to prove. [1]

Back in '33, an unwarranted massacre of a Kiowa village by Osages, coupled with the burning of a Pawnee town by Delawares that same year, and notwithstanding incessant hostility between other tribes, had caused the American Government to act. Complaints and compensation claims were all too frequent items on the agenda of Congress, as more and more trappers, traders and white settlers lost livestock and their lives to marauding Indians.

In summer of '34, Colonel Leavenworth along with four-hundred dragoons had been dispatched into the Central Plains with orders to meet and hold council with as many tribes as possible; negotiate favourable treaties of non-aggression with them and towards each other, and again, obtain the latter's allegiance to the United States. Four-hundred dragoons might not seem an impressive instrument compared to European standards, but to bands of skulking Indians – many among whom had only rarely if ever seen a uniform – an array of blue-clad soldiers wielding shiny sabres and mounted on massive army chargers looked formidable enough when drawn up in battle order. With the soldiers at this time had ridden the artist George Catlin, who had taken it upon himself to capture the Indian mode of life and their likeness on canvas.

Suffice to say, the expedition of that year met with Kiowas, Comanche, Tonkawa, Witchita and others, and succeeded in securing promises of allegiances. At each confrontation with a respective tribe, Leavenworth had professed the Great White Father's wish for peace and a desire to accommodate the needs and comforts of his `Red Brothers.` The Indians had responded by professing eternal love for the Americans and in some instances, even made peace between themselves, and after which, they graciously accepted presents and medals from the expedition, the medals adorned with the likeness of President Andrew Jackson himself.

CHEYENNE PEACE WITH PAWNEES

The expedition was proving a success and continued on to meet the Pawnee Picts [a branch of the Witchita], Toyash, Pani-Mahas [Skidi] and Waco. Then in the blistering heat of July, malaria had struck the column and being unaccustomed to such humidity and traveling conditions, fever ravaged its ranks. Even the Colonel contracted the disease and within a matter of weeks, less than half the original command was still capable of marching. At this point Colonel Henry Dodge after consultation with Leavenworth, split from the stricken camp at the mouth of what is now known as the False Washita, and continued the intended mission with the remaining two-hundred and fifty dragoons. With them went the later famous Stephen Watts Kearney along with a number of Indian guides from an assortment of East Woodland Tribes, including Cherokee, Osage, Seneca and Delaware.

This party reached the Canadian River in early August, and on the 5th that month, learned of the death of Leavenworth. The Dragoons with Dodge were by then also ailing, and by the time the party returned to Fort Gibson from whence the expedition had started, one-hundred and fifty soldiers had died. Still, however, the original object of the expedition had not been a failure, and subsequent treaties with the Wild Tribes of the Plains had been effected from it.

This being so, the following year of '35, Colonel Dodge set out again on a similar expedition, this time with only one-hundred and twenty-five men, consisting of dragoons, officers and Indian guides and including a notorious whiskey trader named John Gant, along with the Government appointed Pawnee Indian Agent, John Doughty. Again, this was a Government endeavour to meet a number of tribes of the Mid-Western Plains, the idea being to bring peace between the warring tribes and obtain assurances from the latter for the unhampered travel of white emigrants when traversing Indian lands. This time the expedition held councils with the Omaha, Otto and the four bands of Pawnee, and the expedition obtained required promises of Indian allegiance, while as before, a distribution of presents and presidential medals concluded the ceremonies.

At a Skidi earth-lodge village, the latter's chiefs and head men of both the Skidi and their Arickara cousins, expressed to Colonel Dodge their desire to make a more lasting and official peace with the Cheyenne, and suggested that one and more of their chiefs and leading warriors accompany Dodge and his dragoons to that tribe to act as ambassadors regarding the sincere intentions of the Skidi and Arickara in concluding peaceful relationships with them. The Colonel complied with the request and soon after, started forth for Bent's Fort on the Arkansas with several Skidi and Arickara head men in attendance. The expedition moved upstream along the South Platte River by way of what is now Browning valley until they came to the foothills of the Rocky Mountains, and whereupon, they swung south to the Arkansas.

Here on the south side of the Arkansas, the expedition came upon a small band of Arapahoe trading with a large group of *Comancheros* of mixed Mexicans and Indians bartering with each other for stolen cattle, horses, guns and whiskey. Dodge held a brief council with the Arapahoe who agreed to peace with not only the Skidi and Arickara, but also with the Kiowa, Comanche, and Osage. The Colonel was overwhelmed, and with a light heart set off again towards his objective Bent's Fort. Indeed, the Arapahoes' professed commitment to peace, incited Dodge to dispatch the trader John Gantt to go ahead of the column and contact other Arapahoe villages and headmen of neighbouring Southern Cheyennes in the hope of bringing their chiefs to Bent's Fort for an official council among even more Western Tribes. Although Captain Gantt has since come down in history as an unscrupulous whisky trader generally lacking in morals, he was among the very few white men who at that time, knew the country and its peoples like the back of his hand.

As it was, even before the column reached the aforesaid fort, it appeared that word of its coming had gone before it, as Indians were heading towards the Colonel, rather than he to them. A band of Cheyennes came riding up to the dragoons and being informed of their destination, the same Cheyennes accompanied the white men on the rest of their journey to the fort. Thus it was probably Arapahoes among the expedition who persuaded Cheyennes to smoke the pipe of peace with their erstwhile enemy the Osages then accompanying Dodge. But either way, peace was made between the latter and those Cheyennes present, and again, the expedition thought itself a success.

On August 6th the expedition, now increased in number with contingents of Cheyennes, Arapahoes and *Comancheroes,* actually reached Bent's Fort on the north bank of the Arkansas surrounded by a large number of Cheyenne tepees, and among which, was a small band of visiting Atsina and twenty-five

Blackfeet warriors, the latter married to Cheyenne women having lived with the Southern Cheyenne bands since 1826. On the south bank of the Arkansas across the river from the fort, was another village of Cheyennes, the occupants of which were then engaged in bartering whiskey from another group of Mexican traders, and never were two separate Cheyenne villages in such contrast to each other. This was apparent when compared to the solemn and dignified welcome the expedition received on the north bank, to the wild hysteria on the south bank owing to the flow of liquor in that camp, and which so impressed a Lieutenant Kingsbury in company with the said dragoons that he was apt to record,

> "…The Cheyennes will sell their horses, blankets and everything else they possess for a drink of it." [2]

The flats around Bent's Fort itself were swarming with Indians, dogs and horses. So much so that Dodge was obliged to bivouac his force a full mile from the fort. Nevertheless, the dragoons in their leisure crossed to the south side of the river and observed the unbridled revelry and orgies then going on among intoxicated Indians. Upon entering a chieftain's lodge, a dragoon sergeant named Hugh Evans was moved to write in his diary,

> "All [or nearly all] men, women and children were drunk…filling their bowls and horn-spoons and handing it around with as much liberality as a candidate for office…Some reeling, staggering and hollowing, falling down and rising up, frothing and naked, and such gestures and grimaces looked as if they came from fiends of the lower regions…But we found some squaws sober [which is invariably the case for the protection of the rest] who appeared to enjoy the sport of their drunken companions admirably well…" [3]

Four days later, the aforementioned Gantt came in to the fort with around one-hundred other Indians, including Arapahoe and Atsina, Blackfeet, Snakes [Shoshoni] and some Crows, and on August 11th a council was held among the Indian chiefs and head men actually within the walls of the fort and the following day, the council continued in the tent where resided Colonel Dodge himself. It was then that Cheyennes took the hands of two Pawnees among the

CHEYENNE PEACE WITH PAWNEES

Colonel's retinue and promised to war against each other never more; neither to take each other's horses, although the Cheyennes did admit that even then, there was still a Cheyenne war-party out roaming Pawnee country.

According to the diary of another expedition member - a Lieutenant Gaines P. Kingsbury, - Little-Moon; a big Cheyenne chief at that time, declared he was not himself at liberty to make a formal peace with the Pawnees and Arickara without his whole Nation's council of forty-four being in agreement, and that a further two large Cheyenne war-parties were still out, one against the Arickara and another against the Comanche. He would, he said, convey the proposal to other Cheyenne chiefs when appropriate, and in the meantime, welcomed the foreign headmen to his camp. Little-Moon then turned to Dodge and asked him to tell those Pawnees present to send each of the four Cheyenne bands a Sacred Arrow [which Pawnees had captured previously], but which request was misconstrued by Lieutenant Kingsbury who further stated, *"...It is the custom of these wild Indians to exchange arrows when making peace."* [4]

Dodge then urged the Cheyenne chiefs to also make peace with the Osage, Arickara and Mandan as the Arapahoe had earlier done. But if he hoped for an end to the Cheyenne feud with the Kiowa and Comanche, it was to no avail. Indeed, the Cheyennes avoided the issue completely and that part of discussion came to an end.

Dodge later recorded that the Cheyennes were divided into three bands; had recently slain their head chief, High-Backed-Wolf, and were in disorganization. Their numbers, he said, was some two-hundred and twenty lodges with six-hundred and sixty men, and constituted together, two-thousand six-hundred and forty souls.

Due to the demise of High-Backed-Wolf, Dodge proposed that Little-Moon select three chiefs among the three Cheyenne bands then assembled at Bent's Fort, so they could receive medals to commemorate the event and which also, would allow them to be recognised by the Great White Father as Cheyenne chiefs. Little-Moon himself, although having acted in the role of head chief since High-Backed-Wolf's death, declined to continue in that position himself. Instead, he designated three well-respected warriors to take on the official chiefly roles as Dodge had requested. These men chosen by Little-Moon subsequently were, White-Cow, Flying-Arrow and Medicine-Snake, this last named also known as Walking-Whirlwind.

CHEYENNE PEACE WITH PAWNEES

Aided by interpreters from the fort, Dodge repeated his Government's overtures with the customary oratory, concluding with promises of rewards in merchandize and protection of the Red Man's rights and interests.

That night resounded to wild revelry of tribal dances amid ear-splitting celebrations to accompany the newly-established pacts. Indeed, all had seemed to go well. Next morning the expedition left its hosts and continued downstream along the Arkansas towards Big Timbers.

On route, the dragoons met a Cheyenne war-party under the leadership of a warrior later known as White-Man's-Chief returning from a foray against the Kiowa and Comanche. Being informed of the recent consultations at Bent's Fort, these Cheyennes requested Dodge to include them also, to which the Colonel agreed, and likewise, presented White-Man's-Chief with an Andrew Jackson medal.

Pushing on, the expedition came at length to the Big Timbers located some forty miles distant from Bent's Fort. Here was encamped another party of Arapahoe and fifty lodges of Cheyennes led by the famous horse-stealer Yellow-Wolf. The latter had themselves only recently returned from a successful raid on Buffalo-Hump's Comanches, and the *Heviatanio* herds were swollen with Comanche stock. Even though, the inter-tribal peace proposals were repeated by Dodge and who told them that if Yellow-Wolf's Cheyennes went to the aforesaid fort, its proprietors would accommodate them with presents as had been given their kinfolk.

Suddenly, the peaceful atmosphere was shattered by the reports of one-hundred muskets discharging their loads, and a hundred throats screeching war-cries which reverberated across the prairie, and as many bunches of feathers adorning Pawnee scalp-locks on shaven heads then appeared in the distance. Colonel Dodge instinctively ordered his dragoons into battle order with sabres drawn. The resident Cheyennes and Arapahoe, however, were unperturbed. Many actually ran from their camp to meet the Pawnees, for riding in the latter's van rode a proud and justifiably smug *medicine* man, stripped naked but for breech-clout and moccasins and daubed all over with red pigment. It was the Sacred Arrow keeper of the Cheyennes, Grey-Thunder himself.

Many moons before, far to the northeast, Grey-Thunder and his small delegation had safely reached the Skidi Pawnee town on the Loup Fork of

CHEYENNE PEACE WITH PAWNEES

Republican River, Nebraska. Grey-Thunder's few companions on his perilous journey had included his wife and another woman, chief Old-Bark or Ugly, and Doll-Man born in 1769 and married to a Mandan woman. Apparently, the Skidi had relaxed their vigilance somewhat, for the Cheyenne party had reached the very entrance of the town before the Pawnees discovered that foreigners were almost in their midst. The Cheyenne party's arrival and first reception by the Skidi was, one might imagine, mixed with suspicion and curiosity, but the town occupants knew the law of the Plains which demanded that all guests either friend or foe, were to be made welcome and comfortable, and not one Pawnee would dare violate the code.

With solemn dignity and indomitable courage, Grey-Thunder, Old-Bark and Doll-Man rode slowly into the earth-lodge town, twisting their way in and out among the maze of domed-shaped earth-lodges while searching for that of the Skidi head chief, Big-Eagle. The towns folk milled around them, some cheering, others murmuring abuse, while the Cheyenne emissaries themselves being more than careful not to convey the slightest indication of fear, several times paused to ask directions to Big-Eagle's lodge. Reaching at length their destination, they casually dismounted and entered the dark interior of the sought after lodge. They then sat cross-legged with their backs to the entrance, and waited patiently for an audience with the lodge owner.

Looking up, there before Grey-Thunder hanging from the wall at the rear of the lodge and protruding from a kit-fox-skin bundle, were two of the Sacred Arrows he had risked so much to retrieve. Here he sat, within arm's reach of the cherished talismans after nearly five years of hope and prayers. Yet such was the etiquette he and his Cheyenne companions were expected to show, that none among the five emissaries moved from their positions to inspect them.

After a while, the mighty Big-Eagle himself entered majestically through the lodge doorway, and sat with arms folded in front of the Cheyennes with his back to the Arrows. For a few minutes there was utter silence both within and without the lodge. Then a Pawnee woman brought in bowls of food for each of the Cheyennes present, and who readily ate their fill. This was a good sign, as once the visitors had been fed they were safe from danger all the while they remained in the town as guests.

The meal over, Big-Eagle lit his pipe; blew symbolic smoke to the Pawnee powers then offered the stem to the Cheyennes. Up until this point, and until after Grey-Thunder, Old-Bark and Doll-Man had smoked, no words had been spoken by any in the lodge. Now, however, Grey-Thunder himself addressed the Pawnee chief in sign language, for neither could speak each other's tongue. Grey-Thunder told Big-Eagle that his heart had been sick since the Sacred Arrow bundle had been captured and that he had heard that the great Big-Eagle had it hanging in his own lodge as a trophy of that fateful day. He wished the return of the 'Arrows,' Grey-Thunder continued, and if the Skidi chief agreed, then his people the Cheyennes would make peace with all the Pawnee tribes and reward them with many horses.

Big-Eagle, knowing that his tribe wanted peace with Cheyennes more so than with any other at this time, was not hesitant with his reply. He was nonetheless, knowledgeable enough to realise the significance which the said 'Arrows' held for the Cheyennes, and was sceptical in thinking that once they were returned and again in the possession of their rightful owners, the proposed peace might be quickly forgotten. Big-Eagle therefore, permitted Grey-Thunder to select only one of the 'Arrows' as a token of Skidi goodwill, and suggested that he and a number of his warriors should accompany the Cheyenne guests back to the latter's village on the Arkansas at Big Timbers, and where they would consolidate a new friendship with the Cheyenne.

Grey-Thunder, of course, assented as he was in no position to refuse, and standing up, Grey-Thunder, removed one of the war Arrows from the bundle. Handling the shaft with much reverence he then turned to face Big-Eagle and pointing it at him, muttered several words in the Cheyenne tongue. He was in fact, placing a curse on the Skidi chief and his people that if hereafter the peace was broken or the rest of the Arrows not returned, he vowed to exterminate the whole Skidi tribe if such became reality.

Big-Eagle did not understand Grey-Thunder's mumblings, and dismissing the actions as some Cheyenne hocus-pocus connected to the shafts, he remained in the same vein of apparent friendship. The war Arrow, however, was not the one to be finally selected by the Cheyenne holy man, and replacing the arrow in the bundle, Grey-Thunder decided upon one of the Buffalo Arrows instead, probably thinking that only one of the four Arrows would actually be returned, Grey-Thunder had contemplated his choice long before. The Buffalo Arrow would insure good hunting by his tribe and for his people's welfare, while a person could survive without war. His people could flee from attack as

CHEYENNE PEACE WITH PAWNEES

once they had regularly done when fleeing from dreaded *Ho-Hay* [Assiniboine and Chippewa] enemies long ago. But no living human could survive without food, and famine would be a worst disaster than defeat.

Thus, a `Buffalo Arrow` was chosen, and receiving word from Big-Eagle himself that he personally would return it to Grey-Thunder ceremonially when peace was officially made between the Cheyennes and Skidi, the black-feathered and painted `Buffalo Arrow` was returned to the captured bundle for the time being. Grey-Thunder then invited the chief and his head men to go with him and his companions to his people, where a grand celebration would be held to honour the new pact between their two tribes.

It was soon after this that Big-Eagle and one-hundred picked warriors, and among which were a number of Arickara at that time visiting the Skidi, started out on foot towards Cheyenne country now with Grey-Thunder and his comrades leading the way on horseback. The Skidi and Arickara were on foot in anticipation of the great number of horses they would be given at the Cheyenne village and they went in force, not merely to counteract treachery if shown by the Cheyennes, but also as protection against other enemies which might be encountered along the way. Big-Eagle himself carried the fur-wrapped bundle, but containing the red-feathered Sacred Arrow, as he had left the remaining black-feathered `Arrow` in his lodge and the two remaining `Arrows` among two other Pawnee tribes, lest the proposed peace-making should not materialise as planned. As regards the third and fourth Sacred Arrows from the original Cheyenne bundle, they were then among the so-named *Kitkahaki* and *Pictchaurat* Pawnee tribes, and it would be up to them to either return them to the Cheyennes or keep them as was their discretion, the Skidi could not speak for them.

Having said this, the Cheyenne emissaries having left the earth-lodge town, for several days they travelled in two separate bodies, one of Cheyennes, the other of mixed Skidi and Arickara in large number, and journeyed on amicably until, when only a short distance from the Cheyenne camp at Big Timbers, Skidi scouts out scanning for Sioux or other enemies, suddenly came running back to their column, shouting that a large Cheyenne and Arapahoe camp was up ahead. Grey-Thunder hearing this and still stripped down to breech-clout and moccasins with his entire body daubed with red pigment to signify his position as `Arrow` keeper, dismounted from his pony and instead, began walking proudly at the head of the procession.

This was the *Heviatanio* Cheyenne village led by Yellow-Wolf, Little-Moon and Medicine-Snake and whose people, of course, had already discerned the Pawnees from afar, and had actually been preparing for a fight if it should come to that. When, however, the village occupants had observed their revered holy man Grey-Thunder riding proudly at the forefront, they became overwhelmed with excitement at seeing he and his companions still alive, and supposing their tribal talismans were at last returning home, scores of Cheyenne horsemen rode out to welcome their hereditary foes now coming towards them in peace. Such was Cheyenne enthusiasm that at one stage, the affair seemed it would quickly get out of hand and a bloody melee be imminent, as some young Cheyenne bucks rode ever closer to the Pawnees, forcing the latter to jump out of the way of horse's hooves. Cheyennes then rode around and in amongst them, touching certain persons with lances and musket barrels in the act of counting coup. Of this the new arrivals were somewhat embarrassed, if not disgusted at the lack of respect given to visitors coming in peace. Big-Eagle, in fact, was on the verge of calling his men to arms, but at the crucial moment a Cheyenne whose name has been forgotten, took up his quirt and began whipping and scolding the perpetrators for their rudeness, and by so doing, drove the offenders away, thus preventing a bloody calamity occurring.

Composing themselves again, and seemingly still in good humour, the Skidi and Arickara continued on towards the village, the young Cheyennes for their part, now having spent their wild spirits. If the visitors had decided to give up their peaceful intention and had turned around to go home, then not only would they have lost face among all their enemies, but most likely, would have been attacked and wiped out by the combined Cheyenne and Arapahoe warriors who together, vastly outnumbered the new arrivals among them.

As the Skidi and Arickaras marched nearer the village, they then fired their muskets in the air to announce their peaceful intent, and it was this, as previously mentioned, which had alerted Colonel Dodge and his dragoons to the Pawnee arrival.

As the Pawnees and Cheyennes continued on, albeit now in a somewhat more frigid harmony, a Cheyenne warrior named *Buk-Sit-Su* rode up to Big-Eagle and offered to carry the bundle the Skidi chief was carrying, saying that

CHEYENNE PEACE WITH PAWNEES

he had carried it long enough and should be pleased to be relieved of his load until they reached the village. Big-Eagle was no fool. He was wary of the lone Cheyenne's intention and so declined the offer. *Buk-Sit-Su*, however, showed great persistence and after continued persuasion, finally got possession of the bundle and next instant, was wading his horse across the Arkansas River, after which he rode over the crest of a distant hill and was soon out of sight.

The Skidi chief was sorely vexed at this unexpected action. Now he was resolved that the Cheyennes would not get their hands on the other Sacred Arrows still among the Pawnees, no matter what forth-coming proposals might be offered. Meanwhile, other Cheyennes riding alongside the pedestrian Skidis, continued in their friendly attitudes towards them, even presenting Pawnee warriors with a number of short sticks to be exchanged for Cheyenne horses when at the camp.

At last the Pawnees and Arickara entered the village of their objective and upon which, Cheyennes and Arapahoe, Arickara and Skidis, embraced each other like long-lost kinfolk. After customary speeches by members of each tribe present, the visitors were fed and Big-Eagle and his head men smoked and held council with the Cheyenne chiefs. Big-Eagle laid on the ground a finely-tanned antelope hide and placed upon it the red-feathered Sacred Arrow he had carried with him all the way. In response, the Cheyennes gave each additional Skidi male other gifts of robes of elk and buffalo tanned hides, beads and trinkets of various sort, while all others among the visitors were regally feasted in several Cheyenne and Arapahoe lodges. In total, fifty guns were given by the Skidi and Arickara in exchange, while delicacies purchased by Cheyennes and Arapahoe from nearby Bent's Fort, were laid out before their guests and consumed. At the same time, Cheyenne women rearranged their tepees to form a large circle, and the warriors of all present then adorned themselves in ceremonial regalia ready to participate in forthcoming dancing, parading and singing, which they knew was to follow in celebration of the pact.

Come sundown, savage drums were throbbing; eagle-bone whistles blowing, while warriors whooped and howled as the ground within the circle of tepees seemed to tremble under the stomping of hundreds of dancing feet. One young Skidi attired only in breech-clout and moccasins, but with an otter-skin cap in the Osage fashion on his head, and because of which, the Cheyennes thereafter named him Otter-Cap, was a great favorite among those assembled.

Repeatedly he threw his tomahawk high in the air above his head and caught it by the handle whilst he himself was still in rapid movement to the fast beat of surrounding drums.

Throughout all, those then gathered together treated each other in the most congenial manner. Many warriors among each tribe present adopted children from each other, while the aforesaid dancer Otter-Cap went so far as to actually marry a Cheyenne woman, and who later gave birth to a son from the mixed tribal liaison who was named Big-Baby. This last later joined for a while the wild conglomerate of Kiowa, Comanche and Mexicans known infamously as *Comancheros*, and was still alive as late as 1914.

As regards Big-Eagle, the Skidi head chief, he was probably the greatest warrior within the Pawnee confederacy at that time and for the rest of that decade. His reputation was recognised by both enemies and friends alike, and among the Cheyennes he was particularly well-known and his personal activities against them already legendary. In his more important battles, he had always been prominent because of his fighting prowess and during the great fight with Cheyennes in 1830 when the Sacred Arrows had been captured, it had been Big-Eagle who kept the Skidi Pawnees together and repelled fanatical Cheyenne charges in their attempts to retrieve the `Arrows.` Whenever Big-Eagle was among Pawnee ranks, then the result was either a Pawnee victory or stale-mate, but rarely a defeat for the Skidi.

The Cheyennes realised this, and it played on their superstitious minds to such extent, they thought the said chief was invulnerable and one to avoid contact with unless sure of success. Indeed, after the battle when the `Arrows` were lost,` Cheyennes had come to a road that if any among them should either slay or even count coup on the Skidi chief, then he would obtain the position of honour among the Cheyennes. Such a prize was not to be scoffed at, and many warriors tried their utmost to claim the prize. As it was, only one man actually professed to having done the deed, by having thrust his lance into Big-Eagle`s buttocks during the 1830 affair. Whether this was a true declaration, no other Cheyennes appeared to show doubt, and the Cheyenne warrior involved did indeed take up an honourable position among his people, and had enjoyed such adulation for several years.

Now, however, having come among Cheyennes with the Dodge expedition five years later, and being quizzed about the affair by Cheyenne chiefs present, Big-Eagle positively denied ever being stuck at the time in question. Certainly, he said, he had never felt the prick of a Cheyenne lance-point on his rump. He went further to drop his robe and breech-clout and invited all to inspect his rear for any scar or other sign of the alleged attack. The Cheyennes could find no scar and were in confusion. Eventually, with some embarrassment, the Cheyenne chiefs apologised to Big-Eagle. They admitted their mistake and immediately stripped the pretender of his chiefly rank who himself, it is said, skulked away in shame. It must not be forgotten here the similar event associated with the Cheyenne Bear-With-Feathers [also known as Old-Bark and Ugly] who, as previously mentioned, claimed to have stolen the same Skidi chief's saddle and mule some thirteen years earlier. Quite likely this story, too, was exposed during the same discussions between Cheyennes and Big-Eagle when in council, but although the supposed deed was likewise realised to have been a fabrication, Bear-With-Feathers because he was one among those who had brought the same head chief to make peace with the Cheyennes, was not personally or severely chastised for having exaggerated his claim.

It was near the break of dawn the following day before festivities finally died down. Indeed, it had been an occasion to remember, yet none but Grey-Thunder himself was more pleased. He had achieved his long-held ambition for peace, and had obtained one of the Sacred Arrows which, hereafter, would help give his people renewed confidence and protection.

How long such a peace would suffice, however, was soon learned.

It is said that the very next day, after the Pawnee and Arickara had packed up and left the allied camp, Big-Eagle and others were not satisfied because, they supposed, the horses they had received from their hosts were comparatively small in number. Indeed, that same night of their leaving, when a sufficient distance from the Cheyenne camp, four of Big-Eagle's warriors went back to the Cheyennes this time undetected, and stole as many extra horses as they could reasonably drive before them. Their raid was successful, but obviously, the old feud was back in full swing. The peace immediately was broken and within a few months, the old feud was being conducted as violently as before. The above-mentioned Otter-Cap very soon after, abandoned his Cheyenne wife and conceived child, and returned to his own people. The

Cheyennes thus, re-opened their war with Pawnees and Arickara, although they appear to have kept peace with the Mandan and Hidatsa for a few years at least.

Having said this, during the actual period of peaceful interaction at the Cheyenne village, Colonel Doge had engaged in a congenial talk with the Cheyenne Chief Little-Moon, and was under the illusion that Cheyennes and Arapahoe were to further meet the Skidi and Arickara on Platte River that coming winter when they would conduct their buffalo hunts together. And so, Dodge thought, his expedition had been of use and soon after, he and his force prepared to leave Big Timbers and wend their way downstream to Fort Gibson and home. Before departing, he handed out a few more medals to Cheyenne and Arapahoe chiefs and head men present, and when exhausting his supply, promised to return in the near future to make up the difference.

From this time forward, Cheyennes as a united entity ceased regular hostilities against the Mandan and Hidatsa, and also, for a while at least, against the Omaha, Otto, Iowa and Osage due solely through persuaions from Colonel Dodge. But against the Arickara and the four Pawnees tribes, Cheyennes remained at logger-heads, and even before the year was out, Cheyennes met a party of horse-stealing Arickara and killed them all but one, and who alone they spared to take word to his people not to molest Cheyennes again, or more serious consequences would surely follow.

Later that year [1835] and north of Big Timbers, the same camp of combined Cheyenne and Arapahoe which had met Colonel Dodge the previous summer, were in residence along Crow Creek flowing into South Platte River. Their warriors had continued their harassment of Kiowas and Comanche to the south, and also against Crows and Shoshoni in the north.

Now it happened that a lone Cheyenne named Plenty-Crows had then gone out to hunt, and after returning to camp, set out the following morning along with his wife to retrieve meat he had bagged and cached the previous night. Plenty-Crows and his wife were both on horseback and leading a pack-mule on which to carry home the meat.

Meanwhile, during the night and unbeknown to the man and wife, a war-party of Crows had discovered the cached carcasses and realised the hunter would return to collect his kill. Sure enough this is what happened, and thus next day, the man and wife did return and began butchering the carcasses and packing the meat on the mule. Such was the large amount of meat provided, Plenty-Crows and his wife after loading the mule, also loaded the horses they had been riding, and so were on foot when deciding to leave the scene. Suddenly, the waiting Crows appeared, and in an instant, had the two Cheyennes surrounded.

Plenty-Crows levelled his musket and for a short while held off the foremost Crows by threatening to shoot first one and then another. But then the enemy all at once charged forward, and after which they killed him with arrows and musket shot, then ripped off his scalp as a trophy.

The Crow party was small, and not knowing how close was the main enemy force within the Cheyenne-Arapahoe camp from which they had intended to steal horses, they satisfied themselves with the one scalp, a Cheyenne female captive and two horses and a mule, and set off at once for their home country along Big Horn River to the northwest. Back at their home camp, the Crow leader of the war-party made the woman his new wife, although this man had two other wives already, and whenever he was away from his lodge, the two other wives abused and beat the captive woman and gave her menial and degrading tasks in order to make her suffer.

There was one, however, a Crow male around seventeen years of age who lived in the same lodge. He took pity on the Cheyenne woman and bade her make extra moccasins and prepare a quantity of dried meat and pemmican to sustain her on a long journey, for, he said, he would help her to escape from bondage as soon as opportunity arose.

The months of captivity dragged on, and it appeared that her captor suspected something was afoot. Thus it was the following spring before a suitable opportunity did arise for her escape. At the time when winter snow melted and buffalo returned to the prairie, most of the Crows went out to hunt. Only young children and old persons remained in camp, and the young man who had pledged to help the Cheyenne woman had also at first gone out with the hunters. But soon afterwards he returned to camp under the pretext that his horse had thrown him and bolted. But before this, he had tethered another horse outside the camp, and now going up to the woman in question, he told her mount the horse and ride away back towards her own country. The young Crow even gave her an additional horse so she could change mounts when one got tired

CHEYENNE PEACE WITH PAWNEES

and thus gain more speed, for if her captor and friends overtook her, she surely would be killed.

All apparently went well. Riding at a gallop all that day towards the south, the following night, she came at last to her own Cheyenne camp on the North Platte which she recognised by painted designs on some of the tepees.

The woman was welcomed back among her people, and whatever else was said of the affair, all Cheyennes agreed that the young Crow who had risked his life by organising her escape had been very brave. This event in turn, actually caused many among the Cheyennes and Arapahoe to become less severe in their current enmity towards that tribe.

- 0 - 0 - 0 - 0 - 0 - 0 - 0 - 0 - 0 - 0 -

CHEYENNE WARRIOR.

Cheyenne Warrior, White-Hawk.

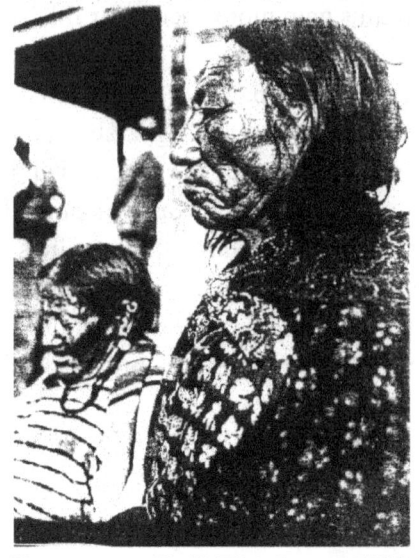
Cheyennes, Bull-Thigh and Wife.

Cheyenne Warrior, [Unidentified].

Touch-The-Clouds, Aka High-Toes.

CHEYENNE CHIEF, BRAVE-BEAR

SOUTHERN CHEYENNE, LITTLE-CHIEF.

NORTHERN CHEYENNE, LITTLE-WOLF.

SOUTHJERN CHEYENNE, PRAIRIE-CHIEF.

NORTHERN CHEYENNE.

NORTHERN CHEYENNE, TWO-MOONS.

HIGH-BACKED-WOLF 2d RAIDS PAWNEES
CHAPTER 18.

HIGH-BACKED-WOLF 2d, RAIDS PAWNEES [1836]

While it is true the aforesaid victory over a Kiowa band in early 1835, had somewhat exhilarated the Cheyennes, life itself was not always the free-wheeling carefree existence the people are often thought to have enjoyed throughout their wandering across the Plains. Due to either severe snow and cold throughout winter, or a prolonged summer drought effecting the grasslands, the people's horse herds suffered accordingly by their mortality, and which, of course, was a severe encumbrance to the people by not being mobile enough to follow the herds and transport their families along with heavy buffalo-hide tepees and belongings. It seems the previous seasons had incurred one or another of the above-mentioned climatic occurrences, and certainly, the more northern Cheyennes at this time [1836], lacked enough horses to satisfy their need. [1]

According to documented data in the guise of letters exchanged between certain white men familiar with Indian country west of the middle Missouri, elements among Cheyennes and Oglala Sioux were now temporarily at logger-heads with one another, due to stealing horses coupled with a movement of Northern Oglala west to Fort John [later Fort Laramie] on the North Platte. We have no finer details and certainly, such hostilities were regarded by the majority of those involved as trivial and unimportant in their outcome. Having said this, a continual need for horses had broken the Cheyenne-Pawnee pact of '35, and by early summer the following year, both peoples were again raiding each other's herds and taking each other's scalps.

So it was later in the year of '36, but further north among Cheyenne bands along Cheyenne River above the Platte, that under the leadership of High-Backed-Wolf 2d [delegated to the role of Sweet-Medicine-Chief after the demise of his uncle of the same name], a large body of warriors went to raid Pawnees, who in mid-summer each year, would be hunting buffalo near the headwaters of the Republican or its Smokey Hill Branch in what is now Nebraska State. Among the Cheyenne war-party at this time, was a renowned *medicine* man named Bear who was the owner of four sacred *Hok'tsim* lances,

HIGH-BACKED-WOLF 2d RAIDS PAWNEES

and with him, an up and coming Cheyenne warrior named Wolf-Pipe who himself, carried one of the aforesaid *Hok`tsim* lances as added protection.

A *Hok`tsim* Lance, was also known as a Wheel-Lance, and consisted of a three-foot long stick with a flint point at one end and carved human face at the other along with a sinew-meshed willow hoop attached half way along its length. The mesh was to enable the carved face end when directed at the foe, to blind those in front, while rendering the holder himself and all with him invisible to the enemy. No more than four *Hok`tsims* were ever in use among the Cheyennes at one time, and were closely related both in symbolism and historically with the tribe`s Sacred Arrow talismans, having likewise, been inaugurated many years before by the original Cheyenne cultural prophet, Sweet-Medicine himself.

CHEYENNE SACRED *HOK`TSIM* LANCE

In this case, the Cheyenne party was a large one, although only a few warriors were horseback and the rest on foot, as the reason for the raid was to

HIGH-BACKED-WOLF 2d RAIDS PAWNEES

capture as many horses from the Pawnees as they could. High-Backed-Wolf had previously planned that the few mounted Cheyennes should feign an attack on a Pawnee tepee hunting camp and then retreat, which by doing, would incite the Pawnee warriors to give chase and be decoyed over a nearby ridge behind which, the rest of the Cheyenne fighting force would be hidden, and thus, able to take the enemy by surprise.

Before finding where their quarry was encamped, High-Backed-Wolf dispatched eight scouts to locate the enemy village, while he and the rest of the party awaited the scout's return. However, three full days went by and still the scouts had not returned. In response, he bade the *shaman* Bear who was also a Spirit Priest, to consult the Spirits themselves inside of what was known as a Spirit Lodge, in order to ascertain the whereabouts of the scouts and what had happened to them. After entering the lodge and consulting with the spirit itself, Bear declared that the scouts were still alive, and had, in fact, gone on further, still looking for the Pawnee camp.

High-Backed-Wolf thus sent out two more warriors named Man-on-the-Hill and Hawk to search for the lost scouts, only this time, the rest of the party would follow their trail some distance behind. *

After traveling some time, the two scouts observed wolves dragging what appeared to be human limbs from a prairie hollow. Upon closer inspection, the two scouts realised the limbs were all that remained of the eight absent scouts. Around about the hollow were many tell-tale moccasin prints peculiar to Pawnee design, along with material evidence that a Pawnee hunting camp had once been sited nearby. The previous day a thick mist had enveloped the Plain, and it seemed obvious that the eight scouts had stumbled on the camp in the fog, and being too late to rectify their mistake, had been rubbed out by the foe.

Man-on-the-Hill and Hawk waited patiently where they were until the bulk of High-Backed-Wolf's party came into view. Then, positioning himself on the crest of a hill, Man-on-the-Hill raised his blanket eight times and let it drop eight times, which was to convey to the on-looking party that they had found the missing scouts, and that all were dead.

*A Spirit Lodge, this was a common sacred amenity among most Algonquin-speaking tribes, and had its origins in more ancient practices among Siberian peoples of the Old World.

HIGH-BACKED-WOLF 2d RAIDS PAWNEES

In response, High-Backed-Wolf led his warriors further downstream to the hollow in question, and there gathered up the scattered limbs and skulls of their comrades. They then buried the remains in a communal prairie hole and covered them with stones, as protection against further despoilment from scavenging animals and passing foes.

As the Cheyenne war-party continued on, now following the Pawnee trail downstream along the Smokey Hill itself, the foremost riders sighted two Pawnee men sitting atop the brow of a hill. A Cheyenne warrior named Black-Horse was first to reach one of the Pawnees and Black-Horse struck this man with his coup stick. As he did so, the other Pawnee shot Black-Horse with his musket, but other Cheyennes then came up, and surrounded the lone Pawnee before killing him and his companion. The Pawnee camp however, was pitched on the far side of the hill. Hearing the sound of gunshots and screams of the exultant Cheyennes, all Pawnee warriors in the camp came out like a swarm of angry bees. The Cheyennes later said that never before could they remember seeing so many Pawnees racing towards them, many of whom were on foot, and the Cheyennes also being on foot, were put to a hard fight to prevent themselves being overrun and slaughtered.

Slowly but surely the Cheyennes were being pushed back owing to the great number of Pawnees, and it was then that the Cheyenne Bear stood his ground ready to face the oncoming foe and attempt to delay their assault while his companions escaped. High-Backed-Wolf seeing him thus, raced his mount forward and began whipping Bear about the head and shoulders with his pony quirt which forced the latter to give up his stand, and mounting up behind High-Backed-Wolf, the two galloped away to safety. Unfortunately, Black-Horse died that night of wounds received, and the Cheyennes, notwithstanding their bravery and resistance, were finally driven back along the north bank of the Smokey Hill and away from the scene completely. Certainly, Pawnees won the day this time, and such was the despondency Cheyennes then felt, they never again camped near the area which they have since named, `Where the Eight Scouts Lay.` Even in after years when with Sioux Allies and in formidable number, Cheyennes have not broken the tradition, while the event of the subsequent battle itself is yet remembered as, *"When We Cheyennes Were Driven."*

-0-0-0-0-0-0-0-0-0-

CHEYENNES RAID KIOWAS and DEMISE OF MOUSE`S-ROAD

CHAPTER 19.

CHEYENNES RAID KIOWAS and DEMISE OF MOUSE`S-ROAD
[1837]

Throughout the hoary months of 1836 -`37, Cheyennes brooded on their misfortunes and contemplated the future. They occupied themselves with whittling and straightening of arrows, dancing, courting and recounting deeds around evening fires, until fear of fate slipped back into the sub-conscious. Then there was talk again of war-trips and of how many heads [scalps] and stolen ponies they would take come spring. Even those lamenting dead relatives ceased their wailings and self-harming acts, as new bloods among the tribe screamed their first defiance at the world. One such blood was White-Bull also known as Ice, destined to earn a deserved reputation as a great fighter and *medicine* man and one who, in later years, would fight Long-Hair Custer in 1876. [1]

Consequently, the spring of `37 saw numerous Cheyenne bucks again straining on the leash, impatient to count coup and bring honour or glory to their names. Such was the ambition of every young Cheyenne brave when the prairie grass once more grew long and thick. With ponies fit and fleet, they would endeavour to counter-act any grief or ill-luck which had dogged the Nation the previous year.

First came victory, when Cheyennes rubbed out a number of Arickara enemies and soon after this, Brule Sioux allies after an attack on a Pawnee town, returned to the Cheyennes what was thought to be one of the `Sacred Arrows,` captured by Pawnees seven years before. Such episodes of good fortune only served to encourage a warrior`s war-like endeavour.

Thus, when came the `*Moon of shedding ponies*` [April], seven snows since the Cheyenne tribal `move` against the Pawnee, and the sun now casting its face on the rolling Plains and scattered camps along the Platte, Cheyenne warriors with bellies full and ponies fit, deemed again it was time for adventure and the long-awaited game of war. Indeed, none gave thoughts of potential sorrow such a time could, and would, inevitably bring to tribal members, and many war-parties started out in one direction and another, returning at length

CHEYENNES RAID KIOWAS and DEMISE OF MOUSE'S-ROAD

with captured horses in tow and waving enemy scalps above their heads. Although some such parties did not return at all.

Indeed, it was in spring 1837, that fourteen young braves then set out from a Cheyenne village on the South Platte, intent on stealing horses from the wily Comanche or the latter's Kiowa and Kiowa-Apache allies, and, no doubt, obtain a few hanks of enemy hair thrown in for good measure.

It had started when Pushing-Ahead and Stone-Forehead visited certain lodges in the *Heviatanio* Cheyenne village, and invited warriors of the Bowstring Society to join with them and go south against the foe, then reported to be encamped along what is now Scott Creek but known to the Cheyennes as Big Sand Creek, being part of the North Fork of Red River, Texas. Twelve *Heviatanio* warriors agreed to go with Pushing-Ahead and Stone-Forehead, both of whom were to carry the pipes [i.e. lead them] and, primarily, as their raid would be for horses, they would go against the enemy on foot in order to ride stolen animals back home. At once, female relatives set about making extra moccasins for the participants, as such footwear did not take long to wear out on the trail, while at the same time, old men in camp raised up prayers to *Ma`heo*, the Great Spirit, to protect those going to war and insure their undertaking be fortunate for all.

A few days later, those in the party slipped secretly from each of their separate lodges and met up a short distance from the village, and thereafter, the fourteen braves started south. They travelled at a dog-trot throughout the daylight hours and rested at night and continued thus until nearing their objective.

On their third day out just before nightfall, they came upon a combined Kiowa-Comanche village. They decided to wait until complete darkness covered the land, then enter the village and take as many horses as possible before returning to a prearranged rendezvous a little distance along the Washita River. This the thieves did with their customary stealth and cunning, and without disturbing any of their sleeping enemies.

Indeed, whilst creeping from lodge to lodge in the interior of the camp, a Cheyenne named Angry who with Stone-Forehead [one of the pipe-carriers], was crawling on hands and knees within the camp, and lifted a Kiowa shield from its tripod outside the very door-flap of its owner's lodge. Strapping it to his back as a trophy, he continued groping around in the pitch dark looking for fine horses to steal. These same two came upon a bunch of fifty or sixty animals,

CHEYENNES RAID KIOWAS and DEMISE OF MOUSE`S-ROAD

and after each mounted a gentle horse in the herd, they led the rest of the bunch out of camp without fuss. A moment later, they were racing towards the predetermined rendezvous point driving the stolen horses before them.

Of the other Cheyenne thieves, Little-Wolf, along with Yellow-Wolf's adopted Ponca captive Walking-Coyote, had captured another, albeit much smaller bunch of horses, and they, too, managed to leave the camp undetected. Likewise, they headed for the predetermined rendezvous near the headwaters of nearby Washita River, but some distance from the first mentioned group, which, however, was a somewhat thoughtless move. Their part of the country was very flat and barren affording no cover from enemy eyes if Kiowa or Comanche should pursue the thieves. Be this as it may, four other Cheyennes including a renowned warrior named Mouse`s-Road, had together also stolen a number of horses and were traveling along the same route, although some distance behind Little-Wolf and Walking-Coyote who were far ahead in the lead.

Meanwhile, at the rendezvous site itself, Stone-Forehead and Angry were waiting patiently for the rest of the party to come in and were cursing the delay. Little-Wolf and Walking-Coyote with a few others did at length reach the rendezvous just as the sun was coming up, and Stone-Forehead, realising the danger of lingering too near the enemy village, decided to push on at once for home, lest Kiowa and Comanches having discovered their loss, were even then preparing to follow the thieves' trail.

Unanimously, the others agreed with Stone-Forehead and these seven Cheyennes in total, started off at a gallop with the two pipe-holders bringing up the rear as was customary on such occasions. Some others rode on each side of the stolen herd to keep it together, and one other was leading the way at the head of the herd setting the pace in the darkness before dawn. When the sky finally cracked wide open and the sun shone bright, each warrior took a long hard look at the animals each had stolen to distinguish their particular prizes from the others, then herded them together into one bunch in an effort to close ranks and elicit more speed. For, as Pushing-Ahead remarked,

"...We are racing the horses far too slow. The enemy will be upon us by the time the sun reaches its highest point in the sky." [2]

Come mid-day, the words of Pushing-Ahead proved prophetic. Suddenly, thirty Kiowa were spotted in the rear of the Cheyennes, coming over the horizon at great speed, and having spied the thieves, were endeavouring to overtake them.

The Cheyennes now resolved to do a brave thing in an effort to escape with the stolen herd. Stone-Forehead sent two braves forward with the stolen animals and directed them to keep on no matter what transpired. Meanwhile, Pushing-Ahead, Angry, Stone-Forehead and the others dismounted, and actually faced the oncoming enemy in a bold attempt to halt their advance. As the first enemy rode into range, one Cheyenne raised his musket to his shoulder; took steady aim and squeezed the trigger, bringing down the horse which threw its Kiowa rider from the saddle. However, before the Cheyenne could get off another shot, a second Kiowa rode up to his unhorsed companion and taking him up on the back of his own mount, rode away, thus rescuing him from the jaws of certain death. The rest of the Kiowa in this group were surprised at the Cheyennes` willingness to fight owing to the latter`s small number. For a while they merely sat their ponies wondering what tactics they should employ. The Cheyennes, though, comprising only six warriors, took full advantage of their enemies` hesitation and charged headlong towards them. In response, the Kiowa wheeled their mounts around and fled in the opposite direction. After this these particular Cheyennes saw no more enemies on their trip and finally, reached home on the South Platte which their companions, - previously sent ahead with the stolen herd - had by then already reached in safety.

At about the same time as the fracas with Stone-Forehead`s group was going on, the two Cheyennes Little-Wolf and Walking-Coyote, were riding together some distance from Stone-Forehead`s group and in another direction, although still towards their home camp on the South Platte. These two spied a second even larger force of Kiowa and Comanche in the distance, streaming across the Plain in two separate groups. But the totems of these two Cheyennes must have been watching. Apparently, the enemy had not seen them, albeit the country through which the two were traveling was also exceedingly flat and open and withal, their stolen horses were very tired having been driven at a gallop throughout the previous night and morning. They could never have hoped to out-run the fresh mounts of their pursuers and desperately, the two fugitives scanned the prairie for some means of concealment or, at least, a place from where they could make a stand.

CHEYENNES RAID KIOWAS and DEMISE OF MOUSE`S-ROAD

When little hope was left to them, they came upon a ravine like a dry wash and immediately taking the initiative, they drove their horses down into it and tied the latter`s halters together to prevent the animals wandering out of the wash and into view of the enemy. The two Cheyennes hid themselves as best they could, but also prepared themselves for combat and perhaps death, as well they knew if the enemy discovered their hastily sought refuge, it would offer the pair little protection.

Still, however, the Great Spirit continued to smile upon them and the eyes of the enemy were suddenly diverted across the open plain in yet another direction. As Little-Wolf and his companion subsequently learned, the eyes of the enemy had, in fact, been cast in the direction of a dust-cloud in the distance, got up by the Cheyenne Mouse`s-Road and three companions driving their own stolen horses some way off. The Kiowa and Comanche allies whooped their war-cries in savage excitement; beat their ponies with quirts, and brandishing twelve-foot lances above their heads, tore after Mouse`s-Road`s group at break-neck speed.

These four Cheyenne including Mouse`s-Road, who himself wore some kind of stuffed bird on his head as a totem, and seeing the large force of Kiowa and Comanche racing towards them along with the fatigue of their own mounts, all at once abandoned most of their stolen horses and urged those they were riding up a convenient knoll. They must have known at this point they would never again see the setting sun, and began preparing themselves to meet their ancestors across the Sand Hills. Dismounting on the crest of the knoll, they hastily smeared their faces and bodies with pigments; entwined eagle-feathers in their hair and began singing death-songs. Yet even before they completed their savage toilettes, the pursuing combined Kiowa-Comanche force stormed the knoll in a great fury. The four gallant Cheyennes at first stood their ground and presented a heroic defence, toppling a number of the enemy from their saddles and which event as a consequence, obliged the rest of the attackers to withdraw out of range from the barrage of arrows and other missiles the four Cheyennes sent among them.

As usual, however, the Cheyennes seem not to have contemplated such a predicament, having spent a good part of their ammunition hunting game during their three-day trek to the enemy villages. They quite soon exhausted their supply of arrows and shot, and at length, were left with only hunting knives with which to defend themselves. They thus decided to make a run for it, and each trust in his own guardian spirit to preserve him.

First they discarded their leggings and other encumbering attire so to be naked but for breech-clout and moccasins to enable them to run and fight more freely, and got ready for the dash. But such an endeavour was in vain. They never had a chance to start from the hill. The enemy saw them undressing and realising their intention they attacked a second time, now with more ferocity and vigour than before.

In a moment the Kiowa and Comanche had dropped three Cheyennes and only Mouse`s-Road remained alive. His bow had been shattered by a musket ball and he stood alone and unarmed but for his knife. He began wailing his death-song and also cried laments over the three corpses of his companions which lay about him. As he did so, a cold chill ran through him and, it is said, tears for his comrades flowed from his eyes. Now he wanted to die; killing the slayers of his friends. He would not go home, he shouted to the enemy, for he would be crying the rest of his days, and like *Achilles* crying over the death of *Patroclus* on the field of Troy, Mouse`s-Road screamed for vengeance or death so to be with his brothers in their last hunting grounds. The enemy, meanwhile, listening to his cries, were determined to satisfy his want.

A Comanche chief clad in all the regalia his rank entitled, rushed at him on horseback and thrust with his lance, but Mouse`s-Road seemed to bare a charmed life. He avoided the stroke; caught hold of the rider and pulled him off his horse, then plunged his hunting knife up to its hilt in the body of his foe several times, until the ground about was red with his victim`s blood. Savage animal instincts swept over Mouse`s-Road as his breathing became more pronounced and his body perspired profusely. He set his teeth wide as the warm blood of his victim congealed over his torso and legs.

Several times, one or more of the enemy would urge their ponies up the knoll in an attempt to get at the Cheyenne, but Mouse`s-road who was a fast runner, would run towards them and so fast, that although each charging enemy turned his mount around to race back down the hill, Mouse`s-Road almost caught up with them before they escaped. When Mouse`s-Road ran towards one or more of his on-coming foes, the dead bird on his head seemed to be fluttering its wings and looked as though it had unattached itself from the Cheyenne and it too, was flying on its own volition towards the foe.

CHEYENNES RAID KIOWAS and DEMISE OF MOUSE`S-ROAD

During all this time his prostrate opponent`s horse had remained still. It now began trotting slowly back to where its dead Comanche master lay within easy reach of the Cheyenne. But Mouse`s-Road had tasted blood and death was with him like a brother and held no fear for him now. Instead of mounting the waiting horse, Mouse`s-Road beat the grazing animal on the rump with the flat of his knife, which caused it to take off and return to the Kiowa and Comanche lines, whose number had since swollen to one-hundred warriors and more, and by then, completely surrounded the lone Cheyenne. Yet even this did not deter Mouse`s-Road from his objective. Showing contempt for the enemy, he signed to them,

"Come on and kill me." [3]

It was then that a Kiowa chief named Lone-Wolf arrived on the scene in company with a Mexican captive named Cuts-With-Knife riding to one side a little way off. Lone-Wolf boasted to those looking on how he alone was going to kill the Cheyenne and for all to witness his deed. But events would prove that this lone Kiowa was ill-fated from the start.

Lone-Wolf`s Mexican captive who probably was unarmed but for a knife, suddenly went charging horseback at the lone Cheyenne, whipping his steed frantically as he did so in an attempt to run his quarry down and trample him under hoof. But Mouse`s-Road remained unnerved and actually ran forward to meet the Mexican which gave the latter no confidence, and the captive could merely bump his horse against the Cheyenne not getting close enough to stab him. Meanwhile other Kiowa and Comanche called out to the Mexican to leave the lone Cheyenne alone, as he was too dangerous an opponent for the Mexican to face with no gun or bow and arrow. They cried to him to let the Cheyenne escape and take news home to his people what had happened to his comrades. But Mouse`s-Road, however, by dodging the flying hooves, managed to wrench his Mexican adversary from the saddle and set about stabbing him repeatedly in every part of the body. Lone-Wolf, seeing the plight of his companion, dismounted and ran towards the Cheyenne with lance raised above his head in both hands to deliver a blow of great force and drive the lance-point right through his opponent. Seeing the Kiowa thus, Mouse`s-Road threw the severely injured Mexican to one side, now that his body was no longer responding to his knife thrusts, and turned to face his new attacker. A moment later, Lone-Wolf was upon him, yet with the agility of a cat, Mouse`s-Road eluded the lance, in

CHEYENNES RAID KIOWAS and DEMISE OF MOUSE`S-ROAD

fact ran under it as the Kiowa brought the weapon down with terrible vengeance nearly toppling him off his feet, such was the force of the thrust which sliced only air. He did not have a second chance.

KIOWA CHIEF, LONE-WOLF

Mouse`s-Road caught hold of Lone-Wolf by the left shoulder and held him fast for an instant, whilst with all his might, he dealt the Kiowa a savage blow on the hip with his knife, hearing the bone splintering as thick blood spurted over him and ran down his legs. In unimagined pain, Lone-Wolf simply turned to flee the Cheyenne`s wrath, but Mouse`s-Road caught hold of his contestant`s flowing hair entwined with large Spanish silver discs, and with great fury while screaming his war-cry, he struck Lone-Wolf in the back with all the force he could muster. Luckily for Lone-Wolf, the Cheyenne`s blade clanged and broke clean in two as it struck one of the silver ornaments, leaving only two or three inches left of the blade. But for this, the lone Kiowa most certainly would have died there and then. The *medicine* of Lone-Wolf was indeed strong that day to have spared him certain death, but the *medicine* of brave Mouse's-Road for the moment, was even stronger.

Still holding the Kowa Lone-Wolf by the hair and blinded with rage, Mouse's-Road began hacking at and slashing his opponent wherever there was an opening, and Lone-Wolf danced, jumped and screamed for help with every blow struck by the merciless Cheyenne with the incompatible name of Mouse's-Road.

Such was fear and dismay now gripping the surrounding enemy that none among them at first offered to help, and at length, Lone-Wolf sank to the ground shamming death, when to all intents and purpose he should have been dead, baring wounds which would scar him for life.

It was only after the watching Kiowa and Comanche saw Lone-Wolf fall, that a single Comanche of some high-standing carrying a lance and bow and arrows, rode forward on a magnificent mare to join in combat with the lone devil of a Cheyenne, but who, seeing his third adversary charging towards him, picked up the discarded lance of Lone-Wolf, and still on foot, actually ran to meet his next contestant. The oncoming Comanche was full of self-confidence and sure of success having the advantage being on horseback. He aimed his lance and thrust, but even his own guardian spirit was powerless against Mouse's-Road, who parried aside the thrust and with the lance he himself was holding, lunged with it at his enemy who he caught fully in the bowels, and in doing, lifted his assailant high out of the saddle with his body pivoting on the lance-point. As the Comanche thudded to the ground, momentum wrenched the lance from the Cheyenne's grip, and there the Comanche lay soaking the ground about him red and withal, twelve-foot of be-feathered lance quivering upright in his corpse.

After this, no one else among the enemy rode out to battle with Mouse's-Road. Here was a man who had brought down four enemy champions by himself and remained unwounded throughout, and yet, was still crying for blood. He had avenged his three comrades, but now fate would even up the odds and finish the job.

The indomitable Mouse's-Road next mounted the fallen Comanche's fine mare; took up the lance of his last victim and without hesitation, trotted towards the enemy, again singing loud his personal death-song. The majority of milling Kiowa and Comanche seeing this, began to withdraw a little to keep distance between themselves and the lone Cheyenne, and some made signs to him for a second time to take the horse he was riding which happened to be prized among them, even offering a saddle for his comfort, and go home to tell his people of his deeds. But Mouse`s-Road had come too far to go back now. Still his one intent was to drench the prairie red where his brothers-in-arms lay close to the blooded corpses of his enemies, albeit mingled with his own. Here the sun shone bright and warm, the sky clear and blue and the sacred beings of the *TsisTsisTsas* were with him, calling him to join them. It was, he thought, a good day to die and he signed once more to the enemy, *"Come on and kill me."*

So saying, he kicked his heels into his pony`s flanks and charged headlong at the foe, who without further ado, whipped up their own mounts and fled. In response to the enemy`s timidity, Mouse`s-Road now pulled the dead bird totem from his head; showed it to the enemy with an out-stretched hand, then actually threw it to the ground. This was done as an act of contempt for his foes by indicating that even without his own protective *medicine*, they dare not come near him, and hereafter, Mouse`s-Road began collecting together the prone corpses of his three comrades and then again, stood motionless in a defiant stance waiting for the Kiowa and Comanche to kill him, but who still remained mounted at the base of the hill, contemplating what else they should do. But alas, the star of Mouse`s-Road was already dimmed. It was indeed time to join his stiff and lifeless brothers, whose spirits were waiting patiently for him to join them in the hereafter of his ancestors.

Two Kiowas, both of whom carried muskets and only recently had ridden up to their fellows and not witnessed the lone Cheyenne`s performance, held their steeds back from those slowly retreating from the field, and were in-between them and the lone Cheyenne. The pair dismounted, and both adopting kneeling positions, levelled their pieces at the lone avenger while calmly awaiting him to draw close. So close, it is said, they could see his dark eyes flashing set in a mask of blood and simultaneously they fired their guns. But so ferocious did their quarry look that fear took hold of the two and marred their aim. Even at such close quarters only one musket ball found its mark, and that in the Cheyenne`s thigh which caused him to topple from his horse.

CHEYENNES RAID KIOWAS and DEMISE OF MOUSE`S-ROAD

The advent of Mouse`s-Road falling to the ground, caused the retreating Kiowa and Comanche to halt their steeds and turn around. Now, being filled with renewed confidence, they sauntered slowly back to where the Cheyenne lay, but Mouse`s-Road was not finished yet.

He sat upright on the ground with legs outstretched, still prepared to defend himself with the captured Kiowa lance, knowing full-well that this would be the end, but hoping he could take one or more extra victims among the enemy to keep him company along the long dark road of no return. Even in such a plight, the enemy still dare not go too near and could only wonder at his bravery.

At length, another Kiowa or Comanche warrior also carrying a musket, crept stealthily around the injured Cheyenne, and taking more careful aim, shot the lone Cheyenne in the back. The head and torso of the great Mouse`s-Road were propelled forward with the impact, and caused him to roll sideways and then lay quite still.

For several moments there was complete silence surrounding the scene. After a while, when the enemy were assured there was no longer need for caution, many Kiowa and Comanche rushed upon the prostrate body and cut the Cheyenne`s head off.

As they did so, the body of Mouse`s-Road suddenly sat upright, still holding the captured lance in both hands as if about to defend himself again, and this gave the antagonists such a fright, they jumped on their horses like fleas to a dog, and scattered in every direction. They lamented aloud they must have slain a great *medicine* man or even a sacred being, and that its ghost would surely come back to haunt them. When word of what had occurred reached the combined Kiowa and Comanche village, the entire population also fled, and in such hast, many of their lodges were left standing and belongings abandoned across the prairie in their panicked flight.

Yet Mouse`s-Road, at last, was truly dead. He had been so in a sense since his three companions had fallen by his side. The Cheyennes remember him to this day, and the Kiowa and Comanche recall that Mouse`s-Road was the bravest warrior they ever met.

Meanwhile, the two Cheyennes Little-Wolf and Walking-Coyote; ignorant of what had been going on, continued hiding in the washout and wondering why the enemy had suddenly raced off in another direction. Even if

CHEYENNES RAID KIOWAS and DEMISE OF MOUSE`S-ROAD

they supposed the Kiowa and Comanche had discovered other members of the original Cheyenne party, they still had no idea as to their fate and come nightfall, the two warriors crept from concealment and on foot started for home. They had earlier abandoned the rest of their stolen horses as being too big a risk in disclosing their hideout, and which they had done as soon as opportunity arose without jeopardising their safety.

Consequently, no one among the Cheyennes knew until sometime after the event what had happened to Mouse`s-Road and his three companions, although a few weeks following the remainder of the war-party`s safe return to its own camp on the South Platte, it was taken for granted that the Mouse`s-Road group must have been overtaken and killed. Indeed, it was three years later before Cheyennes learned the full story of the latter`s demise when finally, they met at a peace-making council with Kiowas and Comanche on the flats close to Bent`s Fort on the Arkansas in 1840.

At first, the Cheyennes as a whole had not mourned the non-return of Mouse`s-Road and his companions. Without tangible proof of their demise, it was considered very bad luck to think the worst while not knowing proper facts. Neither was any retaliation contemplated, as such war-parties were constantly going out and loss among some of their number was a common hazard they undertook. It was, of course, well-known that complete success could not be forthcoming every time, and in all fairness to their enemies, the Cheyennes accepted the ordeal of Mouse`s-Road`s group as simply bad luck. This is not to say that the affair was soon forgotten. On the contrary, when word was finally brought them of Mouse`s-Road and his companion`s demise, relatives and widows of those who had not returned grieved for their departed kinfolk in the traditional manner, and begged one and another of the tribe`s Soldier-Societies to avenge their loss.

-0-0-0-0-0-0-0-0-0-0-

CHEYENNE, RED-BLANKET.

FORTY-EIGHT CHEYENNE BOWSTRINGS WIPED OUT

CHAPTER 20.

FORTY-EIGHT CHEYENNE BOWSTRINGS WIPED OUT [1837].

That summer of '37, Cheyennes held their Sun-Dance or Medicine-Lodge ceremonies at the same time as the Arapahoe. Both peoples were encamped close by each other and participated in each other's rites. Indeed, as if by some magnetic force, all the scattered bands of Cheyenne had come together in a large circle of lodges several ranks deep, it's entrance facing east towards the rising sun. Both Northern and Southern *TsisTsisTsas* along with all their dogs and people were gathered together as one. The Plains about were a patch-work of brown, white, black and grey caused by thousands of milling ponies, while dogs more savage than their Human masters, yelped and scurried in and out among hundreds of buffalo hide lodges outside of which, came forth rich aromas of bison and antelope boiling in large copper cauldrons attached to wooden tripods. The days were hot and long. It was the time for young braves to show their prowess, and for *'swinging at the pole.*'[1]

In due course, after three days of singing and praying and the solemn ritual of raising the centre pole of the Sun-Dance lodge itself, certain tribesmen underwent the self-torture procedure to obtain guarantees from the Great *Ma'heo* for good fortune to attend themselves and all creation, and also, to prove their own manhood amongst the people. A holy man would cut two slits in the breasts of voluntary recipients, and threading hide cords through them, would attach the loose ends to the top of the sacred centre-pole of the Sun-Dance arbour. Each young brave thus attached with heads turned towards the burning sun, would then dance forwards and backwards pulling against the thongs. The cords would grow taught in the blazing sun until, at length, perhaps after five or six hours of pain [if the participant's suffering was short] the flesh was literally ripped away from the slits with a singular 'smacking' sound, and the tormented body propelled backwards to lie flat on its back semi-conscious in the dirt.

In such an unconscious and prostrate state, the 'dancer' or 'swinger,' would be carried by friends to a lodge where his wounds were treated with curing herbs until regaining his faculties. While, however, in an unconscious

FORTY-EIGHT CHEYENNE BOWSTRINGS WIPED OUT

state, it was customary for the young man to receive some kind of vision or portent of a future happening, and also, of course, the respect of the people for undertaking such an arduous and painful ordeal in the first place. In a short time the recipient's body would completely heal, and only two small scars be left on the chest to show his participation. Such scars would thereafter, make him a welcome member of any war-party and an honoured suitor for a tribesman's daughter.

Now it happened at this time, there had been a killing in the Cheyenne camp due to an internal argument, and the tribe's Sacred Medicine Arrows – having supposedly been soiled by such a deed, – were in need of purification by the enactment of a four-day ritual known as "Renewing the Arrows." If any war-party started out before the renewal ceremony was completed, bad luck would most certainly befall its members and who, it was believed, would surely meet disaster. Additionally, if a war-party was still out during the actual 'renewal,' the sacred powers transmitted through the 'Arrows' would be lost and nullified, while any outside encroachment by un-ordained persons but the Arrow priests themselves, or irreverence concerning taboos connected to them, then likewise, power emanating through the 'Sacred Arrows' would also become nullified and lost.

Such a four-day time was trying for young bucks lazing around the village in boredom while the renewal rituals were performed. And so it was, a group of Cheyenne young hot-heads of the Bowstring Warrior Society decided to undertake a horse-stealing expedition against the Kiowa or Comanche, and declared that the non-return of Mouse's-Road was a good excuse to go to war. Thus, the said braves began preparing themselves for a war-trip south.

Before starting out, several Bowstring men requested the Arrow Priest Grey-Thunder to renew the 'Arrows' immediately. But this the latter declined to do, saying the time was not yet propitious as the Arapahoe were then holding their own Sun-Dance ceremonies and *swinging at the pole.* Hearing this, the young bucks began beating and lashing Grey-Thunder with their pony-quirts until he agreed to perform the 'Arrow' rites at once. Grey-Thunder was then in his mid-seventies and, of course, could not endure a severe beating. The soldiers, however, were their own masters and their particular society was known for being impetuous and sometimes reckless. Truly, one old man was powerless against them when their minds were determined to take the road they had decided. Apparently, they paid no heed regarding the great deed performed by Grey-Thunder only a few years before when he had retrieved one of the Sacred Arrows from the Pawnee, and of the ultra-high position he since held within the tribe. Be this as it may, one must remember that the `Arrows` capture in 1830 had for some, shattered a once firm belief in Cheyenne community religion of which the `Arrows` were a central part. What power the `Arrows` now, some Cheyennes thought, when such revered tribal talismans had been in the hands of the enemy who themselves, must have abused and denigrated the powers emanating from them.

Meanwhile, during the Arapahoe Sun-Dances then going on, a number of Arapahoe were also contemplating a war-party in answer to a dancing participant's request, but were soon dissuaded from their resolve by the timely prophecy of another. This man after also dancing and collapsing at the pole, blurted out to those around him that he likewise had received a vision whilst in his unconscious state, and told those looking on,

> "I saw many heads coming into camp from all directions, but they were not the heads of our enemies…There was not a place in this Medicine Lodge from which blood did not flow." [2]

He then addressed the Cheyenne Bowstring warriors specifically, imploring them not to take their intended journey south, for disaster would overtake them all. As it was, the Arapahoe party heeded the dancer's words, but the Bowstrings remained adamant in their undertaking. They showered scorn upon those who hesitated to go to war, and laughed at the superstitions of their people.

One Cheyenne named Hollow-Hip, being an influential brave among the Bowstrings, called on his young comrades to disregard the Arapahoe's warnings, and urged them still to join the proposed war-party of he and his companion Bear-Above against the Kiowa and Comanche. Hollow-Hip retorted them saying,

> "It is not good for a man to grow old…It is not good that his hair turns as white the snows of many winters…It is the time of deciding, whether to sit in our lodges and listen to other men's

brave tales, or become rich in stolen ponies and scalps or, perhaps, be glorified in honourable death...A warrior becomes so only when the blood of his enemies drench him...How can one earn honour when he adheres to woman's talk...If it be our fate this road we are to travel be our last, then let our forefathers prepare to meet us, for we will be decked in glory and not ashamed to meet our brothers who will greet us with many praises...Tarry not...In a few moons hence buffalo will be gone and enthusiasm for war vanished with the sun...The snows will cause a man and beast to seek shelter from the world, to shiver on an empty belly and maybe die of a devil's sickness...What honour in this....A man can die but once...Now who will cry with me over dear Mouse's-Road and his companions slain by the enemy, and dip their lance-points in the blood of those that slew them." [3]

Such stirring words sank deep into the hearts and minds of the young hot-heads, and as soon as the Arapahoe Sun-Dance was over and the different bands of both tribes wandered off in their respective factions to go their separate ways, Cheyenne warriors in small groups of three or four, started slipping away on foot with one objective in mind, being that of stealing horses and taking scalps from one or the other of their southern foes.

Still Grey-Thunder cried warnings to them incessantly, saying that because the sanctity of the `Arrows` had now been vilified by the whipping of their keeper, all power which the `Arrows` invoked would not go with them on the war-path. But his words continued to fall on covered ears.

For their part, Hollow-Hip and Bear-Above at first succeeded in recruiting only a small party and which, without further ado, started south. Having gone only a little way from the site of the disbanded Sun-Dance camp, Hollow-Hip discovered the trails of other small parties also heading south and on foot, and following one of the trails, they found that every so often it became merged with another small trail and then continued on. When at length Hollow-Hip and Bear-Above did catch up with the ever-broader trail, all the warriors heading south were joined together, and in total, they numbered forty-five braves and three young servants, constituting around half the entire number of Bowstring Society members at that time. Included among them were three brothers, whose words always seemed to have much influence over their younger followers. Also among the Bowstrings were four ceremonial staff-carriers, each of whom carrying a be-feathered lance commonly known as a 'banner lance,' had their faces painted red, while wearing deer-hide and bead-decorated war-shirts in recognition of their society order. As regards the entire party, there was not one horse among them.

At length, a council of war was held, during which it was suggested they should let Hollow-Hip and Bear-Above carry the pipes as leaders of the foray, and all having agreed, together they continued south and crossed the Arkansas before following the course of Red River downstream towards a tributary of the latter now known as Scott Creek, and near where, so it had previously been reported, Kiowa and Comanche lodges could be found.

During their trek south, however, such a large number of warriors made it difficult to catch enough game to satisfy the party's needs, and many members soon shot away most of their arrows in their hunting pursuits. Nevertheless, they thought, if all went well they might not need too much ammunition, if that is, they kept far enough ahead of the enemy once they had stolen enough ponies to make their trip worthwhile. Thus they continued on, and coming at last to a narrow ravine near what they thought was a Kiowa camp, the Bowstrings used the ravine as a place of concealment and where they set up their war-camp. *

Here they built a low breastwork of stones facing one edge of the ravine, and at each end, raised a pile of brush and branches covered with buffalo robes to block potential entrance points each end of the party's position.

Having done this, Hollow-Hip and Bear-Above dispatched two scouts to go towards where the enemy camp was thought to be, in order to reconnoitre the camp and surrounding country before attempting their raid on the camp herd itself.

* **In another account from the Kiowa, it is said the Cheyenne lance-carriers were 'Contrary Warriors,' each sporting a sacred 'Thunder Bow Lance' which, supposedly, protected them from thunder itself. There were, however, ever only four such warriors among the Cheyenne at any one time. They were also known as suicide warriors, and it is highly unlikely that all would have been included during the trip in question.**

FORTY-EIGHT CHEYENNE BOWSTRINGS WIPED OUT

Now it happened to be the time the Kiowa themselves were about to undergo their own Sun-Dance ceremonies, and had invited their Kiowa-Apache allies along with a Comanche band and even a group of then still friendly Southern Arapahoe to join them. Thus, a great enemy encampment was in close vicinity to the Bowstring Cheyennes, who as yet were ignorant of that fact. Meanwhile, around the lodges in the combined enemy camp, many among the men-folk were fasting or praying, and elsewhere, life was idle and typical as women cooked, children played and old men sat in the morning sunshine engaged in the straightening and feathering arrows along with various other chores.

It was around day-break the following morning when something happened, and which the Cheyennes must already have contemplated due to their erection of their barricade. A Kiowa brave preparing to go out to hunt, spotted two heads peering over the crest of a nearby hill overlooking the enemy camp below.

Thinking the two persons would be deer-hunters like himself, he mounted his pony and casually rode out from the village to meet them. That he might have suspected them as enemy spies is unlikely, for he continued towards the two without concern for his own safety. The two scouts, however, both carrying muskets, could not risk the Kiowa hunter raising the alarm that enemies were close by, and so each levelled their pieces at him and fired. Their aim was somewhat wild and succeeded in only wounding both man and horse, causing the animal to tumble head over hooves throwing its rider in the process.

At once the two Cheyenne scouts rushed on foot down the hillside in an effort to kill the man before recovering from his fall, but they were too late. The Kiowa's horse got up and as if part of the animal, the Kiowa quickly remounted and raced back to his own people shouting that Cheyennes were in the vicinity, and of his own miraculous escape from death.

The Comanche version of the event states in addition, that a lone Comanche hunter on horseback spied two Cheyennes in the distance ascending a sand hill. The Comanche rode over to them and stopped his pony within hearing distance while he asked then in signs who they were. One of the two answered they were Cheyennes and had come to fight the Kiowa and Comanche to avenge past grievances against their people. This Cheyenne then shot off his musket at the Comanche, while the Cheyenne's companion fired an arrow at

FORTY-EIGHT CHEYENNE BOWSTRINGS WIPED OUT

him. In the event, the Comanche's horse was wounded, but before the Cheyenne with the gun could reload his piece and the other put another arrow to his bow, the Comanche had turned his mount around and was racing it as best he could back to the camp he had left. *

Whatever the case, some others in the combined Kiowa, Comanche, and Kiowa-Apache camp had heard the distant gun-shot, and occupants of the three villages were already in uproar that enemies should venture so near a large confederation of warriors and attempt what the Kiowa regarded an audacious coup in broad daylight. Such bold action thought the vain Kiowa warriors, showed little respect for the latter's prowess as fighters, albeit Kiowas had often proved their worth in many past conflicts against their foes. In another moment, hundreds of warriors from the combined camps were fanning out all over the prairie on horseback in search of the two Cheyennes, and directing the search was a famous Kiowa war-chief named Satank, but in English, better known as Sitting-Bear.

The Allied warriors were spread out in several groups looking for the Cheyennes. But for all their endeavours, the enemy position could not be found. Before Mid-day, all but one of the allied groups had given up the search and were returning back to their lodges. Only a Kiowa group led by Satank refused to abandon the search, and Satank himself was most persuasive in his resolve.

By this time, the grass was starting sharply and all trails of pedestrians were soon lost to view. Aimlessly, Satank and his braves continued to roam the area without avail, when suddenly, a small group of Cheyennes probably out hunting away from their breastworks, were detected running across the plain bobbing up and down in the long grass ahead. A great cry went up from among the Kiowa searchers, and a score of warriors whipped up their ponies and bulldozed their way through the thick undergrowth to reach their quarry.

* **James Mooney in *"The Kiowa Calendar,"* stated from Kiowa information, that the latter's camp was actually on a small tributary of Scott Creek, on the Upper branches of the North Fork of Red River in the panhandle of what is now Texas. This is most likely, as the Kiowa camp in question was a Sun-Dance camp, and such gatherings were often held at that point.**

FORTY-EIGHT CHEYENNE BOWSTRINGS WIPED OUT

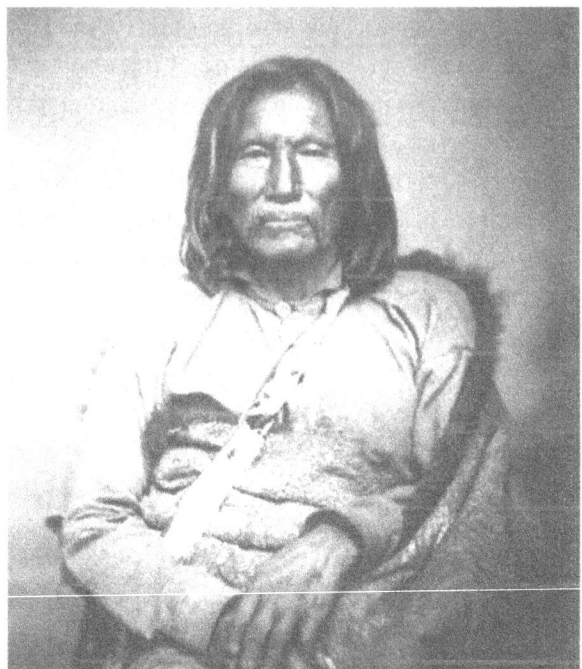

KIOWA CHIEF *SATANK* [i.e, SITTING-BEAR.]

The Cheyennes did not have a chance. Without much ado three of their number were immediately run down and killed, the remainder being hotly pursued across the plain. These few were quickly lost to view in the undergrowth of the rolling landscape and, in fact, managed to reach the breastwork and their entrenched comrades unharmed and unseen.

In response, the searchers split into small groups of twos and threes, and in frustration, spread out even further so they dotted the grassland like so many grazing buffalo. Meanwhile, the remainder of the Bowstrings now all together, continued to hide in the ravine behind their low breastwork and trusted in their individual totems to preserve them. Surprisingly, the pipe-holders Hollow-Hip and Bear-Above were not much perturbed. Each of their comrades carried guns and, it was thought, if they could keep the enemy at bay for long enough and inflict casualties upon them, the enemy would surely give up the fight and the Cheyennes be allowed to return home safely. The three Bowstring brothers previously mentioned, however, were well-versed in game of war. They were

FORTY-EIGHT CHEYENNE BOWSTRINGS WIPED OUT

wise regarding the inevitable outcome of such a predicament they were now in, and quickly, prepared themselves for death.

Very soon more and more of the enemy came upon the scene, some on horseback, many on foot, running over the grassland like so many ants. But still they could not find where the luckless Cheyennes were hiding. Again, after fruitless searching, many of the latter gave up looking and began sauntering back towards their lodges. Satank the Kiowa chief and his group, likewise seemed to lose heart and they too, contemplated abandoning the search completely. The watching Bowstrings seeing many of the enemy departing, breathed a little lighter for their fortune, although it is doubtful they would have given up their original idea of stealing horses from the enemy camps, only to be horse-whipped and ridiculed by the people if they returned empty-handed. Therefore, they decided they would still attempt to raid the enemy's herds and scalp a few village occupants in the event.

Be this as it may, it was as Satank and his Kiowa contingent were actually returning to the combined villages, that an adopted Mexican captive among them, discerned the faint outline of a stone breastwork thrown up by the Cheyennes atop the ravine, and signalled his find to his comrades.

Upon hearing the cries and observing the gesticulations of the Mexican in proclaiming his discovery, the concealed Cheyennes knew at once their game was up. One of their number rose up from concealment and all at once, flashed a mirror towards the enemy in order to attract their attention. He then signalled to them with his blanket by whirling it around above his head as a sign to the waiting Kiowa to 'come forward and fight, for they themselves were not afraid and had been waiting for them.

This, of course, was a quick manoeuvre on part of the Cheyenne pipe-holders to save face as it were, knowing full-well that their whole party was then already as good as dead when the Mexican had first sighted them. The pipe-holder in question waving the blanket above his head and shouting to the enemy was probably Hollow-Hip himself, as it would have been his obligation as leader of the party to offer the lives of his followers to the enemy after he himself had been slain, and, of course, to claim credit for first challenging the enemy on the Cheyenne's own accord. It was, however in response to the actions of the Bowstring chiefs, that the rest of the Kiowa, Comanche and Kiowa-Apache, raced back to where Satank and his whooping comrades were

FORTY-EIGHT CHEYENNE BOWSTRINGS WIPED OUT

positioned so to be in on the kill, and in their hundreds, they surrounded the ravine and the Bowstring barricade.

KIOWA CALENDAR DRAWING FOR 1837, "WHEN CHEYENNES WERE MASSACRED." [The Se'tan Calendar]
[The man figure below in the pictogram, represents a war-bonneted Cheyenne]

They raced their ponies along each side of the ravine, their horse's hooves kicking up clouds of dust and clods of earth which showered the entrenched Cheyennes incessantly. They also screamed excitedly for Cheyenne hair as they rode by, shooting off guns and sending a barrage of arrows among the defenders so there was not a place behind the rock wall where one could take appropriate cover to stage a satisfactory defence.

The Cheyennes were in a very precarious position, and one or another of the three aforesaid Cheyenne brothers told the doomed warriors that if any among them tried to escape rather than meet an honourable death, then the brothers would shoot them themselves. Indeed, in order to show the enemy their defiance and bravery, the entrenched Bowstrings began singing their Society war-songs and these, after the battle was done, were incorporated by the Kiowa and Comanche victors among themselves, and became part of Kiowa Gourd

FORTY-EIGHT CHEYENNE BOWSTRINGS WIPED OUT

Society songs and those connected to the Horse-Dance among the Comanche, but each of which was adopted from these original Cheyenne Bowstring songs.

"CEREMONIAL LANCE CAPTURED BY KIOWAS, 1837."
[From; `A Chronicle of the Kiowa Imdians.` by R.H. Lowie.]

It was not long after this that one after another among the Bowstring warriors began falling to enemy missiles from either gun, bow or lance-thrust, causing several among the defenders to suffer severe wounds or be killed outright by the enemy.

Now and then, one among the attacking force eager to count coup would charge at the breastwork head on, and singularly meet with one or more Cheyenne defender, but only to suffer nigh-instant death himself. Such among the enemy were few, and the majority proved more wary opponents, but of those incapacitated or killed by Cheyenne missiles, it made little impression on the allied ranks. In their defence, the besieged managed to shoot five horses of the enemy, but after which, most of the latter dismounted and continued the fight on foot. One among the Kiowa had a large lump or goitre on his neck and charged the breastworks on foot. A defending Bowstring took steady aim at this man and brought him down, having shot him in the very same area of the goitre and laid him low. But throughout this time slowly but surely, ammunition for the guns of the Bowstrings was running out.

FORTY-EIGHT CHEYENNE BOWSTRINGS WIPED OUT

Another, a young Kiowa who was the son of a renown chief named Black-Horse, was killed instantly when separately, the four Bowstring staff-carriers previously mentioned, each took a stand in front of the breastworks. Standing alone with society staffs before them, each individualy was overwhelmed by the enemy and slain. The first of the Cheyenne staff-carriers to do so wore a magnificent eagle-feathered war-bonnet which trailed majestically down his back. He had stepped out from behind the wall of stones and pinned the trailer of a long red-coloured sash tied around his waist to the ground with his be-feathered staff which had a lance point at one end. Such a red sash was commonly known as a 'dog-rope,' and there he stood, alone and singing his death-song, until he fell mortally injured on the very spot made bloody by his many wounds.

When he fell, a second Bowstring staff-carrier took his place and the act was repeated time and again until all four staff-carriers were laid low. Some other Cheyennes then followed suit, one after the other, they, too, sacrificing their lives against the enemy in front of the breastworks, some with weapons; some with only hunting knives, and each was shot down from a distance either by arrows or musket balls, then ingloriously trampled under-hoof by the mounts of their enemies. Among these last were the same three brothers who previously, had prevented other Cheyennes from fleeing the ravine.

At length, the few Bowstrings left and still crouching behind the defences, had shot away most of their ammunition and only a single musket shot sounded sporadically from their position.

An old man among the Kiowa told one of his sons that the way to become a great man among his people and earn chieftainship, was to deny his fear and attack the entrenched enemy head on. Other Kiowa warriors close by began urging the son to do just that, and finally, the latter did charge the enemy, on foot and head on. He succeeded in lancing a Cheyenne through before he himself received a musket ball in the heart and was killed. The father of the demised son was then overcome with grief. He himself was determined to also assault the enemy alone, and only because his fellow Kiowas restrained him from doing so, he was not killed that day.

There was another, a particularly brave Comanche armed with a lance who was known by the name of Sorrel-Robe. He alone, it is said, rode his mount up to the very breastwork repeatedly, and by stabbing with his weapon down into the ravine, managed to slay or severely injure four Cheyennes. Yet another Comanche dare-devil armed only with a knife, was tussling a lone Cheyenne outside the breastworks who likewise, was armed with a knife. In the event, the Cheyenne stabbed his opponent with such force his blade broke in two, and the Comanche managed to escape back down the hill to his watching comrades to live and fight another day. And then a third Kiowa named Old-Man-Thunder wearing a kind of white sheet tied about his neck and flowing behind him down his back while carrying a lance with an elk-horn as a blade, also ran on foot towards the breastwork. He zig-zagged his way to mar his enemys` aim, but stopped before reaching his objective. Then he ran towards the enemy again and stopped, and this he did four times. After the fourth time when he stopped, a host of Kiowa and Comanche came up behind him and together, with Old-Man-Thunder at their head, they charged towards the ravine and the remaining Cheyennes. In this action even more defenders were killed or seriously maimed, but Old-Man-Thunder was not even wounded, although the white sheet he wore was found later to be riddled with holes made by musket balls shot by the remaining Bowstrings.

At length, however, come mid-afternoon, only one Cheyenne remained alive behind the breastwork.

There was a Comanche crouching outside the defensive wall, and this man carried a yellow-painted shield. From his position, he moved the shield back and forth and up and down and sometimes in a circular motion, in order to draw Cheyenne gun-fire upon him. Whilst so-doing, a Comanche comrade ran past him followed by many Kiowa and Comanche racing on foot right up to the breastwork. Needless to say, they overwhelmed the last of any still-defending Bowstrings, then all jumped into the ravine itself and stood around examining their gory work. They discovered on the last Cheyenne to fall, that tied in his hair was an item symbolising a dragonfly which the Comanche and others recognised as a powerful sacred motif among them. Because of this, it is said, the Comanche were afraid of this dead man, and this being so, they cut him up into pieces so he could not harm them further. The rest of the Cheyenne bodies were dragged out of ravine and laid outside the breastwork in a long row, and there the allied victors left them, open to the sky for the beasts of the prairie and wild fowl of the air.

FORTY-EIGHT CHEYENNE BOWSTRINGS WIPED OUT

Some of the Bowstring corpses were actually tangled up in their dead positions with one and another Kiowa or Comanche corpse with whom they had been fighting and thus, became inter-locked during the last moments of their hand to hand struggles. Indeed, such corpses had to be separated from each other before the dead Cheyennes could be moved.

Yet another dead Bowstring was found lying strangled with a horse-hair lariat tied around his neck, either having taken his own life, or strangled by a comrade to prevent him falling into the hands of the enemy. Forty-eight Cheyenne scalps, according to Kiowa accounts, were then either tied to the end of gun barrels and lance-points belonging to the victors, or whirled above their heads splattering blood and fleshy pellets upon themselves and on those looking on.

The Kiowa and their allies were ecstatic over their victory. All Cheyenne Bowstring warriors lay dead both without and behind the breastworks, some in bunches of two, three or four, others singularly, and some in a pile at one end of the ravine itself. The victors, meanwhile, having torn off the top-knots of their prostrate enemies, did not mutilate the bodies or rob them of clothing or even of artefacts worn about their persons. The Kiowa chief Satank had seen to that. Instead, they collected up the latter's weapons, most of which they threw away except for one richly be-feathered Dog Soldier Society staff found next to a prostrate Cheyenne, and another ornamented lance found while still in its feathered case. The rest of the captured weapons they scattered over the surrounding brush and sandy ground, and withal, wondered among themselves why so many of their foes had sacrificed their lives in such a manner. Whilst rummaging amongst the pile of corpses, they discovered another among the dead Cheyennes who had no wounds on him. Apparently, he had been suffocated to death after a number of bodies consisting of comrades and enemies had fallen on top of him, and had accidently, it seemed, been covered by them.

Later, after returning to their combined camps, the victorious Kiowa and Comanche warriors raced their ponies around the interior and in and out among the lodges, proclaiming aloud their success with typical gusto of the Red Man. It was indeed considered a great event to celebrate. Only six Kiowa had lost their lives including the son of the Kiowa chief Black-Horse, and a like small number of Comanche. They danced and sang for several moons thereafter, and

FORTY-EIGHT CHEYENNE BOWSTRINGS WIPED OUT

proclaimed that surely, their sacred protectors must be greater than those of the Cheyenne.

Several weeks passed, and still the Cheyenne had no inclination as to the fate of the Bowstrings. Indeed, they remained optimistic as to their lot, believing they had gone further south than originally thought in search of horses and adventure, while some others believed that being victorious, they had gone to raid other enemies while their luck held out. Such practices were not uncommon, as had been a war-party of Cheyennes which earlier, had attached itself to that group of Trading Indians made up from members of several different tribes under the influence of the Arapahoe Bear`s-Tooth in the early 1820s. Also, two notable cases of separate Blackfoot and Crow parties which had stayed away from home for two years or more, raiding enemies and stealing horses as far south as Mexico. Besides, it was deemed very bad luck to suppose ill-fortune had befallen a party and consequently, unless there was evidence that the missing in question had met with disaster, absent members were not officially mourned by the tribe as a whole until a prolonged period had elapsed.

Now throughout the time of war between Cheyennes on one side and Kiowa, Kiowa-Apache and Comanche on the other, the Arapahoe, the southern bands at least, had stayed out of the conflict, and had been in the habit of actually trading with each of the afore-mentioned tribes at one or another white man`s forts and trading posts.

It was whilst on one of such trading trip in late summer of `37, that a group of Arapahoe were witness to a spectacular scalp-dance held by the Kiowa camped adjacent to Fort Adobe on the Arkansas River. For a while, the Arapahoe spectators paid little attention, until they happened to scrutinise two scalps over which the warriors were dancing. The Arapahoe recognised the scalps as belonging to two Cheyennes, which by the hair-ornaments and manner of braiding, were distinguished as belonging to two of the absent Bowstring warriors Red-Tracks and Coyote-Ear who only recently, had gone to war with Hollow-Hip and Bear-Above against the Kiowa.

The Arapahoe inquired how the scalps had been obtained, and were proudly told that the great Kiowa war-chief Satank and his warriors, had met forty-eight Cheyennes and annihilated them all. The Arapahoe were amazed to learn the killers had not mutilated the bodies as would have been usual on such occasions, but had laid out the corpses in a row in the open, partly as a mark of respect, but also, so to be easily discernible to any Cheyennes who might come looking for them.

For the two Arapahoe to have spoken out against the slaughter of their allies would surely have resulted in their deaths, as to the frenzy and euphoria the dancers seemed to be in. Consequently, they kept their opinions to themselves and as soon as opportunity arose, rode north back to their own people.

On their journey north, the two Arapahoe met an old Sioux man named Smokey-lodge who was on his way to visit Cheyennes on the South Platte. The Arapahoe informed him what they had seen and heard, and as he was already on his way to visit Cheyennes, they asked him to take the news to them. Hearing this, Smokey-Lodge did not hesitate. He whipped up his horse and continued his journey, eager to inform the Cheyennes of the disaster.

When at last the lone Sioux came to the *Heviatanio* Cheyenne village and burst out his news, he could not have imagined the out-pouring of grief he unleashed, as the Cheyennes absorbed the intelligence that more than half the Bowstring Society was dead. The women-folk began slashing arms and legs with knives and scoring their foreheads with sharp stones until blood streamed from dozens of self-inflicted wounds. They each howled and cried with profound emotion as ever heard in a Cheyenne camp, it is said, and screamed curses and oaths upon the slayers. The whole village was in confusion, but impatient for revenge. In accordance with custom, the women rubbed their bloody hands over the faces and bodies of warriors present, and implored them take pity on their sufferings and end their incessant wailing by avenging their slaughtered kinfolk.

The cry was for Kiowa blood and such was the enthusiasm, it was decided to 'move' the Cheyenne Sacred Arrows against the Kiowa, and if need be, against the latter's Comanche and Kiowa-Apache allies also.

The warrior society chiefs of the Red-Shields were first to take up the proffered war-pipe, but for some unknown reason, they passed it on to the *Hotomtami* or Dog-Soldiers, whose head-chief at that time was a noted fighter named Porcupine-Bear. None was regarded braver then he and certainly, he had counted more coups than any other among his people. However, he was also noticed for being somewhat hot-headed and for his impetuosity, which facts alone had previously prevented him commanding much sway within the councils. Nevertheless, this time he was duly elected to take the war-council's decision of 'Moving the Arrows' to the rest of the scattered Cheyenne bands and their chiefs, a task which would take several moons to accomplish.

For a time all went well. Whenever Porcupine-Bear came upon a village, a large council lodge was erected and the entire occupants of the camp would gather around both inside and out to hear what he had to say. Porcupine-Bear would tell the assembly all what had happened to the Bowstrings, then urge the chiefs and warriors present to accept the war-pipe and smoke it and, thereby, join the other Cheyenne bands in mounting a grand crusade against the perpetrators to exact revenge. In response, the chiefs and head-men of the soldier societies would each voice their opinions and grievances, and after which, they, too, would either take up the pipe or refuse it according to their own whims at the time. As it was, as Porcupine-Bear continued on his mission to each of the bands in turn, of which none hesitated to smoke and pledge themselves to war.

The last and most distant Cheyenne band Porcupine-Bear reached was that of the *Omissis* in camp on the North Platte, and among which resided some of his relatives. At the same time he came upon them, white men traders in the employ of the American Fur Company were entrenched on the south side of the river, and were trading trinkets and raw whiskey to the Cheyennes in exchange for buffalo robes and pelts. The result of such trading was already well-known among both Indians and Whites, many among whom had oft-times witnessed the frenzied drunken orgies that such trading spawned. Indeed, by as early as 1832, the white trader Gantt had amassed a fortune by selling liquor to Indians, moreover to Cheyennes, and only three years later, the whole tribe had been described by educated observers as being, *"...a nation of drunkards."*

Alas, therefore, it was not long after Porcupine-Bear's arrival that the whole *Omissis* camp became roaring drunk, including Porcupine-Bear himself. He was sitting alone in a lodge singing and humming war-songs in a drunken stupor when, outside the lodge, two among his cousins named Little-Creek and Around, began rolling over the ground grappling with and beating each other with their fists. Around was getting the worst of the tussle and called incessantly to Porcupine-Bear to assist him. Suddenly, Little-Creek got on top of Around;

drew his knife and raised his arm to stab. This was enough for Porcupine-Bear who all at once, reared up in his drunken state and began bellowing like an enraged bull. He then ran from his lodge and falling upon Little-Creek, gained possession of the knife and proceeded to stab him several times. He then gave the bloodied weapon to Around, and commanded him to finish Little-Creek off. This his accomplice did and after which, the relatives of Porcupine-Bear and Around each set upon the corpse, and likewise, stabbed it repeatedly with their knives.

Porcupine-Bear, albeit then head-chief of the Dog-Soldier Society, had now ran afoul of what was considered among his people the most contemptuous and heinous of crimes, that of committing murder within the tribe, and his relatives in a moment of excitement had dipped their hands in his guilt.

The following morning after the drunken orgy and revelry in camp had subdued, the guilty parties involved felt heavy in their hearts for what they had done. There was no need for an enquiry by chiefs and elders to establish the facts of the matter, neither was there cause for soldiers of one or another society to enforce the prescribed punishment for such a deed. The consequences were already well known by all Cheyennes without the telling.

Being himself a Society chief, Porcupine-Bear accepted the judgement upon him without complaint and in accordance with the pride and outward impression he was obliged to exercise due to his rank in the tribe. Thus, he and his whole family packed their tepees and belongings on pony-drags and without much more ado, left the camp circle, banished from the rest of the tribe for a period of four years.

The Sacred Arrows, being regarded as the symbol of unity and for safeguarding the very existence of the tribe, were, of course, soiled by the above homicide, and as the entire essence of Porcupine-Bear's task had been to rally the tribe around the 'Arrows' themselves, all his previous work in bringing the tribal fighting force together was now invalid. The Sacred Arrows were once again spotted with blood. Subsequently, they would have to be renewed a second time, and the whole procedure of carrying the war-pipe to the scattered bands taken up again.

Porcupine-Bear's deed had disgraced the Dog-Soldier Society which, therefore, had forfeited its right to summon the bands to council. This being so, Little-Wolf, a Southern Cheyenne and second chief of the Dog-Soldiers, [later known as Old-Little-Wolf so not to confuse him with a younger Suhtai brave of the same name] now offered the said pipe to the Bowstrings. But as the latter's number of warriors had been recently decimated, they themselves declined the offer. Old-Little-Wolf in response is said by some Cheyenne informants to have then created a new society to replace that of the Bowstrings, and named it the Wolf Society instead. He further agreed to bring in the respective bands himself.

By the time Old-Little-Wolf started out on his mission, winter had arrived and there was deep snow over all the country. Nevertheless, he was undeterred in his objective and although suffering much physical hardship, he managed to accomplish the task. The following year [`38] even before the snows had fully melted, one by one the different bands came in to a prearranged rendezvous site not far north of the South Platte, and by spring, all Cheyenne and Suhtaio bands were again united as one Nation.

The last to come in was the *Masiskota* Cheyenne band two days after the largest and most important band the *Omissis* had also made their arrival. As with the other bands, the *Masiskota* met with screeching, wailing and lamenting women-folk who again slashed themselves with knives and sharp stones to show how sad they were for the slaughtered warriors of the Bowstrings. A large buffalo-hide council lodge was duly set up, and all the tribe's chiefs and head warriors of the different Soldier Societies held heated conversations within. The lamenting women once more begged them to avenge their lost relatives and wiped their bloody hands over them. A respected veteran warrior named Hole-in-the-Back, then rode around the circle of lodges, calling out the names of the separate warrior Societies four time each, and urged the young men not yet affiliated to one or the other, to now do so and join them. Later on, the soldiers themselves were showered with presents and praises to further encourage them to act, and soon, it seemed, the whole Nation was clamouring for war.

Unfortunately, such was the immensity of the camp, the occupants soon drained all immediate game resources dry, it still being the early days of spring, and soon the populous was bordering on starvation. The great encampment was obliged to split into a dozen and more bands, each wandering far and wide in search of food. Also, while each Cheyenne band was separated from each other, protection by their previous unity was greatly diminished, and each camp was at the mercy of horse-stealing foes, including Crows and Pawnee and even

FORTY-EIGHT CHEYENNE BOWSTRINGS WIPED OUT

Blackfeet raiders from north of the Missouri. One entire Cheyenne band, it is said, lost every one of its horses to stealthy thieves during this particular period of isolation.

However, in due course, the last of the snows melted and both deer and buffalo returned to the grazing country at their leisure. With full bellies and warm early summer sunshine, warriors once more began feeling the loss of sons and brothers killed by Kiowas the previous summer, and the lust for vengeance came upon them yet again.

Runners were again now dispatched by Old-Little-Wolf to call together the scattered bands for a second time, and one moon later, the whole Cheyenne Nation was once more camped together along with a large band of Southern Arapahoe encamped close by. The chiefs of these last named had asked the Cheyenne chiefs specifically to offer them the war-pipe, owing to the recent killing of an Arapahoe by Kiowas during the winter, and his severed head suffering humiliation by being dragged behind a horseman through the Kiowa camp. Thus, for some unexplained reason, the Kiowa also had since commenced hostilities with the Arapahoe, an action which the latter would never completely forgive. Having said this, with the Kiowa-Apache who were close allies and relatives to the Kiowa through intermarriage, the Arapahoe continued their friendship, but with the Comanche they also were now indifferent, and held no qualms of treating them as enemies too, because they were allied to the Kiowa.

- 0 - 0 - 0 - 0 - 0 - 0 - 0 - 0 - 0 - 0 -

CHEYENNE CHIEF, MAD-BULL.

MEDICINE-SNAKE IS KILLED AND PICTURED

CHAPTER 21.

MEDICINE-SNAKE IS KILLED AND PICTURED [1837-'38].

Meanwhile, since 1836 when `Cheyennes had been driven,` Cheyenne war-parties had left the Pawnees much to themselves, and this, coupled to the recent humiliation of losing the Nation`s Sacred Arrows` at the hands of the same Pawnee foe, had sometimes been too much to bare. [1]

There was one, however, having waited to avenge himself on the Pawnee for some time until an appropriate opportunity arose, who set off from the *Heviatanio* Cheyenne village then sited outside Bent`s trading post on the Arkansas during winter of `37-`38, and with five companions, attempted to raid a Pawnee hunting camp in retribution for the affair of `36. This was nearly two years after the latter event and at a time when most other Cheyennes instead, were psyching themselves up for a grand hostile expedition against the Kiowa and Comanche in return for the killing of forty-eight Bowstring warriors the previous summer. In the current case against the Pawnee, the Cheyenne Pipe-Holder was named Medicine-Snake but who also was known as Walking-Whirlwind, the same who jointly with Yellow-Wolf and Afraid-of-Beavers over ten years earlier, had led the *Heviatanio* on their migration north to south, and was a prominent chief and orator loved and honoured among his people. Thus the said five-man party after three days of dog-trotting, reached the Solomon River of what is now the western part of Kansas State, where Pawnees were then reported to be hunting and encamped in a tepee village.

On the party`s second day out, a heavy mist came up and as the party travelled on, it grew thicker and thicker until a fog enveloped the prairie and became so dense, they could not see the way ahead more than a few yards. Without knowing, the Cheyennes, unwittingly, stumbled upon their quarry, which was the same Pawnee hunting camp with its occupants only just stirring with the break of dawn. Too late the Cheyennes realised their blunder. They halted then turned back, but as fate would have it a Pawnee man out early with his wife gathering firewood, spied the hazy shapes of footmen and discerning the latter`s style of dress as foreign, ran back into camp and raised the alarm.

MEDICINE-SNAKE IS KILLED AND PICTURED

Within minutes scores of Pawnee warriors were mounted and searching in the grey murky light for the interlopers. Pawnee women and children joined in the search and camp dogs bounded over the grassland also searching for the foe. Medicine-Snake had been caught unawares and indeed, his whole Cheyenne party was in a quandary what to do next.

Blindly they took to their heels and ran away in the opposite direction of enemy voices, neighing horses and barking dogs, and towards the Republican River, although the river unfortunately, was running far too high to wade across and carry them to safety, if that is, the pursuing Pawnees would have let them get that far in the first place, and very soon the fog began to lift. All of a sudden, it seemed, the thick haze disappeared and a winding narrow steam came into view semi-obscured by rocks and over-growing foliage over-shadowed by a small bluff. Desperate for a place of concealment, the five Cheyennes immediately splashed through the smaller stream to reach the bluff, for if the rocks could not conceal them, then the crest of the bluff itself was deemed as good a site as any from where to make a stand.

All the while the lingering fog still remained in patches over the prairie, the Cheyennes were safe, albeit their antagonists were searching around for their whereabouts. It was indeed around mid-day before the fog finally lifted completely and a pale sun gleamed over the waters. But it was then that the keen eyes of a few Pawnees spotted the tips of eagle feathers and the glint on metal lance-points atop the bluff. The luckless Cheyennes could hear clearly the enemy whooping their discovery, and thus, they prepared themselves for battle and as they supposed, their imminent deaths. By the time the Pawnees did attack, Medicine-Snake and his companions had re-braided their hair and fixed their savage regalia ready to look their finest when they entered the Spirit land of their ancestors.

The brave Medicine-Snake stood up from cover and cried out to the surrounding enemy to kill him first, for as he was the Cheyenne leader, it was considered his duty to be first to die. Upon this a lone Pawnee dismounted and ran headlong up the slope towards the chief. But Medicine-Snake sent him crashing to the ground with one stroke from his war-club. But this was Medicine-Snake`s last deed before he himself was felled amid a howling mob of enemies. His followers were quickly felled in his wake and cut-up limb from limb whilst still breathing by the vengeful Pawnees.

MEDICINE-SNAKE IS KILLED AND PICTURED

This had happened in the winter of '37-'38, but Medicine-Snake's relatives knew nothing about it. As time went on and there came no word of the latter's fate, the people became worried and sceptical as to what had occurred. They at length requested certain holy men to enquire through their deities as to the missing persons' lot and this the holy men did. However, they each returned verdicts contradictory to each other, some saying that Medicine-Snake and his party were still alive, others declaring the whole party was dead. Dissatisfied, the relatives then carried a pipe to a revered *medicine* man named Elk-River, and entering the Sacred Arrow lodge, they implored him to smoke and invoke the spirits to determine the whereabouts of the missing party. After putting himself through a somewhat baffling ceremony necessary to communicate with one or more departed spirits, Elk-River declared that Medicine-Snake was indeed dead, slain one winter before with his companions laying around him. Even though Elk-River could only have been surmising, he had convinced himself and those around him that words he had uttered came from the spirits themselves, and being in the presence of the Sacred Arrow bundle, the people believed him whole-heartedly. As a consequence those who felt obliged to, entered into a prolonged period of mourning, some even amputating a finger joint as if there was no doubt that their relatives were no more. Medicine-Snake's son thereupon, took the name of Walking-Whirlwind which had been Medicine-Snake's other name, and was known thereafter as Young-Whirlwind. He himself became recognised as a formidable Cheyenne warrior and Society Chief and at a later date, was more commonly known as Old-Whirlwind.

Meanwhile, some weeks after Elk-River's decleration, a war-party of Sioux on its way home from raiding Pawnees, stopped off at the *Heviatanio* village with interesting news. Whilst on the Solomon River, they said, they had come upon an abandoned Pawnee hunting camp. Nearby etched in charcoal on the dead limb of a fallen tree, was a mass of picture-writing symbols and a branch pointing it's way downstream. The pictures told in a simple yet fascinating way the actual story of Medicine-Snake's killing. The Sioux party did not venture further downstream to view the bodies themselves, lest it be a ruse to ambush them by waiting Pawnees, but all agreed that the slain so indicated on the tree limb, was the event of the demise of Medicine-Snake's party.

MEDICINE-SNAKE IS KILLED AND PICTURED

Upon this intelligence, the great Cheyenne warrior Standing-on-the-Hill got together a small party and started out to the place of slaughter on the Solomon in an attempt to retrieve the corpses.

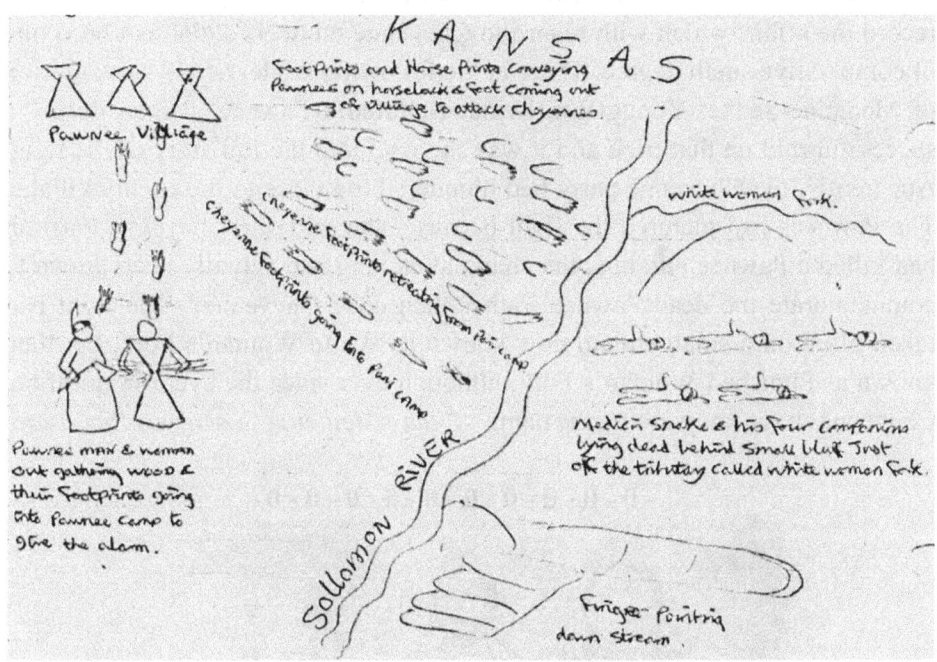

PICTOGRAPH BY PAWNEE OF KILLING OF MEDICINE-SNAKE AND PARTY.

After several days travel following directions from the Sioux, they came across the old hunting camp and exposed log depicting dead Cheyennes just as the Sioux narrators had said. Standing-on-the-Hill led his party further downstream and turning up an even smaller creek, discovered the bleaching remains of Medicine-Snake and his companions. Wolves and buzzards had picked the bones clean and scattered them far and wide, although small piles of stones or cairns had been erected on the very spots where each Cheyenne had fallen, obviously by the victorious Pawnees as a show of respect for the dead Cheyenne braves. The recovery party, however, was a small group in hostile territory and therefore, it ignored the customary wailing and mourning which usually would have accompanied such a discovery. Hastily they collected up the bones and skulls and buried them in a hollow in the creek bank. The party

MEDICINE-SNAKE IS KILLED AND PICTURED

then whipped up their ponies and took verification back to their village. On the party's return, there was much sadness among all the *Heviatanio,* as Medicine-Snake had been much loved and a highly respected member of the tribe.

The Cheyennes were curious as to why the Pawnees had taken trouble to record the affair, which with regard to Cheyenne numbers slain, had been one of comparative small degree. Then, in the following winter of `39 -`40, the son of Medicine-Snake, Young-Whirlwind, captured a Pawnee woman during a successful raid on that tribe and it was she who told the full story of the fight. Apparently, the Cheyenne party had blundered too close to the enemy village. The Pawnees had pictured the fight because, she said, the Cheyenne Partisan had killed a Pawnee and thus the charcoal etching had actually been drawn to commemorate the dead Pawnee, rather than dead Cheyennes. The fight had taken place on a small stream now known as White Woman's Fork, but then known as Punished Woman's Fork, although ever since the event in question, Cheyennes have known it by the name *"Where Medicine-Snake was Pictured."*

- 0 - 0 - 0 - 0 - 0 - 0 - 0 - 0 - 0 - 0 –

CHEYENNES, OLD-WHIRLWIND AND FAMILY.

CHAPTER 22.

PREPARATIONS AGAINST THE KIOWA [1838]

As regards the great crusade proposed against the Kiowa and Comanche, so it was in mid-summer 1838, somewhere on the South Platte north of Bent's Fort on the Arkansas, Cheyennes pitched over seven-hundred tepees in a great circle several ranks deep. Their Southern Arapahoe confederates in a like manner, albeit with around two-hundred tepees and led by their head chief, Little-Raven, were positioned about one-mile away. [1]

Once more the tribal din of mourning for dead kinfolk echoed through the camps. The women opened up old scars on arms, legs and thighs; tore out hanks of hair from their heads and ripped their clothes as they stomped and crawled around the lodges on hands and knees, yelling hideous laments until they were hoarse or collapsed from sheer exhaustion. Meanwhile, the war-pipe, yet again, was duly passed among all Cheyenne chiefs and to the Arapahoe, and quite likely, to some wandering Sioux until all present had smoked.

An important man among the Cheyenne, probably the second High-Backed-Wolf, but whose name has since been forgotten, invoked his personal totems to bring victory to his people. He took up a quantity of feathers from the ground in both hands and threw them into the air above him, and when settled back on the ground, the feathers were seen to each have what seemed like specks of blood on them. The specks of blood, the important man declared, represented the blood of the enemy, which the Cheyennes and their allies would shed in the coming fight.

At length, the formidable gathering of the entire Cheyenne Nation and Arapahoe allies started forth. At their head rode the Cheyenne Sacred Arrow priest Grey-Thunder – an Aorta band member and holiest of holy men then riding alongside his wife Tail-Woman, carrying the Sacred Arrows in a bundle strapped to her back. Sun-Getting-Out-of-Bed, being the holy keeper of the Suhtai *Issiwun* or Sacred Hat also with his wife, were riding at Grey-Thunder's side and together, along with many of their tribes-folk, they rode into and milled around outside the white man's trading post Bent's Fort on the north bank of the Arkansas. There they purchased guns, powder, ball, metal arrow-points,

PREPARATIONS AGAINST THE KIOWA

steel hatchets and other objects of war, including several cap and ball single-shot pistols from the traders in exchange for spare horses and hides. All the Cheyenne women, children and old persons were with them, while the surrounding flats both north and south of the fort were covered with tepees, horses and Indians.

If the traders tried to dissuade the Cheyennes to abandon their proposed venture, it was to no avail, and soon the grand ensemble continued on its way, eager as ever to meet the foe. The traders were involved in so much that the war might smash completely any potential Kiowa and Comanche trade at the fort, for the latter would surely stay away from where Cheyennes were apt to trade, unless they themselves were in formidable number and more than ready for a fight.

Meanwhile, the Cheyennes moved south across the Arkansas River and that night, went into camp about six miles above that known as Chouteau`s Island, with their Southern Arapahoe allies again encamped one mile away.

In the centre of the Cheyenne village, a large buffalo-hide lodge fashioned from the skins of two tepees, was erected as a place of gathering for the chiefs and head men, and having done this, runners were sent over to the Arapahoe camp to summon their chiefs to another council of war.

Now among the Arapahoe was a young man, handsome and dashing, a true `Cavallero` of the Plains. His name was Flat-War-Club owing a particular bludgeon he carried wherever he went, and was held in some kind of awe by his tribesmen. Cheyennes knew him also, although for their part, they had regarded him somewhat as a topic of ridicule. They had heard his many and unfulfilled boasts of valour, but as yet had, not bourn witness to any of his deeds.

When runners did reach the Arapahoe camp, Flat-War-Club gave them a message to take back to the Cheyenne chiefs. He requested that four Cheyenne braves should be delegated to come and carry him in a blanket over to the council lodge. Such a request astounded the Cheyennes, especially as the Arapahoe in question was not a chief or even a proven warrior. But nevertheless, they realised he was intending to do something important to dare make such a demand in the first place, and thus, the chiefs acceded to his request.

PREPARATIONS AGAINST THE KIOWA

Four Cheyennes walked over to the Arapahoe camp, placed a fine blanket on the ground and bade the man sit upon it. Whereupon, each picked up a corner and proceeded to carry him over to the said council lodge. As has been stated, the two camps were one-mile apart, and so large a man was Flat-War-Club, the bearers had to put him down several times and rest before reaching the Cheyenne camp. Upon entering the Cheyenne village, the bearers of Flat-War-Club headed straight for the council lodge along a route lined with hundreds of inquisitive women, men and children. Still carrying the Arapahoe on the blanket, they entered the great council tepee and placed their burden on the ground at the rear of the lodge, albeit this being the customary place of honour preserved for guests and surrounded by the headmen of both Cheyennes and Arapahoe.

When all was quiet and traditional formalities of receiving guests concluded, Flat-War-Club arose to his feet and addressed the gathering. He told them how deeply honoured he was that they had complied with his wishes and acted as servants to someone yet unknown for his prowess as a warrior. But, he continued, there was good reason for his request. He was going to give his body to the enemy by sacrificing his life in the coming battle, in order to gain victory for his Cheyenne brothers.

The Cheyenne chiefs professed they were very grateful and flattered by his words. They each congratulated him with shouts of *"Ha-ho, Ha-ho"* i. e. Thank you, Thank you, and the Arapahoe Bushido, as he was, then asked the Cheyenne headmen if they would grant him the privilege of `talking to their wives,` as he had vowed to do a great thing for them. `Talking to a woman` was a Plains Indian metaphor for making love, and probably, he more than others of his tribe, knew how chaste and incorruptible women among the Cheyennes were known to be. Indeed, Cheyenne women had earned respect among all tribes and even white men with whom they came in contact for their rigid chastity and decorum. Naturally then, this was an even greater request from Flat-War-Club for the chiefs to grant. But realising such a favour was to be returned by the said Arapahoe shedding his blood and even life on their behalf, they reluctantly consented and bade their men-folk and even husbands not to interfere while he did indeed, `talk` to any Cheyenne woman of his choice. The white historian George Grinnell, who interviewed Cheyennes who had actually been present during the occasion in question, mentioned that in 1914 he had

PREPARATIONS AGAINST THE KIOWA

interviewed a Cheyenne woman who recalled her meeting with Flat-War-Club, and even those many years later she portrayed a certain amount of smugness at having been chosen by him, and which, when an old person, she still regarded as having been a great honour bestowed upon her.

There was also a Cheyenne warrior named Big-Breast who, likewise, made a suicide vow. He rode around the inner circle of tepees proclaiming his decision while singing *medicine* songs and raising loud his death-chant.

Meanwhile, in the council lodge itself, all great fighters of both tribes swore vengeance on the Kiowa, not only for the slaughter of Bowstrings the previous summer, but for all other past grievances against that tribe. All present voiced their eagerness to shed their enemies` blood or to die in the attempt. One of the Cheyenne leading chiefs, the *Hevitanio* Yellow-Wolf, then acting as the most prominent spokesman among them, summed up the situation and concluded the council by saying,

> "My brothers, we have made this road to attack the enemy and that no prisoners shall be taken. These people have killed our young men for many winters past, and that is why we have made this road, to take no one alive." [2]

The following day both Cheyenne and Arapahoe took down their tepees, packed them and effects on pony-drags and before mid-morning, all started south in two great bodies with Porcupine-Bear and his recently out-lawed relatives in company with a number of loyal adherents creating a third and marching on the flank of the Cheyenne column about one mile distant.

Now among one of the Southern Cheyenne bands, were included two young male relatives of the earlier slaughtered Medicine-Snake and his comrades slain by Pawnees the previous winter. These two young men named Left-Hand and Stands-on-the-Hill, had since vowed to give their lives in the next confrontation with Pawnees, in an endeavour to kill one or more of the enemy in revenge for Medicine-Snake`s demise. The Cheyennes said of such persons, *"He is a young man, but also an old man...He is young, but is going out to die."*

PREPARATIONS AGAINST THE KIOWA

While the grand Cheyenne and Arapahoe cavalcade was traveling east downstream along the Arkansas, and ultimately heading further east to Wolf Creek where it had been reported, their Kiowa and Kiowa-Apache quarry would be encamped, Cheyenne scouts discovered a hunting camp of Pawnee in the process of hunting buffalo and wild horses further down the Arkansas on that river's north bank. Skidi Pawnees had since been allowed to roam such country due to a recent peace initiative effected between that particular Pawnee tribe and certain Comanche bands, and this was the opportunity the two traveling Cheyenne suicide warriors had been hoping for.

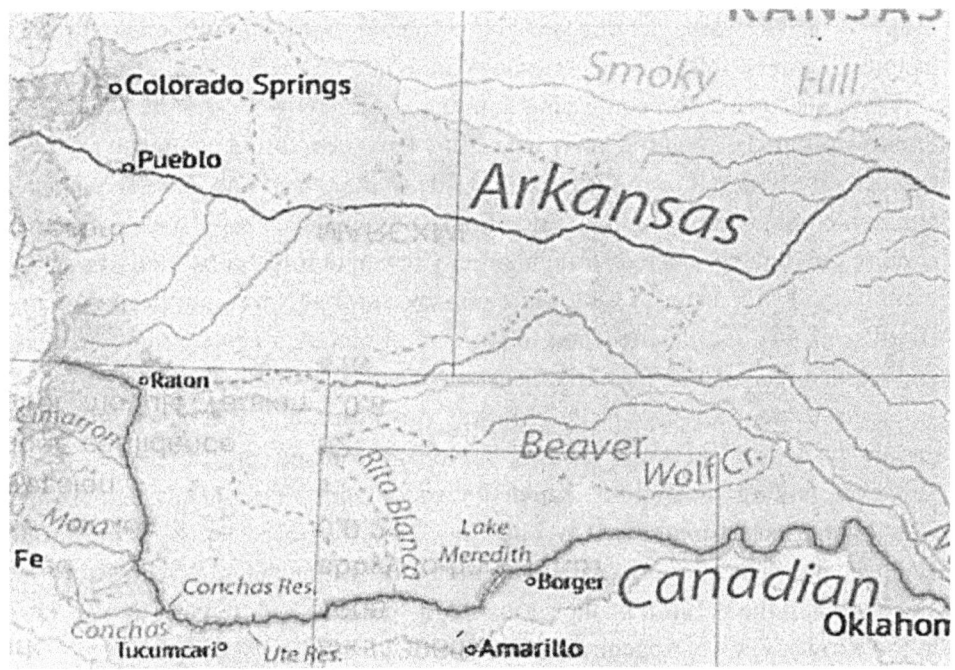

MAP OF WOLF CREEK AND BEAVER CREEK AND SURROUNDING COUNTRY.

The closeness of the Pawnee hunting camp caused a significant number of Cheyennes to break from the grand party's original route, and instead, decide to attack the Pawnee hunters in order to accommodate the vows made by Left-Hand and Stands-on-the-Hill.

Meanwhile, Pawnee fighters in the nearby hunting camp had discerned a large body of Cheyennes coming slowly on horseback across the plains from the west, and in their front some thirty yards distant, rode the two Suicide braves leading the way, heading directly towards the Pawnee hunting camp.

Left-Hand, one of the leading Cheyennes continued riding forward, and a number of Pawnees rode out to meet him. Left-Hand ran his horse into that being ridden by a Pawnee who shot his gun at the lone Cheyenne, and the bullet struck its target in the stomach. But the wounded Cheyenne remained in the saddle and while hanging on to his mount, other Cheyennes caught up with his horse; turned it around and led it and rider back to the main group of Cheyennes who were watching some distance in the rear. Left-Hand, however, knew he had got his death wound. He asked his Cheyenne companions to lead him on his horse back towards the Pawnees, but as he did so, blood pumped up through his mouth and he fell from his steed a dead man.

While this had been going on, the other avowed suicide Cheyenne Stands-on-the-Hill, had rode on towards the Pawnee hunting camp and by then, had actually ridden through it from one side to the other. The Pawnee warriors and non-combatants of women and children having seen only two Cheyennes at close quarters, suspected a much larger Cheyenne force must likely be in the vicinity, and preparing to take the camp by surprise from another direction. Because of this, the Pawnees ran to seek cover among a nearby stand of trees, and readied themselves for a more sustained attack upon them.

As it was, Stands-on-the-Hill was not killed and returned among his people who still sat their mounts stationary looking on from a distance. However, having allowed the suicide boys to attempt their endeavours in what was thought an honourable way, the Cheyennes retrieved the corpse of Left-Hand, and with the surviving Stands-on-the-Hill among them, gave up the fight, and re-joined the column of their kinsfolk as it continued towards Wolf Creek to the Kiowa, Kiowa-Apache and Comanche villages on Wolf Creek.

- 0 - 0 - 0 - 0 - 0 - 0 - 0 - 0 - 0 - 0 -

BIG FIGHT AT WOLF CREEK

CHAPTER 23.

BIG FIGHT AT WOLF CREEK [1838]

In the aftermath of the attack on the Pawnee, the grand Cheyenne and Arapahoe crusading columns turned southeast. They travelled throughout the daylight hours until reaching a point south of the Arkansas around dusk. It was then that the Cheyenne chiefs dispatched Pushing-Ahead, Howling-Wolf and Crooked-Neck along with one other [whose name has been forgotten], to go forward on foot and locate the enemy village or villages Their recognisance, however, was unfruitful, but whilst returning to the Cheyenne camp, they observed a party of three Kiowa carrying lances and shields and on foot, leading their horses through the long grass. This, the Cheyenne scouts thought, determined them a war-party going north on a raid. The three Kiowa were in a valley of Wolf Creek and this being so, the scouts guessed the enemy village would not be far away. [1]

Patiently, the scouts continued watching the war-party as it moved up the creek. As soon as it was out of sight, they themselves set off at a dog-trot back to their own village, which had since moved further south than its previous night's stop to a new location on Crooked Creek, only a few miles from the Cimarron River in what is now south-western Oklahoma.

The Cheyenne and Arapahoe camps were now pitched in one great circle several tepees deep, and in the centre of which, was again a large council lodge made from the skins of two tepees. Herein, the headmen of both tribes were once more assembled in council, and it was to the chiefs that the scouts made their report and related all they had seen. Upon this intelligence, another detachment of scouts, three in number including a young Cheyenne named Wolf-Road who was regarded as a fast runner, and another known as Gentle-Horse, were sent out to determine the exact position of the enemy camp.

This time, the Cheyenne chiefs advised the scouts to pick up the trail of the three Kiowa and back-track it to the actual village it had come from. But Pushing-Ahead who led the scouts, instead told Gentle-Horse he was sure the Kiowa were camped on or very near Wolf Creek, and consequently, led his companions towards that stream in order to save a great deal of time searching

BIG FIGHT AT WOLF CREEK

for their quarry. Having said this, the three Cheyennes moved too far west, and even they failed to locate the camp they were looking for. In fact, they themselves incurred a narrow escape from disaster.

A Kiowa hunting party was suddenly sighted in the distance, but for some unaccountable reason failed to see the Cheyenne scouts posing in full view on the crest of a hill. Luckily, the scouts saw the hunting party first and raced down the blind side of the hill and into the dry shallow bed of a nearby creek. The Kiowa hunters, meanwhile, having spotted a small buffalo herd in the vicinity, gave chase to the animals and began cutting out prime bulls oblivious to their hidden enemies. One among the hunters rode so close to the scout's position, so the scouts later told their people, that if the Kiowas had looked in their direction instead of towards the herd, the three scouts would certainly have been discovered and killed.

Their Cheyenne *medicine* protectors must have been watching over them, they said, for the scouts remained undetected. When after the Kiowa hunters had made their kill; butchered and packed the meat on ponies and started back to their camp, the three Cheyennes followed behind at a safe distance from them. Sometime later, a long belt of timber came into view which stretched along the same stream known as Wolf Creek with hundreds of Indian ponies grazing on surrounding flats. By this the scouts knew a very large village must be close at hand. Immediately they returned to their own camp which had since moved again, this time further south to a point on what was then known as Beaver Creek.

Even as the scouts came in, all Cheyenne and Arapahoe warriors having noticed the scouts returning from afar, were already dressing for war and mounting horses ready to race around the centre of camp and strike a customary pile of buffalo chips representing the enemy, and thereby, claim the first coup of their hostile expedition. Now, after the scouts again made their report and the Cheyenne and Arapahoe chiefs had definite knowledge where their objective was, the the camp crier was directed to inform the people of the chiefs' decision that their combined fighting force would start towards the foe as soon as the sun went down, and thus, by marching through the night, they would be in a favourable position to attack the enemy at dawn.

With all hast, the women-folk began erecting crude scaffolds upon which belongings that would not be needed were placed away from the reach of scavenging animals, while the bottom of tepees were rolled up so gnawing rodents and wolves could not reach them. While such activity was going on, young warriors paraded around on horseback bedecked in all their finery and proclaiming what great deeds they intended to perform. At the same time, other women sang Brave-Heart songs to encourage their sweethearts and sons in the coming conflict.

At length, however, after travelling through the night, it was evident in the dim light of dawn that during the process of their march, they had become somewhat divided, and the column was now separated into at least four groups as their later mode of attack indicated. There was now one body of Arapahoe including a few Cheyennes which had moved southeast; a column of Cheyenne Red-Shield Soldiers with some Arapahoe to the southwest, and another of mixed Cheyenne Crooked-Lance [or Elk Soldiers] and Bowstrings [newly-formed by Little-Old-Wolf with the alternative new name of Wolf Soldiers] in yet another group further southwest. These bodies did not include Porcupine-Bear and his outlawed Dog-Soldiers, who themselves, had been moving directly south from the other groups on their own volition.

For some reason or other, the grand cavalcade had a little difficulty finding the exact whereabouts of the enemy camp, and it was some two or three hours after sunrise before it was eventually located at the junction of Wolf Creek and that of the Beaver.

In response, the Cheyenne and Arapahoe set up another temporary war-camp composed of brush and hide bivouacs on the north bank of the Beaver, with the Cheyenne outlaw group led by Porcupine-Bear positioned some one-hundred yards off to one side, as by custom due to their being classed as exiles, they must remain separated from the main body. No one officially had notified this outlaw group what the scouts had reported or of the chief's decision to move, although through spurious means they knew of everything then going on, and were availing themselves accordingly with their own plan of attack.

By mid-day the grand avenging force set off again, this time towards the Kiowa village itself, but which unbeknown to the Cheyenne and Arapahoe, had since been augmented with a number of allied Comanche and Kiowa-Apache. The Cheyennes and Arapahoe were now riding and marching together again in one long twisting column stretching more than a mile across the prairie, and at their head was Grey-Thunder and his wife with the Cheyennes' Sacred

BIG FIGHT AT WOLF CREEK

Arrow bundle, while on grey-thunder's right was Sun-Getting-Out-of-Bed and his wife, carrying the Sacred Buffalo-Hat of the Suhtaio.

Directly behind these two couples and being the position of honour for guests, was the Arapahoe contingent of chiefs and warriors, while Cheyenne braves in their respective Warrior Societies rode in the rear. Between these two groups were positioned a good number of women, children and old-folk along with the majority of spare horses, the Arapahoe herd being kept separate from those of the Cheyenne by the efforts of industrious boy herders. The rest of the non-combatants meanwhile, lagged behind the main column, content to follow the cavalcade at their own pace, while at all times, scouts from both tribes were out in front; at the rear and on the flanks, and one or another group of society soldiers kept young bucks from breaking away and attacking the enemy before necessary rites pertaining to the 'Arrows' and 'Buffalo Hat' had been performed to ensure the crusade's good fortune. Indeed, if any among the warriors became impetuous to begin the conflict before such rituals were performed, they would surely destroy the element of surprise and any potency the tribal talismans might have against the foe.

Now at this time, a small number of Cheyenne fighting men constituting seven in total, were traveling horseback cautiously across the ridge-broken plain looking for enemy sign. Soon these same men raced into Porcupine-Bear's camp, shouting excitedly that enemies had been sighted over a hill a little way ahead. Hastily, other Cheyenne warriors with Porcupine-Bear at their head, mounted ponies and galloped to the base of the hill. Porcupine-Bear then urged his mount up to its crest and scanned the open prairie on the far side sweeping away into the distance.

Some way off, a bunch of riders could be seen heading towards the same hill, and by a number of running-horses and pack-mules they were leading along with the presence of women among them, showed them to be a hunting party after buffalo. The hunters were clearly Kiowa or Comanche and actually out-numbered the Cheyennes around three to one. But even so, Porcupine-Bear decided to attack them.

Porcupine-Bear told his comrades to keep below the crest and wait patiently for his signal. He himself remained where he was atop the ridge within full-view of the enemy. He concealed his lance in the long grass and turned his back to the hunters, while pretending to be looking at something in the distance. The hunters saw him and paused for a moment discussing among themselves whether he be an enemy or not. Porcupine-Bear then began riding his horse in a circle, which was Indian sign that he had sighted either buffalo or enemies, and the Kiowa hunters; now supposing he was one of their own people also out hunting, albeit separately and on his own, stopped what they were doing and rode casually towards him.

Keeping his face turned away from the hunters, Porcupine-Bear relied solely on his hearing and instincts to tell how close the enemy were. Soon they were so close he could hear them talking to one another and knew by their language they were indeed Kiowa.

When the hunters were no more than thirty or forty yards away, the lone Cheyenne picked up his lance and signed to the rest of his hidden comrades to charge. He himself then let out a high-pitched war-whoop, turned his horse around and rode straight down the ridge slope towards the enemy with his comrades now a short way behind, screaming at his heels.

Such was the momentum of the charge and total surprise which took them, the Kiowa hunters some thirty in number, did not have time to string their bows or even change to running-horses to make an escape. The Cheyennes smashed into them, lancing them through or knocking them from their mounts with tomahawks. The Cheyenne Crooked-Neck carried a white man's sabre and was slashing away at as many enemy hunters as he could reach. Within moments, all but one of the hunters both men and women, were dead. The last Kiowa in this bunch to die had been at the rear of his party, and when attacked, had managed to change mounts to that of his running-horse and ride away. The Cheyennes said at a later date that if he had kept going then none among the Cheyennes could have caught him. Instead, the wife of the same Kiowa - who herself was about to be surrounded - called to her husband for help. The Kiowa man heard her pleas and showing utmost gallantry, stopped his horse then raced back to rescue her, and thus, he, too, went careering to his death. There were then only six Cheyennes in Porcupine-Bear's group, but who caused such slaughter among the Kiowa at that time, most of them including women were killed. There was, however, so the Kiowa later asserted, a young Kiowa boy and two women among the hunters that escaped death. The boy then around nine or ten years old, it is said, was taken up by a Cheyenne and carried back to the Cheyenne camp on the beaver, and from where later in the day, he was either allowed by his captor to return to his own people unharmed, or simply made his escape. The two Kiowa women meanwhile, had hid themselves in the long grass while the slaughter of the hunters had been going on, and later made it safely back to the Kiowa village, albeit that one of the said women had suffered a great gash on her head caused by the white man's sabre the Cheyenne Crooked-Neck had been wielding. Porcupine-Bear is accredited to having alone killed twelve of the hunters both women and men, whilst his comrade Crooked-Neck in the same fight, is said to have killed eight.

Certainly, Porcupine-Bear had now counted the first coup of the coming battle against the Kiowa and Comanche. But owing to the fact he was considered an outlaw, Cheyenne custom denied him the honour and gave it to another who earned the distinction a little time later. In addition to this, Porcupine-Bear's assault had been activated before the Sacred Arrow rituals which should have preceded any such attack, had not been properly performed, and consequently, once again as was the case against the Pawnee in 1830, the sacred power emanating through the 'Arrows' necessary to obtain victory, was rendered impotent. Grey-Thunder, the 'Arrow' priest was much perturbed. In his mind the whole hostile venture was now doomed to failure. For him, at least, the tribal talismans had been violated one too many times. He was too old himself to personally chastise the culprits and therefore, not capable of enforcing the associated taboos on the younger sacrilegious element of the tribe. From here on, he was resolved to pay penance for, as he supposed, was his own inefficiency at being the revered 'Arrow Keeper' itself, and as it was, no official 'Arrow' ceremony was performed against the enemy at this time before the battle proper began.

Meanwhile, the most eastern column of Cheyenne and Arapahoe warriors was nearing the enemy village, but although the sun had been up three or four hours, still they had not found their objective owing to a miscalculation of their route. Among this combined party was the *Hevietanio* Cheyenne Yellow-Wolf and his adopted son who had been a Ponca captive named Walking-Coyote, and with these two were the majority of Cheyenne Crooked-Lance Soldiers. It was, in fact, about mid-day when these warriors first sighted their objective. They could, however, only see a part of the enemy encampment at the south end of the village, and still could not have known that further along the creek stood an alignment of Comanche lodges and even a short distance further, the whole Kiowa-Apache tribe.

MEDICINE-WATER, SOUTHERN CHEYENNE.

These enemy camps combined, was the largest the Cheyenne had seen for many a year. The Kiowa were in the process of holding their annual Sun-Dance ceremony, and were waiting the arrival of the Osage who earlier, had promised to attend and make peace with the Kiowa, Comanche and Kiowa-Apache. It is also said that the Kiowa Chief Black-Horse, who had lost his son in the fight with Cheyenne Bowstrings soldiers the previous year, had himself been calling for the Kiowa and their allies to mount their own crusade against the Cheyennes, and thus, the Cheyenne and Arapahoe would find that their combined southern foes could match them well.

It was at this point that the Suhtaio Sacred Buffalo Hat was given to a warrior named Elk-River to wear on his head and be first to attack the foe, while

BIG FIGHT AT WOLF CREEK

Grey-Thunder got ready to direct the two 'man arrows' of the Sacred Arrow bundle at the foe when finally confronted, and so blind the enemy when firing their missiles and make all those behind the 'Arrows' invisible to the foe.

At the same time, the Cheyennes could see a number of enemy women on the south side of the stream digging roots and berry-picking, along with several young couples making love among the trees at the south end of the village. A force of combined Cheyenne and Arapahoe broke away from the aforesaid column and splashing across the stream proceeded to attack these unsuspecting non-combatants. However, before actually crossing the stream, the attackers discovered two Kiowa males hiding in the long grass on the north side of the river. The couple only had one horse between them and after seeing they were discovered, both mounted the animal and raced away to cross the stream and reach their nearby village. The double weight on the horse, of course, severely hampered its speed, and just as they entered the water, Cheyenne and Arapahoe warriors came up alongside. One Cheyenne named Two-Tassels [aka Two-Twists], counted coup on them both with a single blow from his lance striking at a sideways angle, and then a second Cheyenne warrior struck them also counting coup, before Two-Tassels sent a musket-shot into the back of the rear rider and at such close range, the ball went clear through the man and into the rider in front, also causing a death wound. Both men were subsequently scalped and mutilated by other Cheyennes coming behind.

The third Allied column including two Cheyennes named Old-Little-Wolf and Medicine-Water, the latter wearing a famous iron-shirt, went careering through the stream and smashed into the aforesaid group of women digging roots. The women without adequate weapons to protect themselves, fell like corn under the sickle's edge, while those amorous couples among the trees met a similar gory fate, and twelve more enemy scalps dangled from Cheyenne waist-belts.

This episode probably relates to an event mentioned later by Comanche participants in the same fight, but who stated in addition, that the women were berry-pickers who were attacked by surprise and among them was a lone Comanche warrior who realising enemies were near, took up a shepherds crook-shaped lance with a feather fluttering and spinning at its pointed end; mounted his nearby pony and headed over the brow of a hill towards where the commotion was coming from. Only a short time later his horse came racing back to the Comanche end of the camp, having left its rider scalped, bloody and dead on the far side of the stream. One other Comanche man then came up and passed a lone woman survivor of the berry-picking group stumbling along trying to reach the protection of her village. She had herself been scalped by a vengeful Cheyenne and all her clothes were bloody. The Comanche man, however, did not stop to assist her. Instead, he also with a shepherd`s-crook lance rode on, and he, too, disappeared among the enemy and was killed.

By this time, both Kiowa and Comanche persons in the villages were digging fox-holes both within and without their tepees in which to take cover while defending themselves, and were strengthening brush and timber barricades previously erected in fear of just such an allied assault upon them.

Meanwhile, those Cheyenne and Arapahoe who had not crossed the river with Old-Little-Wolf as one of their leaders, continued on from a northeast direction and towards another part of the Kiowa village where many loose ponies were gathered. The Kiowa and their allies had not had time to drive the animals into some safe recess before the enemy attacked, and here the Cheyenne Gentle-Horse rode right in amongst the herd and drove off a large number of animals back across the river from whence he came, and where Cheyenne and Arapahoe non-combatants of women and old men were watching the conflict from afar.

Meanwhile, even while the besieged were re-enforcing their barricades, Porcupine-Bear and his comrades now augmented with increased numbers of warriors, had already heard of Porcupine-Bear`s deed of wiping out the Kiowa hunters and believing his totems would be all-powerful that day, had since attached themselves to his band eager for honours they hoped to share with him. Together, they now hurled themselves into the upper end of the combined villages which was predominantly occupied by the Kiowa-Apache. The Cheyennes and Arapahoe rode around and right up to the barricades and encroached some way into the village itself, shooting off guns and arrows into the tepees and were pressing the defenders hard. At the same time, the party which had attacked the buffalo hunters now attempted to re-cross the creek a little further downstream and attack the lower end of the villages which was the Kiowa encampment itself, and where stood the red-painted tepee of a young Kiowa chief named Satanta [White-Bear] along with a number of Comanche allies.

BIG FIGHT AT WOLF CREEK

At the point where this group of Cheyenne and Arapahoe crossed the stream, it proved deeper than expected, the bank being high and the way up exceedingly muddy and slippery. They were severely hampered in their advance towards the enemy, and whilst thus engaged, a large body of Kiowa charged out from the village, some on horseback; many on foot, and spread out atop the bank in order to check the advance. A few Kiowa actually descended the bank and fought with Cheyennes and Arapahoe in the water.

Standing atop the south bank stood a brave and renowned Kiowa named Sleeping-Bear, bedecked in feathers and paint and wearing a magnificent yellow-painted and beaded hide war-shirt and because of which, the Cheyennes called him Yellow-Shirt. As two Cheyennes named Wolf-Chief and Medicine-Water came riding along at the base of the bank searching for a way up, Wolf-Chief saw the Kiowa man above him and attempted to count coup with his lance. Sleeping-Bear, however, took hold of the lance; wrenched it from the Cheyenne's grip and with it poised above his head in both hands, looked hard at Medicine-Water for a place uncovered by the latter's coat-of-mail where he might severely wound his adversary. Unfortunately for Medicine-Water, the iron-shirt he was wearing was styled with a wide open neck and it was here, close to the collar-bone, that the Kiowa at last made his strike. However, Sleeping-Bear managed to inflict only a flesh wound and before he could finish the job, two other Cheyennes one of which again was Old-Little-Wolf, rode over to Medicine-Water's assistance. Old-Little-Wolf counted coup on the lone Kiowa with his lance, but Sleeping-Bear then dropped the lance and using instead his bow and arrows, shot a feathered shaft which struck Medicine-Water in the cheek. Notwithstanding this, both Wolf-Chief and Medicine-Water together drove the Kiowa back, each counting coup on him as they did so, but the Kiowa Sleeping-Bear then remounted his waiting pony and managed to escape back among his own people. Just then, yet another large body of Kiowa, Comanche and Kiowa-Apache came rushing from the village, and charged forward amass, forcing the Cheyennes and Arapahoe on that part of the field to give way.

Before the Cheyenne contingent at this point had been forced to retreat, the same Kiowa Sleeping-Bear was shot with a musket ball in the thigh and was toppled from his horse. He then sat upright on the ground with legs outstretched and prepared to defend himself with bow and arrows. Cheyennes coming close to him counted yet another three coups on his person, bringing the total times to nine, and then he was killed as others among the Cheyenne and Arapahoe rode by. Such respect did the Cheyennes have for this particular Kiowa fighter, that each of those who counted `coup` on him that day, named one of their sons after him, but by their own name for the man who they themselves knew as Yellow-Shirt.

Others among those Cheyennes retreating across the ford back from whence they came, were the afore-mentioned Pushing-Ahead and Crooked-Neck. They and their comrades retreated only so far when they reigned in their ponies and turning them around, charged straight at their pursuers and drove them back to the barricades. During this event, the Cheyenne named Sun-Maker shot a horseback Comanche in the back with an arrow, and although the rider continued racing his steed across the creek towards his village, before he could reach his own people, he suddenly threw up both arms in the air and fell from his horse a dead man.

The battle now went back and forth between those warriors engaged within and outside the breastworks; some mounted, others on foot, sometimes to the advantage of the Cheyennes and Arapahoe, sometimes to the enemy. Several times either a Cheyenne, Arapahoe, Kiowa, Comanche or Kiowa-Apache was dismounted and put on foot, and was at the mercy of the foe when his horse had been shot from under him. Often when such an event occurred, a fellow warrior would bravely face the enemy missiles, ride up to a dismounted comrade and taking him up behind him on his horse, would gallop off to safety within his own lines. Some others, nonetheless, having at first been rescued, did not actually make it back before being killed.

At one stage while the fighting around the Kiowa breastworks was raging, a lone Comanche returning from a hunt and seeing what was going on, rode straight towards the attacking Cheyennes and Arapahoe to join in the fray. This man`s horse was shot from under him and he ran on foot back to the beleaguered village; promptly mounted another horse and returned once again racing towards the foe, although at this time, with a host of Kiowa and Comanche following behind. At another time still around the breastworks, a middle-aged Comanche riding a fine black horse also rode towards the enemy and disappeared among them. Soon, however, his black steed returned at a gallop to the Comanche tepees, but without its rider who had been killed in the melee then going on.

This man had four sons, three of which were fighting in another part of the field. When word was brought them of their father's death, they raced over to where he lay and transported the corpse back to the village from whence he came. Leaving the body in the care of relatives, one of the sons mounted the same black horse and without hesitation, rode into the fight. In a short time, it is said, the black horse again came galloping back, but without its rider, indicating the death of the son who had recently ridden out. Upon this, the second son mounted the returned horse and also rode off into the thick of the fighting.

Again, the black horse returned with no rider and likewise, the third son mounted up and disappeared among the foe. Needless to say, the said horse returned yet again on its own. But this time as the fourth and youngest son attempted to mount the animal, his relatives held him fast and instead cut the horse's throat, as the animal had proved, so they thought, a very bad omen and in such a way, they prevented the last son from likewise riding to his death.

As the fighting continued to rage up and down along the banks on both sides of the creek and around the barricades themselves, the Kiowa and Comanche were driven back towards the outskirts of the tepees and sometimes back into the villages themselves with Cheyennes and Arapahoe in hot pursuit.

It was then that a lone Kiowa held his pony back in the rear of his comrades. He called to them to halt and witness his deeds. He then dismounted, took an arrow from his quiver and thrust it through the trailing end of a red quill-ornamented long sash tied about his waist. There he stood, facing the oncoming Cheyennes and Arapahoe alone with bow and arrows in hand, and beckoned to the enemy to come forward and fight. Most of the Cheyennes and Arapahoe knowing his suicide intention dare not go near him, and actually rode past him in pursuit of the still fleeing bulk of enemies. Others, though, coming behind their fellows, rode right up to the lone Kiowa and flaying about him with tomahawks and lances, finally brought him low and gleefully took his scalp. Now the fleeing enemy looking back, and seeing a Cheyenne racing atop the bank on the north side of the stream holding a long willow-wand with the suicide Kiowa's long hank of hair trailing from its end, turned their mounts around and again charged back across the stream. A *Yamparika* Comanche named Baby's-Neck then rode close to the Cheyenne displaying the scalp, and managed to lance him through and kill him.

It is said that among the Cheyennes then fighting around the barricades were four warriors of the Dog-Soldier Society. Each of whom had made a vow to sacrifice their lives against the enemy and by so doing, bring victory to the Cheyennes. One of these men held only a sacred pipe pertaining to that society, and another, was a brave young man named Whistling-Arrow. These two warriors charged in amongst the host of Kiowa and Comanche confronting them, and subsequently, were both killed outright in the event. Of the remaining two who also had vowed suicide, one survived, but the other, wearing a Dog-Soldier Society crow-feathered bonnet, staked himself to the ground close to the entrenched enemy and holding a Society staff, prepared to meet his doom alone and on foot. The Kiowa defenders and their allies endeavoured to accommodate his wish and the Dog-Soldier did indeed die where he stood. On his demise, a number of on-looking Cheyennes raced over to him and managed to retrieve the latter's society staff before the enemy could claim it. Another Cheyenne, the son of Porcupine-Bear himself, who was simply named Porcupine, rode right into the Kiowa village battling with the foe and likewise, was killed whilst doing so.

The momentum, however, of this fresh Kiowa, Kiowa-Apache and Comanche charge, drove the Cheyennes and Arapahoe away from that part of the field. Now, during the latter's retreat, Grey-Thunder the Cheyenne high-priest reigned up, and paused for a moment on one side of the melee. Because Porcupine-Bear and his followers had attacked the enemy prematurely, the required 'Arrow' rituals needed to be performed, had not been carried out, and all around him his people seemed to be in confusion. Warriors were dropping to the ground wounded or killed, while others were unhorsed and set on foot or left squirming and splashing in the water which by now was flowing red. Alongside Grey-Thunder rode Tail-Woman his wife with the Sacred Arrow bundle still strapped to her back. Turning to her, Grey-Thunder spoke in a proud yet meaningful tone,

> "The young men are calling me a fool…I am a man of many winters and thinking maybe they are right…It is time to join our ancestors and let the people chose a new Arrow Keeper." [2]

BIG FIGHT AT WOLF CREEK

CHEYENNE WOMAN, BLACK-BELLY
[Born circa; 1807] Edward S. Curtis Photo, 1907]
[A Cheyenne woman eye-witness to most events recounted herein]

Thereupon, after giving blessings to his wife, he turned his horse to face a thick bunch of the enemy and with a sudden high-pitched war-cry, went splashing back across the stream to where the enemy villages were. He was singing loud his death-song and shouting it was a good day to die. He intended to literally hurl himself and his steed into the midst of the enemy, but he did not make the far bank. Grey-Thunder's horse began to balk and a Comanche named Not-Exhausted came close and lanced the priest through. A dozen and more Kiowa and Comanche then fell upon Grey-Thunder as he lay on the ground, and within a matter of minutes, left his scalped and mutilated body face downwards half in and half out of the water on the muddy step running up the south bank. Without thoughts of compassion, Kiowa and Comanche pony hooves trampled over the blood-drenched corpse and alas it was, such a revered old man's death went at first unnoticed by his own people. The Kiowa and their allies saw that the Cheyenne they had killed had some form of scrofula around his crutch and on top of his thighs, and so have since referred to him by the term, White-Marked-Loins.

Soon, however, the cry did go up that the revered Grey-Thunder had fallen, and only cries of anger from Cheyenne throats could be heard above the din of battle. Their confidence now somewhat shattered, the Cheyennes held back their mounts and hesitated a while as they wondered what to do next. At last with renewed vigour, Cheyennes and Arapahoe did again charge forward and this time, swept over the then stationary and whooping Kiowa and Comanche in a desperate attempt to retrieve the body of their shaman. The enemy force weltered away under the fury of this counter-charge and at length, Grey-Thunder's body was recovered. Grey-Thunder was the first important Cheyenne among them to be slain that day.

Then all at once, enemy numbers swelled with the arrival of an even larger Comanche contingent which had been out hunting buffalo and having just returned, now entered the fray. When coming to the ford, this enemy group of re-enforcements forced the Cheyenne and Arapahoe once more to retreat.

At this point, the Kiowa war-chief Black-Horse, who earlier because his son had been killed in the fight with Bowstrings the previous summer had tried to instigate a Kiowa and Comanche crusade against the Cheyennes, received a mortal gun-shot wound, but managed to stay in the saddle and was rescued by comrades who took him back within the entrenchments of the Kiowa village, although he succumbed to his injury a short time later.

As the Cheyennes raced back across Wolf Creek to its north bank pursued by these fresh enemy fighters, the Cheyenne Big-Breast turned in the saddle and gazing upon the very emissaries of death, he welcomed what he saw. Suddenly, he spurred his horse to splash back across the creek while calling to the Kiowa and Comanche to give him battle and send him to his dead brothers across the Sand Hills of the After World. His totems were pleased with Big-Breast and put great courage in his heart and for a while, he fought well and hard against countless adversaries at the ford, and several were the enemy laid low by his hand. But the will to live had left Big-Breast long ago and for several moons he had been a man in love with death. Soon his torso and arms sprouted feathered-shafts; blood flowed from his many wounds down his legs and over his horse's withers and he knew he had got his death wound. Toppling from his horse, the steed that once so nobly bore so great a man wrested free of its fallen

BIG FIGHT AT WOLF CREEK

rider. It galloped away from the tentacles of hell, leaving its master to shed his life-blood in the crimson water which was now the ford at Wolf Creek.

The Cheyennes and Arapahoe meanwhile, having fallen back across the creek re-grouped along the north bank. In this retreat two more Cheyennes other than Big-Breast were slain and many more suffered wounds of various degree, while their pursuing enemies were actually spared any sizable number of casualties during this particular phase of their counter-attack.

The Kiowa and allies then raced their ponies back and forth along the crest of the south bank, whooping savagely at their killing of Big-Breast and jeering at the Cheyennes and Arapahoe, who themselves, had halted along the north bank and were returning the insults and taunts heaped upon them by the foe. Yet they dare not retrieve the body of Big-Breast which bobbed up and down in the water in full view, pin-cushioned with arrows with its head scalped and body bloody.

It was during this phase of Cheyenne and Arapahoe retreat back across the stream, that a veteran Cheyenne fighter named Medicine-Bear received an arrow in the face, but lived to tell the tale, while a Cheyenne comrade named Howling-Wolf, got a musket ball in the chest but also survived. The Cheyenne Muskrat had his horse shot from under him, but was rescued by a comrade, and among other Cheyennes slain by the enemy at this time, was an old and highly respected holy man known as Deaf-Man and another chief named Grey-Hair. A Comanche who struck coup on one of the retreating enemy with the barrel of his empty gun, was also killed during this part of the fracas.

While the Cheyenne and Arapahoe were forcing their mounts up the slippery north bank, the Arapahoe Flat-War-Club who also had pledged himself to die, sat his magnificent horse in the wake of his comrades with only his famous war-club to protect him. Near him, likewise making a stand, was a lone mounted Cheyenne. Together, Flat-War-Club and his companion warded off those among the pursuing enemy who were brave enough to confront them. Flat-War-Club was wielding his gigantic weapon with both hands, and brought it crashing down full into the face of his first attacker, who with a tremendous howl of pain, literally spun around in the saddle before toppling into the water, his legs and arms kicking and waving frantically with every bone in his bloodied face smashed to fragments. After this, few were those who ventured close enough for combat and of those that did, they also were sent spinning off their mounts and into a watery grave.

In the middle of the ford, Flat-War-Club's Cheyenne companion had his horse shot from under him. He was floundering in the stream endeavouring to reach the north bank and safety. A group of Kiowa and Comanche seeing his disadvantage, spurred their ponies forward eager for his scalp. Desperately the Cheyenne tried to gain the bank before they overtook him, but his haste only hampered his speed and lessened his chance of life. Flat-War-Club was first to see his comrade's predicament. Immediately he took the initiative and without heed for his own safety, the lone Arapahoe whipped up his mount and splashed through the water to give assistance to his ally.

Groups of Kiowa and Comanche racing their ponies to and fro along the south bank and realising Flat-War-Club's intention, all at once rode pell-mell into the water and screaming insults and defiance at him, joined their foremost comrades in charging the fleeing Cheyennes, now that two enemy scalps seemed imminent. The lone Cheyenne knew that whoever first reached him, either Flat-War-Club of the foe, would be the answer whether he lived or died, for by the time those Cheyennes and Arapahoe on the north side realised what was going on, it was too late for them to be of any assistance. The Kiowa and their allies were too close to their quarry. The Cheyennes could only shout encouragement to the pair and continue slating the enemy, and the result of the unequal duel about to transpire was entirely in the hands of Flat-War-Club.

The Gods were watching the lone Arapahoe, and putting the swiftness of the hawk into his steed, and while his adversaries were some way off they allowed Flat-War-Club to reach his Cheyenne comrade. Edging his mount backwards, he bade the Cheyenne climb up behind him and when both were settled on the animal's back, they set off towards the north bank and safety. But the Gods remembered the personal vow the lone Arapahoe had made, and now called on him to keep it.

The oncoming Kiowas let fly a barrage of arrows and musketry at the pair, but appearing to bare charmed lives, they rode on towards the north bank unscathed. Then, only twenty or so yards from their objective, another fusillade from their pursuers sent both men and horse stumbling head over heels into the water with half-a-dozen feathered flights quivering in the Cheyenne's back, and two or three in that of the Arapahoe. One musket ball had actually gone right through the Cheyenne and entered the Arapahoe Flat-War-Club through his back, and was itself enough to cause a death wound.

The great `Dandy` of the Plains was dead.

Those Cheyennes and Arapahoe on the north bank cried to the heavens in grief and anger. Their whole body then charged into the creek to exact revenge against the foe, and caused the latter in turn to flee precipitously back to the south bank and their barricaded village, with all the haste they could muster.

Now, of course, the Cheyennes and Arapahoe as a combined host, were in the fight again.

A Cheyenne known as Two-Crows envisaged playing the same role as had others by sacrificing his life in order to obtain lasting honour such a deed would bring him. At the time when Two-Crows decided the road he was destined to take, the besieged Kiowa and the latter`s allies realised their position was desperate. Thus, yet another attempt to counter-attack was executed and although not as successful as those previous, such was its suddenness and momentum it did manage to stem the current Cheyenne and Arapahoe assault, who in response, again gave up the front and effected a short and sharp retreat. This was, so thought Two-Crows, the ideal moment to make his stand.

It was then that a Kiowa-Apache contingent was leading the counter-attack. Turning his horse around and facing them, Two-Crows reigned in his pony between an oncoming group of Kiowa-Apaches and his fleeing comrades. He cried out to his people that he alone would hold the enemy back, while they and the Arapahoe made good their escape. This lone Cheyenne; already loved and honoured by his people and armed with only a lance and hunting knife stayed his ground, and was quickly surrounded by his oncoming foes. He presented an imposing sight, sitting erect in the saddle with a full-blown bonnet of eagle feathers on his head nodding gently in the breeze. His raven-black hair fell loose over his shoulders and down to his middle, while a polished white-bone breastplate contrasted against his copper-coloured torso, albeit his tarnished yellow-hide leggings adorned with numerous horizontal black stripes representing many `coups` stood out predominant over all.

He had set his heart upon dying this day, and swinging his left leg over his horse`s shoulder he dismounted on the right-hand side, then struck his steed on the rump with the flat of his lance-point so it took off towards his watching people, cutting off any chance of escape.

Kiowa-Apaches galloped their ponies towards him from every angle, it seemed, and a score of arrows flew past and thudded into the ground about him. Two-Crows turned continuously with the agility of a cat to check an assailant's lance-thrust or dodge an arrow. Yet for every strike he avoided, one was received and at last, his stamina failed him. Slowly he began sinking to the ground and next moment, was on one knee, still parrying enemy spears and tomahawk blows with his body oozing blood from many savage cuts and gashes. He then disappeared under a writhing mass of Kiowa-Apaches, who threw themselves at him and literally, hacked him to pieces.

At the same time, those Cheyennes and Arapahoe that had ridden further along the north bank downstream, were disputing another ford with detachments of Kiowa and Comanche. The Cheyennes and Arapahoe continued their advance and got right up to the village breastworks once again. But the enemy defenders were reinforced by yet another body of Comanche on fresh mounts which came smashing into the fray, and there was much hand to hand fighting at that point. Thus, back and forth the contest still swayed, sometimes occasioning brief periods of inactivity to give their mounts a breathing space, and whereupon, both sides communicated with each other by shouting across the creek or by signs as to who and how they were fighting.

Around twilight as the sun began dipping behind the western hills, the whole congregation of Cheyenne and Arapahoe non-combatants appeared atop a crest over-looking the bloody arena below. The Kiowa and their allies were greatly perturbed at the sight, supposing them to be an additional enemy force now coming to carry on the fight. A Kiowa camp crier went through his village telling the women to leave their lodges standing and take the horses and children further up the creek to a Comanche camp on the South Canadian River some distance away, and there prepare to make yet another stand against the foe.

This proposed move, however, was unnecessary. A cry went up that the Arapahoe had signalled they were prepared to end the contest and actually make peace with the foe. Cheyennes by then, were also retiring from the scene of conflict and soon after, the whole force of Cheyenne and Arapahoe fighters crossed the creek to its north bank, and began heading for their own camps on Beaver Creek a little to the west.

BIG FIGHT AT WOLF CREEK

After crossing Wolf Creek, a Kiowa woman was discovered hiding among some driftwood and was promptly shot and killed. The Cheyennes had lost too many important warriors for them to show mercy. Indeed, no enemy prisoners were taken and none among the enemy that fell into their grasp were spared. Even when another enemy female was sniffed out from hiding by Cheyenne dogs while the latter's non-combatants had been ascending the hills to observe the last phase of battle, no pity or remorse was shown. The wife of the earlier killed Cheyenne chief Medicine-Snake, threw her arms around her to hold her tight, and calling to others to help, still held the captive while other female Cheyennes came up and cut the unarmed defenceless woman to death.

Yellow-Wolf the *Heviatanio* band chieftain then, too, spurred his tired mount away from the scene of slaughter, his face-paint and body-paint running and stained with perspiration. He sat his horse atop a small rise which offered a panoramic view of the entire scene. Below him in the twilight of the day, fatigued warriors of both Cheyennes and Arapahoe having given up the fight, were straggling back west across the open ground to their lodges on the Beaver. Dusk became apparent, and only those from each tribe involved in retrieving or looking for bodies of dead and severely wounded relatives and friends remained on the field of conflict. Occasionally, a musket shot or insult was exchanged if either parties got too close to one another.

Turning slowly from the line of retreat, Old-Little-Wolf who had proved his prowess as both fighter and leader many times that day, headed his mount towards a rise where sat Yellow-Wolf still motionless on his steed. Old-Little-Wolf reigned up beside him, and he, too, gazed with eyes of pity over the blood-drenched battle-ground. Many thoughts flashed through their minds, but gory honours earned that day which might have caused their chests to swell, were over-shadowed by grief they both harboured for love-ones slain and maimed. At length, Old-Little-Wolf greeted Yellow-Wolf with the traditional Cheyenne colloquium, and after a pause continued,

> "It is not good that Yellow-Wolf is not with his people to show how strong is his *medicine*, for he has survived this day of slaughter."

BIG FIGHT AT WOLF CREEK

"My heart is heavy," replied Yellow-Wolf. "...Many of my brothers-in-arms have crossed to the Sand Hills this day...The great *Ma`he`o* does not smile upon his children."

For a moment Old-Little-Wolf himself was silent, and although his eyes were dry and countenance impassive, he was crying within himself. He raised his gaze to the western horizon and answered,

"Now the fighting is done...I am thinking of my woman and warm lodge across the river."
"*Doh*," concurred Yellow-Wolf, "...I also am thinking these things...The sun hides its face from this place and goes away to sleep....I am thinking that is what we, too, should do."
"It is so," said Old-Little-Wolf, and both agreed it was time to go home.

- 0 - 0 - 0 - 0 - 0 - 0 - 0 - 0 - 0 - 0 –

CHEYENNE WARRIOR, FIRE-WOLF

INTERTRIBAL PEACE ON THE SOUTHERN PLAINS

CHAPTER 24.

INTERTRIBAL PEACE ON THE SOUTHERN PLAINS [1839-'40]

From the moment fighting ceased along Wolf Creek, warriors had come limping into the Cheyenne and Arapahoe villages north from across that river. Even after darkness had covered the land for many hours, groups of horsemen and lone riders still straggled into camp, many bringing news of one and another's death by bloodied corpses lying stiff across the backs of ponies. It was indeed a sad time for the Cheyennes. There would be much mourning throughout the rest of the summer season.

Come morning, the air again was fresh and clean. The sun smiled on lush prairies causing the waters of the Beaver to sparkle as if sprinkled with numerous diamonds. But the Cheyennes and Arapahoe were not free from expectation of defeat. Scouts came in at sunrise having lingered around the Kiowa village the previous three days and nights, lest the enemy attempted a counter-attack, and now they brought with them discouraging news. On the third day a large party of Osage along with a number of Comanche and white men, had arrived at the Kiowa and Kiowa-Apache village on a peace mission, and were haggling the Kiowa and their allies to resume the battle.

Such discourse troubled the Cheyennes and Arapahoe. Their lodges were immediately struck, and their whole ensemble began moving hastily away.

The white men referred to were led by E. L. Chouteau, a nephew of Auguste Pierre Chouteau then Agent for those tribes in what was called Indian Territory, but now known as Oklahoma. With them were thirty Osage and eight Comanche along with twelve Government dragoons under a Lieutenant Lucius B. Northrop. The white men's mission was to prevent an exceleration of intertribal warfare after, earlier that spring, Comanches and Kiowa had made it known they intended to launch their own crusade against Cheyennes and Arapahoe, while the Osage themselves comprised a delegation intending to make peace with their erdtwhile Kiowa and Comanche foes.

As the aforesaid party entered the Kiowa camp, they were told of forty-three Kiowa warriors killed in the recent battle, along with a number of women and children also slain. Twelve Cheyenne corpses and one Arapahoe were still lying in various parts of the conflict area having not been carried away by the Cheyenne and Arapahoe attackers, and also, at least one-hundred dead horses still littered the same area. The Comanche dead by the time of the white men's arrival had already been interred and the white men visited their fresh graves. The Kiowas further informed Chouteau that had it not been for a supply of arms and ammunition received while on a recent visit to Camp Holmes, then the Kiowa and their Kiowa-Apache and Comanche allies could not have driven off their foes.

The Kiowa and their allies were still very tired and grieving over their dead and wounded, and when the Osage contingent suggested getting together a large retaliatory force to follow up the retreating Cheyennes and Arapahoe and exact revenge, the Kiowa chiefs declared that enough blood had already been spilt, and that the enemy should be allowed to move out of the country without further molestation.

The Cheyennes and Arapahoe for their part, had not, however, waited to determine their enemies' intentions. Even though their number could still match the combined forces of the latter, the stamina of their own warriors would most certainly fail them. Thus, they themselves had no stomach for a continuation of hostilities.

The Cheyennes and Arapahoe in response split their forces and continued north in a dozen and more lamenting bands. Once back on home soil on the South Platte, they buried the dead bodies they had carried all the way from Wolf Creek and continued to lament their losses in the customary manner.

The wife of the deceased Grey-Thunder had taken possession of the 'Sacred Arrows' after her husband's demise, and bore them safely home to Arkansas River and Bent's Fort. At that place, the shaman named Elk-River took temporary charge of the talismans, until, that is, some few months later, the Cheyenne chief's council of forty-four selected another as permenant 'Arrow Keeper' and this man thereafter, was known among the Cheyennes as Lame-Medicine-Man, who owing to being lame in one leg due to a wound sustained during the recent Kiowa fight, was often referred to simply by white men of his aquaintence as The-Lame.[1]

However, the following summer of '39, smallpox struck each of the Southern Plains Tribes which included Cheyennes. Previously, since the peace effected at the end of the Wolf Creek fight of '38 between visiting Osage and

Kiowa, Kiowa-Apache and Comanche, the pact had proved a success, as since then, the above Nations began regularly visiting each other's camps. It was not unusual then, that Osages with a number of allied Kaws visited the Kiowa Sun-Dance camp on Wolf Creek that following summer of '39. Innocently, the visitors brought gifts to their hosts of tobacco, horses and goodwill, but, unwittingly, also brought the smallpox and subsequent disaster to all those gathered together.

The Southern Arapahoe, having always been in some kind of harmony with the Kiowa-Apache long before the fight at Wolf Creek, had already sued for peace with each other and with the Kiowa and Comanche at the close of the aforementioned fight of '38. Indeed, Arapahoes had previously inter-married among the Kiowa-Apache for many years, and the Arapahoe had since realised their own rashness of declaring war on the Kiowa and Comanche since the dragging of an Arapahoe head through a Kiowa village the previous winter, albeit after the victim had been caught stealing Kiowa horses. Added to this, during the winter of '38 -'39, Kiowas had wiped out a whole party of Arapahoe, and the latter thereafter, lost no time in patching up their quarrel with the Kiowa-Apache. Thus, by summer of '39, Arapahoes were again actually visiting and trading with Kowa-Apaches, Kiowa and Comanches in perfect harmony, as they had done so in the past.

Cheyennes, nonetheless, continued in hostility against all the allied Southern Tribes and during which, they slew a famous Comanche chief named *Peyevirou*. Having said this, still Cheyennes were visitors and allies to their ancient friends the Arapahoe.

Then in spring 1840 it happened.

A group of Kiowa-Apache arrived at a Southern Arapahoe camp to visit a woman of their tribe married to a kinsman of the head Arapahoe chief, Little-Raven. One of Little-Raven's subordinate chiefs named Bull, took the visitors into his own lodge and welcomed them as guests.

It was not long after this that a group of eight Cheyennes led by a warrior named Seven-Bulls rode proudly into the same Arapahoe camp, but painted and armed for war. Seeing the aforesaid Kiowa-Apache visitors, the Cheyennes became arrogant and aggressive, and the once congenial atmosphere in the Arapahoe camp became tense and ominous.

INTERTRIBAL PEACE ON THE SOUTHERN PLAINS

The Arapahoe Bull tactically intervened, and greeting the Cheyennes as friends, reminded them of the universal Indian custom among all tribes of treating visitors with hospitality if they came in peace, and further, he said, the Kiowa-Apache in their camp would be protected by their Arapahoe hosts. Neither Kiowa-Apaches nor Cheyennes would dare violate such a law, and especially so, as one day the same law might well protect their own lives if in a similar situation. Bull's persuasions were effective. He even managed to get both rival parties to sit down together in his lodge and talk.

All apparently went well. The village occupants loitering outside Bull's tepee, eager to witness the outcome whatever it might be.

After much discourse between those in the lodge, the Arapahoe Bull filled his pipe; lit it, and handed it in turn to each Cheyenne and Kiowa-Apache present with an offer to smoke. A spokesman for the Kiowa-Apache stood up and declared that his people along with the Kiowa and Comanche had long wished peace with the Cheyennes, and further said that the Kiowa would return the forty-eight Cheyenne scalps taken when the Bowstrings had been killed two years earlier, while the Comanche themselves had promised to give the Cheyennes many horses if the latter accepted their proposal of peace.

However, refusing the offered pipe, Seven-Bulls next stood up and addressed the Kiowa-Apaches around him.

> "Friends" he said, "You know we ourselves are not chiefs...We cannot smoke with these Kiowa-Apache for we do not have power to do so...As warriors only, we have no authority here within us...We can only carry the messages you give us and relay them to our chiefs. I have listened to what you have said, and when the sun next rises, I and my comrades will start back to our village and repeat the words you have told us...Our chiefs alone must decide what will be done...We ourselves are but young men and cannot make agreements with you by ourselves, but we will take your words of goodwill to our chiefs." [2]

Both the Arapahoe and Kiowa-Apache understood the words of Seven-Bulls and next morning, the Cheyennes departed from the camp in good faith. Of course, the Cheyennes abandoned their proposed sortie on a Kiowa or

INTERTRIBAL PEACE ON THE SOUTHERN PLAINS

Comanche horse herd, and instead, they raced back home to their own village recently left on Shawnee Creek, a small tributary of the Republican to the north.

Back at the Cheyenne village, Seven-Bulls told his chiefs of their encounter at the Arapahoe camp, and the rest of his party collaborated what he said. The very next day, a large council lodge the size of two joined-together hbuffalo ide tepees was erected in the centre of the Cheyenne village, and all the Cheyenne chiefs, forty-four in number having come from far and near, were invited to attend.

At length, with all the Nation's chiefs from scattered camps across the land sitting cross-legged in a circle in the great lodge, the council commenced. As each chief rose in turn and spoke, there ensued much heated debate. Some haggled for peace, whilst others were against such a move, and after many hours of discussion both for and against, the chiefs as a unanimous body could still not reach a decision.

The then head Cheyenne Chief High-Backed-Wolf 2d, who was acting as spokesman and co-ordinator of the council, suggested leaving the ultimate decision to the most prominent Warrior Society, the Dog-Soldiers. The Dog-Soldiers, however, themselves began arguing over the same question, and at length, Beard, an old and the most respected warrior among them, finally persuaded two other prominent men with the honorary title of 'Door-Keepers' of the Dog-Soldier lodge, named White-Antelope and Little-Old-Man, to decide the issue among themselves and have the last word on the matter. Both White-Antelope and Little-Old-Man were leading old-time warriors and very wise, always holding the welfare of the people foremost in their minds and deeds. This all the Cheyenne people knew, and were ready and willing to agree with which ever road they happened to come to. As it was, the two old veterans did not hesitate to answer.

"Yes," they said, "...It will be peace with the Kiowa, Kiowa-Apache and Comanche."

The decision was welcomed by the vast majority of Cheyennes with exclamations of *"Ha-Ho, Ha-Ho,"* [Thank you, Thank you], and High-Backed-Wolf 2d, took it upon himself as elected Sweet-Medicine-Chief of the Nation, to inform the people of the council's final decision. This he did by riding around the great circle of lodges crying aloud the news, and forbidding any to start on a war-trip against either of the southern tribes involved.

Runners were dispatched to nearby Arapahoe camps informing them of the chiefs' decision, and who were then expected to inform the Kiowa-Apache with whom the Arapahoe had themselves already made peace. The Cheyennes, so the Arapahoe chiefs reported, would meet with the Southern Nations at a place known to the Indians as Two Butte Creek about fifty miles below Bent's Fort, and thereafter, the Cheyennes disbanded their great Medicine Lodge camp and in separate bodies, started for the said Creek. On route, they stopped off at the Bent's Fort itself, and from there they purchased through trade and on credit, hundreds of guns, knives, steel hatchets, rolls of calico, Navaho blankets, brass kettles and a vast assortment of the white man's delicacies, such as sugar, molasses and coffee. All to present to the Southern Tribes as tokens of Cheyenne goodwill.

The Cheyennes now with their Arapahoe allies and when reaching the afore-mentioned trysting site, again erected their tepees in two large circles several ranks deep with their openings facing east, and patiently waited the arrival of Kiowas, Comanche and Kiowa-Apaches. They had been in camp only two days when from over the hills to the south, came eight strange Indians riding leisurely towards them. From a distance the Cheyennes could distinguish by the latter's hair-styles and dress that they were selected emissaries of their expected guests.

The riders rode slowly and majestically onto the open ground in the middle of the Cheyenne camp circle as befitted their status, and all Cheyennes and Arapahoe then present, including men, women and children, crowded around to eye the solemn spectacle. When the riders reached the centre of the circle, they each dismounted and sat in a row, cross-legged and poker-faced, awaiting an audience with the Cheyenne chiefs.

These eight men had shown much bravery riding alone into the very midst of their one-time enemies, and, no doubt, were prepared to meet their deaths if the whole affair proved merely a rouse for treachery, or that a group of Cheyenne warriors attempted to extract retribution for kinfolk slain in previous conflicts, and kill them all. But such was not to be.

After a space of several minutes, the whole ensemble of forty-four Cheyenne chiefs appeared, bedecked in all their finery and feathers, and each holding in the crook of his left arm a long-stemmed pipe. In their other hand each held a long staff, some befeathered; others adorned perculier to their respective warrior societies and of personal status among the tribe. These men sat down on either side of the eight foreign dignitaries and together, formed a long row.

When all were seated and after a pipe had been passed around and all members had inhaled a few puffs from it, one of the foreign chiefs stood up with a more elaborately decorated long-stemmed pipe cradled in the crook of his left arm. He strode forward a few feet from his seated row of comrades ready to address those Cheyennes assembled around him. This man was a noted Kiowa chief named *Dohausan* or Little-Mountain, and others of his Kiowa tribesmen sitting close by were Satank [Sitting-Bear], Yellow-Hair, Eagle-Feather and a son of the aforesaid Yellow-Hair. Of the Comanche were chiefs Buffalo-Hump and Shaved-Head, while of the Kiowa-Apaches was a chief known as Leading-Bear. A second pipe was given to the son of Yellow-Hair who filled its bowl with sacred tobacco; lit the contents, then offered it first to the head Cheyenne Chief High-Backed-Wolf 2d to smoke. After High-Backed-Wolf had inhaled and exhaled the first ceremonial puffs, the pipe was handed around to the other leading Cheyenne and allied chiefs, who in turn also smoked, and by so doing, peace between the erstwhile warring tribes now sat together in a row, was duly confirmed.

Next, the Kiowa chief, Eagle-Feather, offered the head Cheyenne chief a bundle in which were dried scalps once belonging to the slaughtered Bowstring warriors killed three years before. The scalps were meant as a token of Kiowa good will, but the bundle was refused by High-Backed-Wolf, lest its contents inflame relatives of the deseased and possibly, change the congenial atmosphere to one of intertribal strife. High-Backed-Wolf then told his chiefs that all those wishing to give presents to their foreign visitors should now do so, and pile them around the Kiowa boy.

In response, many among the Cheyenne populous took forward their presents, which included striped Navaho blankets and were so many, they obscured the Kiowa boy from view. The head Kiowa Chief Little-Mountain then replied that when Cheyennes again met the Kiowa, Comanche and Kiowa-Apache in the near future, an official ceremony would be held to solidify peace-making between the five tribes present, and then the Southern tribes would reward their Cheyenne friends by giving them many presents in return, including horses and guns. Thus, the first stage of this particular time of intertribal harmony was enacted. The foreign dignitaries after staying the night with their hosts, finally left the latter's camp that following sunrise, having previously agreed that their entire tribes would meet together a few days hence on a broad grassy flat adjacent to the north side of the Arkansas, close to a thirty-mile growth of cottonwood trees and brush known as Big Timbers about five miles south-east of Bent's Fort.

Three days after this, the whole Cheyenne Nation and Southern Arapahoe erected their tepees yet again in two large circles adjacent to one another near Big Timbers, and later that same day, a few Kiowa runners came into the Cheyenne camp with word that the rest of their people along with three bands of Comanche and the Kiowa-Apache were not far distant. Certainly, before mid-afternoon the following day, the latter did arrive and set their lodges on an adjacent flat on the south side of the Arkansas across from the Cheyennes and Arapahoe on the north bank.

When all the visitors' tepees were up, High-Backed-Wolf rode alone over to the Southern tribal camps and invited chiefs of the three southern tribes to a grand buffalo-hide canopy fashioned from three tepee coverings standing in the centre of the Cheyenne camp, and where, the Cheyenne head chief said, their newly-arrived guests would be feasted and made welcome as was the custom. The respective chiefs and head men of the foreign guests accepted the invitation, and when the feast was concluded, Little-Mountain invited all the Cheyenne chiefs and head men to cross the river on foot next morning, and then in turn, they would be feasted and rewarded by the Southern allies.

Thus, the following day, a great body of Cheyennes including men, women and children went to the Allies' camp, and sitting in rows many ranks deep, all were feasted as promised.

When the grand feasting was over, Satank, the great Kiowa warrior, gave each Cheyenne a small stick and for the return of which, warriors from among each of the three Southern tribes would present the holder with a horse to take its place. Indeed, so old Cheyennes used to say, they were given so many horses by their guests at that time, they lacked enough ropes to lead them away. Satank alone, they said, gave over two-hundred and fifty head.

INTERTRIBAL PEACE ON THE SOUTHERN PLAINS

CHEYENNE HOWLING-WOLF'S PICTOGRAM OF MAKING PEACE WITH KIOWA
[Section 1]

"GIVING PRESENTS ACROSS THE RIVER." HOWLING-WOLF'S PICTOGRAM.
[Section 2.]

INTERTRIBAL PEACE ON THE SOUTHERN PLAINS

Old Cheyenne participants further said, that they as a tribe, then owned more horses than any other they were acquainted with. On the other hand, within a comparatively short period, the Kiowa, Comanche and Kiowa-Apache replenished the number of horses they had given away by their warriors raiding other tribes' stock, and also, from both Mexican and Texan herds further south.

After this period of 'Horse-giving across the river,' as the Cheyennes knew it, High-Backed-Wolf requested that next day, the three allied tribes should themselves gather in the centre of the Cheyenne village, and further told them to bring many pack-ponies in order to carry away gifts they would receive from the Cheyennes. The Cheyennes then departed back across the river to their own camp, and where their women-folk began cooking vast quantities of various meats in preparation of giving their new-found friends another, albeit, an even more gargantuan feast the following day.

Thus next morning around Ten o' Clock by the white man's time, Kiowas, Comanches and Kiowa-Apaches crossed the river to the north bank in a great mixed mass. Together they thronged the inner circle of Cheyenne tepees, while the camp women brought forth great quantities of food, including the white man's sweet foods such as sugar and molasses and certain fruits, much desired by the Indians. Even while the guests were still eating, they were presented many brass kettles, rolls of brightly-coloured calico and strouding-cloth and also, coats, trouses and shirts of the white man's varied fashions and materials, and withal, iron implements of swords, metal arrow pints and spear blades, knives and iron-bladed tomahawks.

Suddenly, there was heard a fusillade of musket shot, as one-hundred and fifty Cheyennes fired guns into the air, and this was just before presenting the same firearms to their guests.

It would have seemed that old enmities between all those now gathered together had never before existed, as the whole assembly treated each other like long-lost relatives having returned to the fold.

Later that day at dusk, the southern visitors returned to their camps on the south side of the river over-laden with merchandise, and next morning, a grand trading fair was arranged on another part of the flats, while on yet another, competitive horse races were held, games of shoots-the-arrow and the hand game, whilst other warriors sat in harmony with each other discussing past conflicts and of their personal adventures. Certain children among each tribe were adopted by members of another, and throughout all was intertribal dancing, singing, the beating of drums and of whooping in wild excitement.

White trappers and traders meanwhile, watched the affair with interest, while the doors of Fort Bent itself were flung wide open for trade with Indian customers, particularly with Comanches, who took immediate advantage of looking over the white men`s wares as they had wished to do since the fort`s erection, but dissuaded from doing so by Cheyennes in the vicinity.

The whole affair proved a great success, and especially so, when the fort occupants fired off a small canon time and again, to the great delight of the Indians.

On a more serious note, during the congenial atmosphere then presiding over the multi-tribal gathering, the trader William Bent himself managed to ransom several white child captives from the Comanches, and entered into a lasting peace with them and their Kiowa and Kiowa-Apache allies. However, at one stage, a small quantity of liquor got among the Indians and a brief scuffle ensued. The whole peace-making may then have collapsed and the flat lands made bloody by a large-scale intertribal battle. But the trader Bent intervened and put all existing alcohol under lock and key, thus preventing mayhem caused by a drunken orgy.

After two or three days more of continuous celebratioin, the great gathering at last came to an end. One by one the respective bands pulled down their lodges and began their weary treks back to their own domains. The Kiowa, Comanches and Kiowa-Apaches went south across the Red and Cimarron rivers and from where, they continued depredations against the Mexicans and Texans. The Cheyennes and Arapahoe for their part, went north against the Shoshoni, Crows and Pawnees, and indeed, any other Indian foes on hand.

The peace, however, then effected between Cheyennes, Arapahoe, Kiowa, Comanche and Kiowa-Apache at Big Timbers on the Arkansas, was since that summer of 1838, and but for minor temporary squabbles, has never yet been broken and thus, still holds firm today.

$$- 0 - 0 - 0 - 0 - 0 - 0 - 0 - 0 - 0 -$$

NOTES AND SOURCES

Introduction.
1. Originally published in varied form in, *"Ma'heo's Children,"* The Choir Press, Gloucester, England. 2018. And information supplied from archival *"papers"* and published works by George Bird Grinnell, Truman Michelson, James Mooney and others.

Chapter 1.
1. Originally published in varied form in, *"Ma'heo's Children,"* The Choir Press, Gloucester, England. 2018.

Chapter 2.
1. Originally published in varied form in, *"Ma'heo's Children,"* The Choir Press, Gloucester, England. 2018.

Chapter 3.
1. Information from *"The LaVerenderye Journals."* And; from the present Author's Crow Indian informant Joe Medicine Crow.
2. *"The American-Horse winter-count."* Smithsonian Institution. Washington D.C.

Chapter 4.
1. Information from Edwin James, *"The Major Long Expedition."* Washington D.C. And; both Crow and Cheyenne sources narrated to the present Author. Originally published in varied form in *"Red Was the Blood of our Forefathers."* The Caxton Press, Idaho. U.S.A. 2010.
2. Captain William Clark Journal. Washington D.C.
3. Joe Medicine Crow to Author.
4. George Bird Grinnell, *"Papers"* In; Southwest Museum, Los Angeles, California. U.S.A.

Chapter 5.
1. Llewelin and Hoebel, *"The Cheyenne Way."* Oklahoma University Press.
2. Joe Medicine Crow to Author.
3. George Bird Grinnell *"Papers."* In; The Southwest Museum, Los Angeles, California. U.S.A.
4. Sioux Winter-Counts. Smithsonian Institution. Washington D.C.
5. James H. Bradley *Ms.* Montana Historical Society. U.S.A.
6. Winona Plenty-Hoops [Crow informant] to Author.
7. Winona Plenty-Hoops [Crow informant] to Author.

    The Cheyennes always declared that if there had been only one village of Crows in the fight, then a good number of Cheyennes would have escaped. The presence of the whole Mountain Crow division had made their annihilation a certainty. When discussing the fight some years later at the Fort Laramie Treaty of 1851, Crow veterans who had taken part in the fight, described to the Cheyennes the man who had acted like a bird in front of the breastworks, but the Cheyennes could not determine who it had been. They did recognize One-Eyed-Antelope, when the Crows sang the song which the Cheyenne with the gun had sung each time he fired his weapon and killed a Crow. Why fire-power among the Crows had not annihilated the Cheyenne party much earlier than the two days and nights required, was probably due to the fact that old-time flintlock guns employed by Indians at the time were of the smooth-bore type, obtained from Fur Company posts and manufactured specifically for the Indian trade. These firearms were generally of an inferior quality and being un-rifled, proved extremely inaccurate over fifty yards or so. Additionally, they often suffered the barrel being cut down to be handled more easily from horseback, while both lead shot and wadding was rarely rammed home sufficiently, thus further reducing the gun's accuracy and velocity, and rendering such weapons ineffectual other than in close combat situations.

Hitherto, there has been confusion as to whether the Cheyenne party was composed of Crooked-Lance or Bowstring Society warriors. Grinnell stated they were the former, whilst George Bent said Bowstrings, and John Stands-In-Timber stated they were Crazy-Dogs. This last-named society belonged specifically to the Northern Cheyennes, and was the equivalent of the Bowstrings among the Southerners. However, the Crazy-Dogs did not come into being until after the separation of the Cheyennes into their Northern and Southern divisions about the date 1834. Neither were the Bowstrings in any great number in the North Country during the time of the aforesaid fight. It must be admitted, though, that the Crooked-Lances and Bowstrings were very closely connected, and that the original Crazy-Dogs had been made up in the first instance, from ex-Crooked-Lance and Bowstring soldiers combined. It is indicative also that two Cheyenne brothers slain in the fight had been Suhtaio band members, and that the punitive expedition undertaken thereafter by the Cheyenne Nation in order to avenge its loss, was, primarily, instigated and organized by the Suhtaio. It must then be assumed that the fight at Prairie Dog Creek had been a Suhtaio affair, and thus involved Crooked-Lance warriors which, certainly, was the predominant society among the Suhtaio and included at the date in question, i.e. 1819, for the most part only Suhtaio band members.

According to the Grinnell account, the Crows once called the site of the battle and its nearby stream, "Crow Standing Butte" and "Crow Standing Creek" respectively, in memory of the Cheyenne brave who had ran around outside the breastworks imitating a bird. The Cheyennes of old used similar appellations, but declared that the meaning was "Where they [Cheyennes] Stood off the Crows." On the other hand, a Crow informant of Joe Medicine Crow named Plain-Feather, stated that the Crow name should more properly be rendered "Where Owner-of-Raven was Killed," as for a long time the Crows had thought that the Cheyenne warrior prancing outside the breastworks had been soliciting the aid of his personal medicine helper, which, the Crows believed, took the form of a raven. Having said this, yet another Crow name for the site – as told to Tim McCleary by a Crow informant, is rendered "Where Raven-Owner was attacked," referring to the initial assault upon the Crooked-Lance Cheyennes, and is said by the same source to have occurred near the foothills just south of the present-day town of Story in the northern part of Wyoming.

The stream today is marked on modern day maps as Prairie Dog Creek, although in the 1860s when the military post Fort Phil Kearney stood nearby, it was known to troops stationed there as "Peno Creek." It is also said that the fight actually took place very close to where the Crow Cultural Hero No-Intestines [or a later protégé] first planted the Crow Nation's Sacred Tobacco Seeds. For this reason, the fight in question may have had a more significant impact on the Crows, who would have regarded the presence of enemies in that vicinity as a sacrilegious

NOTES AND SOURCES

violation and trespass into an area revered by the Crows as a holy and inviolable place of worship and of religious mystery.

Chapter 6.
1. Information from Edwin James, *"The Major Long Expedition."* Washington D.C. And; both Crow and Cheyenne sources narrated to the present Author.

Chapter 7.
1. George Bird Grinnell *"Papers."* In; Southwest Museum, Los Angeles, California. U.S.A.
2. Lowie, Robert H. *"Crow Texts."* California University Press, 1960. And; Bradley, James H. *"Papers."* Montana Historical Society. U.S.A.
3. Joe Medicine Crow to Author.
4. Lowie, Robert H. *"Crow Texts."* California University Press, 1960.
5. Lowie, Robert H. *"Crow Texts."* California University Press, 1960.
6. Lowie, Robert H. *"Crow Texts."* California University Press, 1960.

Chapter 8.
1. George Bird Grinnell *"Papers."* In; Southwest Museum, Los Angeles, California. U.S.A.
2, Catlin, George. *"The North American Indian."* Smithsonian Institution. Washington D.C.
3. Lieutenant Welch *"Papers."* On Line.

Chapter 9.
1. John-Stands-In-Timber, *"Cheyenne Memories."* Oklahoma University Press.
2. George Bird Grinnell, *"By Cheyenne Campfires."* Oklahoma University Press.

Chapter 10.
1. George Bird Grinnell *"Papers."* In; Southwest Museum, Los Angeles, California. U.S.A.
2. George Bent, *"Letters."* Denver Public Library, [Archival Collections] Colorado. U.S.A.
3. Lieutenant James Abert, *"Journal."* Smithsonian Institution. Washington D.C.

Chapter 11.
1. George Bird Grinnell *"Papers."* In; Southwest Museum, Los Angeles, California.

Chapter 12.
1. George Bird Grinnell *"Papers,"* In Southwest Museum, Los Angeles, California. And; James H. Dorsey. *"How the Pawnees Captured the Cheyenne Medicine Arrows."* Smithsonian Institution. Washington D.C.

Chapter 13.
1. George Bird Grinnell *"Papers."* In; Southwest Museum, Los Angeles, California.

NOTES AND SOURCES

2. Edwin Denig, *"Five Indian Tribes of the Upper Missouri."* Oklahoma University Press.And; Robert H. Lowie, *"Crow Texts."* California University Press, 1960. And; Stanley Vestal *"Papers."* Oklahoma University, U.S.A.

Chapter 14.
1. George Bird Grinnell *"Papers."* In; Southwest Museum, Los Angeles, California.

Chapter 15.
1. Grinnell, George Bird, *"The Cheyenne Indians."* Vol. 1. P.30.
  See also; Marquia, Thomas B. *"Wooden-Leg."* Here Wooden-leg indicates the same trip to Washington D.C., and notes the name No-Braids as one of the Cheyenne delegates.
  In 1832, the white trader Kenneth McKenzie at Fort Union at the mouth of Yellowstone River on the Upper Missouri, along with the then Indian Agent John F.A. Sanford, invited dignitaries from several tribes to return with Agent Sanford to Washington D,C. and meet with the Great White Father, President Andrew Jackson. For some reason, Crow chiefs could not be contacted, but chiefs of the Blackfoot, Cheyenne, Cree, Assiniboine and Chippewa were, and who agreed to go with the Agent to Washington D.C. However, both the Blackfoot and Cheyenne delegates went no further than the Missouri, while the Cree, Chippewa and Assiniboine continued on. Some few weeks later that same year of `32, after the three tribal chiefs left the Capitol, they were returning to their own countries up the Missouri on the steamboat *Yellowstone*, and on board was the traveling the white man artist George Catlin. At the mouth of Teton [Bad] River on the west side of the Missouri, the said artist actually met the Cheyenne Chief High-Backed-Wolf [who he referred to as Wolf-on-the-Hill] and the latter`s wife Bathes-Her-Knees, and painted both their likeness on canvas.

Chapter 16.
1. Beckwourth, James P. *"Life and Adventures."* And; George Bent *"Letters" Ibid.* And; James Mooney, *"Kiowa Calendar."* Smithsonian Institution. Washington D.C.

Chapter 17.
1. *"The Dragoon Expedition."* Washington D.C. And; George Bird Grinnell *"Papers." Ibid.* And; George Bent, *"Letters," Ibid.* And; James H. Dorsey *"Papers."* Smithsonian Institution. Washington D.C.

Chapter 18.
1. George Bird Grinnell *"Papers."* In; Southwest Museum, Los Angeles, California.

Chapter 19.
1. George Bird Grinnell *"Papers."* In; Southwest Museum, Los Angeles, California. .And; *"Life of Ten Bears,"* By Attocknie, Francis Joseph. University of Neb; Press, 2016.

Chapter 20.

NOTES AND SOURCES

1. George Bird Grinnell *"Papers."Ibid.*

Chapter 21.
1. George Bird Grinnell *"Papers."* In; The Southwest Museum, Los Angeles, California. And; *"Life of Ten Bears,"* By Attocknie, Francis Joseph. University of Neb; Press, 2016. And; James Mooney, *"Kiowa Calendar."* Smithsonian Institution. Washington D.C. And; George Bent *"Letters." Ibid.*

Chapter 22.
1. George Bird Grinnell *"Papers." Ibid.* And; George Bent, *"Letters." Ibid.*

Chapter 23.
1. With the death of Grey-Thunder, his wife Tail-Woman [died during the Cholera epidemic of 1849] carried the sacred talismans in their kit-fox hide bundle to her home camp outside Bent's Fort on the Arkansas. At first, the Cheyenne Elk-River took temporary charge of the 'Arrows' until the chief's council selected another permenant keeper. This man was named Lame-Medicine or, Lame-Medicine-Man. It seems from circumstantial evidence, that earlier, he was known as Running-Wolf, [See *Hoistah*, by J. M .Bartlett] a well-recognised veteran of many war-parties against the Kiowa and Comanche. Also, he had been one of the Cheyennes who with High-Backed-Wolf 1st and other Cheyenne chiefs, signed the so-called Friendship Treaty with the Atkinson-O'Fallon expedition of 1825. During the battle of Wolf Creek, 1838, he had been severely wounded in the affray and having recovered, suffered a noticeable limp thereafter. Hence, when being appointed Arrow Keeper, he became known colloquially among his tribesmen as Lame-Medicine-Man, and was often referred to by white men of his acquaintance simply as, 'The Lame.' When in 1848 and again in '49, Cheyennes had been invited by the then Government Agent Thomas Fitzpatrick to attend a proposed treaty-signing of tribes at Fort Laramie on the North Platte in late summer of '51, of which several Cheyenne chiefs were sceptical of attending, Lame-Medicine-Man spoke eloquently in favour of their doing so, and his persuasion was successful. He died soon after the aforesaid Cholera epidemic which swept across the Plains in 1849, but not from the contagion itself, although before the treaty gathering of '51 took place.
2. George Bird Grinnell *"Papers." Ibid.* And; George Bent, *"Letters." Ibid.* And; *"Life of Ten Bears,"* By Attocknie, Francis Joseph. University of Neb; Press, 2016. And; James Mooney, *"Kiowa Calendar."* Smithsonian Institution. Washington D.C.
3. George Bird Grinnell *"Papers." Ibid.*

Chapter 24.
1. Bartlett, J. M *"Hoistah, an Indian Girl."*
2. George Bird Grinnell *"Papers." Ibid.*
3. George Bird Grinnell *"Papers." Ibid.*
4. Information from George Bird Grinnell *"Papers." Ibid.* And; George Bent, *"Letters." Ibid.* And; *"Life of Ten Bears,"* By Attocknie, Francis Joseph. University of Neb; Press, 2016. And; James Mooney, *"Kiowa Calendar."* Smithsonian Institution. Washington D.C.

INDEX

Abert, Lieutenant J. 138
"Arrows", xii
Above World,, xiii
Afraid-of-Beavers, 127, 252
Algonquian, 5, 8, 9, 14, 15, 20, 21
Alimouspigoiak, 29
American Government, 77, 85, 97, 117, 118, 119, 120, 121, 161, 186, 195
American-Horse, 13, 14, 15, 17, 33
Angry, 220, 221, 222
Aorta, xi, xii, 15, 18
Apache, 4, 7, 12, 34
Arapahoe,12, 21, 30, 34, 39, 40, 42, 43, 46, 80, 81, 82, 83, 84, 102, 126, 128, 129, 131, 137, 140. 151, 152, 153, 194, 197, 199, 200, 203, 204, 205, 208, 231, 232, 233, 234, 236, 245, 246, 250, 257, 258, 259, 260, 261, 263, 264, 265, 266, 269, 270, 271, 272, 273, 274, 275, 277, 278, 279, 280, 281, 282, 284, 285, 286, 287, 288, 289
Arickara, 30, 34, 37, 40, 42, 44, 99, 102, 103, 122, 123, 124, 172, 184, 185, 197, 199, 203, 204, 205, 207, 219
Arkansas River, 31, 46, 98, 128, 137, 168, 188, 195, 205, 246, 258, 285
Around, xii, 126, 217, 248, 281
Arrow Keeper, 12, 15, 16, 17, 19, 44, 268, 275
Arrow Priest, 65, 232
Assiniboine, 39, 126
Atkinson, General, 117
Atsina, 2, 39, 126, 198
Baby's-Neck, 275
Baron de Lery, 13
Bear, 4, 7, 24, 26, 42, 43, 58, 71, 82, 83, 84, 92, 95, 100, 101, 103, 106, 118, 176, 207, 215, 217, 218, 233, 234, 235, 236, 239, 245, 246, 247, 248, 249, 260, 265, 266, 267, 268, 271, 272, 275, 278
Bear Butte, 4, 7, 24, 26
Bear's-Head, 95
Beard, 288
Bear-Feathers, 100, 101
Beaver Creek, 264, 281
Beckwourth, James P. 189
Bell, Captain, 82
Belle Fourch Branch, 167
Belle Point, 82, 85

Below World,, xiii
Bent, Charles, 136
Bent, George, 10, 11, 21, 44, 48, 72, 76, 79, 103, 136, 167, 195, 259
Bent, Robert, 136
Bent, William, viii, 44, 128, 132, 133, 135, 136, 138, 161, 168, 172, 176, 186, 189, 197, 198, 199, 200, 205, 229, 252, 257, 285, 289, 294, 295
Bent's Fort, viii, 128, 138, 186, 189, 197, 198, 199, 200, 205, 229, 257, 285, 289, 294.
Big Cheyenne River, 31, 34, 42, 47
Big Horn River, 192
Big Timbers, 137, 138, 159, 168, 176, 188, 200, 202, 203, 208
Big-Baby, 206
Big-Bellies, 126
Big-Breast, 260, 277, 278
Big-Eagle, 157, 158, 182, 183, 201, 202, 203, 204, 205, 206, 207
Big-Foot, 131, 132, 136
Big-Hand, 118, 161
Big-Head, viii, 161, 162, 163, 164, 165
Big-Old-Man, 133, 135
Big-Prisoner, 74
Big-Shadow, 97
Big-Spotted-Horse, 101, 157
Big Timbers, 292, 295
Bijeau, Joseph, 81, 82, 83, 84
Billings, 86
Birchwood Creek, 152
Black Hills, 4, 30, 31, 33, 39, 42, 47, 55, 110, 126, 140, 167, 168, 175
Black Lake, 133
Black Mountain, 26
Blackbird-Woman, 172
Blackduck, 27
Blackfeet, 39, 126, 127, 128, 129, 198, 250
Black-Horse, 218, 242, 245, 269, 277
Black-Kettle, 22
Black-Shin, 22, 192, 193, 194
Blind-Bull, 140
Blood, 2, 39
Bob-Tailed-Bull, 70
Bowstrings, 5, 14, 16, 17
Bowstring Lake, 5, 14, 17
Bowstring River, 5, 14

300

INDEX

Bowstring Society, 92, 220, 235, 241, 246
Bowstrings, xiii, 14, 15, 16, 17, 18, 19, 93, 233, 235, 238, 239, 241, 242, 244, 245, 247, 249, 260, 265, 269, 277, 286, 287
Box-Elder, 140, 141, 142
Bradley, James H., 77, 78
Brave-Wolf, 140
Brule, 31, 33, 42, 56, 151, 219
buffalo, 35, 53, 56, 58, 61, 88, 140, 172, 173
Buffalo Arrows, 3, 18, 202
Buffalo-Head, 118
Buffalo-Hump, 130, 131, 133, 135, 138, 190, 200, 291
Buffalo Men, xi
Bull, 287, 288
Bull or Buffalo Soldiers, xii
Bull-Bear, 57
Bull-Head, 182.
Bull-Thigh, 18
Burnt Aorta, xi, xii
Camp Holmes, 286
Canada, 2, 30
Canadian River, 196, 281
Cartier, Jaques, 8
Catlin, George, 11, 79, 103, 195
Cayuse, 161
Celtic, 10
Central Algonquian, 26
Cherry Creek, 31, 122
Cheyenne River, 31, 42, 56, 98, 110, 122, 126, 159, 167, 169, 188, 215
Cheyenne-proper, x, xiii, 5, 9, 17, 21, 22, 24, 29
Cheyennes, v, viii, ix, x, xi, 2, 3, 4, 5, 7, 8, 9, 10, 12, 13, 14, 15, 17, 18, 21, 22, 24, 25, 26, 29, 30, 33, 34, 39, 40, 41, 42, 43, 44, 45, 46, 47, 48, 49, 50, 51, 52, 53, 55, 56, 57, 58, 59, 61, 62, 63, 65, 67, 68, 69, 71, 72, 73, 74, 75, 76, 77, 80, 81, 82, 83, 84, 85, 86, 87, 88, 89, 90, 91, 92, 93, 94, 95, 96, 97, 98, 99, 100, 101, 102, 103, 104, 105, 107, 109, 110, 111, 112, 117, 118, 119, 120, 121, 122, 123, 124, 126, 127, 128, 129, 130, 131, 132, 133, 134, 135, 136, 137, 138, 140, 141, 142, 149, 150, 151, 153, 154, 155, 156, 157, 158, 161, 162, 163, 164, 165, 167, 168, 169, 170, 171, 172, 174, 180, 181, 182, 184, 185, 186, 187, 188, 189, 190, 191, 192, 193, 194, 196, 197, 198, 199, 200, 201, 202, 203, 204, 205, 206, 207, 208, 215, 216, 218, 219, 220, 221, 222, 223, 224, 229, 231, 236, 237, 238, 239, 240, 241, 242, 243, 244, 245, 246, 247, 248, 250, 252, 253, 255, 256, 257, 258, 259, 260, 261, 262, 264, 265, 266, 267, 269, 270, 271, 272, 273, 274, 275, 277, 278, 279, 280, 281, 282, 284, 285, 286, 287, 289
Cheyenne-Suhtaio, 48
Chief Little-Man, 12
Chief Soldiers, xiii
Chippewa, 18, 25, 27, 29
Chouteau, Auguste Pierre, 285.
Chouteau, E.L, 285, 286
Chouteau's Island, 258
Cimarron River, 131, 263, 295
Clark, 40, 41, 85, 99, 121
Colorado, 80, 98, 128, 138, 159
Columbia River, 42
Comanche, 12, 30, 31, 42, 81, 82, 85, 126, 127, 128, 129, 130, 131, 132, 133, 134, 135, 136, 137, 160, 168, 189, 190, 191, 195, 199, 200, 220, 221, 222, 223, 224, 225, 226, 227, 228, 229, 232, 233, 235, 236, 237, 240, 241, 243, 244, 245, 247, 251, 252, 258, 261, 265, 266, 268, 269, 270, 271, 272, 273, 274, 275, 276, 277, 278, 279, 281, 284, 285, 286, 287, 288, 289
Comancheros, 197, 206
Contraries, xiii
Contrary Warrior Society, 63, 235
Coronado, Francisco, 13
Coteau des Prairies, 5
Crazy-Dogs, xiii
Cree, 5, 9, 15, 16, 17, 21, 22, 29, 126
Crooked Creek, 263
Crooked-Lance, 52, 54, 55, 56, 66, 149, 265, 268
Crooked-Lance Society, xii, 48, 55,
Crooked-Neck, 263, 267, 273
Crows, viii, ix, 30, 31, 32, 33, 34, 35, 36, 37, 38, 39, 42, 47, 48, 49, 50, 51, 52, 53, 54, 56, 57, 58, 59, 60, 61, 62, 63, 64, 65, 66, 67, 68, 69, 70, 71, 72, 73, 75, 76, 77, 78, 80, 84, 86, 87, 88, 89,

INDEX

91, 92, 93, 94, 95, 96, 97, 98, 101, 103, 126, 128, 129,131, 137, 140, 141, 142, 149, 151, 161, 167, 168, 169, 170, 171, 172, 173, 174, 175, 176, 177, 178, 179, 180, 185, 186, 189, 190, 191, 192, 194, 198, 208, 250, 280, 281
Culbertson, Thadeus, 77, 78
Curly-Bear, 161
Custer, George A. 172
Dakota, 140
Dangling-Foot, 167, 168, 169, 170, 171, 172, 173, 175, 180
Deaf-Man, 278
Delawares, 195
Denig, Edwin, 168, 180
Devil's Lake, 5
Dodge, Colonel Henry 196, 199, 200, 204
Dog Den, 7
Dog-Soldiers, xiii, 247, 249, 265, 288
Doll-Man, 201, 202
Dougerhty, John, 182, 196
Dried-Out-Furs, 171
Eagle-Feather, 291
Eagle's-Peak, 3
Earth Renewal ceremonies, xiii
Elk-Horn Scrapers, xii, 24.
Elk-River, 138, 254, 269, 285, 287
Elks, xii, 14, 16, 17, 18
English, 2, 32, 237
Erect-Horns, xi, xii, 24
False Washita, 196
Fitzpatrick, Thomas, 97
Fitzpatrick Treaty, 97
Flatheads, 126, 171
Flat-War-Club, 258, 259, 278, 279, 280
Flint Men, xii
Flying-Arrow, 200
Fort Gibson, 196, 208
Fort John, 161
Fort Smith, 85, 98
Fountain Creek, 136
Four-Bears, 103, 104, 105, 106, 107, 109, 110, 111, 112
Four-Dancers, 89
Fowler, Jacob, 98
Fox, xiii, 14, 15, 16, 17, 18, 25, 27
Fox Society, 15, 17, 25, 161
French, 8, 13, 32, 81, 82
Friendship Treaty, viii, 120, 121, 161

Frog-Woman, 33
Gantt, John, 197
Gattacka, 34
Gens L'Arc, 15
Gentle-Horse, 22, 263, 271
Glenn, Captain Hugh, 98
Grand Camp Creek, 80
Grand River, 42, 122
Great Plains, 14, 15, 22
Green Man, 10
Green-Bird, 136
Grey-Hair, 278
Grey-Thunder, 12, 151, 152, 155, 157, 160, 188, 189, 195, 200, 201, 202, 203, 204, 207, 232, 234, 257, 265, 268, 270, 275, 276, 277, 285
Grinnell, George Bird, 21, 44, 48, 259
Gros Ventres of the Prairies, 126
Guts, 111
Hair-Rope band, xi, 127, 137
Half Sioux / Half Heviatanio, xi
Hanging-Raven, 89, 90, 91, 92, 97, 98
Hat *[issiwun]* ,viii, xii, 23, 24, 25, 26, 27, 29, 56, 64, 65, 136, 151, 153, 257, 266
Hawk, 217
Heviatanio, xi, 127-129, 137, 162, 167, 200, 204, 220, 246, 252, 254, 256, 282
Heviqsnipahis, xi, xii
Hi - mo`weyuhks, xii
Hidatsa, 4, 5, 7, 33, 39, 40, 42, 44, 50, 85, 91, 92, 96, 107, 111, 112, 208
High-Backbone, 88
High-Backed-Wolf 1st ix, 12, 22, 56, 57, 58, 86, 117, 118, 120, 152, 153, 161, 186, 187, 188, 199, 215, 216, 217, 218, 257, 288
High-Backed-Wolf II, 120, 215, 289, 292, 298
High-Lance, 88
Himatanohis, xiii
Hi-mo`weyuhks, xii
Hofnowa, xi, 128
Hohnuhk`e., xiii
Hok`tsim lances, 215
Hollow-Hip, 233, 234, 235, 236, 238, 240, 246
Holy Mountain, 4
Horse Creek, 42, 43, 81, 89, 90, 176
Hota`mita`niu, xiii

INDEX

Hotami`-Massau, xiii
Hotomtami, 247
Howling-Wolf, 263, 278
Huefeno Creek, 98
Hunkpapa, 37
Huron, 8
Ice, 63, 67, 70, 72
Island, 13, 70, 258
Issiometanui, xi
Issiwun, xii, 23, 24, 56, 151, 257
Jackson, 41, 195, 200
Joe Medicine-Crow, 171
Kamchatka, 9
Kaw or Kansa, 84
Kearney, Stephen Watts, 196
Kicked-in-the-Belly Crows, 77
King, James [Jim], x
Kingsbury, Lieutenant, 199
Kiowa, ix, 4, 7, 12, 30, 34, 42, 43, 80, 81, 82, 83, 126, 127, 128, 129, 130, 131, 133, 136, 137, 160, 172, 175, 191, 192, 193, 194, 195, 197, 199, 206, 215, 220, 221, 222, 223, 224, 225, 226, 227, 228, 229, 232, 233, 235, 236, 237, 238, 239, 240, 241, 242, 243, 244, 245, 246, 247, 250, 252, 258, 260, 261, 262, 263, 264, 265, 266, 267, 268, 269, 270, 271, 272, 273, 274, 275, 276, 277, 278, 279, 280, 281, 282, 284, 285, 286, 287, 288, 289
Kiowa-Apache, 34, 81, 82, 83, 128, 129, 137, 160, 220, 237, 240, 245, 247, 250, 261, 262, 265, 269, 271, 272, 273, 275, 280, 284, 285, 286, 287, 288, 289
Kipp, Joseph, 103
Kit-Fox, xii, 15, 16, 17, 18, 24, 162
Kit-Fox Warrior Society, xiii, 16
Kitkahaki, 203
Koisenko, 193
Lake Superior, 27
Lakota, 31, 33, 34, 37, 40, 56, 59, 62, 69, 74, 76, 77, 140, 219, 246, 257
Lame Deer, x, 77
Lame-Medicine-Man, 286, 299.
Lame-White-Man, 172
Laramie Fork, 159, 161
Leading-Bear, 291
Left-Hand, 260, 261, 262
Lesharroco, 42
Leavenworth, Colonel, 195

Lewis, 33, 40, 41, 85, 99, 121
Lewis and Clark, 33, 40
Light, 153
Likes-the-Old-Women, 88
Limber-Lance, 182
Lipan, 34
Lisa, Manuel, 42, 81
Little Big Horn, 172
Little Missouri, 102
Little-Beaver, 136
Little-Moon, 118, 199
Little-Mountain, 291
Little-Old-Man, 289
Little-Raven, 286, 287
Little-White-Bear, 95, 118, 176, 178
Little-White-Bull, 87, 89, 91, 92
Little-Wolf, 22, 131, 133, 135, 162, 221, 222, 223, 229, 249, 282
Lone-Bear, 162, 165
Lone-Wolf, 225, 226
Long, Major, 81, 82, 85, 98, 100, 149
Long-Hair, 37, 48, 50, 57, 58, 59, 61, 62, 64, 68, 69, 75, 78, 86, 88, 90, 95, 96, 97, 98, 171, 172, 173, 174, 219
Long-Jaw, 74
Loup Fork, 47, 80, 182, 184, 201
Lousy-Man [aka Scabby], 118
Lower Red Lake, 5, 14, 17, 20, 21
Lower St. Lawrence, 8
Luttig, Charles, 42
Ma`heo, 2, v, x, xiii, 3, 8, 220, 231
Mad-Wolf, 131
Mahohe`was, xii
Man Arrows, 18
Man-Above, 162, 193
Mandan, 4, 7, 34, 40, 41, 42, 85, 99, 102, 103, 104, 105, 106, 107, 109, 110, 111, 112, 121, 122, 123, 124, 137, 199, 201
Man-on-the-Hill, 217
Many-Magpies, 162
Mashikota, xi, 14, 15, 16, 17, 18, 19, 29
Massaum, 9, 10
Mato-Topa, 103, 104, 105, 111, 112
Maximillian Zu Weid, 103
Medicine Arrows, xii, 151, 232
[Mahuts], xii
Medicine Crow, 49, 86
Medicine Lodge` or `Willow Dance, xiii

303

INDEX

Medicine-Elk, 120
Medicine-Man, 42, 285.
Medicine-Snake [aka Walking-Whirlwind, ix, 127, 200, 204, 252, 253, 254, 255, 256, 260, 282
Medicine-Water, 270, 272
Mexicans, 82, 83, 100, 192, 197, 206
Michelson, Truman, 18
Middle Missouri, 30
Miniconjou, 31, 33, 56
Minnesota, 4, 5, 7, 20, 25, 26
Minnesota River, 5, 20
Mississippi headwaters, 4, 5, 11, 14, 16
Missouri River 7, 13, 15, 21, 22, 30, 31, 34, 40, 42, 80, 98, 99, 100, 102, 107, 109, 110, 117, 118, 122, 124, 126, 128, 182, 184, 192, 250
Moiseo, xi, 8, 9, 13, 15, 16, 17, 18, 20, 21, 29
Monsoni, 5, 16, 18, 29
Montagnais, 13, 18, 21
Montreal, 8
Mooney, James, 20, 237
Morning Star deity, 182
Motsounetaniu, xii
Mountain Crows, 48, 50, 61, 86
Mouse`s-Road, ix, 221, 223, 224, 225, 226, 227, 228, 229, 232
Navaho, 24, 185
Nebraska, 42, 80, 99, 152, 154, 201, 215
Neo-Atlantic period, 25
Nez-Perce, 126, 161
No-Braids, 296.
No Colds, 22
North Dakota, 5
North Fork of Red River, 130
North Platte River, 42, 151
Northern Cheyenne, x, 77, 128, 140, 159
northern Minnesota, 2, 4, 7, 9, 14, 17, 20, 21, 25, 29
Northern Plains, 31
O`Fallon, Benjamin, 117
Oglala, 31, 33, 56, 57
Oivimana, xi, 128, 167
Okhtsin, 10
Oklahoma, x, 3, 77, 263
Oktouna, xi, 128
Old Lady Rondo, 120
Old-Bark, 101, 201, 202, 207

Old-Horn, 140, 141
Old-Little-Wolf, 133, 135, 136, 138, 193, 249, 250, 270, 271, 272, 282, 283
Old-Smoke, 57
Omissis, xi, xii, 14, 15, 16, 17, 18, 19, 29, 140, 150, 247, 248, 249
One-Eyed-Antelope, 51, 52
One-Who-Walks-Against-the-Others, 118
Ontario, 2, 4, 5, 7, 8, 18, 20
Osage, 84, 85, 99, 149, 185, 196, 199, 205, 284, 285
Otoe, 84
Ottawa, 27
Otter Creek, 59, 60, 62, 74, 86, 98, 174
Otter-Cap, 206, 207
Pacific Ocean, 40, 121
Padaux, 34
Pani-Mahas, 196
Papillion, 42
Passes-Women, 88, 95
Pawnee, 30, 45, 46, 80, 81, 82, 84, 99, 100, 101, 103, 131, 149, 151, 152, 153, 154, 156, 157, 158, 160, 182, 184, 189, 195, 196, 199, 200, 201, 202, 203, 205, 206, 207, 215, 216, 217, 218, 219, 233, 250, 252, 253, 254, 256, 261, 262, 263, 268
People of the Bow, 15
Petelasharo, 81
Pile-of-Buffalo-Bones, 118
Pipe-Stem-Men, 18
Platte River, 89, 167, 168, 181
Plays-With-His-Face, 88, 89, 90, 91, 92, 93, 94, 95, 96, 97, 98
Plenty-Coups, 208, 209
Plenty-Hoops, 70
Pompey`s Pillar, 174, 176
Ponca, 138, 221, 268
Poor-Little-Wolf, 42
Porcupine-Bear, 247, 248, 266, 267, 268, 271
Powder River, 32, 33, 77, 78, 140
Powell, Father Peter, 23
Powell, William, 23
Prairie Dog Creek, 48, 49, 54
Pretty-Lance, 172
Pryor Creek, 35
Pryor Gap, 35, 38, 40
Pueblo County, 98

INDEX

Pushing-Ahead, 220, 221, 222, 263, 273
Quebec, 8
Radisson, Pierre, 29
Raises-the-Club, 118
Raven-Face, 171
Rawlins, Wyoming, 169
Red Lakes, 2, 4, 7, 17, 20.
Red River, 82, 85, 130, 220, 235
Red-Dog-Rope, viii, 122, 124
Red-Hat, 14, 17
Red-Moon, 138
Red-Owl, 60, 61, 62, 63, 73, 78
Red-Painted-Robe, 53, 55, 71
Red River, 294.
Red-Shields, xii, 14, 16-18, 247
Red-Sun, 138
Republican Loup, 99, 100
Republican Pawnee, 203
Ridge Men, xi, 18
River Crows, 77, 86, 87
Roasting, 153
Rock-Forehead, 130
Rocky Mountains, 31, 80, 161, 162, 171, 191, 192, 197
Roman-Nose, 22
Running-Wolf, 118
Rustling-Corn-Leaf, 3
Sacagawea, 33
Sacred Arrow bundle, 10, 15, 97, 156, 254, 266, 270, 275
Sacred Arrow keeper, 200, 204
Sacred Arrows, viii, 2, 5, 7, 9, 10, 15, 16, 18, 19, 21, 23, 24, 26, 29, 44, 56, 64, 65, 128, 138, 151, 154, 159, 160, 188, 201, 203, 205, 206, 207, 219, 232, 233, 247, 249, 252, 257, 285
Sacred Buffalo Hat, xii, 23, 44, 151, 152, 154, 159, 269
Sacred Morning Star bundle, 158
Sacred Mountain, 7
Sand Creek, 133, 138, 220
Sans-Arc, 31, 33
Santa Fe, 132
Sarsi, 126
Saskatchewan River, 126
Satank, 237, 239, 240, 244, 246, 291, 292
Sauk, 25, 27
Sault St. Marie, 20, 27
Scout Creek, 192

Seneca, 196
Seven-Bulls, 286, 287, 288
Shawnee Creek, 288
Shaved-Head, 291
Shoots-the-Arrow Rock,", 35
Shoshoni, viii, 30, 33, 39, 42, 43, 44, 45, 81, 126, 128, 129, 131, 137, 140, 141, 142, 159, 161, 162, 163, 164, 165, 188, 189, 198
Siksika, 39, 126
Sioux, xi, 16, 17, 18, 21, 29, 30, 31, 32, 33, 34, 37, 38, 39, 40, 42, 43, 44, 56, 57, 58, 59, 60, 61, 62, 63, 67, 68, 69, 72, 73, 74, 75, 76, 78, 80, 81, 98, 102, 117, 128, 129, 131, 132, 136, 151, 152, 153, 167, 184, 203, 218, 254, 255
Sitting-Bear, 162, 165, 237
Skidi, ix, 45, 46, 47, 80, 81, 82, 83, 99, 100, 101, 103, 149, 150, 153, 154, 156, 157, 158, 182, 183, 184, 185, 196, 197, 201, 202, 203, 204, 205, 206, 207, 261
Skutani or Flyers, 47
Sleeping-Bear, 272
Small-Back, 87
Smallpox, 8, 43, 98, 168, 185, 285
Smokey Hill River, 215, 218
Snake-Woman, 194
Soldiers, xi, 118, 230, 248, 249, 250, 275, 288
Solomon River, 252, 254
Sore-Belly, 51, 52, 59, 75, 86, 87, 88, 89, 93, 94, 95, 98, 140, 171, 174, 176, 180
South Platte, viii, 127, 128, 129, 130, 131, 133, 134, 158, 197, 220, 222, 229, 246, 249, 252, 257, 285
Southern Arapahoe, 257
Southern Cheyenne, x, 3, 14, 101, 128, 159, 161, 172, 184, 249, 260
Spanish, 13, 40, 42, 45, 65, 71, 82, 83, 101, 226
Staihitans, 47
Standing-All-Night, 21, 22
Standing-Medicine, 3
Standing-Sweet-Grass, 3
Stands in Timber, John, 26, 48, 117
Stands-All-Night, 172
Stands-on-the-Hill, 260, 261, 262
Stone, 26, 135, 162, 163, 220, 221, 222
Stone Hammer Mountain,, 26

INDEX

Stone-Calf, 162, 163
Stone-Forehead, 220, 221, 222
Stohr, A. C. 120
Stripped-Arrow-People, 173
Sublette, William, 140
Suhtaio, xii, 9, 13, 14, 17, 18, 21, 22, 23, 24, 25, 26, 27, 29, 30, 47, 48, 53, 55, 56, 57, 58, 60, 63, 65, 67, 71, 81, 128, 140, 151, 152, 159, 161, 167, 168, 169, 170, 171, 172, 175, 176, 177, 178, 179, 180, 185, 188, 192, 193, 215, 249, 266, 269
Sun Dance, xiii, 9
Sun`s-Road, 22
Sun-Getting-Out-of-Bed, 56, 257, 266
Sun-Maker, 273
Sweet-Medicine, x, xii, 2, 3, 4, 7, 10, 11, 12, 13, 14, 16, 17, 118, 159, 161, 215, 216, 288
Sweet-Root-Standing, 3
Swift Hawks, xiii
Tail-Woman, 257, 275
Teton Sioux, 30, 34, 39, 102, 167
Tongue River, x, 24, 47, 48, 49, 57
Tonkawa, 195
Toyash, 196
Trading Indians, 46, 80, 81, 82, 83, 98, 99
TsisTsisTsas, x, xii, xiii, 18, 24, 25, 26, 27, 139, 227, 231
Twines-His-Horses-Tail, 95
Two Butte Creek, 290
Two-Crows, 280
Two-Face, 88
Two-Tassels, 270
Two-Twists, 55, 56, 57, 65, 66, 67, 270
Ugly, 101, 201, 207
Upper Great Lakes, 21, 25, 27, 29
Upper Mississippi, 2, 4, 13, 16, 17, 24, 27, 29
Utes, 128, 185
Waco, 196

Walking-Coyote, 133, 134, 135, 138, 221, 222, 229, 268
Walking-Whirlwind, 200, 252, 254
Walks-Out, 162, 164
Wants-To-Die, 88, 95
War-Path-Bear, 56, 64, 92
Watapio, xi, 18, 101, 128, 131, 167
Wheskerinni, 15, 18, 21
Whiiu`Nutkiu, xiii
Whistling-Arrow, 275
Whistling-Elk, 56, 60, 61
White-Antelope, 118, 130, 131, 28, 289
White-Buffalo-Woman, 55, 71
White-Bull, 22
White-Cow, 194, 200
White-Cow-Woman, 194
White-Haired-Killer, 63, 67
White-Hat, 136
White-Tail, Ralph, 12
Whkesh`hetaniu, xii
Wind River, 140
Winter, 33
Witchita, 84, 195, 196
Wolf Creek, ix, 261, 262, 263, 264, 265, 277, 282, 284, 285, 286
Wolf Soldiers,, xiii
Wolf-Chief, 272
Wolf-Pipe, 215
Wolf-Road, 263
Wyoming, 169
Yamparika, 190, 274
Yankton, 34, 42
Yellow-Belly, 189, 191
Yellow-Hair, 291
Yellow-Haired Maiden, 25
Yellow-Shirt, 272
Yellowstone, 2, 33, 57, 86, 96, 112, 167, 171, 172, 174, 191
Yellow-Wolf, 127, 129, 130, 131, 133, 134, 135, 136, 137, 138, 162, 192, 200, 204, 221, 252, 260, 268, 282, 283

www.ingramcontent.com/pod-product-compliance
Lightning Source LLC
Chambersburg PA
CBHW070632160426
43194CB00009B/1437